MW01620251

Beatrix Potter

DRAWN TO NATURE

Published to accompany the exhibition *Beatrix Potter: Drawn to Nature* at the Victoria and Albert Museum, London, from February 12, 2022 to January 8, 2023

First published in the United States of America in 2022 by
Rizzoli Electa, a division of Rizzoli International Publications, Inc.
300 Park Avenue South
New York, NY 10010
www.rizzoliusa.com

Originally published in the United Kingdom in 2021 by
V&A Publishing,
Victoria and Albert Museum
South Kensington
London SW7 2RL
vam.ac.uk/publishing

ISBN 978-0-8478-7143-8
Library of Congress Control Number: 2021942098

2022 2023 2024 2025/10 9 8 7 6 5 4 3 2 1

Visit us online:
Facebook.com/RizzoliNewYork
Twitter: @Rizzoli_Books
Instagram.com/RizzoliBooks
Pinterest.com/RizzoliBooks
Youtube.com/user/RizzoliNY
Issuu.com/Rizzoli

Front cover illustration: detail of no.157
Back cover illustration: Rupert Potter, Beatrix Potter with Benjamin Bouncer ('Bounce') on a leash, September 1891; photograph in an album, albumen print on paper; Cotsen Children's Library, Special Collections, Princeton University Library, 10005.161
p.10, detail of no.97
p.18, detail of no.31
p.56, detail of no.5
p.92, detail of no.95
p.138, detail of no.133
p.170, detail of no.145
p.198, detail of Water lilies, probably at Esthwaite Water, Cumbria, c.1906; watercolour, ink wash and ink; V&A: LC 3/A/2, given by the Linder Collection
p.216, detail of no.100

Designer: Charlie Smith Design
Copy-editor: Linda Schofield
Origination: DL Imaging
Index: Nic Nicholas
New photography by Sarah Duncan and Kieron Boyle, V&A Photographic Studio

Printed in China by Toppan Leefung

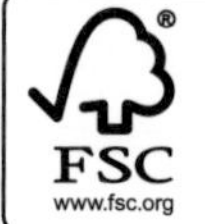

MIX
Paper from responsible sources
FSC® C104723

V&A Publishing

Supporting the world's leading museum of art and design, the Victoria and Albert Museum, London

Beatrix Potter

DRAWN TO NATURE

Edited by Annemarie Bilclough with contributions from
Richard Fortey, Sara Glenn, Emma Laws, Liz Hunter MacFarlane,
James Rebanks and Lucy Shaw

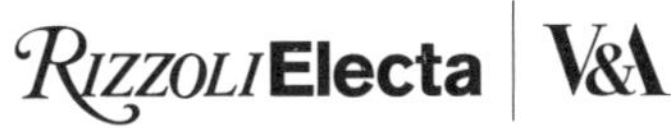

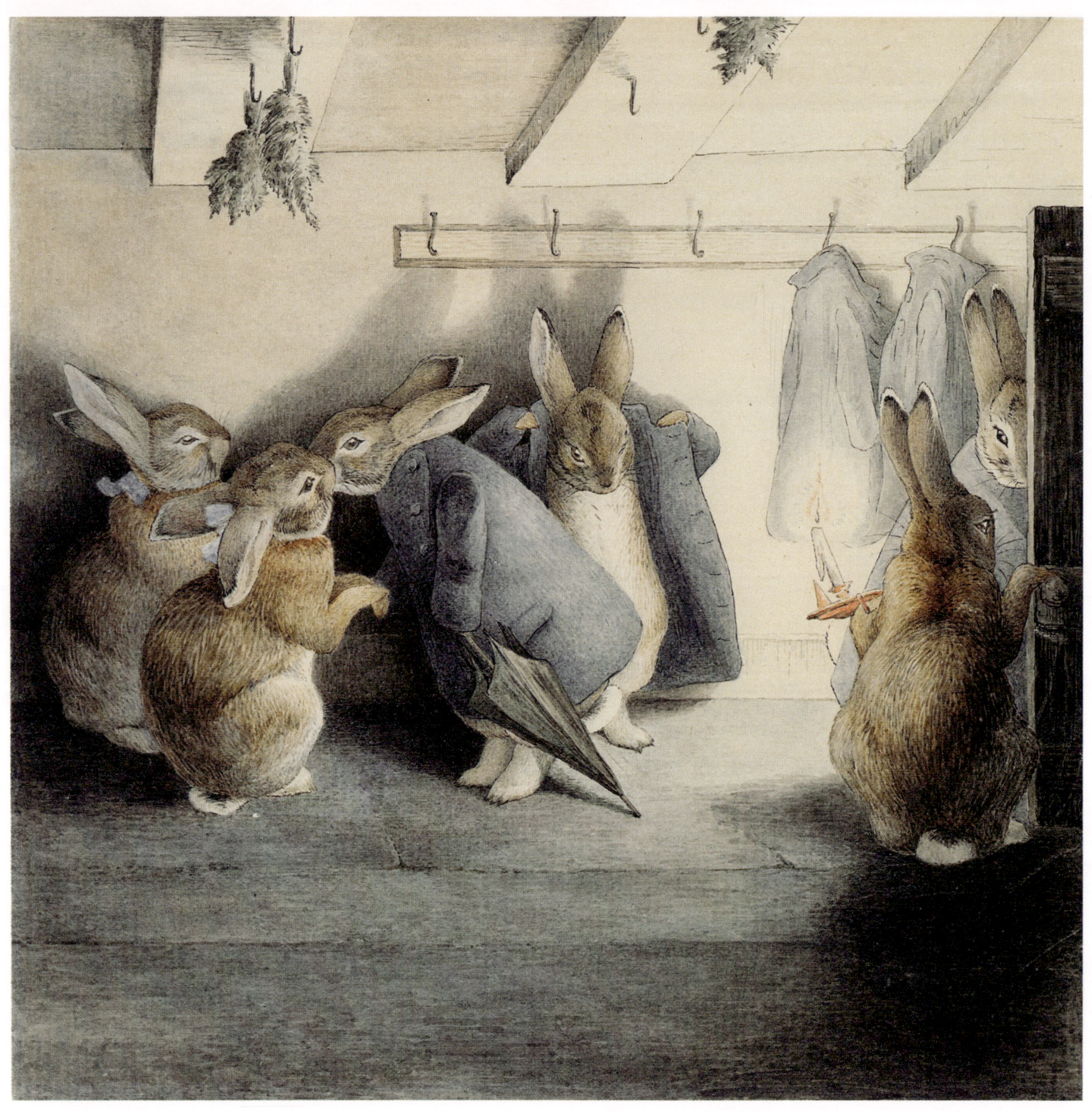

1.
'The Rabbits' Christmas Party: The Departure'
From a set, c.1892
Watercolour and ink on paper
V&A: BP.1471(d), Linder Bequest LB 1006

DIRECTOR'S FOREWORD

Almost 120 years after the first publication of her books, Beatrix Potter (1866-1943) remains among the most famous of British children's book creators. Over 250 million copies of her books have sold worldwide, and they have been translated into 46 languages. Yet, there is much more to Potter than Peter Rabbit, Jemima Puddle-Duck and the other charming characters imagined through her storybooks. In the family-friendly exhibition *Beatrix Potter: Drawn to Nature*, young and mature alike are invited to delve into Potter's complete life story and her own incredible journey from town mouse to country mouse.

The V&A is privileged to hold the largest collection of Beatrix Potter artworks in the world. The origins of such a rich archive stem from the research of the scholar and engineer Leslie Linder, whose discovery and decoding of Potter's diary – kept from her mid-teenage years in 1882 until 1897 – gifted the world a remarkable first-hand insight into the day-to-day life, character, humour, dreams and anxieties of a young middle-class Victorian woman during her formative years. Linder tracked down and meticulously studied Potter's surviving manuscripts and drawings, helping in the process to reveal the diversity of her creative output.

In 1973, he bequeathed to the V&A a remarkable collection comprising around 3000 items: drawings and sketchbooks from Potter's childhood into adulthood; manuscripts; rare first editions; and family photographs taken by her father and amateur photographer, Rupert. Natural history studies and landscape drawings join the background research and preliminary character sketches for Potter's world-famous storybooks. A significant collection in its own right, the Linder Bequest (as it is known) has been supplemented over the years by other notable donations, including objects once owned by the Potter family, donated by Joan Duke, and Leslie Linder's specially curated selection of artworks, given to the museum in 2019 by the Linder Collection, by which it is also known. The V&A is also fortunate to hold several key loans such as the archive of the publisher Frederick Warne.

It is apt that so much of Beatrix Potter's artwork has a home at the V&A, since she grew up in nearby Bolton Gardens and visited the museums of Albertopolis – the South Kensington Museum (now the V&A) and the museum of Natural History – for inspiration, studying at the associated Schools of Art.

The V&A is thrilled to have worked in partnership with the National Trust, to whom Potter bequeathed the finished watercolours and manuscripts for most of her storybooks, her archives relating to the management of her farm estates, and a large tract of the Lake District National Park. As a result, *Beatrix Potter: Drawn to Nature* marries together two of the world's largest collections of Potter artworks and archives to showcase the full breadth of her life achievements. This wealth of material is supplemented by significant international loans, including the important collection of Potter's mycology drawings from the Armitt Library.

Potter will always be loved for her imaginative and charismatic literary creations, from the 'terribly tidy' Tomasina Tittlemouse to the 'charming rascal' Benjamin Bunny. We continue to marvel at her admirable gift for capturing the beauty of the natural world. Yet, through this exhibition and the expansive collections on display, we can celebrate Potter's wider life and legacy – her passions, inspirations and accomplishments – that stretch far beyond the pages of her storybooks.

Tristram Hunt,
Director, V&A

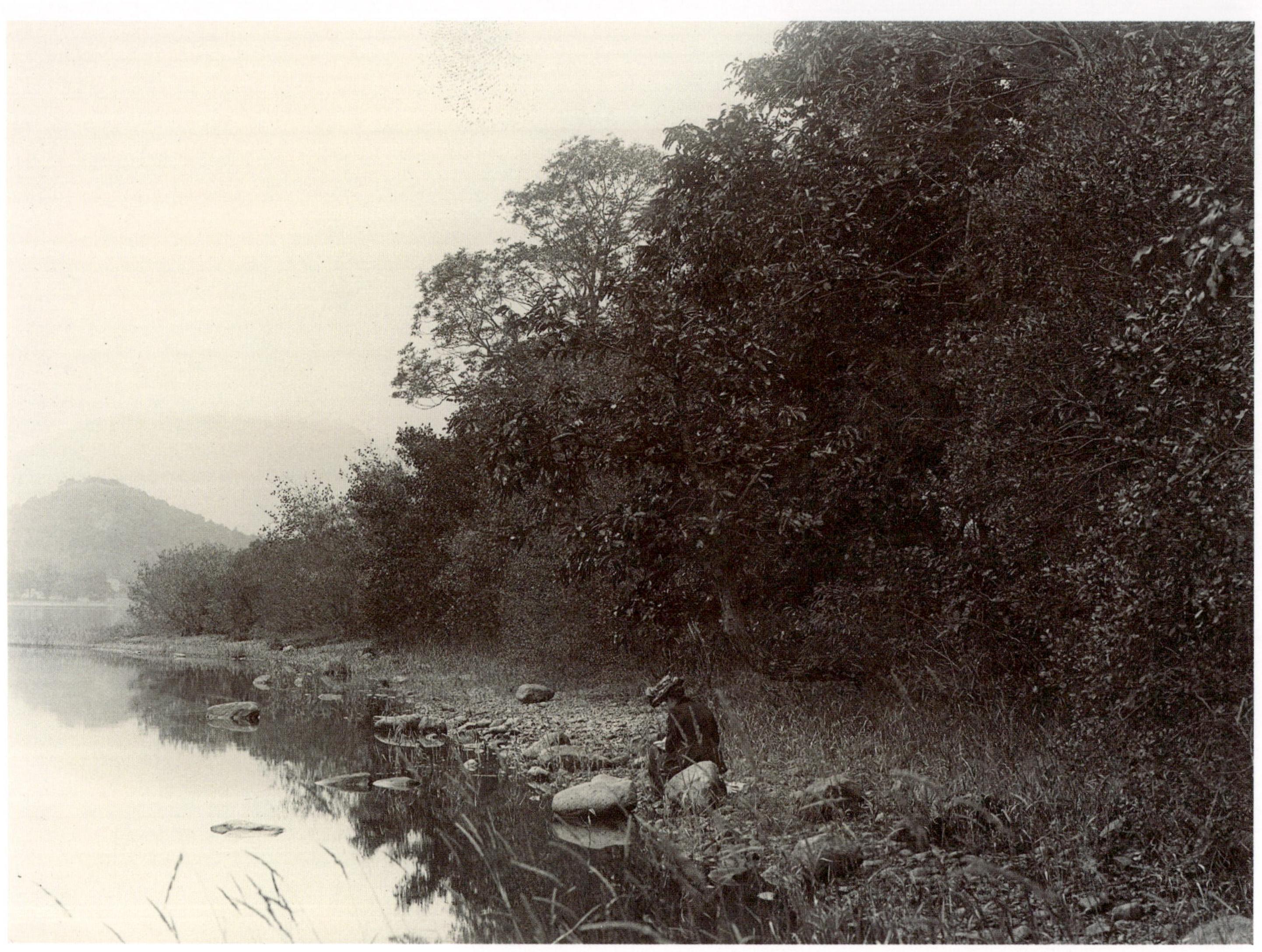

2.
Rupert Potter (1832–1914)
Beatrix Potter drawing on the shore of Derwentwater, 26 September 1903
Photograph in an album, albumen print on paper
Cotsen Children's Library, Special Collections, Princeton University Library, 10005.138

PARTNER FOREWORD

Beatrix Potter's connection with the Lake District began when she was 16, during the first of many family holidays spent in this intoxicating place. It was on that visit in 1882 that the Potters stayed at Wray Castle, where they met Canon Hardwicke Rawnsley – later to be a co-founder of the National Trust. So began a lifetime of friendship and shared interests that led to a strong desire to protect this unique landscape.

We are delighted to have the opportunity to share Potter's story through our partnership with the Victoria and Albert Museum.

A shy and insatiably curious girl, Potter drew deep inspiration from the Lake District which was, in so many ways, different to her family's home in London. It was of crucial importance to the wonderful worlds she created through her stories. Climbing craggy fells and exploring tranquil woodlands, she sketched along the way, capturing views and features in the landscape that would then often appear in her 'little books' and that can often still be seen today. Potter is known principally as the illustrator and writer of these iconic books, which are just as much a part of children's lives now as when they were first published. However, at her farmhouse, Hill Top, and in the wider Lake District we can explore her many other passions and interests, such as farming, vernacular buildings and, of course, conservation.

In 1905, Potter bought the working farm at Hill Top in Near Sawrey, having first visited the village many years earlier and fallen in love with it, describing it as 'as nearly perfect a place as I have ever lived in'. In the farmhouse she created a precious sanctuary for herself, filling it with family heirlooms and rescued pieces of local, traditional furniture. There are many things in the collection to surprise the visitor that reveal much of the woman herself, from tiny pieces of knitting for dolls, to the clogs she wore trudging the footpaths she both loved and protected as a longterm member of the Footpath Association – and even the smit markers she used for branding her flock of prize-winning Herdwick Sheep (nos 139, 140).

Potter spent the last 30 years of her life protecting as much land in the Lake District as she could – often buying it herself using royalties from the sales of her books or merchandise. She focussed especially on the acquisition of farms and farming heritage, including the associated flocks. She maintained a close relationship with the National Trust and, while she did not always agree with our decisions at a local level, she supported many campaigns and often worked hand in hand with the Trust. One of the most important instances was the purchase and ongoing preservation of Monk Coniston, which includes one of the most beloved features of the Lake District, Tarn Hows, and several important farms.

The Lake District is now recognized as a World Heritage Site by UNESCO, in appreciation of the outstanding universal value of its farming traditions and local industry, set against the most spectacular landscape of mountains, valleys and lakes. This is the place Beatrix Potter sought to protect and preserve during her life. Thanks partly to her exceptional bequest, the National Trust now cares for almost a quarter of this remarkable place, for everyone, for ever.

Hilary McGrady
Director-General, National Trust

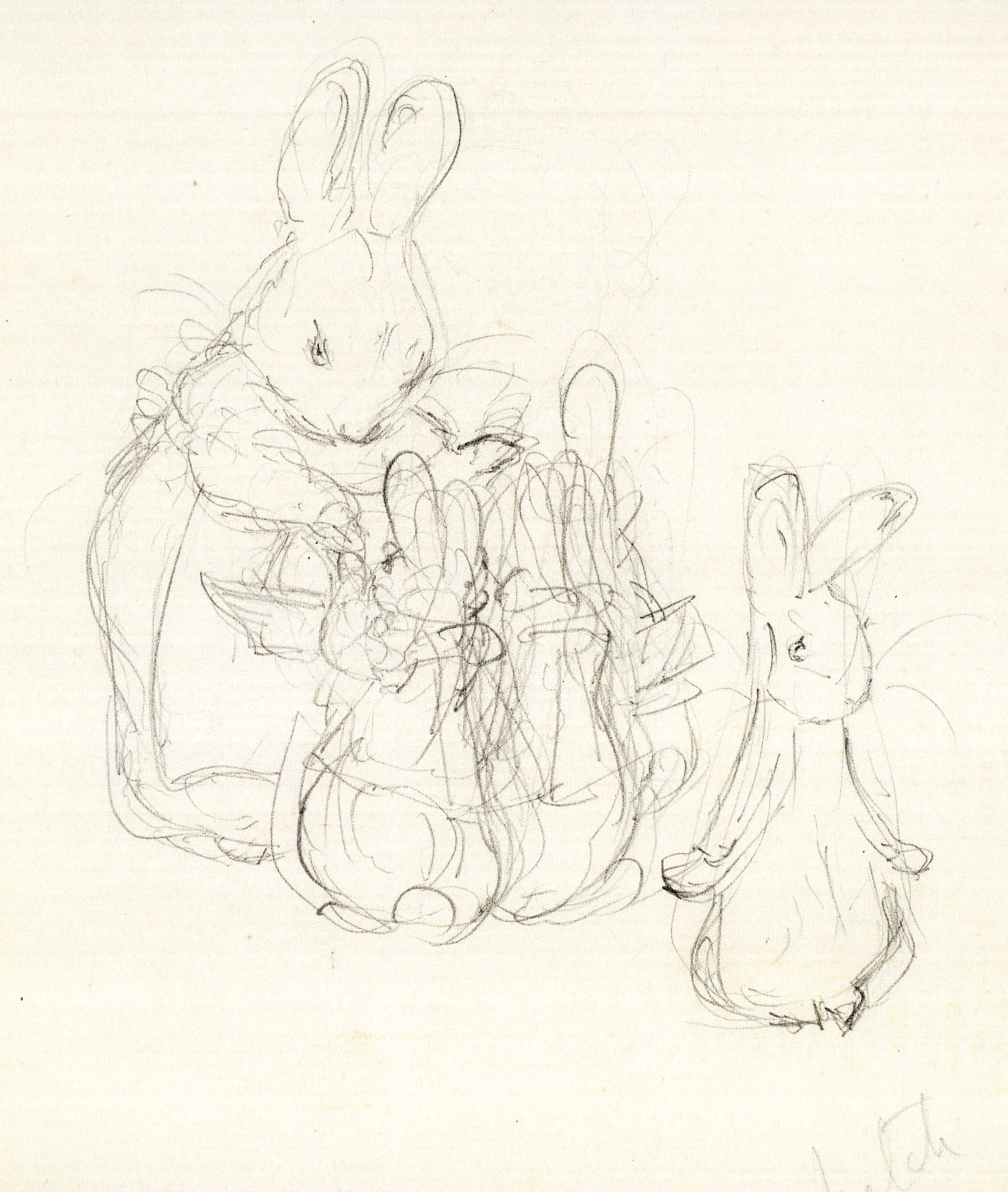
sketch

Introduction

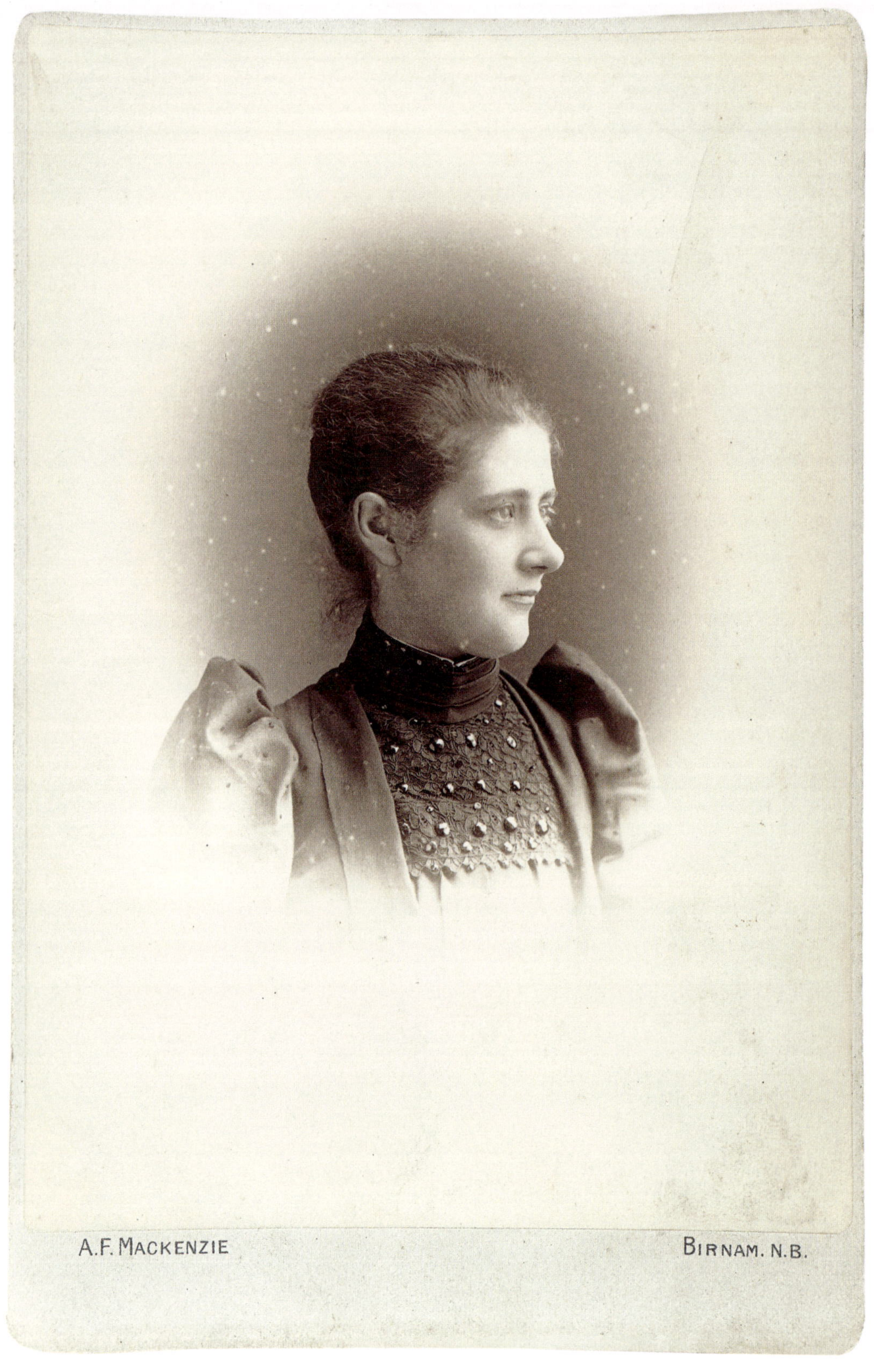
A.F. MACKENZIE
BIRNAM. N.B.

3.
Andrew Finlay Mackenzie (1846–1940)
Studio portrait of Beatrix Potter, c.1890
Albumen print on card
V&A: AAD/2006/4/472, given by Joan Duke

As a rule each takes his own style, and screws it occasionally into prettiness, but very few see the beauty of nature.

(BEATRIX POTTER, *JOURNAL*, 28 APRIL 1883)

Beatrix Potter: Drawn to Nature follows Beatrix Potter from her childhood home in London into the rural Lake District, on the way discovering a natural scientist, an author and illustrator, a farmer, and a conservationist. It explores the inspirations behind her accomplishments and reveals how she combined an abiding and all-consuming passion for nature and the animal world with her natural shrewdness, perseverance and imagination.

Helen Beatrix Potter (1866–1943) (no.3) spent much of the first 47 years of her life in the same town house in a genteel enclave of Kensington, in south-west London (no.7). However, as she once explained: 'My brother and I were born in London because my father was a lawyer there. But our descent – our interests and our joy was in the north country.'[1] Although no audio recording of Potter survives, she joked in her *Journal* that her brother returned from his first term at school speaking with a long vowel ('rather inclined to say pāth, grāss'), suggesting that, despite her London birth and upper-middle-class background, she was used to hearing northern accents.[2] This should not be surprising, since both of her parents and their families hailed from the north of England: her paternal grandfather, Edmund Potter, established a large calico printing firm at Dinting Vale in Glossop, Derbyshire, while her maternal grandfather, John Leech, was a merchant from Stalybridge, near Manchester, and related by marriage to cotton manufacturers from Hyde in Cheshire. When considering her connections, however, Potter went even further back to the 'generations of Lancashire yeoman [*sic*] and weavers; obstinate, hard headed, *matter of fact* folk [and]...Dissenters'.[3] Thus, even as

4.
The Tailor of Gloucester artwork, c.1902
Watercolour, ink and gouache on paper
Tate, A01089

she was compiling an autobiographical article about her world-famous storybooks, she saw her roots in farming:

> The question of 'roots' interests me! I am a believer in 'breed'; I hold that a strongly marked personality can influence descendants for generations. In the same way that we farmers know that certain sires – bulls – stallions – rams – have been 'prepotent' in forming breeds of shorthorns, thoroughbreds, and the numerous varieties of sheep.[4]

Later in life, Potter's home was a farmhouse in a corner of the Lake District, in Sawrey, then part of Lancashire, and she was, in actuality, a farmer and prizewinning sheep breeder. Potter's growing interest in sheep farming and an understanding of its importance in shaping the land led to a conscious determination to preserve the landscape of her beloved Lake District for posterity.

Before her journey towards a life in farming Potter's early career developed organically or even by accident. She became for a decade immersed in scientific drawing, microscopy and the world of mycology as intellectually stimulating pastimes, making good use of family connections to forge associations and push her studies.

Then came her significant but somewhat accidental career as author and illustrator of almost two dozen children's books, the majority of which were published between 1902 and 1913. *The Tale of Peter Rabbit* evolved from a letter and a privately printed storybook, which Potter gave away or sold to friends of the family. The first Frederick Warne edition, in July 1902, was already quite large at 8,000, but rapidly grew by a further 20,000 by December of the same year; by 1904 the figure had risen to 90,000, revealing how quickly the book captured the public's imagination. *Peter Rabbit* even drew attention and a compliment of sorts from the United States in pirated editions, which appeared from as early as 1904. Potter's subsequent storybooks, arriving at a rate of two a year, followed the winning formula of charting the adventures of animals in lightly moral tales; her second book, *The Tailor of Gloucester* (1903), even earned the distinction of a review in the *Tailor and Cutter* magazine ('by far the prettiest story connected with tailoring we have ever read') (no.4) and by the time of *The Tale of Benjamin Bunny* (1904) Potter was receiving attention from the *Times Literary Supplement*.[5]

Potter remained surprised at the continuing popularity of her storybooks. The success of the books can be put down to a combination of Potter's sublime watercolour imagery with a sophisticated use of language and humour, as well as her acknowledgement of the harsh realities of the animal world and her knowledge of animals' physiognomy and habits, which ensures that her characters are more than merely anthropomorphic (see no.1). The *Tales* were variously influenced by or composed during holidays at the seaside, or in Scotland or the Lake District, but increasingly the imagery and sources of inspiration reflected her growing attachment to the latter and overlapped with her burgeoning interest in farming.

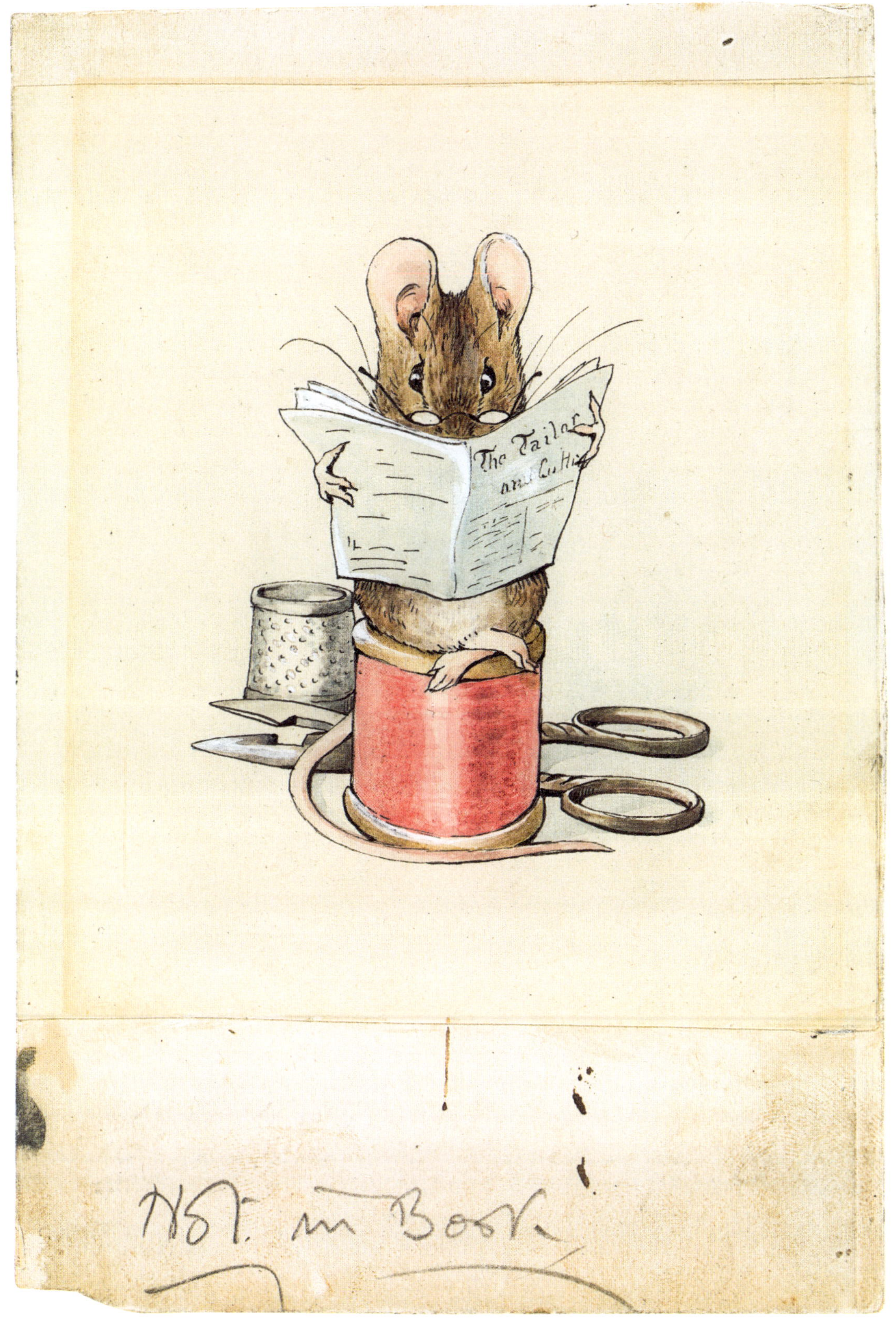
The Tailor
Not in Book

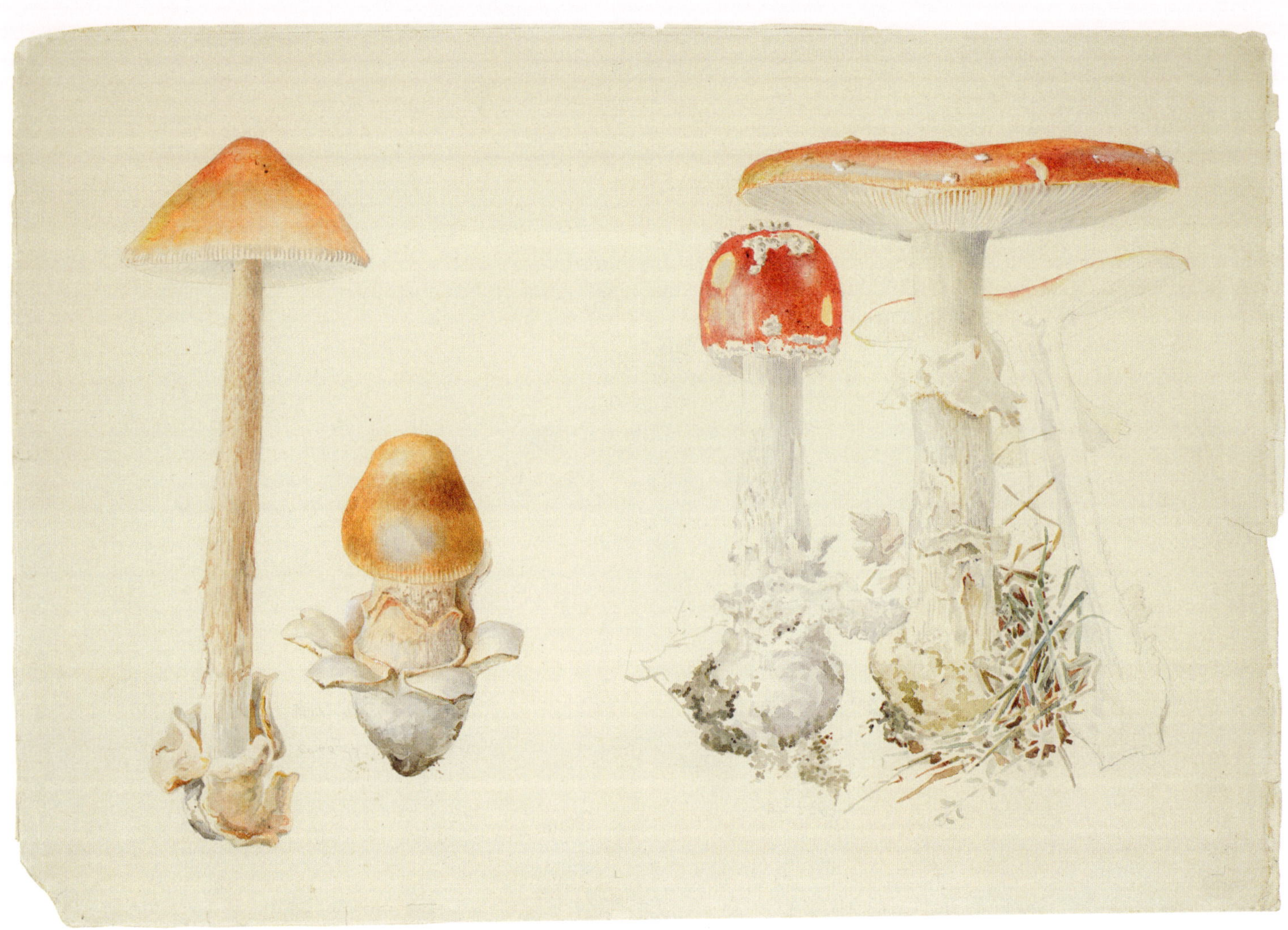

5.
Amanita crocea, 'Orange Grisette',
and *Amanita muscaria*, 'Fly Agaric',
2–3 September 1897
Watercolour and ink over pencil on paper
V&A: BP.244, Linder Bequest LB 292

The chapters in this book are arranged thematically and celebrate Potter's major achievements or legacies.

'Town and Country' provides a backdrop to Potter's home life and her family's artistic and natural history inclinations and annual travels, which had an early and lasting effect on her aesthetic sensibilities (see no.2). Potter's privileged background afforded her opportunities for cultural enrichment but paradoxically it also constrained her, since her family's wealth meant that she had no pressing need to earn a living. However, her thirst for knowledge and continued study of the world around her through drawing led her down a variety of paths. In 'Holiday Haunts' Lucy Shaw explores the subject of nineteenth-century tourism through the lens of the Potters' many holidays around Britain.

'Under the Microscope' begins in the schoolroom, with Beatrix and younger brother Walter Bertram's (1872–1918) childhood pets, and their natural history collecting and study, before turning to Beatrix's expanding intellectual pursuits, ranging from archaeology and geology to microscopy and mycology. These could well have been a testing ground for a potential career as a scientist or scientific illustrator. Professor Richard Fortey focuses on 'Miss Potter, the Mycologist' and considers the accuracy of her fungi drawings and her contribution to the study of spore germination (no.5). Had Potter become a mycologist, as she seemed inclined to in the 1890s, her famous storybooks might never have come about.

Emma Laws describes, in 'A Natural Storyteller', how Potter discovered that she could tell stories through the illustrated letters she wrote to children. This chapter explores the evolution and inspirations behind her storybooks and how she coupled her fascination with language with a, by now, highly tuned skill in drawing. Potter was not only a talented illustrator and writer but also had a pioneering interest in merchandise design and branding. Sara Glenn reflects on this acumen in 'Beatrix Potter, Entrepreneur', using objects mostly drawn from the archives of the publisher Frederick Warne.

Eighteen years of lengthy holidays around Derwentwater and Windermere led Potter ultimately to lay down her roots in the Lake District. In 1905 she bought a small farmhouse there and, as Liz Hunter MacFarlane explains in 'Living Nature', this became her specially curated space, a romantic escape rather than a home. Potter became absorbed in the business of farming and sheep breeding and, realising that revitalising a native, hardy sheep breed had a role to play in the landscape's long-term conservation, used her wealth to ensure a major legacy of land to the National Trust. Potter's marriage to the Hawkshead solicitor William Heelis in 1913 allowed her to focus full-time on farming. In 'Mrs Heelis, Farmer' James Rebanks provides an insight into the world of the Herdwick shepherd and reflects on Beatrix Heelis's place within this world.

Finally, 'Drawn from Nature: Selected Potter Protagonists' introduces the reader to some of the characters from the storybooks who were born from various strands of their creator's life, from her pets and her close study of their natures to her passion for landscapes and the Lake District.

Beatrix Potter: Drawn to Nature tells the story of an individual of enormous sensibility, whose drive and determination to create for herself a meaningful life resulted in more than one enduring legacy. We hope that readers of this book, and visitors to the exhibition that it accompanies, emerge with a sense of the breadth of Potter's achievements, not just her enduring storybooks but also her exquisitely observed scientific drawings and her contribution to the ongoing management of a 'Culture Landscape'[6] resulting from 'the combined works of nature and of man'.[7] It seeks to place Potter's justifiably famous books against the backdrop of a wider legacy: she played no small role in securing the Lake District's long-term conservation, and therefore its eventual designation as a UNESCO World Heritage site. Potter's life story shows that through talent, perseverance and passion great things can grow from inconsequential beginnings.

Annemarie Bilclough

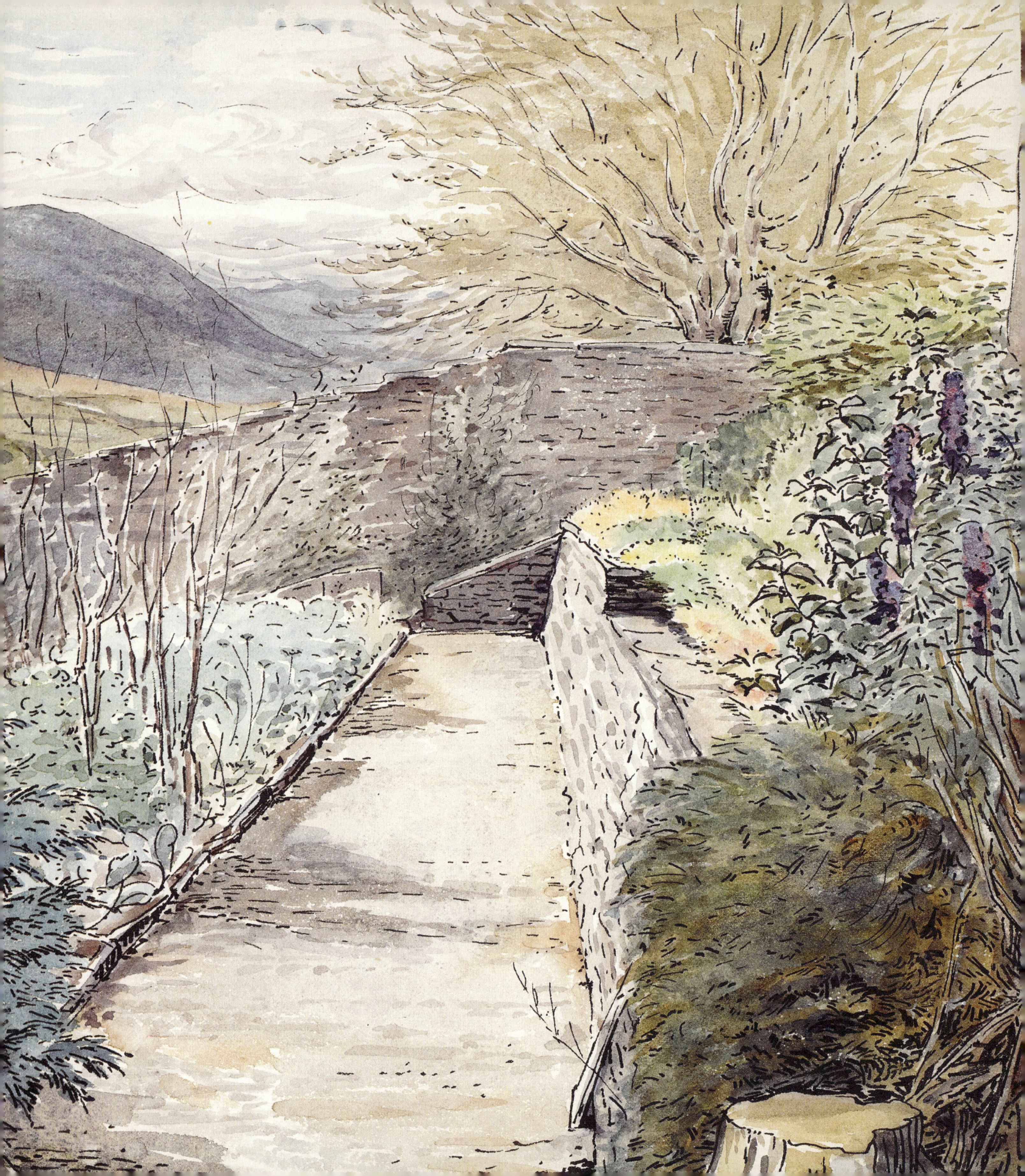

Town and Country

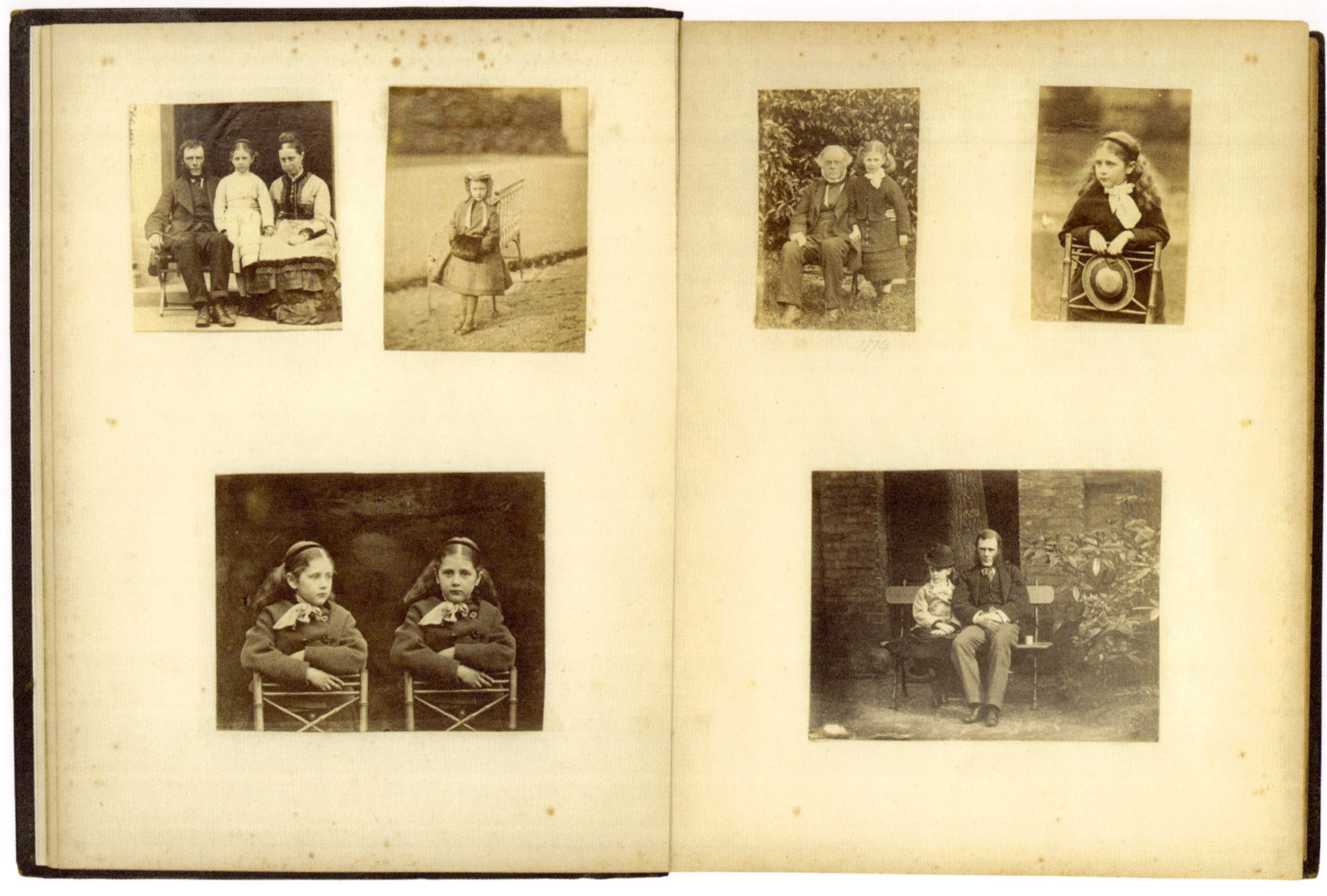

6. Above
Rupert Potter (1832–1914)
Beatrix Potter as a young girl, and with her parents Rupert and Helen Potter (top left), William Gaskell (top, third from left), and Rupert Potter (bottom right), 1870s
Pages from a photograph album, albumen prints on paper
V&A: AAD/2006/4/459/11–16, given by Joan Duke

7. Opposite
Unknown photographer
2 (porch) and 3–6 Bolton Gardens, London, January 1933
Photographic print on paper
London Metropolitan Archives, SC_PHL_01_202_92_272

Camfield, country most beautiful, flowers and birds' nests. Why do people live in London so much?... Head suddenly completely better without apparent cause.

(BEATRIX POTTER, *JOURNAL*, 19 MAY 1884)[1]

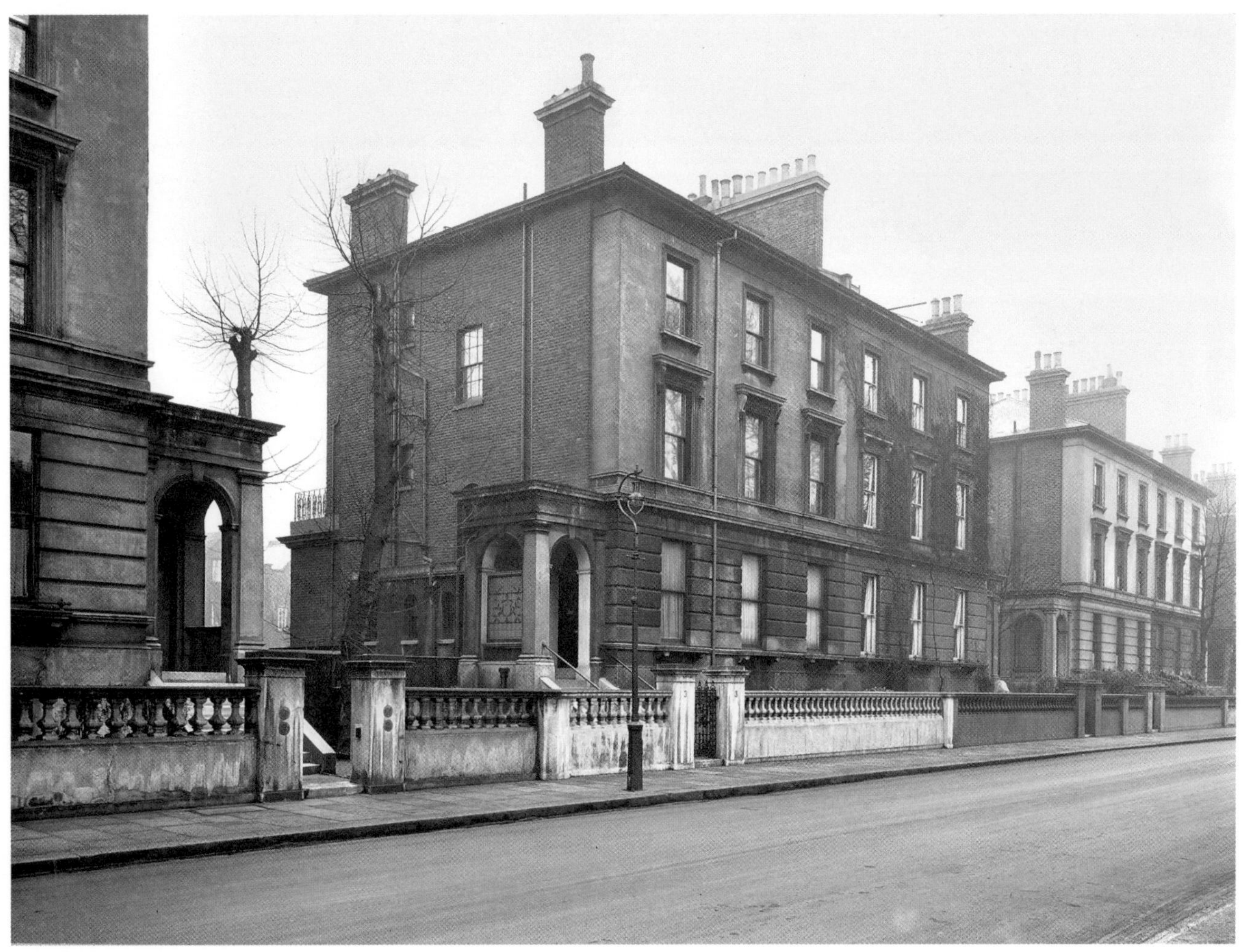

Beatrix Potter spent the first half of her life in a large semi-detached house in Bolton Gardens just off the Old Brompton Road in Kensington, London (no.7).[2] Her father Rupert, a barrister, and mother Helen moved into the newly built house on a steadily growing estate in around 1865, shortly before Beatrix's birth (no.6).[3]

The Kensington development was intended to attract the wealthy middle classes and it transformed a semi-rural parish of market gardens into a London suburb, served by several railway stations. During the most intense period of construction from 1860 to 1880, the area's population more than doubled.[4] However, as late as 1883, the 16-year-old Potter referred to 'the last bit of the orchards left' and to builders 'cutting a road across the field, preparatory to building'.[5] It is little wonder, growing up surrounded by such works, that Potter complained her 'unloved' home was the source of frequent illness; dust and dirt combined with the ubiquitous London smog, not to mention smoke from the frequent chimney fires of their next-door neighbours – the Saunders.[6] Potter had no love for London and was 'discontented and never strong as a young person'.[7] The regular political unrest and occasional violence also caused her some anxiety.[8]

In her early years, Potter's London horizons were evidently quite limited, as at 19 she was surprised to find herself driving past Horse Guards, Whitehall, and along the Strand for the very first time; she did not venture further east until 1890.[9] Nonetheless, she went swimming, and visited the Round Pond in Kensington Gardens and the Zoological Gardens in Regent's Park, the sorts of places frequented

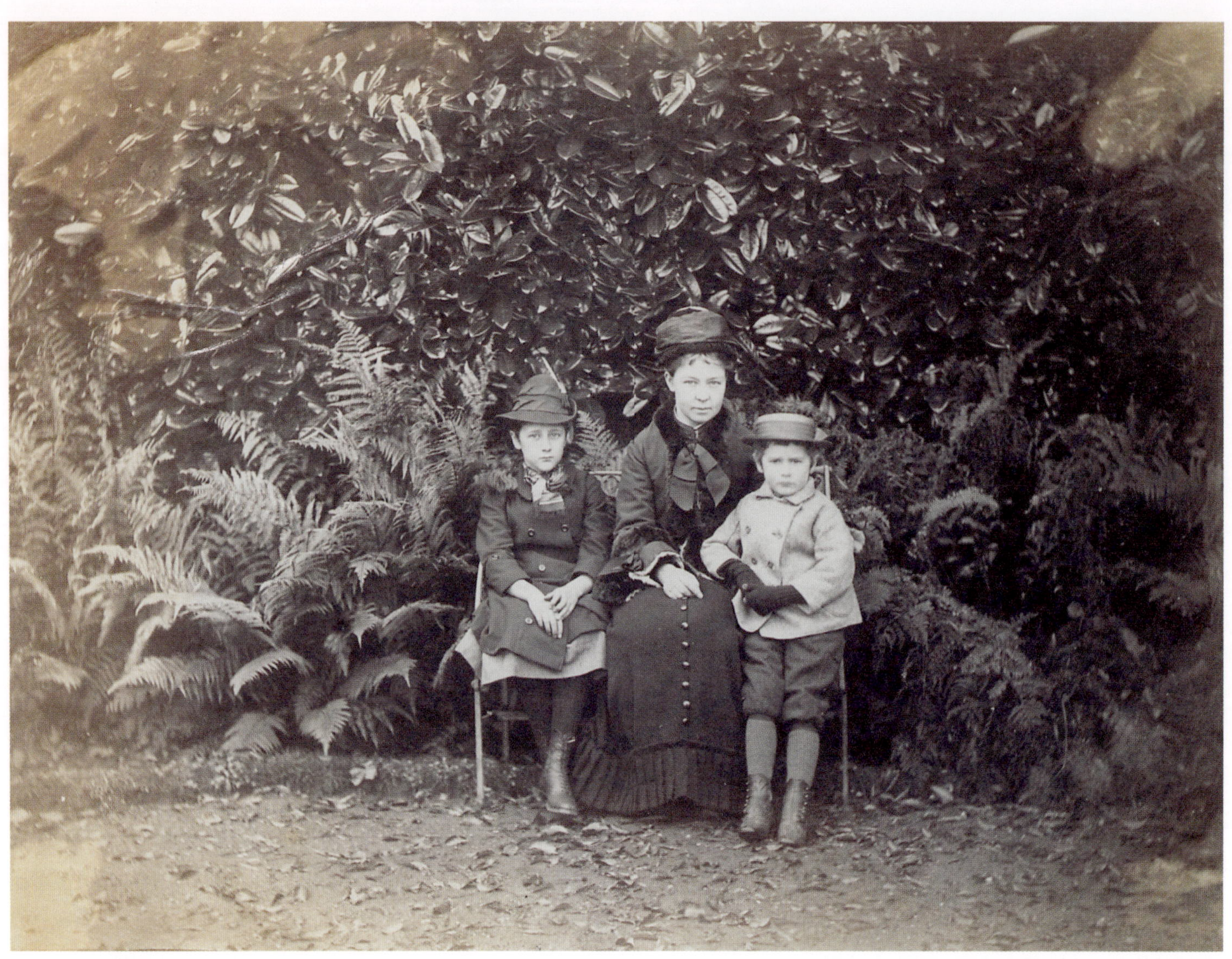

8.
Rupert Potter (1832–1914)
Beatrix and Bertram Potter with their governess, Miss Davidson, c.1878
Photograph in an album, albumen print on paper
Cotsen Children's Library, Special Collections, Princeton University Library, 10005.178

My education finished 9th. July... I regret German very much, history I can read alone, French is still going on,...there is no general word to express the feelings I have always entertained towards arithmetic.

(BEATRIX POTTER, *JOURNAL*, 10 JULY 1885)

by nannies and their charges.[10] The district also benefited from a major cultural centre nearby known as 'Albertopolis', a cluster of schools and museums established to advance art, design and science, which afforded Beatrix relatively easy access to opportunities for self-improvement as she grew older.[11]

Potter's home life continued in much the same way for more than 40 years: as an unmarried and dutiful daughter, she remained at home, dependent on family money and in a household run according to her mother's direction.[12] On the other hand, at 18 she took her first driving lesson in a 'little carriage' drawn by a 16-year-old pony. She enjoyed it very much, noting '[have] had no misfortune yet', and it seems that she sometimes drove herself, albeit chaperoned, around London. Later, after an accident in the Lake District, she wrote, '[I] never touched anything in my life', despite having 'driven in much funnier traffic in London'.[13] A well-connected family also ensured leisure and travel opportunities and contact with an artistic, scientific and political milieu; as she entered adulthood Potter accompanied her mother on social visits and went to art exhibitions and occasional cultural events.[14]

Beatrix was homeschooled and was joined from the age of five by her brother Walter Bertram (known as Bertram). The pair were looked after first by a nursemaid (Ann Mackenzie) and then by governesses, Madeline Davidson (no.8) and Florence ('Florrie') Hammond.[15] Bertram went to boarding school when Beatrix was 16, but despite the pair being close, Beatrix gives little impression in her journal of the impact his absence must have had on her.

Potter's journal entries indicate that her education was not as 'neglected' as she later claimed.[16] She was taught geography, grammar, French dictation and Latin, including poetry by Cicero and Virgil.[17] She may have had music lessons, and while she lamented her lack of German, she had a good enough grasp of it to form a critical impression of Julius Oscar Brefeld's multivolume work on mycology: 'discursive and unstable as – as *Dacromyces deliquescens*'.[18] A surviving exercise book (which she used later to press ferns) contains carefully copied passages of history and poetry (see no.57).

By her teenage years, Potter's education must have been structured, since she celebrated the days' shortening: 'believe shall not do [lessons] in the afternoon any more. A delightful prospect for the drawing'.[19] Where her education was limited was in its reliance on the individual abilities of her various governesses.

Florence Hammond left in June 1883 when she found her charge's level of knowledge had outstripped her own.[20] By this time, Potter felt that she had 'set in view German, English Reading, and General Knowledge, cutting off more and more time for painting', and was dismayed when her mother found yet another governess for her.[21] Her last, though, was more like a companion. Sophisticated and well-travelled, Annie Carter must have been a revelation to Potter, whose life was so sheltered.[23]

There is, of course, more to education than the schoolroom, and Potter's home life offered her a

I learned to read on the Waverly [sic] novels; I had had a horrid large print primer and a stodgy fat book...by Mrs Trimmer. I know I hated it – then I was let loose on 'Rob Roy'.

(BEATRIX POTTER, '"ROOTS" OF THE PETER RABBIT TALES', 1929)[22]

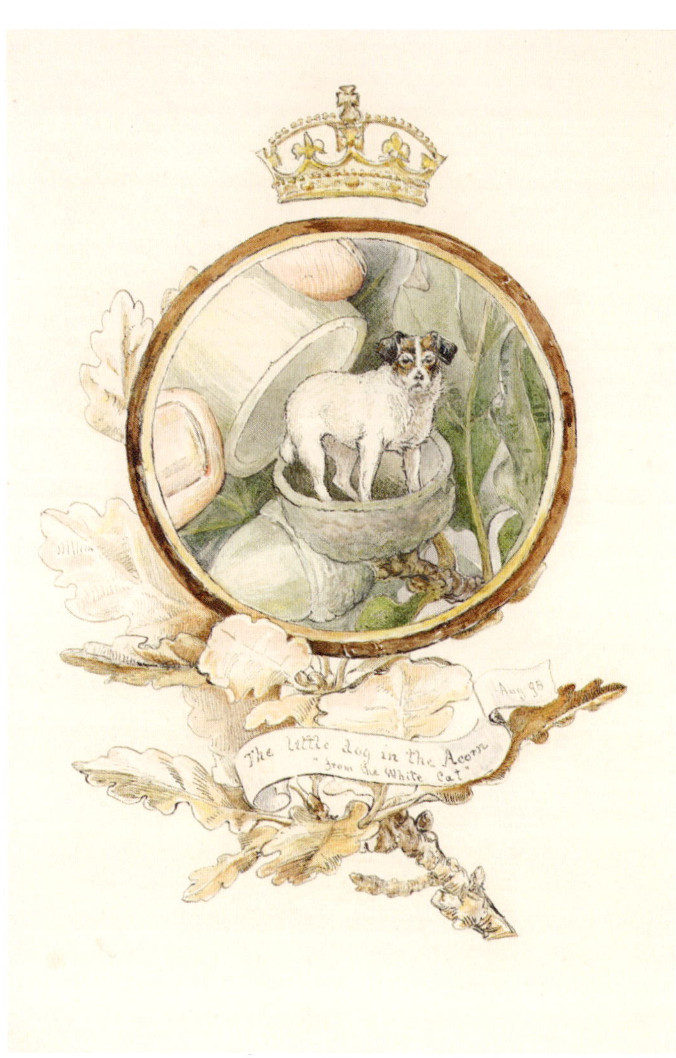

particular advantage in access to books. Some were her own, but she would have seen others in libraries belonging to her family and even in holiday homes.[24] In fact, she seems to have encountered a wealth of books, in spite of a later claim to have had 'very few'.[25]

As 'a small child of 3 or 4' she read 'Trash...silly stories about other little girls' doings', and as she grew older, she 'carefully kept' the books of authors Juliana Horatia Ewing and Maria Edgeworth.[26] In her sixties, she re-read Edgeworth's *Simple Susan* (1800) with 'as much pleasure as ever, in an old dumpy edition that belonged to my grandmother.'[27] She remembered trying to imitate the hymns of Isaac Watts and 'sentimental ballad descriptions of Scottish scenery',[28] and further back in the mists of memory her Scottish nurse Ann Mackenzie told her fairy tales. These in later life became a source of more sustained study and inspiration for her art (no.9), as did Edward Lear's poem 'The Owl and the Pussy-Cat' (1871) (no.10). She certainly owned a copy of Lear's *A Book of Nonsense* (1846).

Besides all this standard children's fare, Potter remembered having *Uncle Tom's Cabin* (1852) by Harriet Beecher Stowe read to her and being 'fond' of international-selling American novels such as Elizabeth Wetherell's *The Wide, Wide World* (1850). The Uncle Remus stories (1881–1907) compiled by Joel Chandler Harris delighted her with their combination of humorous storytelling and dialect, and inspired some of her earliest imaginative illustrations (no.104, see 'A Natural Storyteller', pp.130–31).[31]

9. Opposite
Illustration to Madame d'Aulnoy's 'The White Cat' (1698), 1898
Watercolour, ink and pencil on paper
Free Library, Philadelphia, RBD BP ART 24

10. Below
Illustrated manuscript based on Edward's Lear's verse, 'The Owl and the Pussy-Cat', c.1897
Ink and pencil on paper
V&A: BP.619(a), Linder Bequest LB 981

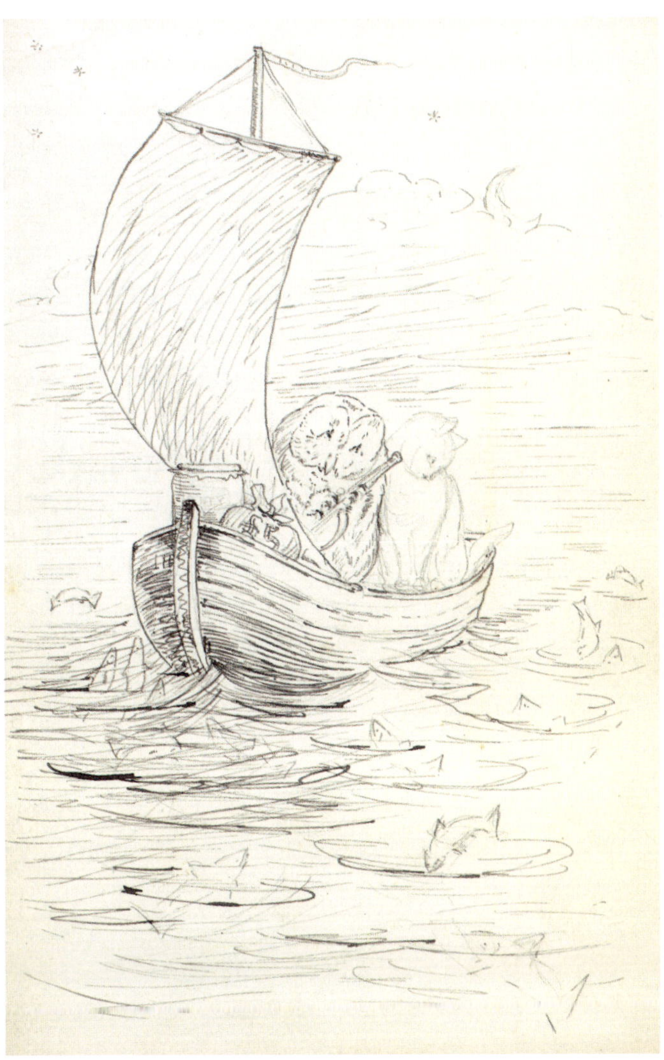

Yet despite having books intended for children her own age, it was through Sir Walter Scott's *Waverley* novels (1814–32) that Potter actually learned to read: 'I spelled through a few pages painfully; then I tried "Ivanhoe" – and the "Talisman" – then I tried "Rob Roy" again; all at once I began to READ (missing the long words of course)'.[32] She memorized Scott's poem 'The Lady of the Lake' (1810) when she was as young as seven and must also have absorbed Shakespeare early on because an accomplished watercolour from 1878 survives, inspired by Macbeth (no.12).[33]

Of course, access to books sometimes also meant exposure to illustrations. Potter admired Richard Doyle's cartoons for *Punch* magazine 'from a little child',[34] and growing up in the late 1860s she had the advantage of colourful toy books, such as 'all of the Walter Crane' books (written by Mrs Molesworth), which she got 'as they came out'.[35] She was thought 'too young, or the book too old' for Lewis Carroll's *Through the Looking-Glass, and What Alice Found There* (1871), but later she remembered being 'absorbed' by John Tenniel's wood-engraved illustrations when, aged nine, she was given a copy of the book by a visiting Oxford don, Professor Wilson (she received the previous book, *Alice's Adventures in Wonderland* [1865] a few years later).[36] When she was 10, Potter's pride and joy was Jemima Blackburn's *Birds Drawn from Nature* (1862), and at some point she must have come across Thomas Bewick's illustrations, since she observed later that Blackburn's birds 'do not on the average stand on their legs so well...but he is her only possible rival.' (no.13)[37]

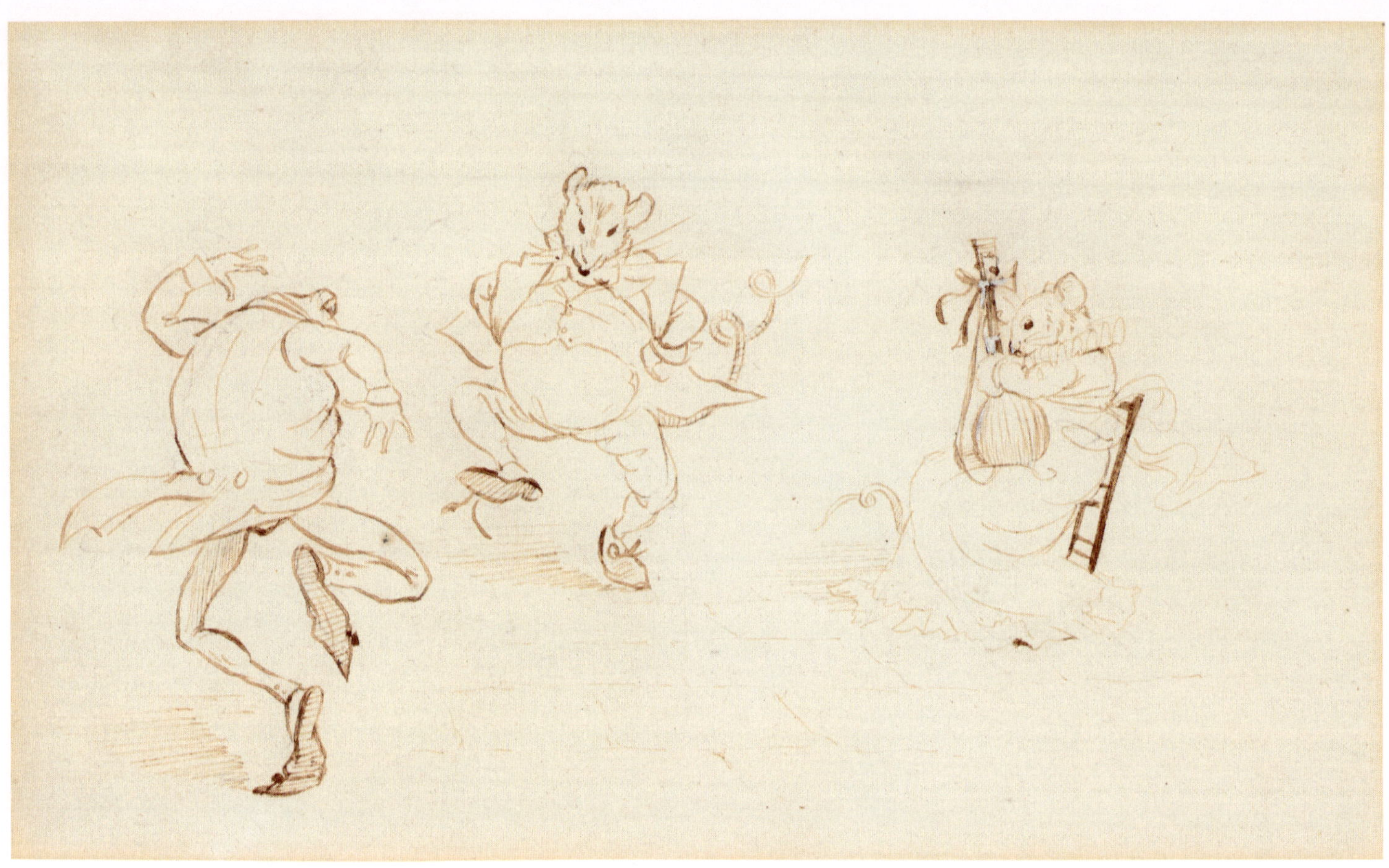

11. Above
Randolph Caldecott (1846–1886)
'But While They Were Thus Merry-Making',
for *A Frog He Would A-Wooing Go*, c.1875
Ink on paper
Manchester Art Gallery, 1933.25,
formerly belonging to Rupert and Helen Potter

12. Opposite
The Three Witches of Birnam Wood
(inspired by William Shakespeare's *Macbeth*), 1878
Watercolour over pencil on paper
Cotsen Children's Library, Special Collections,
Princeton University Library, 33207

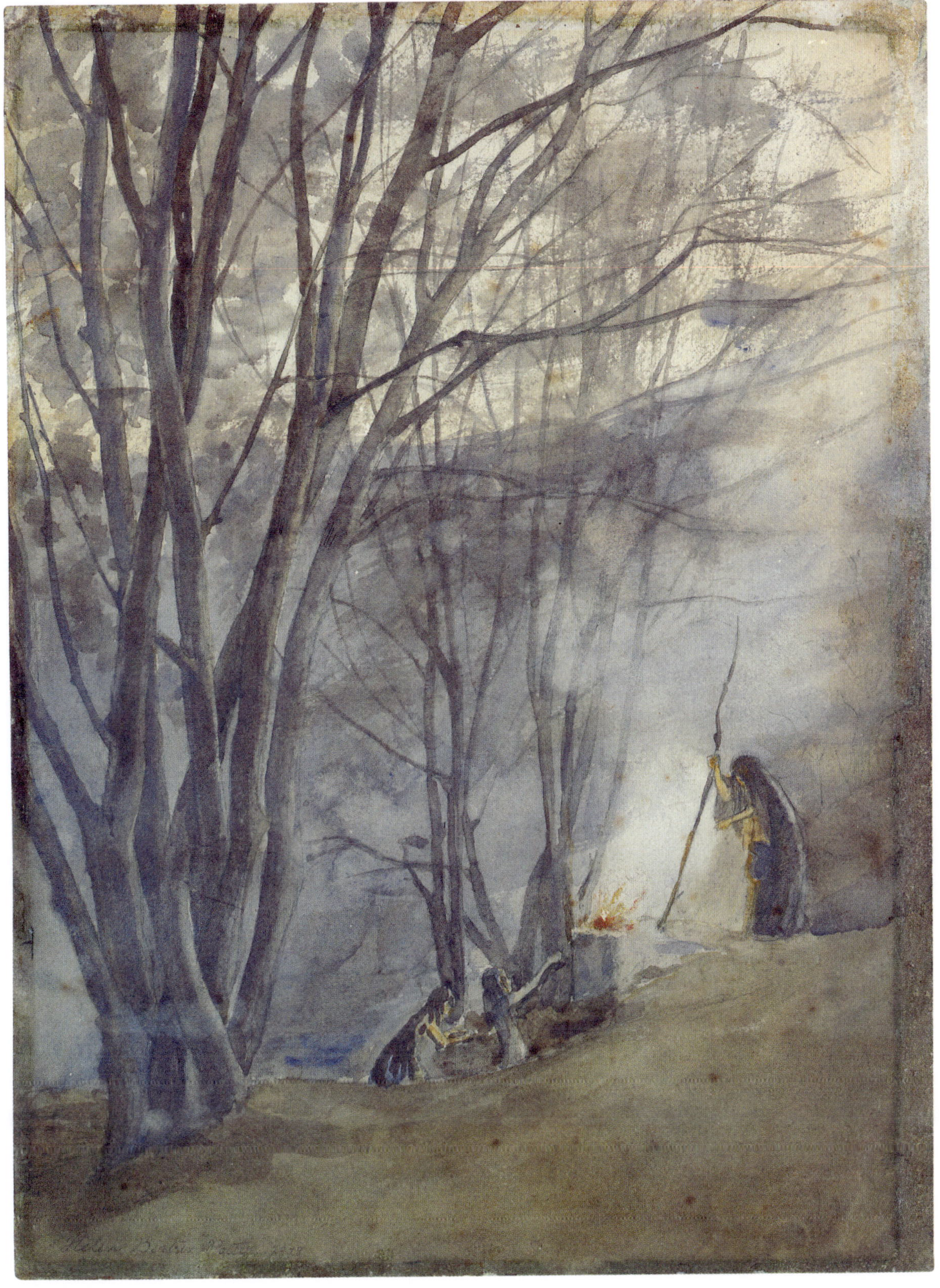

13. Below
Tracing of The Red Breast from Jemima Blackburn's *Birds Drawn from Nature*, c.1876
Pencil on paper
V&A: BP.419(B), Linder Bequest LB 1131

14. Right
Page from a sketchbook, c.1875
Watercolour over pencil on paper
V&A: BP.740, Linder Bequest LB 1090

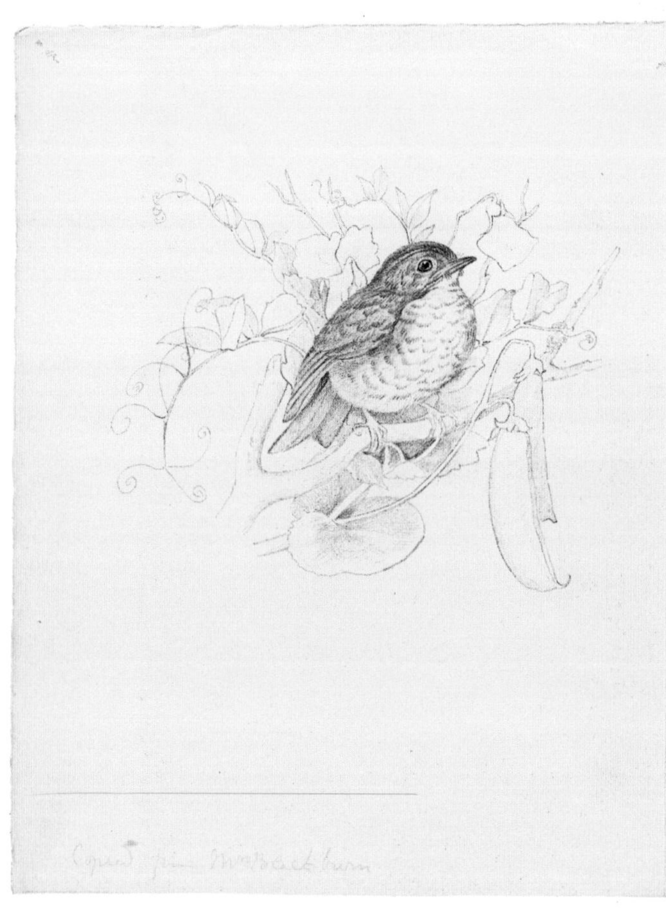

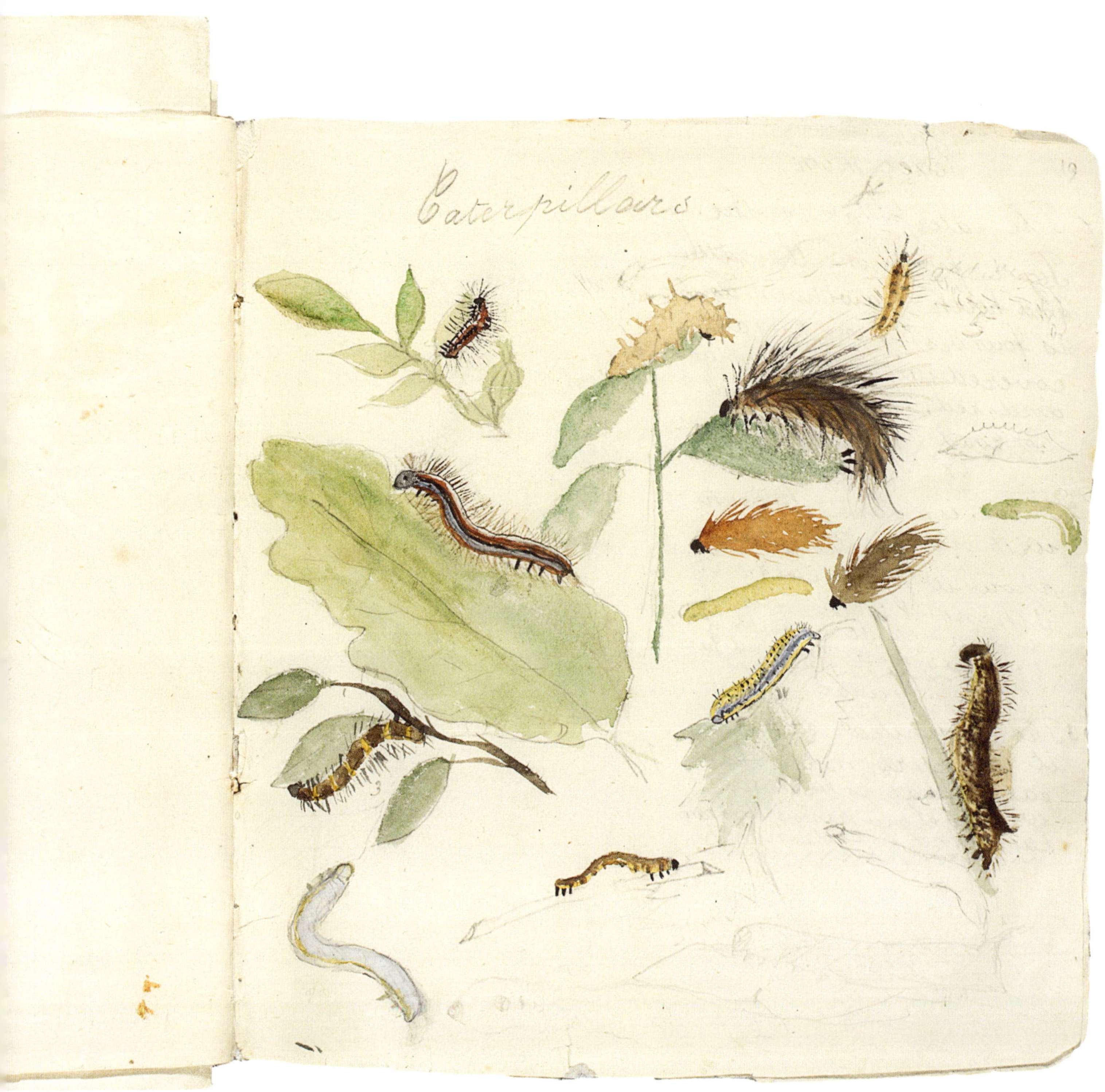
Caterpillars
19

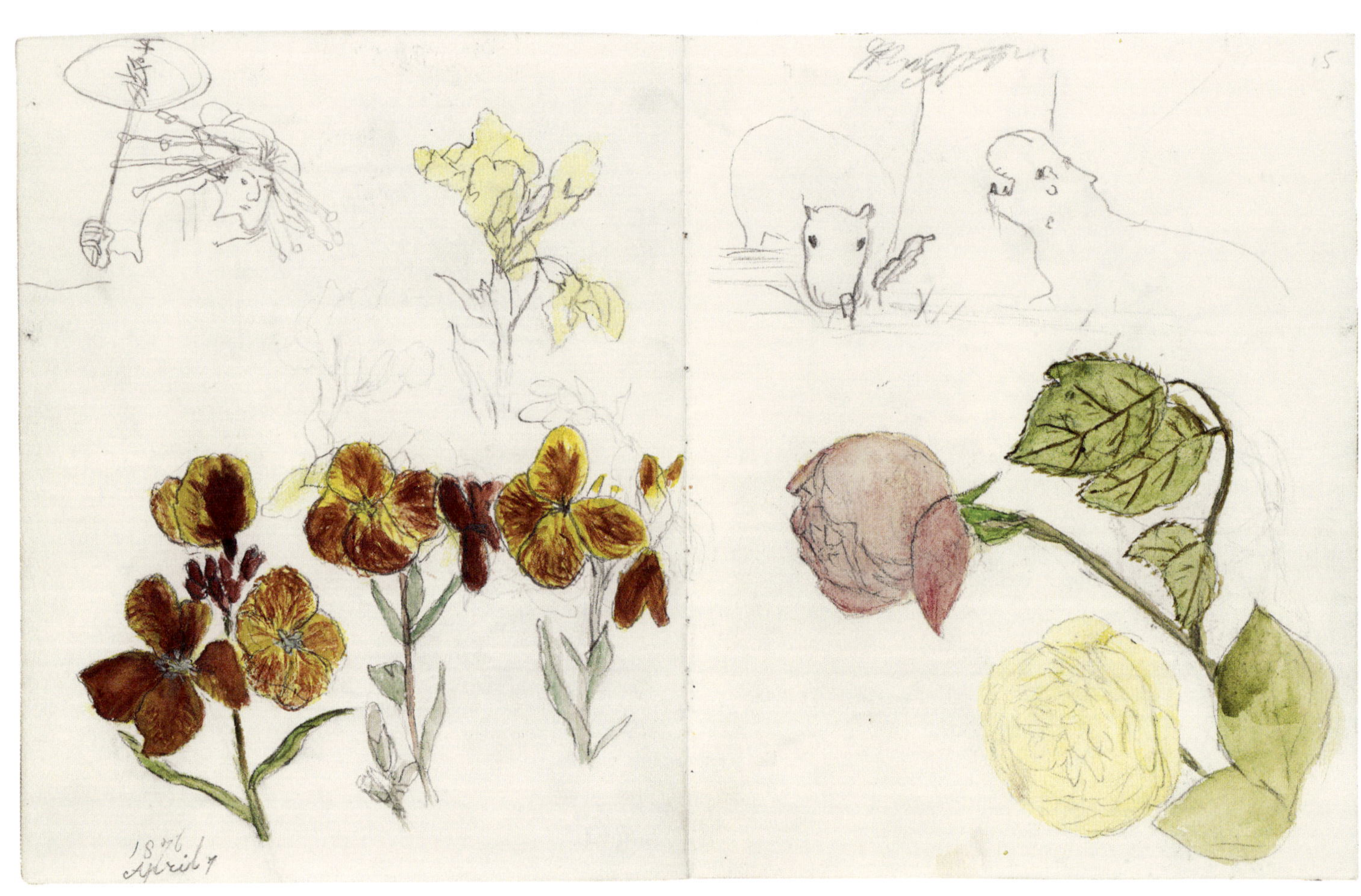

15.
Page from a sketchbook, dated 7 April 1876
Watercolour and pencil on paper
V&A: BP.741, Linder Bequest LB 1091

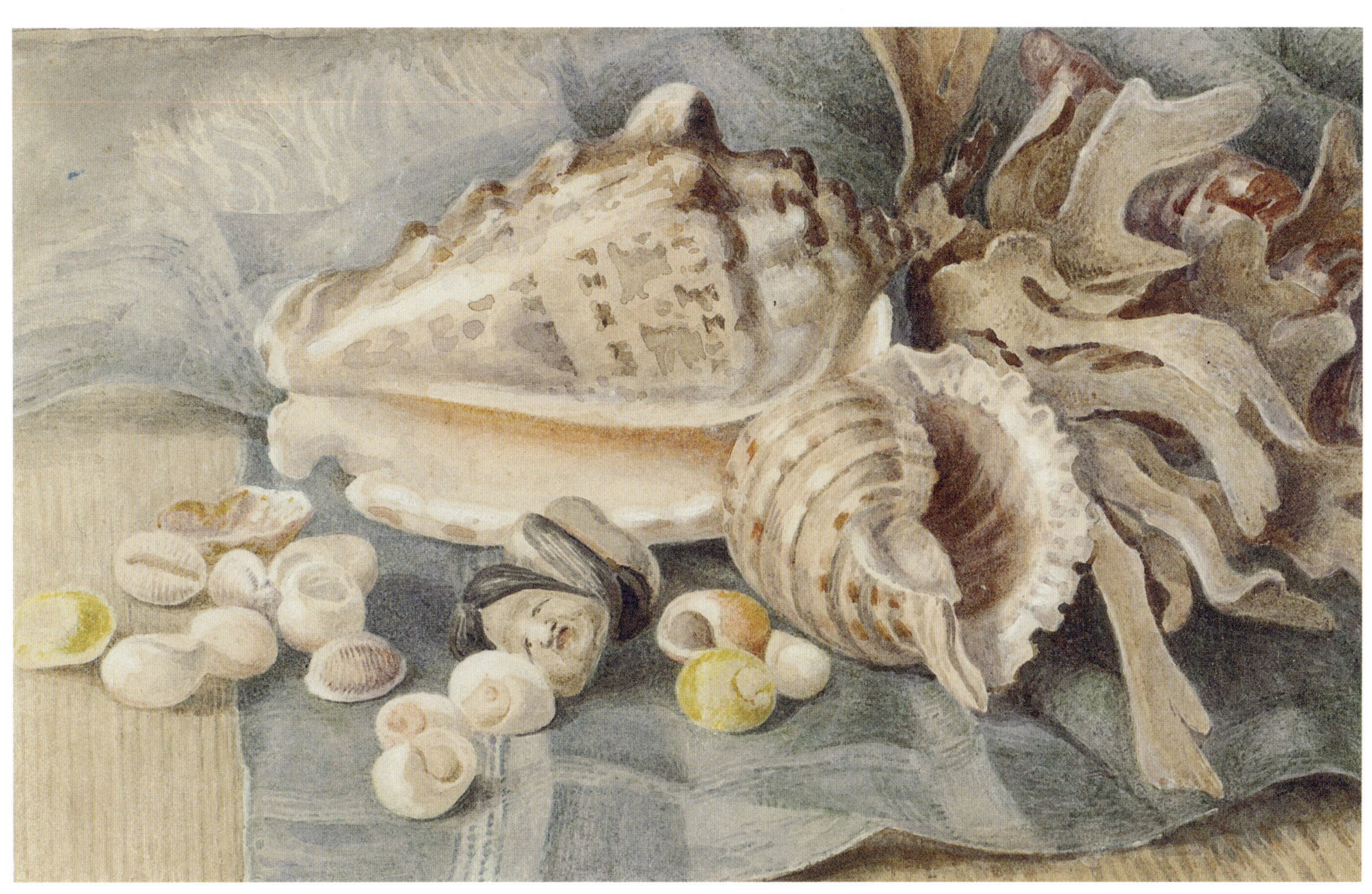

16.
Shells, seaweed and Japanese netsuke masks, c.1885
Watercolour over pencil on paper
V&A: LC 16/A/5, given by the Linder Collection

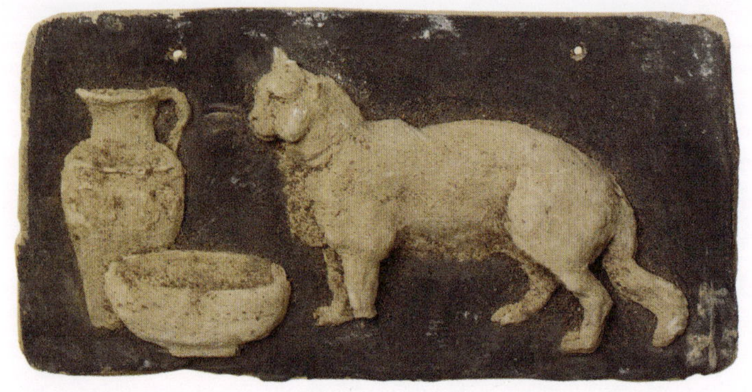

17. Above
Modelled copy of Wedgwood jasperware design, 1885
Painted clay
V&A: BP.864, Linder Bequest LB 1871

> *I did try to copy [Randolph] Caldecott; but...I did not achieve much resemblance. When I was young...the [Pre-Raphaelites']... meticulous copying of flowers & plants etc influenced me.*
>
> (BEATRIX POTTER, LETTER TO ARTHUR STEPHENS, 7 FEBRUARY 1943)[38]

A constant in Potter's life from an early age was drawing. Her first surviving sketchbook is one she stitched together when she was eight from scraps of drawer lining-paper and stationery (no.14), and in this and other sketchbooks she copied from a variety of illustrations, including those in Walter Crane's *The Baby's Opera* (1877) and Jemima Blackburn's *The Pipits* (1872) (no.15). With his lively and humorous pen and ink outlines, Randolph Caldecott was to Potter 'one of the greatest illustrators of all'.[39] Around 1884 her father bought from the Fine Art Society Gallery two of the artist's pen and ink sketches for *A Frog He Would A-Wooing Go* (1883) to add to a number of watercolours for *The Three Jovial Huntsmen* (1880) he had purchased previously.[40] The Frog story and sketches not only inspired Potter's *The Tale of Mr. Jeremy Fisher* (1906) but also reveal strong similarities to some of her animal characters; his gentleman rat bears an uncanny resemblance to Samuel Whiskers (no.11). Potter received formal art lessons from the age of 12 from Miss Cameron, having:

> great reason to be grateful to her, though we were not on particularly good terms for the last good while. I have learnt from her freehand, model, geometry, perspective and a little water-colour flower painting.[41]

Some carefully executed drawings from 1880 correspond to handwritten notes detailing which colours to use, suggesting that they relate to these lessons.[42] Close to the Potters' house, the schools of art attached to the South Kensington Museum (now the Victoria and Albert Museum) offered

18. Above
Helen Potter (1839–1931)
Drawings in an album belonging to Beatrix's mother Helen Potter, 1873–8
Watercolour over ink and pencil on paper
National Trust, 242512

19. Opposite
Drawing of part of a frieze, June 1882
Watercolour over pencil on paper
V&A: BP.222, Linder Bequest LB 88

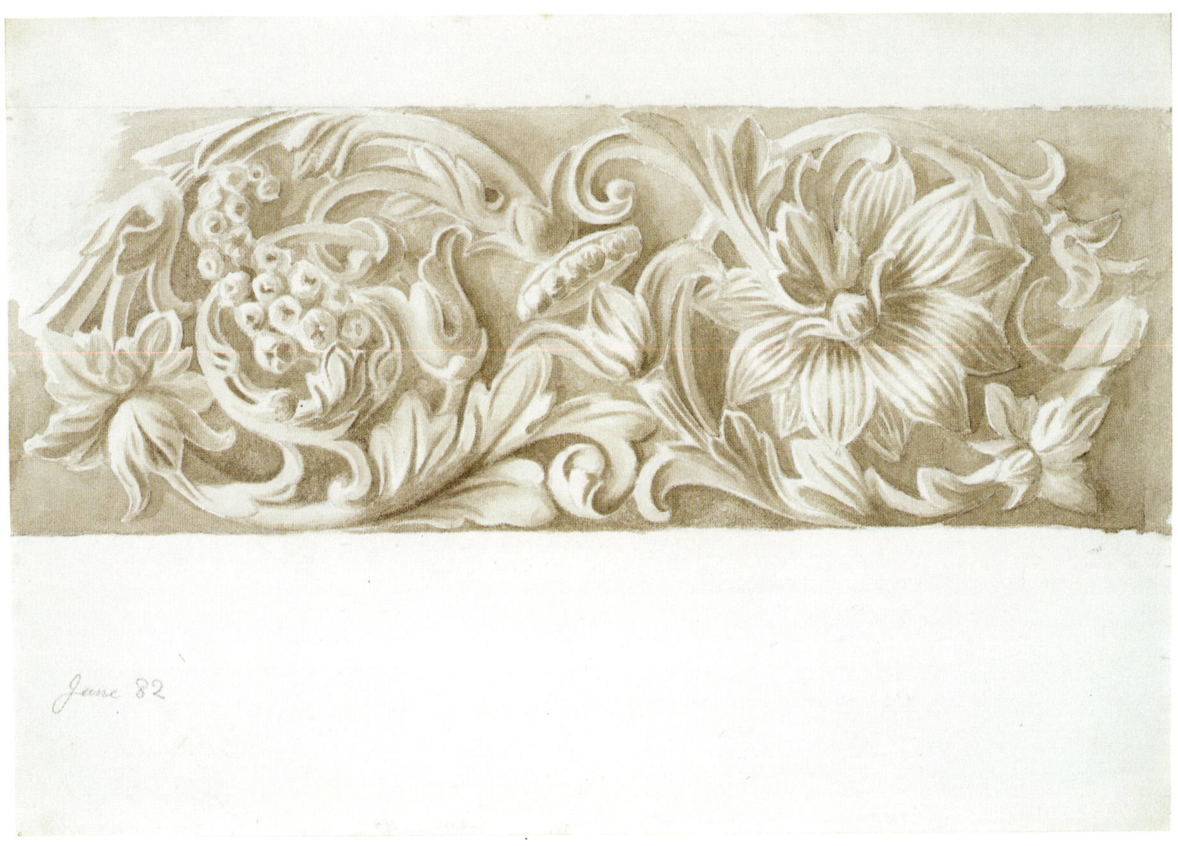

modelling practice from plaster casts of architectural sculpture. When Beatrix was 13, she took evening examinations there in model and freehand drawing, receiving an 'excellent' grade in both (no.19).[43] Copying exemplary works of art was standard practice in art education and examples by Potter from a landscape by John Constable and a portrait by Thomas Gainsborough suggest that she also used the museum's art collection for self-study.[44]

Potter did not distinguish between copying for study and for pleasure. Her sketchbooks include imagery from Japanese prints, and pencil and pen drawings seemingly taken from engraved natural history illustrations (nos 15, 16, 52). As a teenager, browsing in her grandmother's library, she came across and copied the outline designs for Homer's *Iliad* and *Odyssey* by John Flaxman, the 'greatest English draughtsman that has ever lived',[45] and she used white clay found near a holiday home in Hertfordshire to reproduce designs seen on Wedgwood jasperware:

'It is all the same, drawing, painting, modelling, the irresistible desire to copy any beautiful object which strikes the eye.' (no.17)[46]

In keeping sketchbooks and learning from other illustrators, Potter no doubt received encouragement, practical or by example, from her parents. Helen was a proficient landscape watercolourist and she illustrated a page of the household visitors' book of 'favourites' to reflect her interests (no.18).[47] As a student in his twenties, Rupert had kept a sketchbook, which he filled with pen and ink copies of book illustrations and natural history engravings, including a watercolour drawing of a tulip copied from a Vere Foster drawing book, as well as landscapes drawn from observation and some inventions of his own, such as flying puddle ducks in bonnets (no.20). Copying also inspired shared projects between Rupert and the children: they traced birds and animals from Foster's books for transfer onto linen and ceramics (nos 21, 22).

I never thought there could be such pictures. It is almost too much to see them all at once – just fancy seeing five magnificent Van Dyck's [sic] side by side, before me who never thought to see one. It is rather a painful pleasure, but I have seldom felt such a great one.

(BEATRIX POTTER, *JOURNAL*, 13 JANUARY 1883)[48]

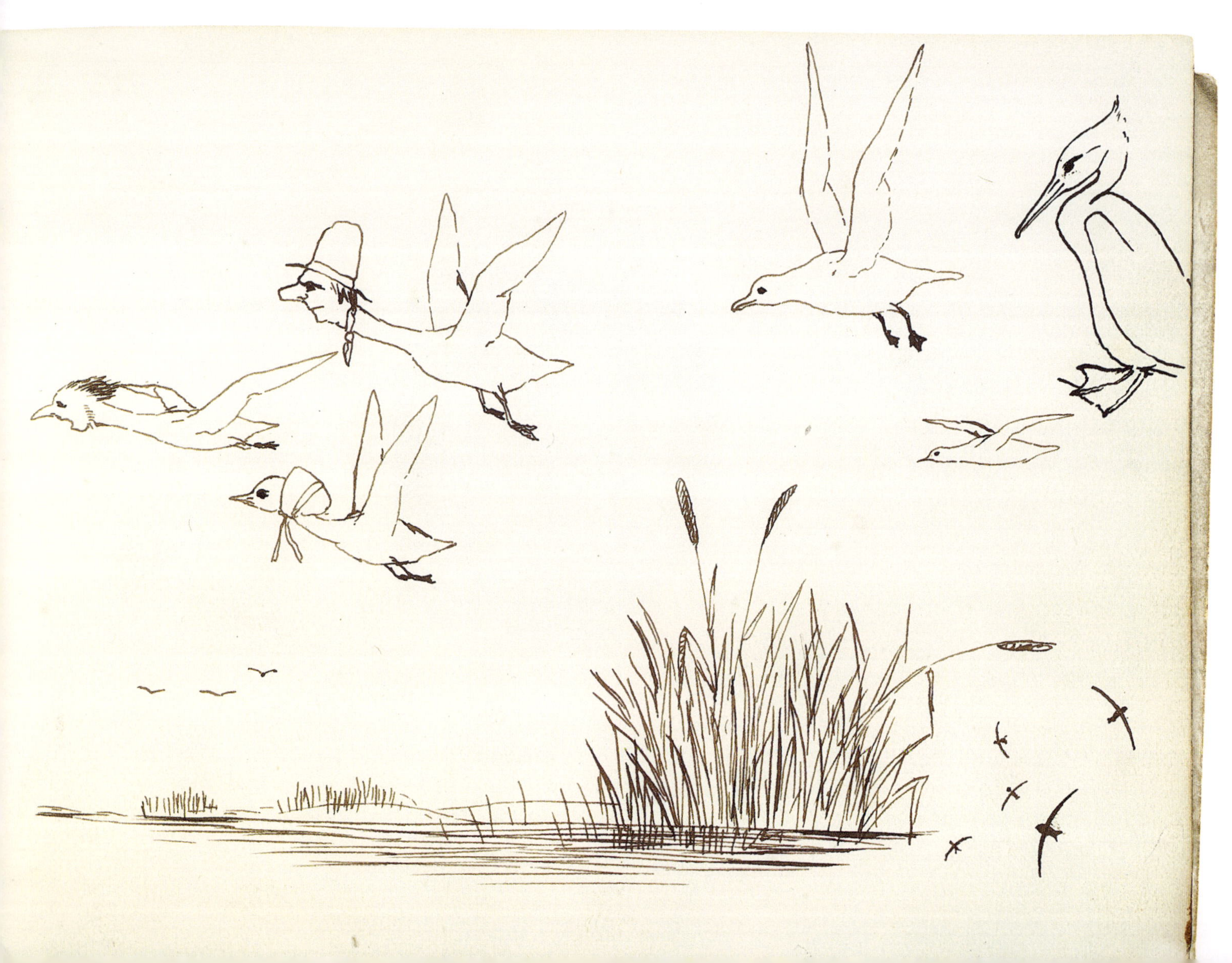

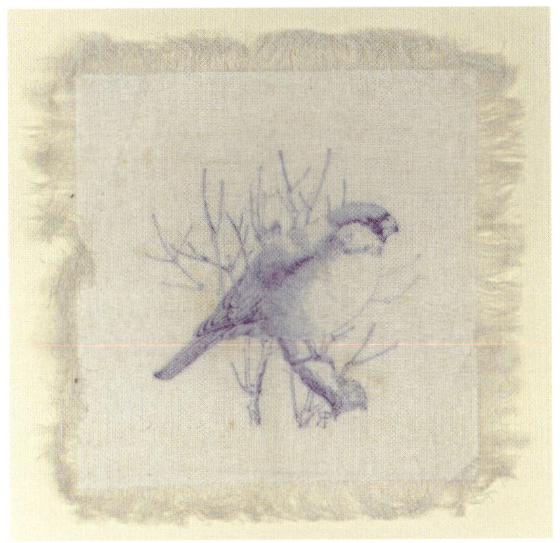

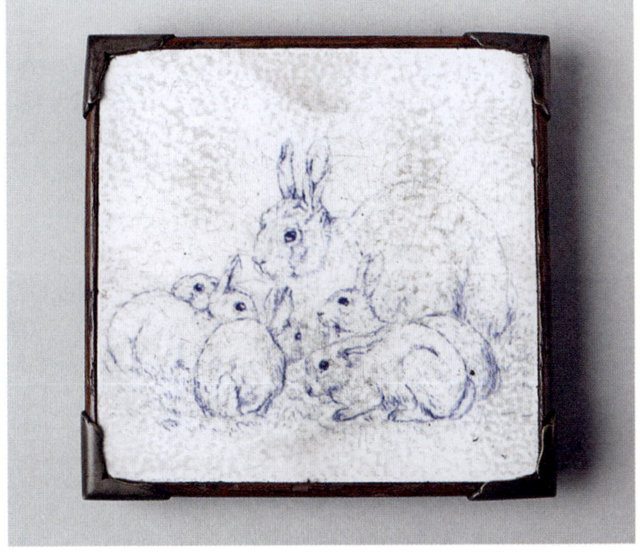

20. Opposite
Rupert Potter (1832–1914)
Page from a sketchbook, 1853
Ink on paper
V&A: BP.782, Linder Bequest LB 1121

21. Top
Rupert Potter (1832–1914)
Outline of a bird, c.1873
Transfer print on linen
V&A: AAD/2006/4/350, given by Joan Duke

22. Above
Family of rabbits, copied from
a Vere Foster drawing book, 1881
Transfer-printed ceramic tile
National Trust, 641377.1

Besides having access to libraries, Potter benefited from art collections in her relatives' various homes. Her parents had a modest collection, which included William Henry Hunt's meticulous *Bird's Nest and Blossom* (c.1851) and landscapes by David Cox.[49] Her uncle, Edmund Crompton Potter, owned a substantial collection that ranged from Chinese enamels to paintings by modern artists such as the Pre-Raphaelites. Following his death, the Potters visited the auction rooms of Christie, Manson and Woods in London to see the collection for one last time prior to its sale in 1884: 'To think that *Stella* [by Millais] has once been in our family and is going.'[50] 'Grandmama' Leech's house at Gorse Hall in Stalybridge, Greater Manchester, also had 'engravings on the stair'.[51]

Where the nine-year-old Beatrix came across Japanese prints is not known, but may have been through her grandfather John Leech's trading business (no.15).[52] Her family owned japanned furniture and she clearly had access to decorative pieces and continued to hold the Japanese style in high regard.[53] In her diary she described Blackburn's illustrations of the hooded crow and herring gull as 'worthy of the Japanese', and when she admired landscapes she compared them to the 'Japanese method' in a manner suggesting she considered the style to be the pinnacle of quality.[54] Potter's earliest experience of art must have come mostly from the pieces owned by the family:

> It was a singular thing, when I had always shown a taste for drawing, that I should have reached the age of seventeen without being taken to see any collection of pictures other than... *[text is unfinished but suggestive of visits to her family]*[55]

She was, however, able to see a practising artist's studio through her father's friendship with Pre-Raphaelite painter John Everett Millais, whose studio was in nearby Cromwell Place. An amateur photographer, Rupert Potter sometimes provided Millais with landscape and portrait photographs to serve as source material and Beatrix had a 'most affectionate remembrance' of the artist. She recalled that when she was little he had given her tips on the use of colours and 'the kindest encouragement with my drawing... [saying] "plenty of people can *draw*, but you and my son John have observation".'[56]

23. Below
Coat, c.1790–1800
Embroidered silk
V&A: 295–1898

24. Opposite
Sketch of a waistcoat, 1902
Taken from the 18th-century waistcoat, see no.25
Watercolour and pencil on paper
V&A: LC 9/A/2, given by the Linder Collection

25. Overleaf left
Detail from a waistcoat, 1780–9
Embroidered silk, linen, chenille, warp-frame woven net
V&A: 652A–1898

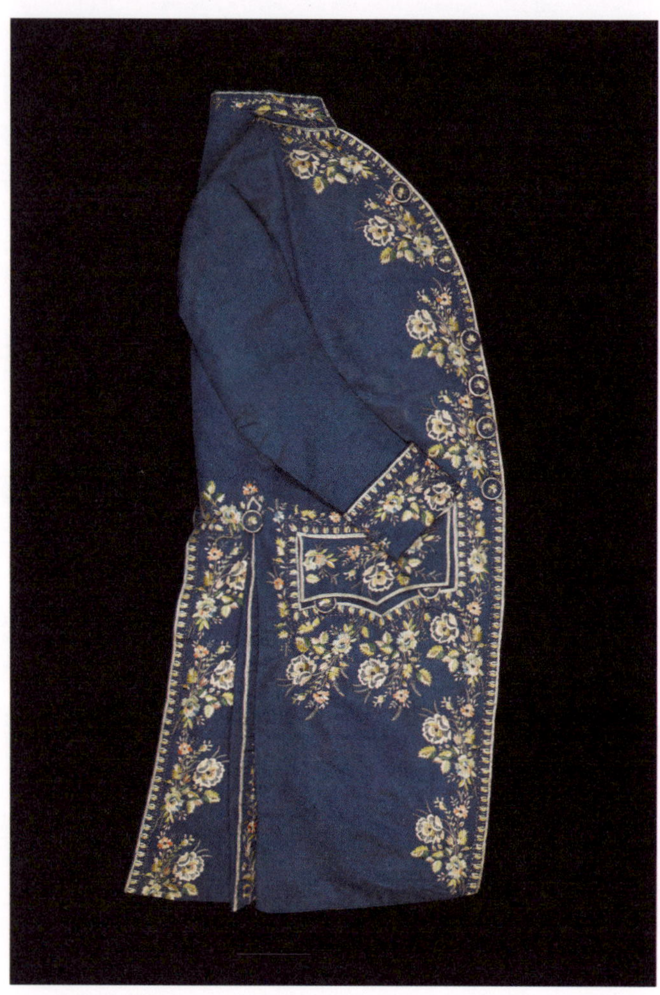

26. Overleaf right
The Tailor of Gloucester artwork, 1902
Watercolour, ink and gouache on paper
Tate, A01100

As Potter reached her late teens and began visiting galleries in London with one or other of her parents, her appreciation of art became more serious and she wrote detailed critical accounts in her diary. Her first ever gallery trip – to the Royal Academy of Art's Winter Exhibition – astounded her. Although it left her slightly 'disheartened', at the same time it was a stimulus to improvement: 'It has raised my idea of art', and the work of artist Angelica Kauffman showed her 'what a woman has done'.[57] On 15 December 1883 she visited four galleries in a single day: the Fine Art Society Gallery to see some illustrations by 'Phiz' (pen name of Hablot Knight Browne) for Charles Dickens's books ('simply marvellous...a wonderful difference of expression in the faces'), as well as the Doré, Pall Mall and McLean's Galleries.[58] She developed strong opinions, growing to dislike the 'greenery yallery Grosvenor Gallery' artists of the Aesthetic movement.[50]

Closer to home, Albertopolis provided Potter with other sources of inspiration, including the South Kensington Museum with its decorative arts, prints collections and art library.[60] She found herself drawn to a 'dark corner' of the museum containing embroidered costumes, which would become immortalized in *The Tailor of Gloucester* (1903; nos 23–6).[61]

Elizabeth, Lady Eastlake, an art historian and connoisseur, introduced Potter to a professional artist, the unidentified Mrs A, for her '*first* lessons in oil or figure drawing':

> Of course, I shall paint just as I like when not with her...I am convinced it lies chiefly with oneself. Technical difficulties can be taught, and a model will be an immense advantage. We shall see.[62]

Potter thoroughly disliked these painting lessons – 'She speaks of nothing but smoothness, softness, breaking the colours, and the lightness of the shadows, till there is nothing left' – but they gave her a useful introduction to oils and probably helped direct her firmly towards drawing in watercolour and pen.[63] Around 1900, and as late as 1902 when she was enjoying success with *The Tale of Peter Rabbit* (1902), Potter was still inclined to self-improvement: she belonged to a mutual art appreciation society in which the participants submitted drawings under

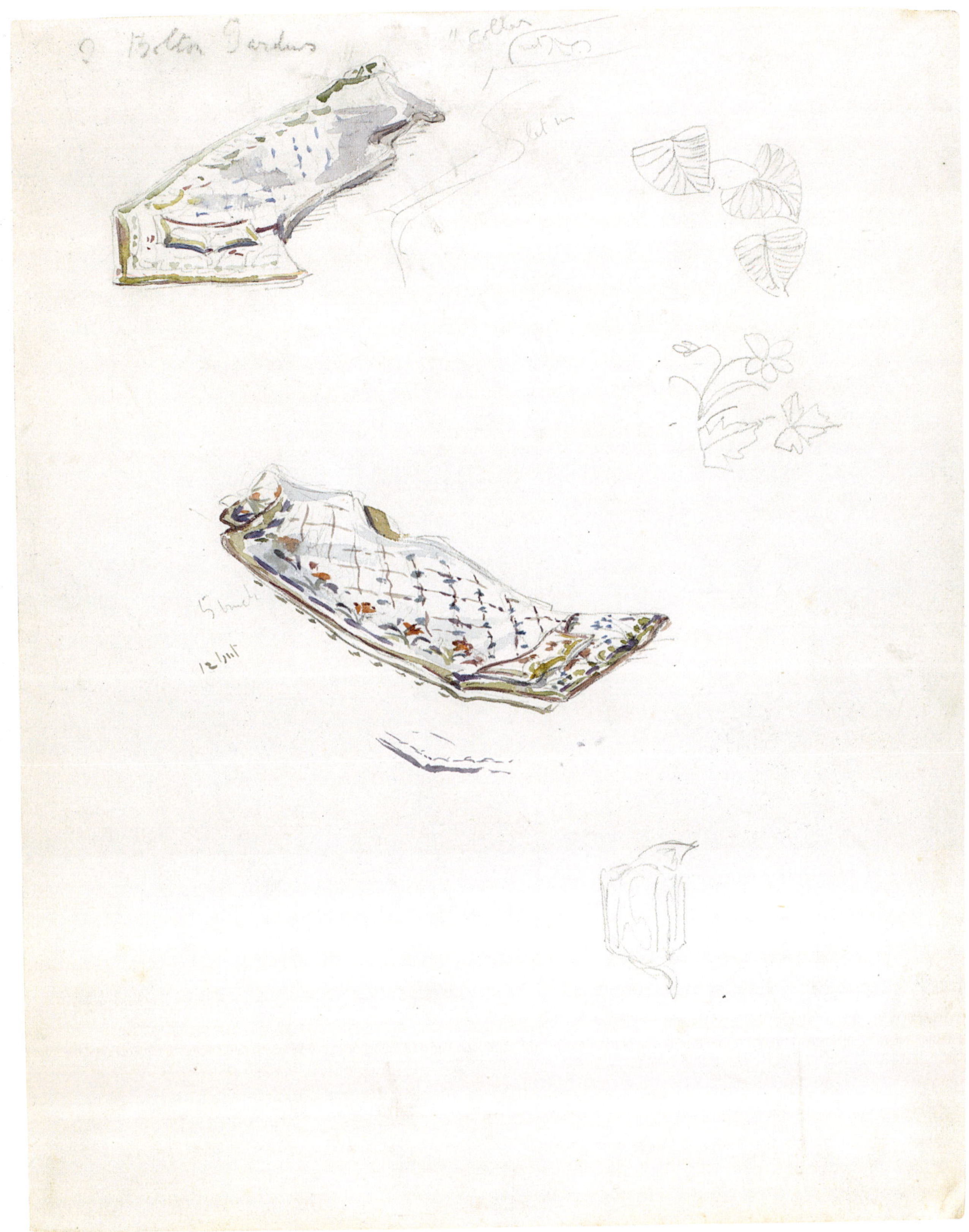

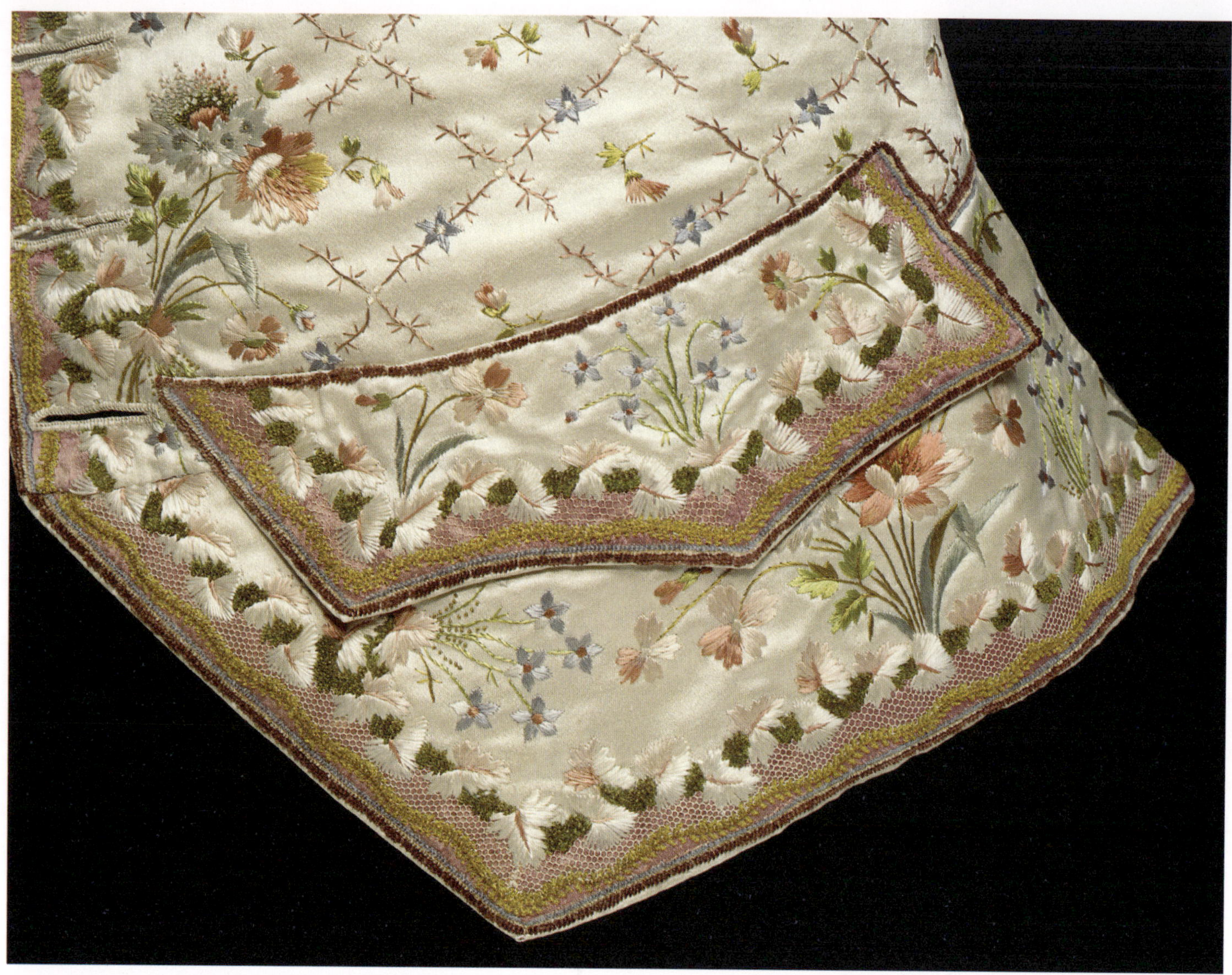

pseudonyms for critical comment (hers was 'Bunny'). A drawing of a garden in Tenby (no.27), which partly inspired the one visited by Peter Rabbit, attracted the following observations from members calling themselves 'Sphinx' and 'Stuffed Monkey: 'Very well done. I think the outline of the cat is too sharply defined it does not look fluffy enough'; 'Charming colouring – but overworked.'[64]

Potter's various activities and visits to museums and art galleries channelled her curiosity and creativity, as well as alleviating the boredom of a life of imposed leisure. A journal entry made as she approached the age of 18 reveals a sense of anxiety about an uncertain future.[65] Despite her dislike of formal lessons, Potter's journal suggests that, for her, drawing was a form of therapy:

> I cannot rest, I must draw, however poor the result, and when I have a bad time come over me it is a stronger desire than ever, and settles on the queerest things...Last time, in the middle of September, I caught myself in the back yard making a careful and admiring copy of the swill bucket, and the laugh it gave me brought me round.[66]

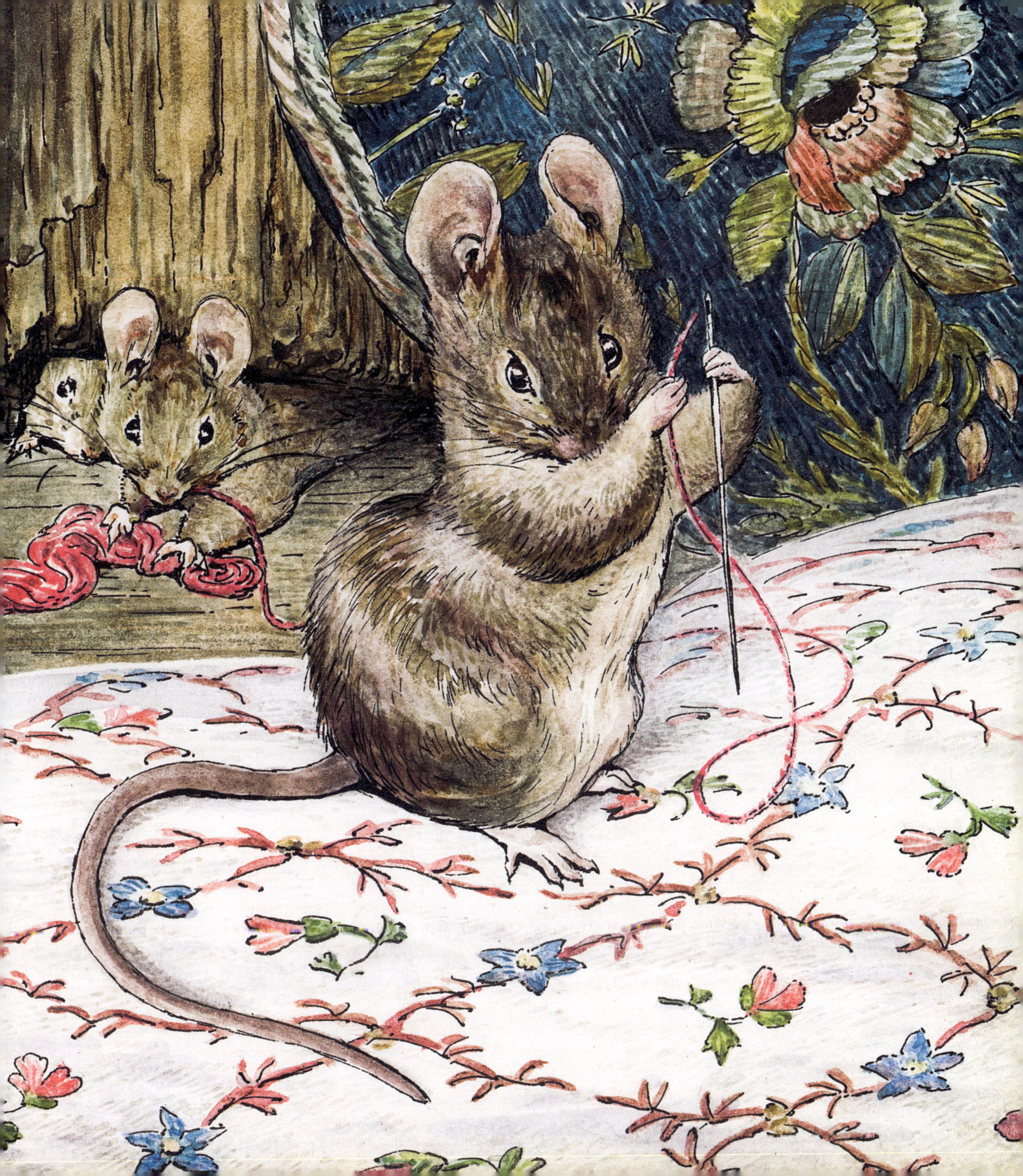

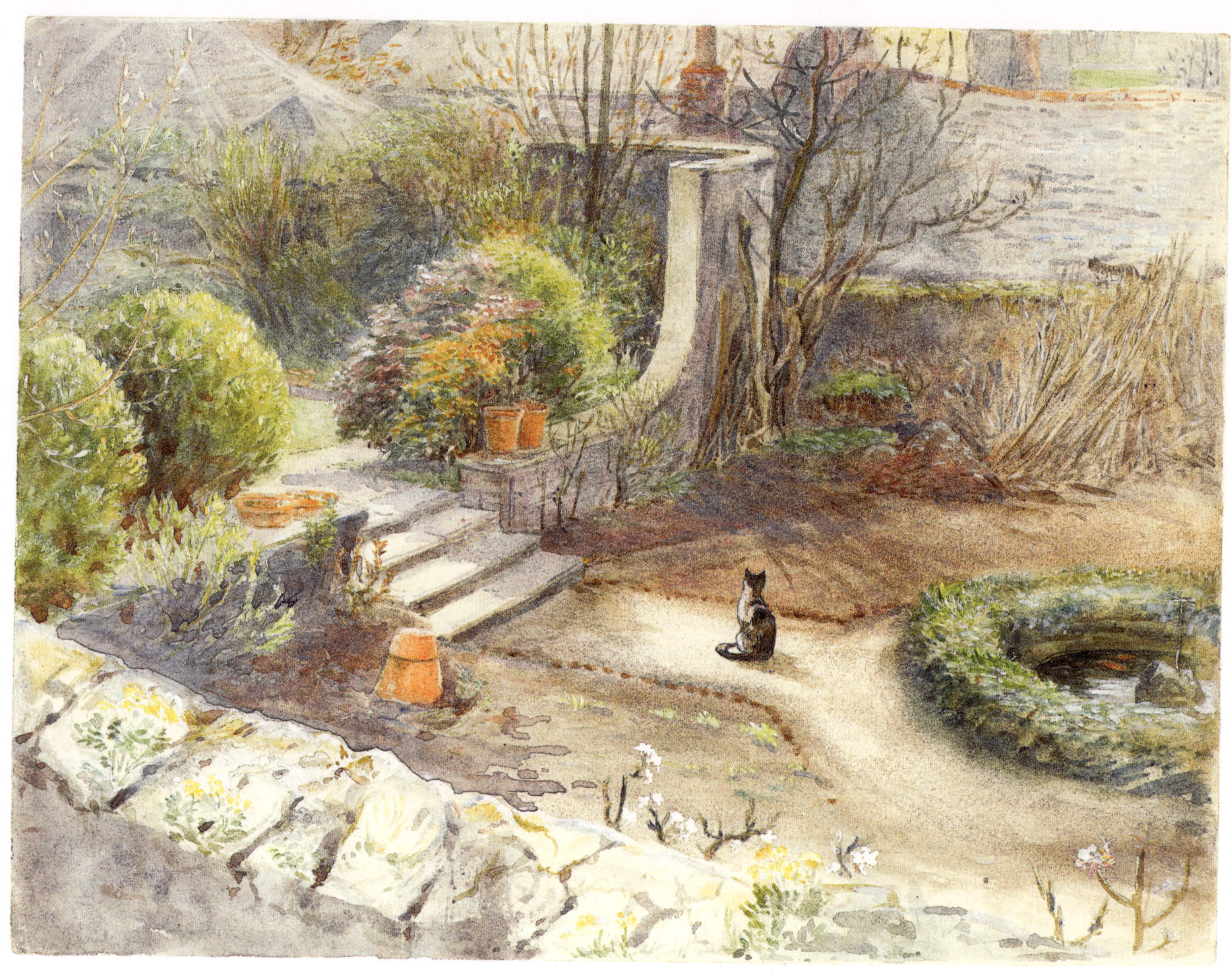

[T]here was a story called Little Sunshine's Holiday. She went by train at night, just like the journeys I was taken, and when she got there at some unearthly hour, instead of having bread and milk…she was given a basin of cream with a large spoonful of strawberry jam…

(BEATRIX POTTER, LETTER TO MRS RAMSAY DUFF, JUNE 1943)[67]

27.
Garden at Tenby, April 1900
Watercolour on paper
V&A: BP.241, Linder Bequest LB 467

A large part of the Potter family's calendar involved travel and extended stays in leased holiday homes. Beatrix's diary and 'picture letters' provide lengthy descriptions of some of her holiday experiences and suggest that on the whole she enjoyed them. She was fascinated by the different regional customs and dialects, the variations in farmland practice and the minutiae of day-to-day working lives, from those of fishermen's wives to sailors.

While the servants spring-cleaned during March or April, the family vacated their home, pursuing a somewhat itinerant lifestyle in towns along the south or east coast. The accommodation sometimes proved insalubrious: 'it is possible to have too much Natural History in a bed'.[68] As she entered her thirties, Potter tolerated these holidays with decreasing patience because she had little control over where the family went. She 'poked about...delightfully' in woods and quarries, hunting for fossils or collecting snails; to 'slither and slide' unladylike down hillsides was a pleasure and a kind of freedom.[69] In this later period the family split up to pursue different interests and Beatrix and her father, sharing the same passion for 'antiquities' and wildlife, occasionally escaped together.[70] During a spring stay in Torquay, having endured a day driving round 'a most dreary suburb' with her mother and a family friend Ada Smallfield, Beatrix was:

> so disgusted with my drive that I privately incited papa to going into [the cavern] Kent's Hole next morning by way of a reviver. We slunk out after breakfast...We afterwards lost our way which was a judgement.[71]

Potter was fortunate in having a wealthy extended family with large homes and gardens, where she could feed her senses and imagination. It was while staying with her relatives, the Huttons, in Gloucestershire that she kindled a friendship with her distant cousin, Caroline Hutton, who shared the same interest in getting 'dirty to our heart's content' following badger tracks in the copse behind the Huttons' home, Harescombe Grange.[72] Similarly, beyond her aunt and uncle's garden at Gwaynynog Hall, Denbighshire, there was parkland, a rich source for the collection of 'fossils, corals, encrinites and a few shells'.[73]

Camfield Place in Hertfordshire, which became her grandparents' home following Edmund Potter's retirement as a member of Parliament, had a 'hideous' artificial grotto and two summer houses down by the ponds but there was broad open countryside beyond to clear the head. Memories of this home were wrapped up in an immense fondness for her grandmother, Jessie, whose miniature portrait Beatrix sometimes carried about with her:

> How pretty she does look with her grey curls, under her muslin cap...with her gentle face and waken, twinkling eyes...She always seems to me as near perfect as is possible here...[74]

One of her favourite places, where her happiness was 'bound up together in fact and fancy', Camfield inspired a descriptive romantic epistle to a fictional friend called Esther, in which Potter imagined herself as a young Regency-era girl, dressed in muslin, exploring the house's corridors.[75] Her memories of

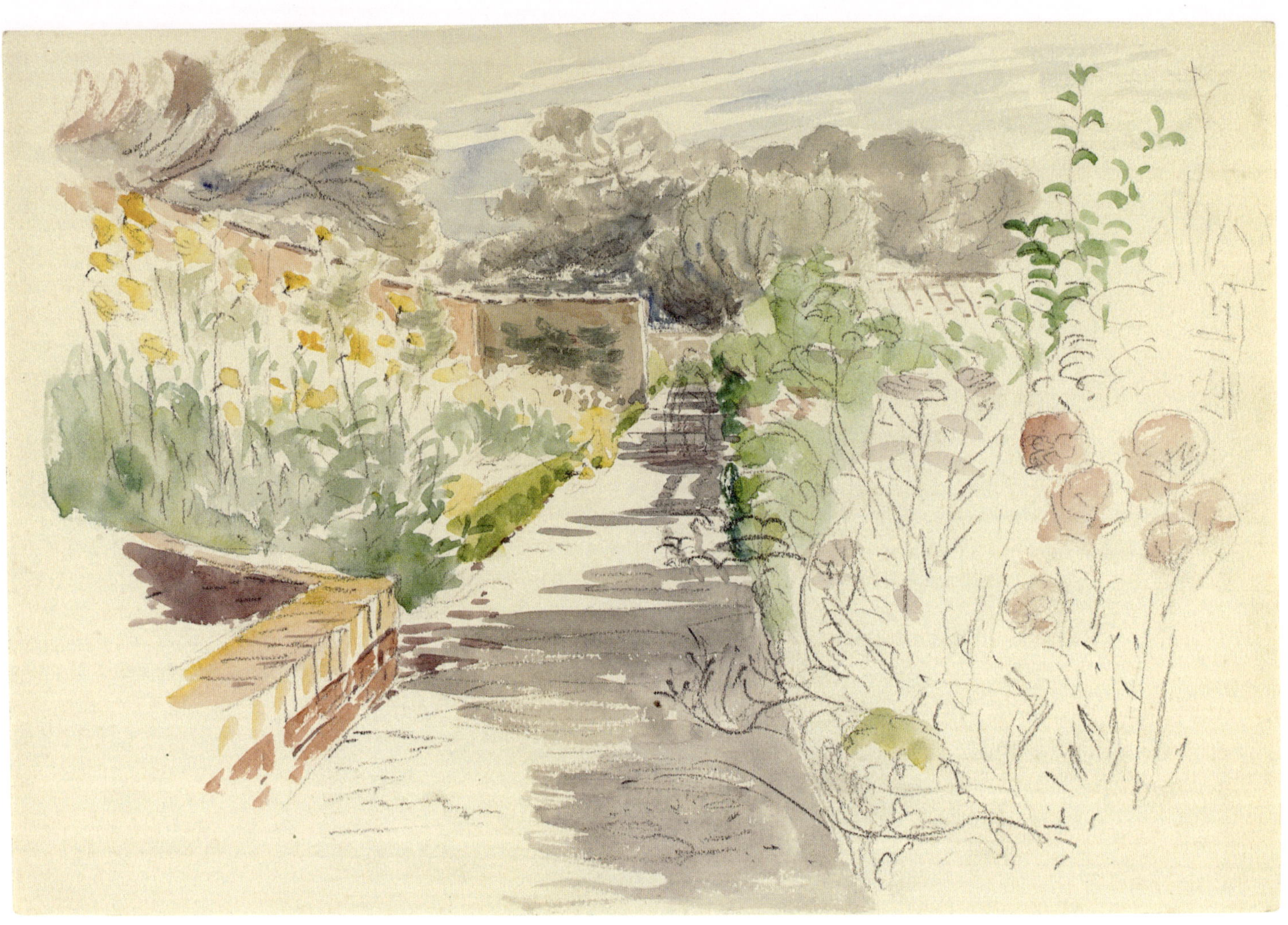

28.
Garden at Gwaynynog Hall, Denbighshire, probably March 1909
Watercolour and pencil on paper
V&A: LC 27/B/3, given by the Linder Collection

the surrounding countryside, as described in her journal, were notably drenched in colour:

> In summer the distant landscapes are intensely blue. The autumn frost spreads a ruddy glow over the land...miles upon miles of golden oak wood, with here and there a yellow streak of stubble, and a clump of russet walnut trees behind the red gable, and thin blue smoke of a farm.
> Not less beautiful is the winter, when the oaks are clothed in a delicate tracery of snow and hoar-frost, they sometimes look quite orange-coloured in the sunshine against the sky...[76]

Less frequently the Potters visited other members of the family near their home town of Manchester and, like Camfield, her grandparent Leechs' home, Gorse Hall in Stalybridge aroused childhood memories, with the 'dark and mysterious' passage 'I used to patter along so kindly on the way to bed'.[77] Gwaynynog in Denbighshire was a more practical influence, owing to her uncle Fred Burton's interest in collecting antiques. The rooms – 'never...more faultless in scheme of colour or Sheraton, more elegant without being flimsy' – developed in her an appreciation of furniture.[78] The garden (no.28) inspired both the setting for *The Tale of the Flopsy Bunnies* (1909) and Potter's own cottage garden at Hill Top: 'very productive but not tidy, the prettiest kind of garden, where bright old fashioned flowers grow amongst the currant bushes.'[79]

For at least three months of the year, like many middle- and upper-class families, the Potters leased a home in the country to escape the unhealthy London summers. Usually the houses were large and their servants stayed with them.[80] From these bases the Potters could explore the countryside, fish and shoot, and play host to friends, including the families of Reverend William Gaskell (1805–1884) and the politician John Bright (1811–1889).[81] For a decade from 1871, Dalguise House in Perthshire was the family's regular summer home, chosen for its exceptional access to fishing.[82] The area played a significant part in Potter's life during her formative years, and aroused strong romantic feelings. She preserved a fairy-tale vision of:

> woods...peopled by the mysterious good folk. The Lords and Ladies of the last century walked with me...among the box and rose hedges of the garden...I lived in a separate world...Even when the thunder growled in the distance, and the wind swept up the valley in fitful gusts, oh, it was always beautiful, home sweet home...[83]

Then, in 1882, the family switched location from Scotland to the Lake District. When Dalguise was available only for a 'ridiculous' rent of £450, 'Papa took Wray Castle', a mock-Gothic folly on the shore of Lake Windermere (no.35).[84] Potter, disappointed not to be returning to Dalguise, absorbed impressions of the Lake District countryside with little enthusiasm. In the nearby village of Hawkshead she had 'a series of adventures. Inquired the way three times, lost continually, alarmed by collies at every farm, stuck in stiles, chased once by cows.'[85]

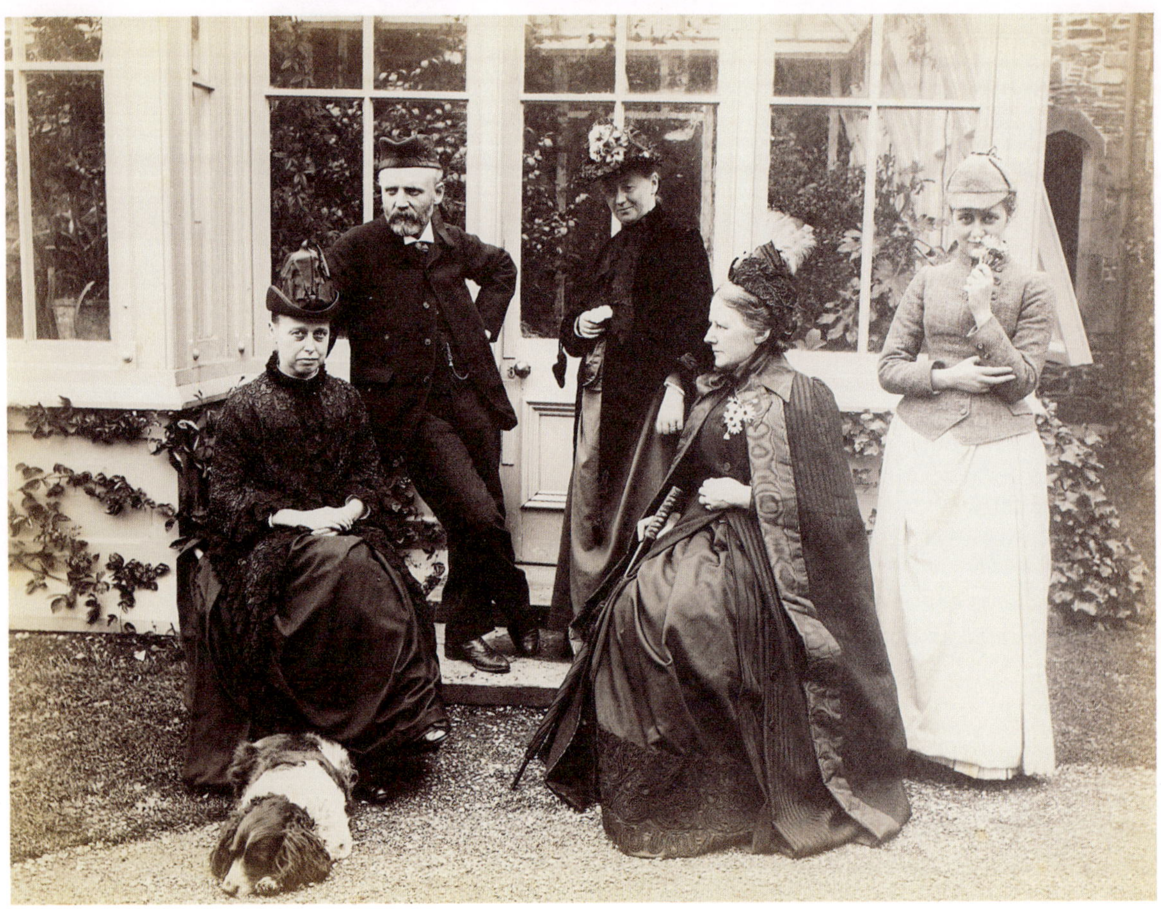

29.
Rupert Potter (1832–1914)
Beatrix Potter (right), her mother Helen (left) with their dog Spot and friends at Holehird, near Windermere, September 1889
Photograph in an album, albumen print on paper
National Trust, 242368

The holiday itself was the occasion for making an important acquaintance, however (see 'Living Nature', pp.153–5). Hardwicke Drummond Rawnsley was then the local vicar, described as Europe's 'most active volcano' for his passionate, energetic advocacy for the poor and campaigns for conservation. His romantic vision and love of the Lake District would have a lasting impact on the area.[86] Potter's own opinion of the landscape at this time was less than favourable: 'Do not care for the Peaks, a poor starved country, extraordinary number of dead sheep.'[87]

The Potters continued to stay in the Lake District for some years. At Holehird, near Windermere (no.29), they searched for fungi in the woods, while at Lingholm or Fawe Park (nos 2, 30), both on the shore of Derwentwater, they fished or sketched from boats. Beatrix gradually began to revise her impressions of the area and became drawn towards Troutbeck's 'largeness and silence going up into the hills'.

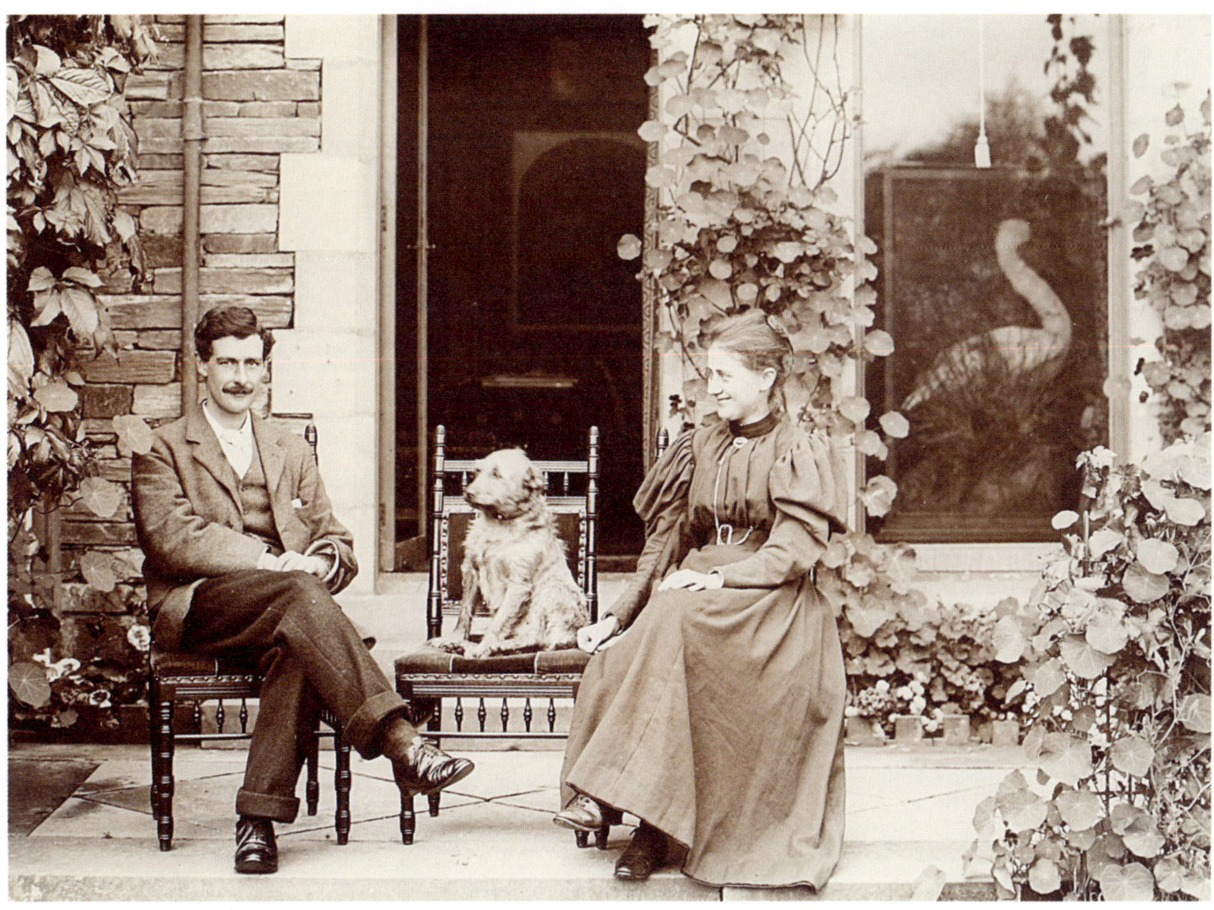

30.
Rupert Potter (1832–1914)
Beatrix and Bertram Potter with Bertram's terrier at Lingholm, near Derwentwater, probably October 1897
Photograph in an album, albumen print on paper
National Trust, 242368

Of Esthwaite Water she wrote: 'it really strikes me that some scenery is almost theatrical, or ultra-romantic', while a holiday home called Ees Wyke (or Lakefield, see no.31), on the edge of Esthwaite and close to the village of Near Sawrey, was 'as nearly perfect a little place as I ever lived in, and such nice old-fashioned people in the village.'[88]

Potter's reflections on the Lake District landscape are recorded in watercolours that are mostly impressionistic and dominated by an overwhelming sense of colour (nos 32, 33), much like her written descriptions:

> The sunset was still fiery in the west and south, the moon was rising, the reflections of the great blue mountains lay broad and motionless in the water, undisturbed save now and then by the ripple of a passing boat.[89]

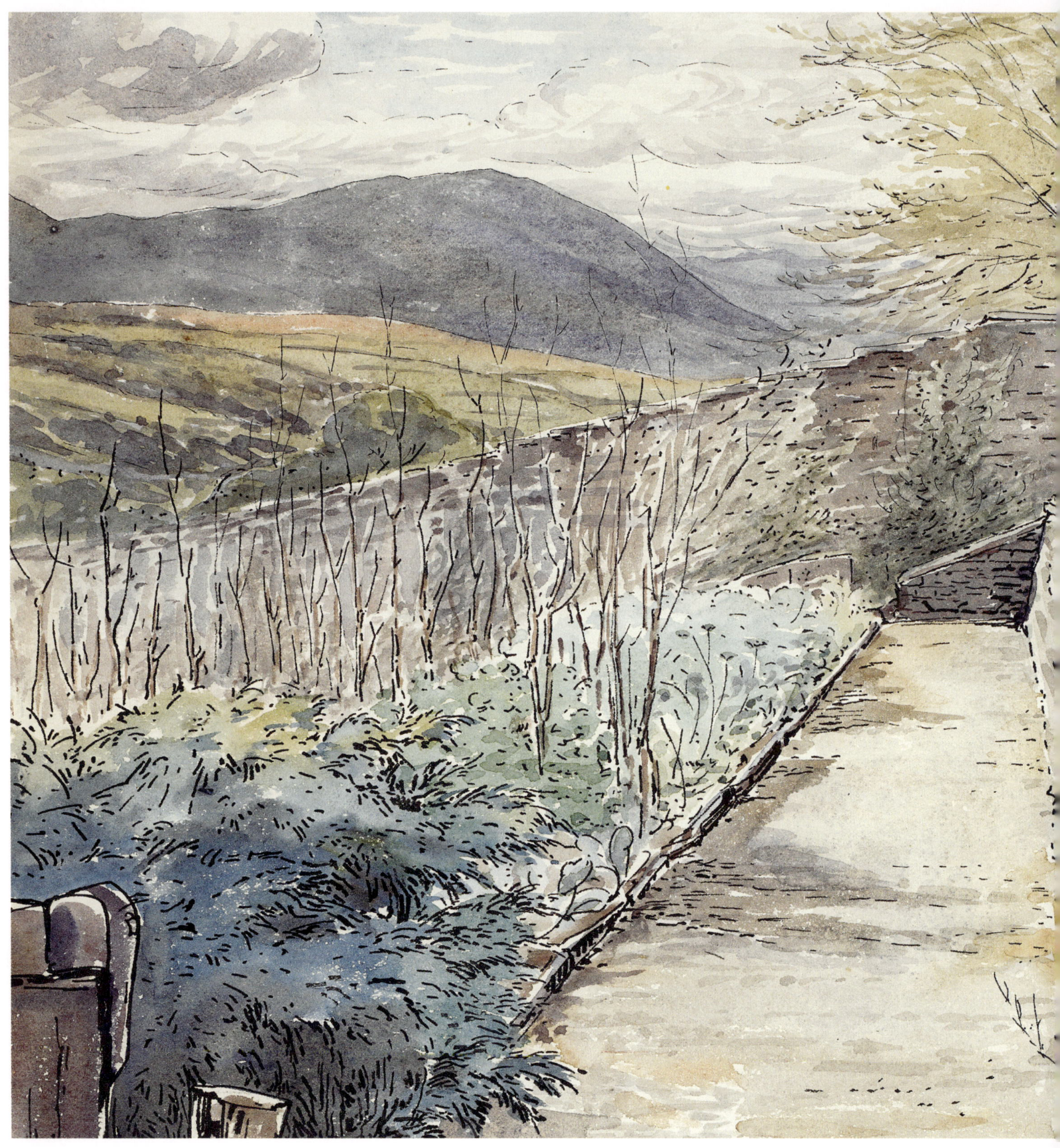

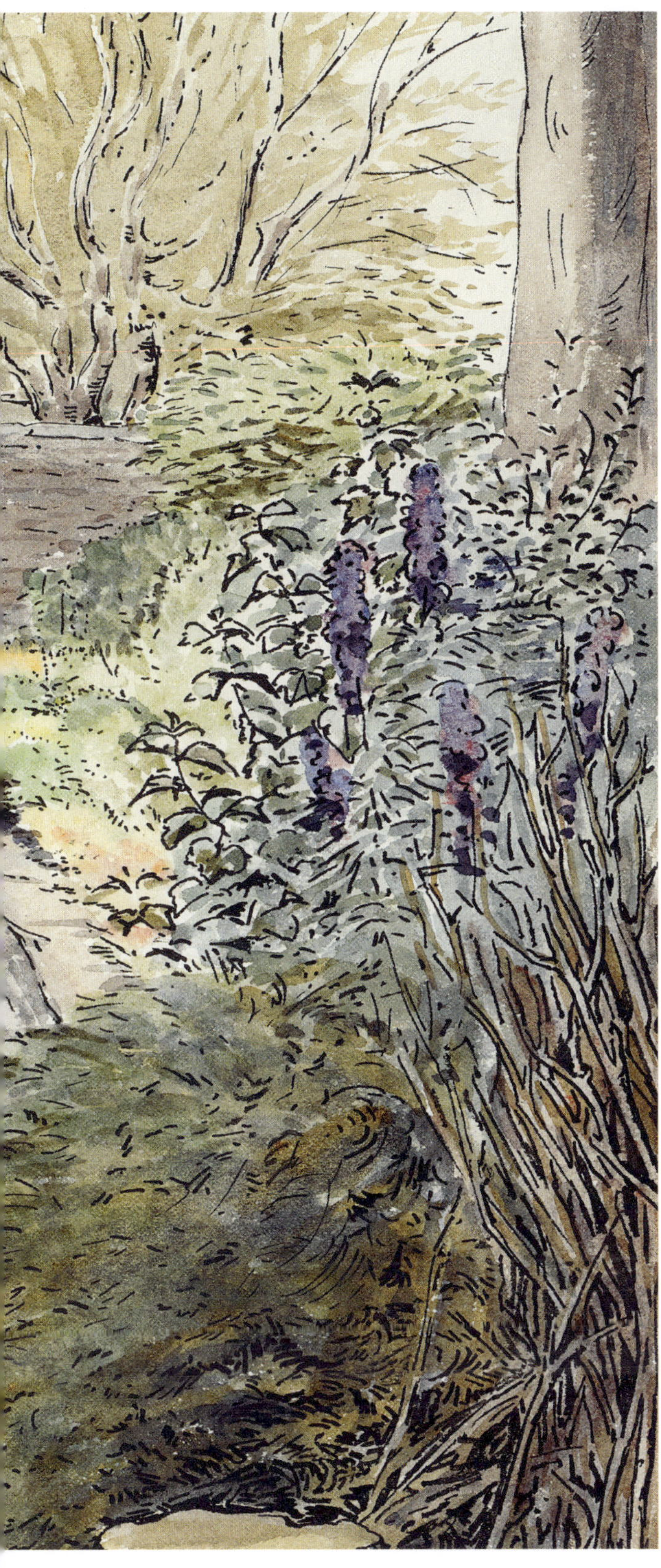

31.
Garden at Lakefield, Sawrey, in August, c.1900
Watercolour and ink on paper
V&A: BP.238, Linder Bequest LB 465

Visits to the countryside provided Potter with pleasures she could not experience in London. Driving out in a pony and trap gave her freedom to explore (no.36). She would go fossil hunting, sometimes accompanied by her father, while he took landscape photographs and showed her how to use a camera. The two would also observe the wildlife – 'we had great pleasure watching a pair of buzzards sailing round and round over the top of Wansfell' – or shepherds at work:

> Four or five sheep...escaped the dog's observation, whereupon the ancient shepherd, a mere speck in the slanting sunlight down the great hillside, this aged Wordsworthian worthy, awoke the echoes with a flood of the most singularly bad language.[90]

Potter once remarked that, although she and her brother were born and bred Londoners, 'our interests and our joy was in the north country'.[91] It is no surprise that the more romantic descriptions in her journal were in response to her holidays. Her 'unloved' London home life cannot be entirely dismissed, though, since it gave her the chance to increase her cultural and scientific knowledge.[92] However, for someone with a profound emotional connection with the natural world, the bricks and mortar and ever-shrinking greenery of the city must have felt increasingly restrictive. Fortunately, while Potter was allowed to keep animals in her London home, the gardens and the countryside surrounding both her relatives' homes and family holiday leases provided her with the means to venture beyond the urban environment, literally expanding her horizons.

Annemarie Bilclough

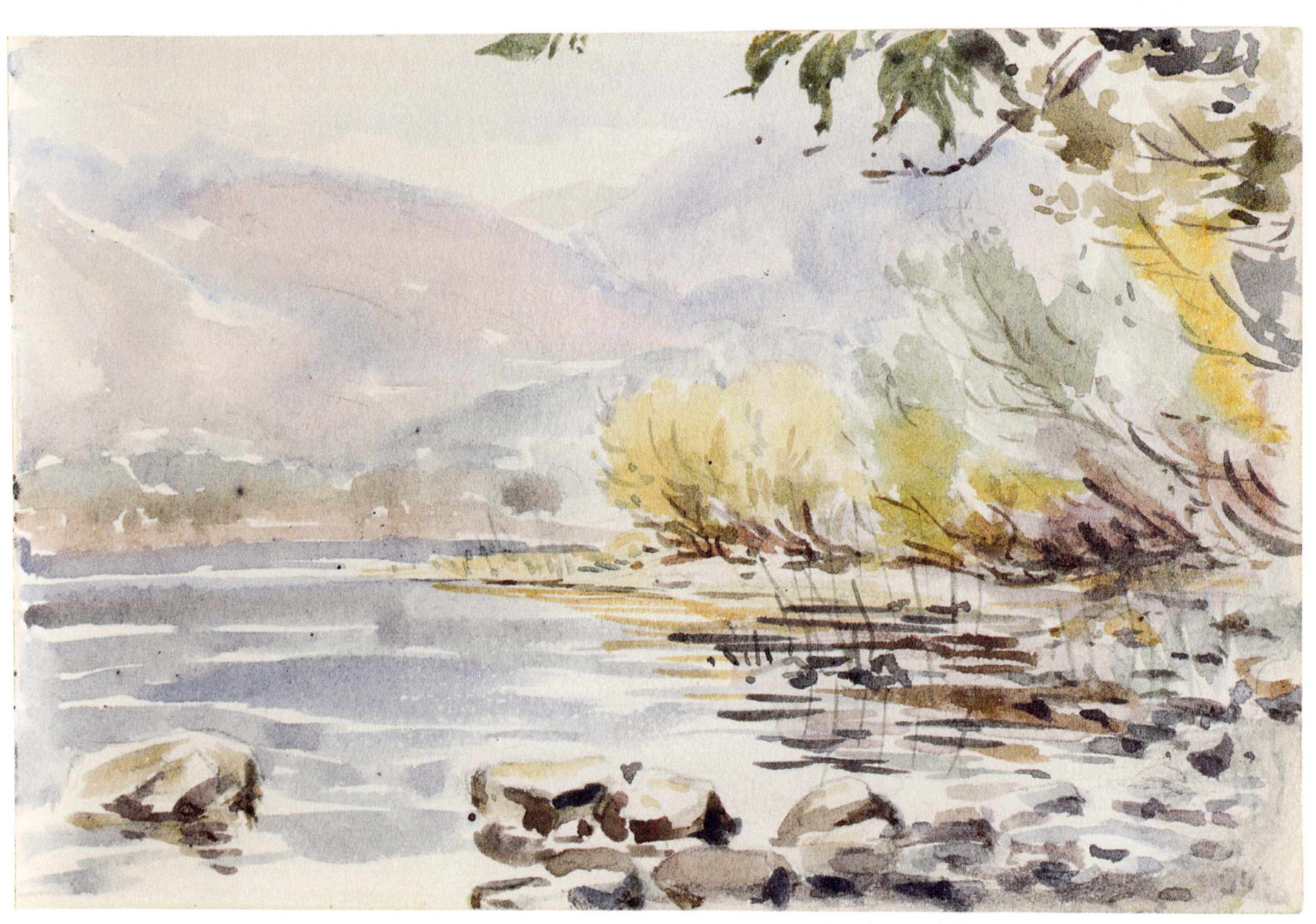

32.
The shore of Derwentwater, 1903
Watercolour over pencil on paper
National Trust, 242727

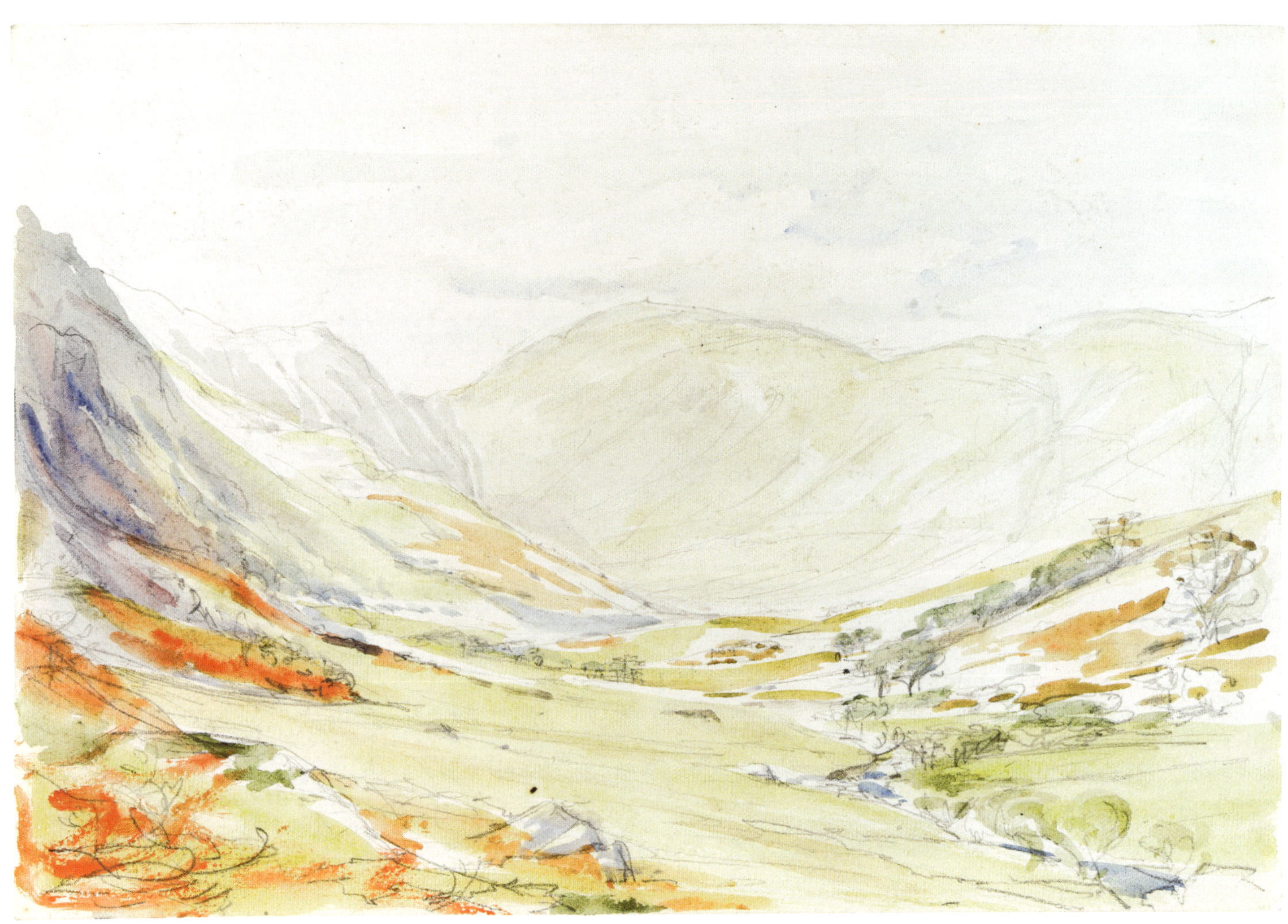

33.
Landscape, probably Newlands Valley, near Derwentwater, c.1905
Watercolour and pencil on paper
V&A: BP.1129(VI), Linder Bequest LB 864

Holiday Haunts

Every year the Potter family took extended stays, usually in rural Scotland or the Lake District. In spring they spent two weeks on England's south coast.

In the nineteenth century Scotland became an increasingly popular tourist destination stimulated by its favour with the monarchy. King George IV visited in 1822, and after their initial trips to Scotland in the 1840s Queen Victoria and Prince Albert were so enamoured that they bought the Balmoral estate in 1852. This, along with an economic upturn in the 1850s, inspired many wealthy people to buy or rent estates in Scotland, where they would spend long periods of time over the summer enjoying the fashionable country pursuits of fishing and hunting, just like the royals.[1] A boom in train travel to the area boosted the growth of tourism, with Perth becoming a major junction for trains coming from London to travel all across Perthshire and central Scotland.

The Lake District was not always a popular tourist destination. Daniel Defoe in 1724–6 wrote pejoratively that with the 'impassable hills…all the pleasant part of England was at an end'.[2] The poet Thomas Gray's journal of his tour of the English lakes (1769) changed all that. To Gray the landscape was 'a picture, that if I could transmit it to you…& fix it in all its softness of its living colours, would fairly sell for a thousand pounds.'[3] His diary inspired poets and writers, as well as Joseph Farington's landscape paintings, which in turn inspired artists like Joseph Mallord William Turner and John Constable. Guidebooks to the region were published, the most famous by William Wordsworth, and by 1800 the poet Samuel Taylor Coleridge complained that in the summer the area was 'swarming with tourists'.[4] Most visitors were day trippers from nearby cities, but many wealthy people built villas in prime lakeside locations.[5]

By 1900 a trip to the seaside had also become a tradition for many families in England, since it was thought to have health benefits.[6] From the first resorts of Brighton and Margate, development had gradually spread to the West Country by around the time the Potters visited Ilfracombe, Weymouth and Sidmouth. Wealthier families like the Potters ventured even further afield, to towns such as Falmouth in Cornwall, which was not yet a tourist destination when they travelled there in 1892.[7]

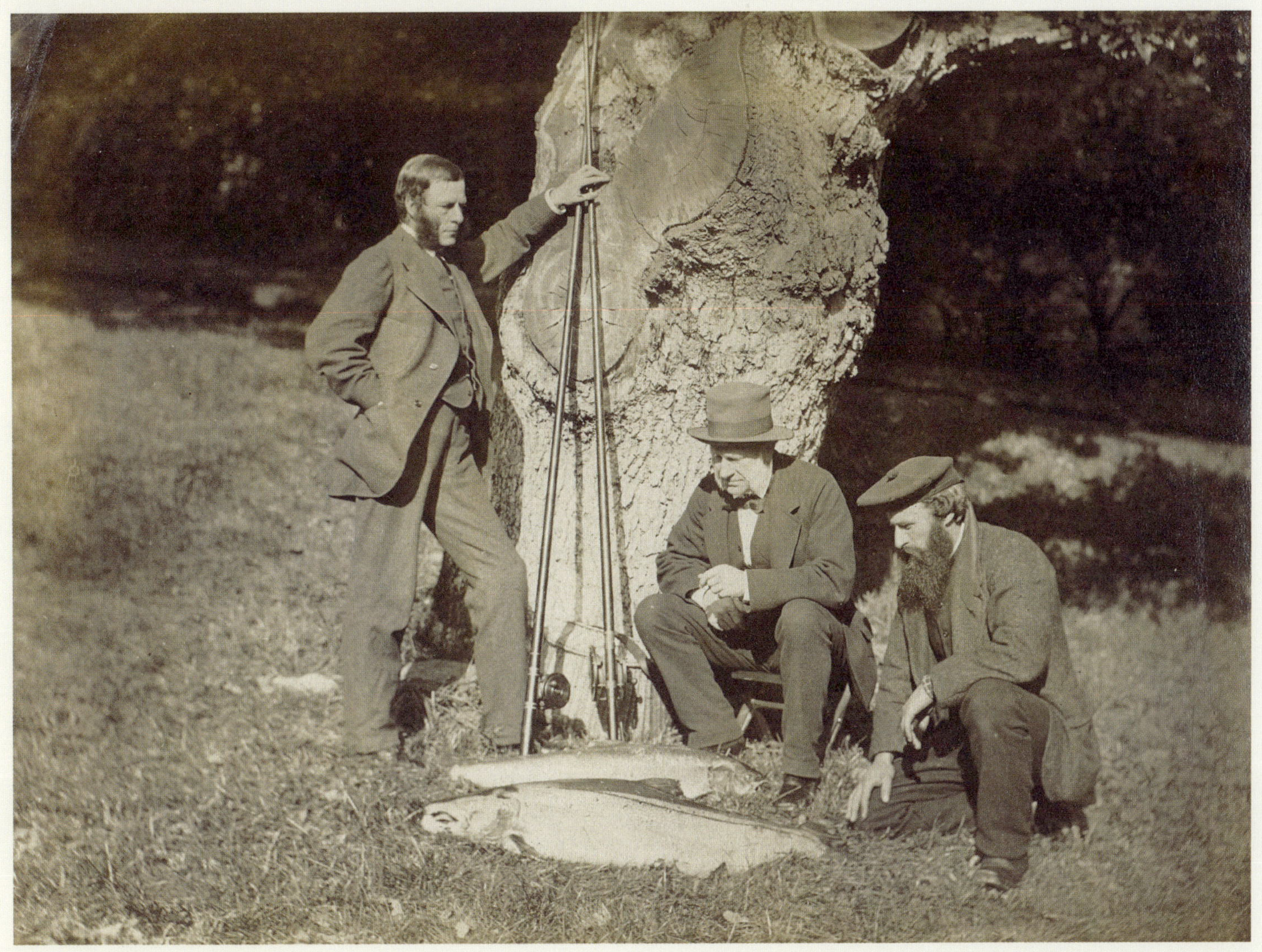

34.
Rupert Potter (1832–1914)
Rupert Potter with Sir William Broun, Baronet (1804–1882) and Dalguise gamekeeper Robert McIntosh (c.1837–1907) with their catch at Dalguise, Dunkeld, 1871
Albumen print on paper
V&A: AAD/2006/4/517, given by Joan Duke

The Potters spent their summers at Dalguise House in Dunkeld, Perthshire, over 10 years from 1871. Dalguise was a very large estate with its own fishing boat on the river. Rupert Potter enjoyed the country pursuits of a gentleman: shooting and fishing. He often invited his friends along, including Reverend William Gaskell, the Radical MP John Bright and artist John Everett Millais. Beatrix went on to base her character of Jeremy Fisher on the 'leisured gentlemen' who would spend their summer fishing in Perthshire rivers.[8] In 1882 the new owners demanded an exorbitant lease of £450 and the Potters went elsewhere, including Wray Castle in the Lake District.

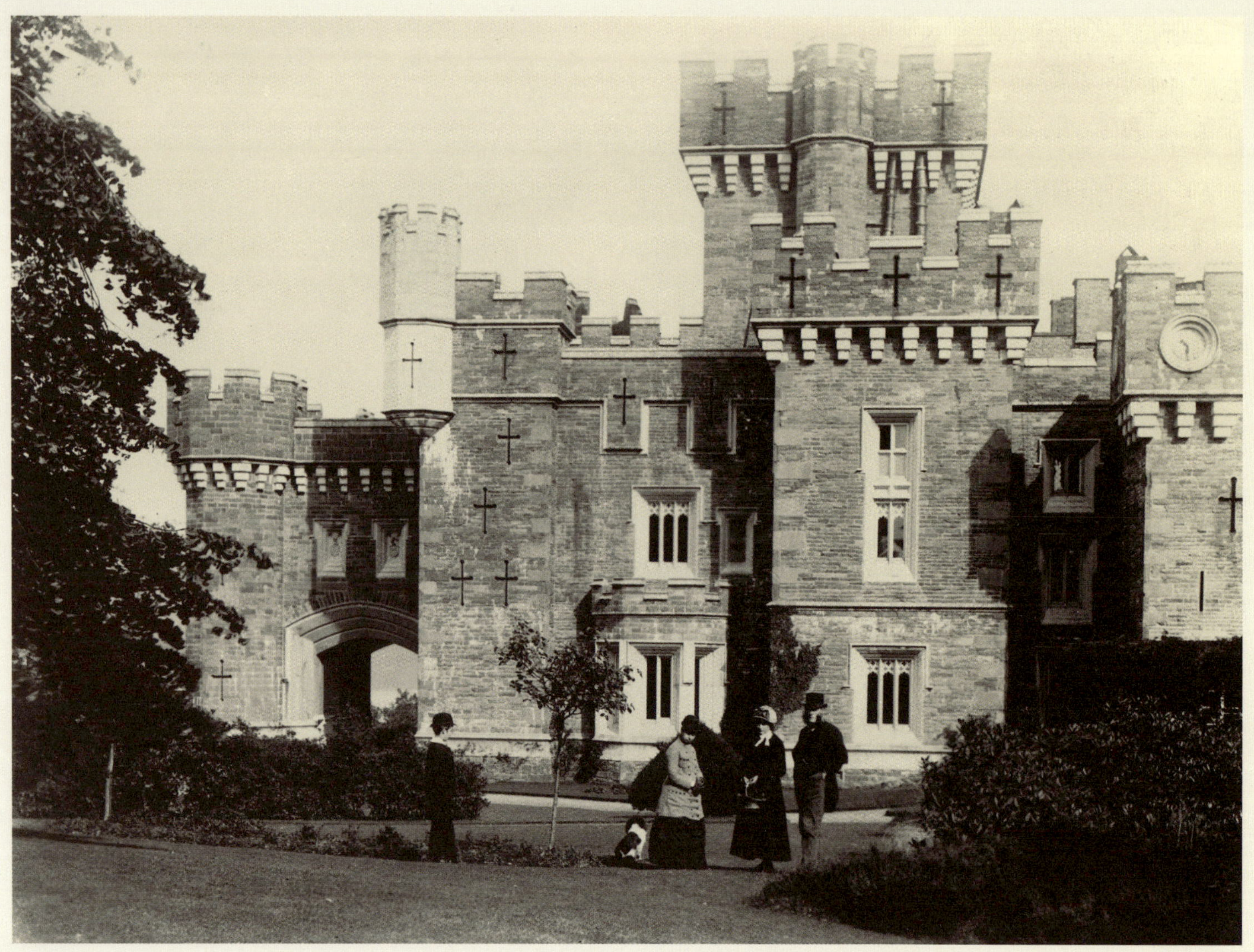

35.
Rupert Potter (1832–1914)
Beatrix and Bertram Potter at Wray Castle, near Windermere, August 1882
Albumen print on paper
V&A: BP.1318, Linder Bequest LB 2051

Built in an extravagant mock-Gothic style, Wray Castle was described by poet William Wordsworth as 'a dignified feature to the landscape scenery on which it stands'.[9] Many places associated with Wordsworth attracted particular attention from tourists, and Potter herself recalled in her journal how the castle's garden was home to a 'Mulberry bush planted by Wordsworth'.[10] Her response to the house was more matter-of-fact; she commented that its alleged cost of £60,000 'might have built a village'.[11]

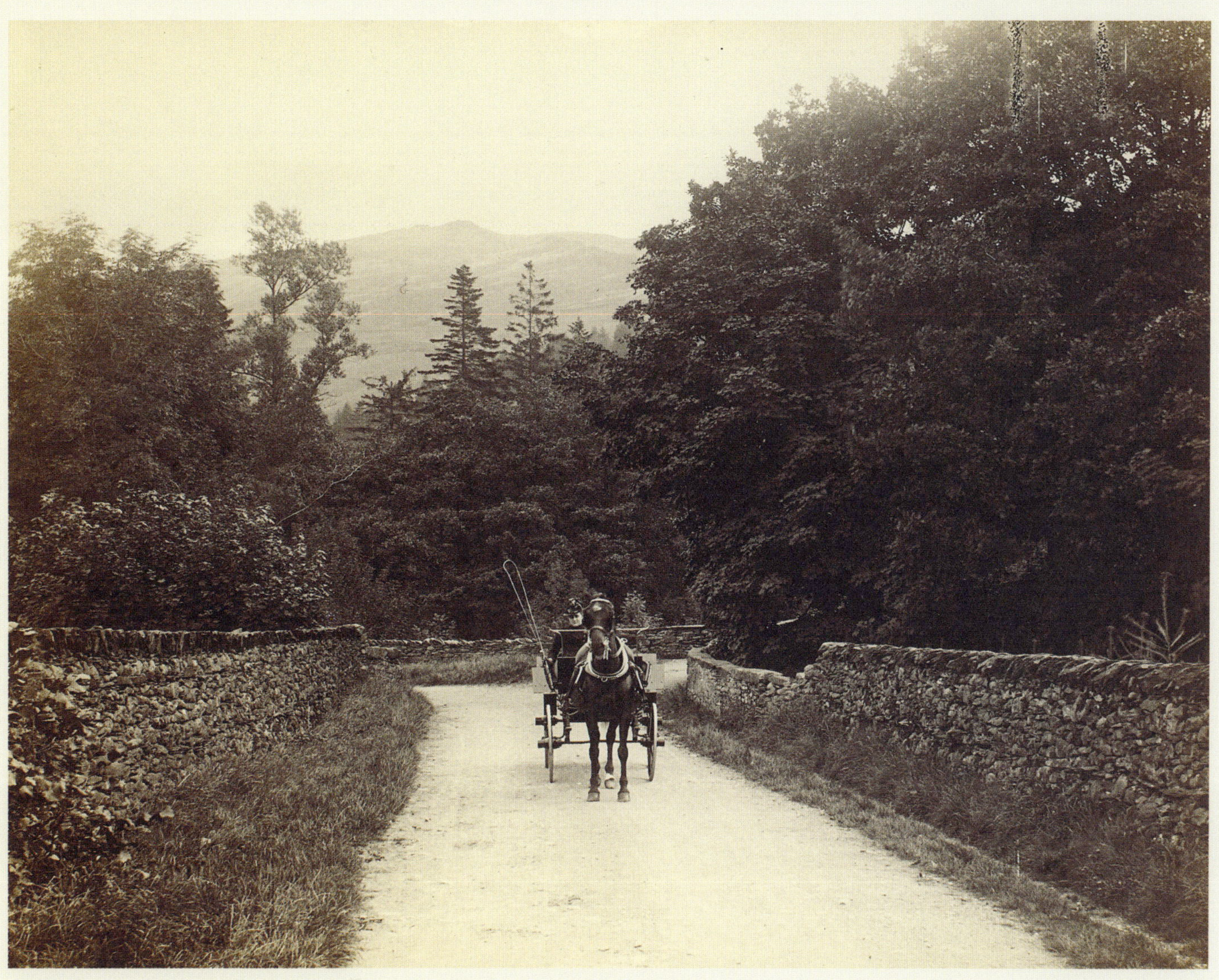

36.
Rupert Potter (1832–1914)
Beatrix Potter with her pony and trap at Holehird, near Windermere, 1889
Photograph in an album, albumen print on paper
V&A: BP.1525, Linder Bequest LB 2027

As she grew older, Potter enjoyed the freedom of driving herself and sometimes her father around the Lake District. The narrow roads could make for a bumpy ride. In her diary she described a close encounter:

> at one of the corners between Out Gate and Randy Pike, was banged into by another female driving a gig...she was so rude, asked me why I did not get out of the way...We were dragging up hill at a walk, she coming down very fast...I could [not] have gone three inches nearer the ditch.[12]

Falmouth Hotel
Falmouth
March 11th. 92

My dear Noel,

Thank you for your very interesting letter, which you sent me a long time ago.

I have come a very long way in a puff-puff to a place in Cornwall, where it is very hot, and there are palm trees in the gardens & camellias & rhododendrons in flower which are very pretty.

37. Left
Picture letter by Beatrix Potter sent to Noel Moore from Falmouth Hotel, 11 March 1892
Ink on paper
Morgan Library and Museum, New York, MA 2009.1

In her earliest surviving picture letter, to Noel Moore, son of her final governess, Annie Moore (née Carter), Potter gave an account of her holiday to Falmouth, Cornwall, during the Easter of 1892. She described the very long train journey and included silhouettes of the family walking in a garden, one of whom was using an umbrella for shade. The weather was extremely hot and Beatrix was surprised to see palm and eucalyptus trees, and to experience a climate so mild that she 'could sit out till nine o'clock watching the waves in the moonlight'; it seemed like a foreign country to her.[13] She collected a large bag full of shells – their 'variety ... doubtless due to the warm sea' – which she sent to Noel's brother, Eric, in the post.[14]

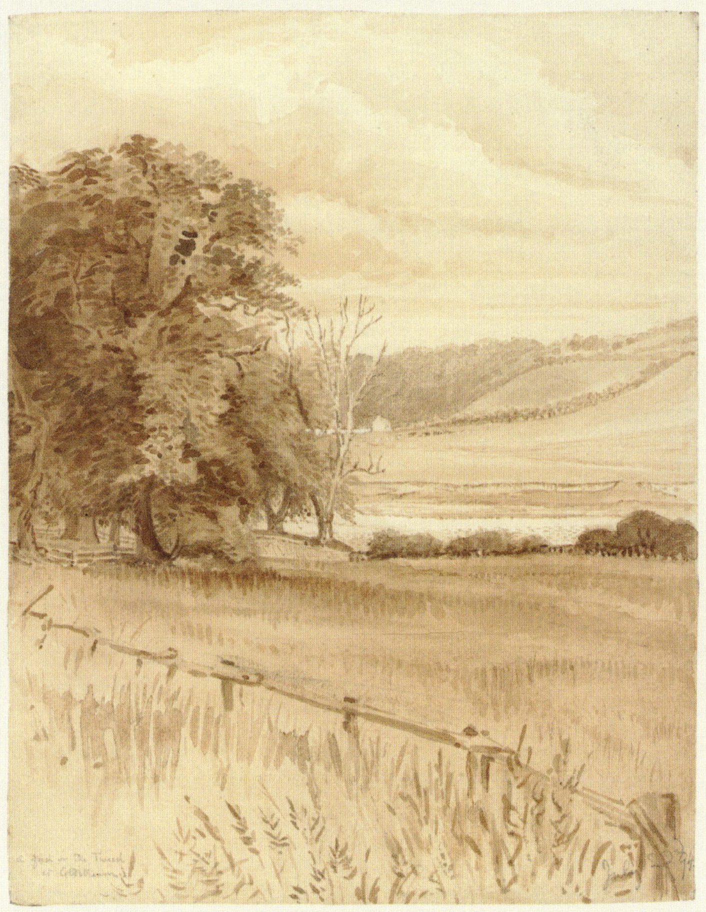

38. Right
Landscape at Coldstream, 22 January 1894
Brown wash over pencil on paper
V&A: BP.312, Linder Bequest LB 567

In 1894 the Potters stayed near Coldstream in the Tweed Valley on the Scottish Borders. Beatrix 'never was in such a delightful country for driving'.[15] She went out most mornings in a carriage and with her pony Mistress Nelly, who could 'go any distance, face the steepest road and never stumble once ... and take an amusing interest in geography'.[16] Beatrix explored the farmland, found a 'heavenly dream' of fungi in the woods, and studied the geology of the landscape and the battlefield of Flodden. She was 'very sorry indeed to come away'.[17]

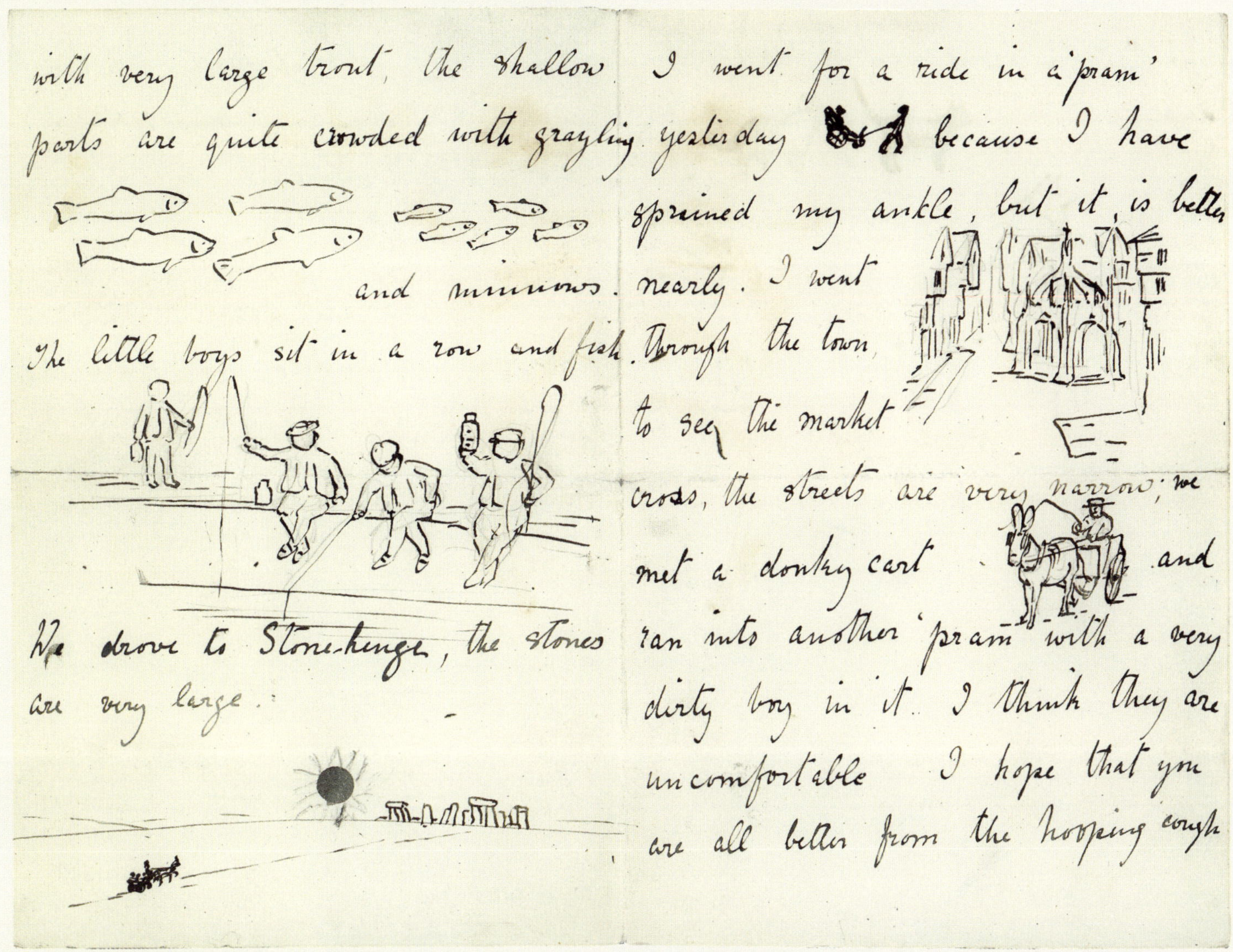

with very large trout, the shallow parts are quite crowded with grayling and minnows.

The little boys sit in a row and fish.

We drove to Stone-henge, the stones are very large.

I went for a ride in a 'pram' yesterday because I have sprained my ankle, but it is better nearly. I went through the town to see the market cross, the streets are very narrow; we met a donkey cart and ran into another 'pram' with a very dirty boy in it. I think they are uncomfortable. I hope that you are all better from the hooping cough

39.
Picture letter by Beatrix Potter sent to Eric Moore from the White Hart Hotel, Salisbury, 21 April 1895
Ink over pencil on paper
Cotsen Children's Library, Special Collections, Princeton University Library, 35896

In a picture letter to Eric Moore, Potter sketched scenes of her family's trip to Stonehenge by coach. Although long a cultural obsession, by 1739 Stonehenge had a hut 'dispensing liquors'. [18] When Potter visited there was a dedicated guidebook seller and camera with darkroom on wheels.[19] She 'was more impressed by the Plain' than by the henge with its 'ubiquitous game of golf, two other carriages and a camping-photographer.'[20] At this time the monument was still in private hands; it did not belong to the nation until 1918.[21]

Lucy Shaw

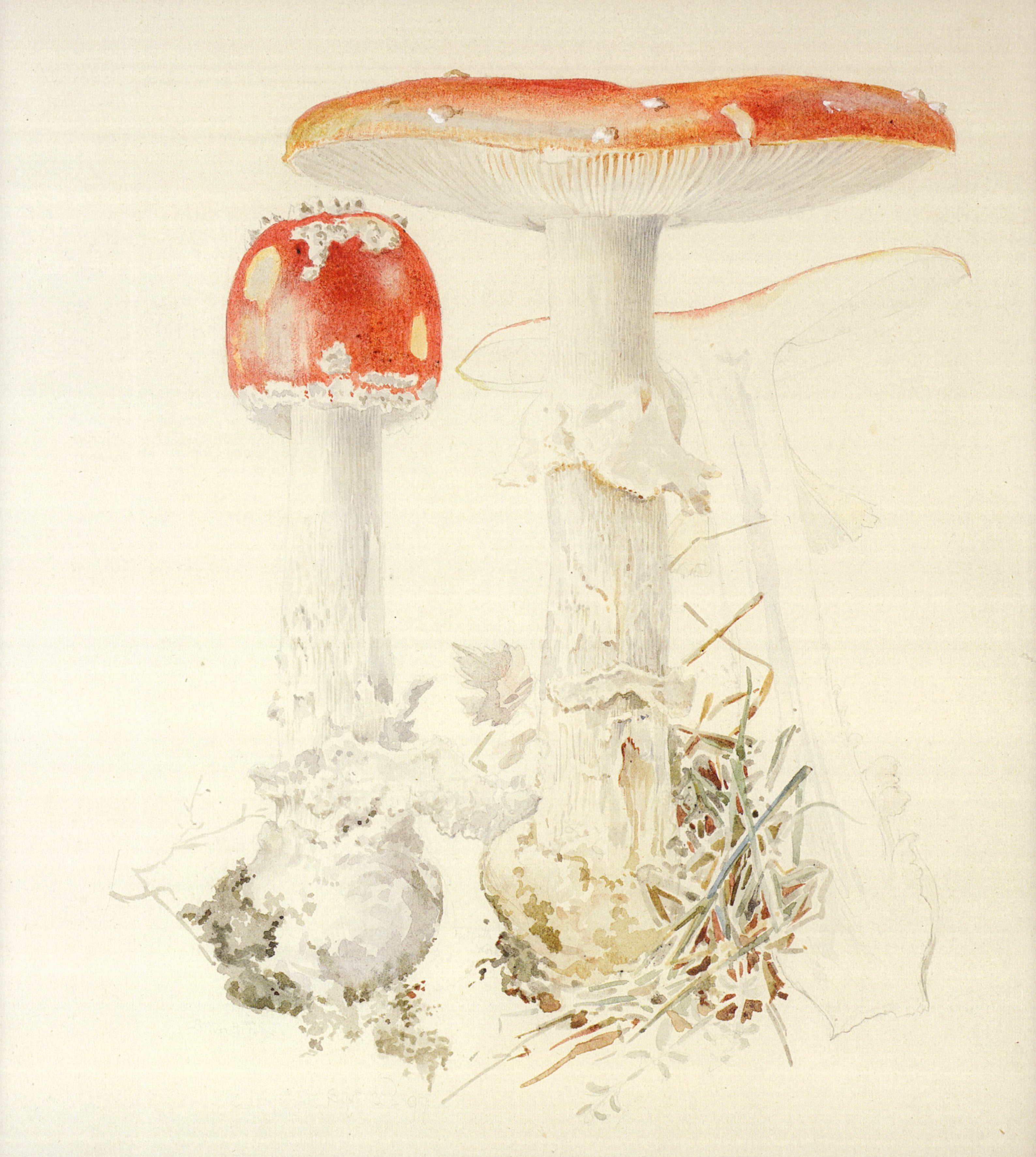

Under the Microscope

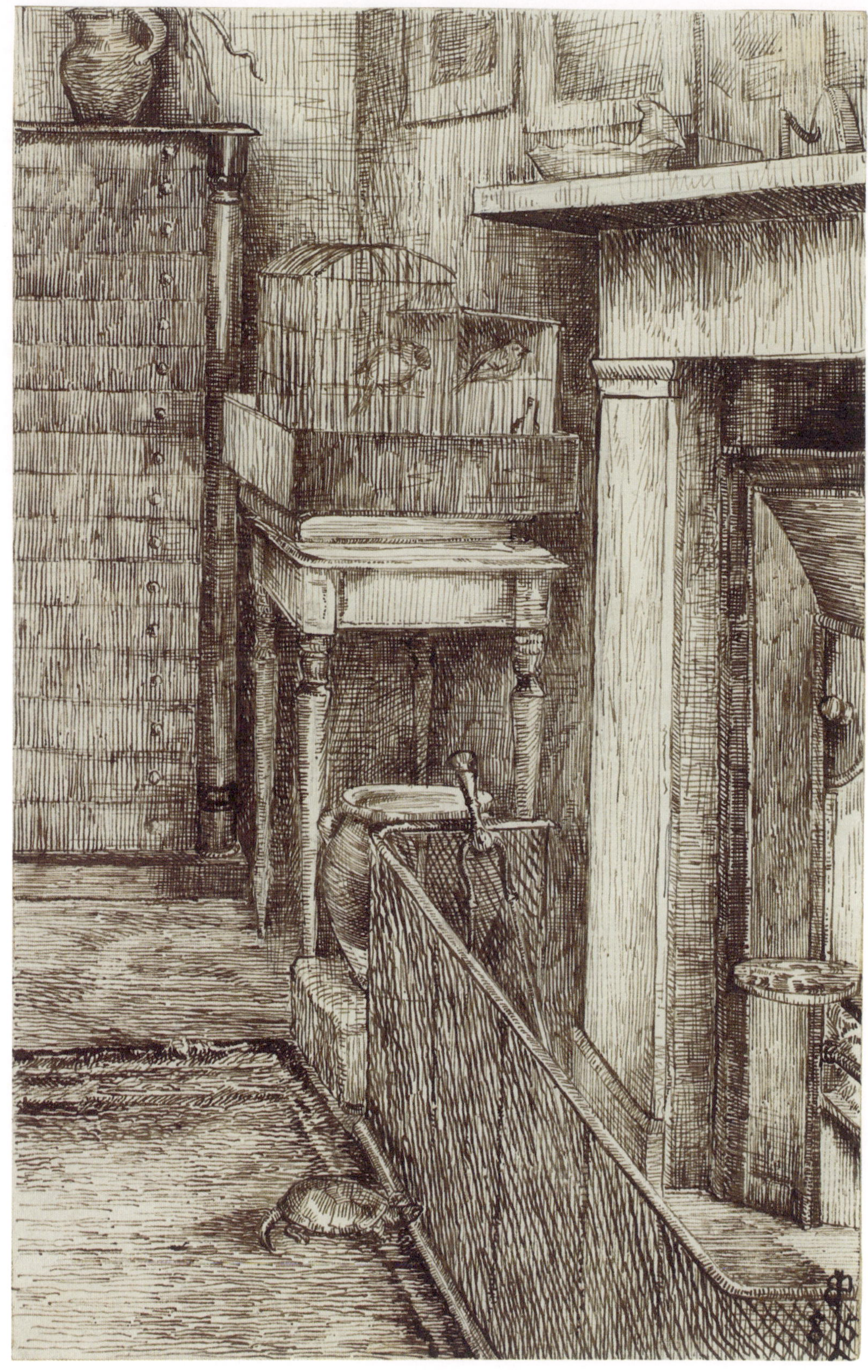

[O]ut came a little wild rabbit to talk to him...but the stupid Benjamin did nothing but stuff cabbage...[he] at length caught sight of it round a cabbage, and immediately bolted.

(BEATRIX POTTER, *JOURNAL*, 20 AUGUST 1892)

40.
Corner of the schoolroom, 2 Bolton Gardens, London, 26 November 1885
Indian ink on paper
V&A: LC 12/A/1, given by the Linder Collection

On an upper floor at the back of the house in Bolton Gardens, Beatrix and her brother Bertram's nursery-cum-schoolroom was a mostly parent-free space – and their nature reserve.[1] Near the fireplace in the corner, beside some animal cages, was a tall dresser with 10 shallow drawers: a collector's cabinet of butterflies, beetles and other insects, birds' eggs, rocks and fossils (no.40). Judging by Beatrix's various descriptions of her pets, the room might have been quite a noisy environment.

It has been estimated that Potter kept at least 92 pets over the course of her lifetime and some of them would inspire her imagination in picture letters, as well as provide the names and even characters of some of the animals in her storybooks (nos 41–3).[2] Her assortment featured a number of domesticated rabbits, which usually stayed in hutches in the back garden (no.46), although when the family was on holiday one of them, Peter Piper, was partial to lying in a box by the fireside (no.44). Benjamin and Peter are of course the most famous, but Beatrix had kept rabbits from a young age, including, in 1877, one called Tommy.[3] By the time she was 16 and writing in her diary, her current rabbit was Benjamin H. Bouncer, brought home 'in a paper bag' and 'not observed by the nursery authorities for a week' (nos 45, 74).[4] Though immortalized by name in Potter's fourth storybook, he was in fact the first official model for her illustrations.[5] A handsome Belgian hare – a breed of domesticated long-legged rabbit – Benjamin was 'revered' by Potter, albeit 'absolute vermin as regards eating'.[6] By around 1892 a new member of the household was talented at 'jumping (stick, hands, hoop, back and forward), ringing little

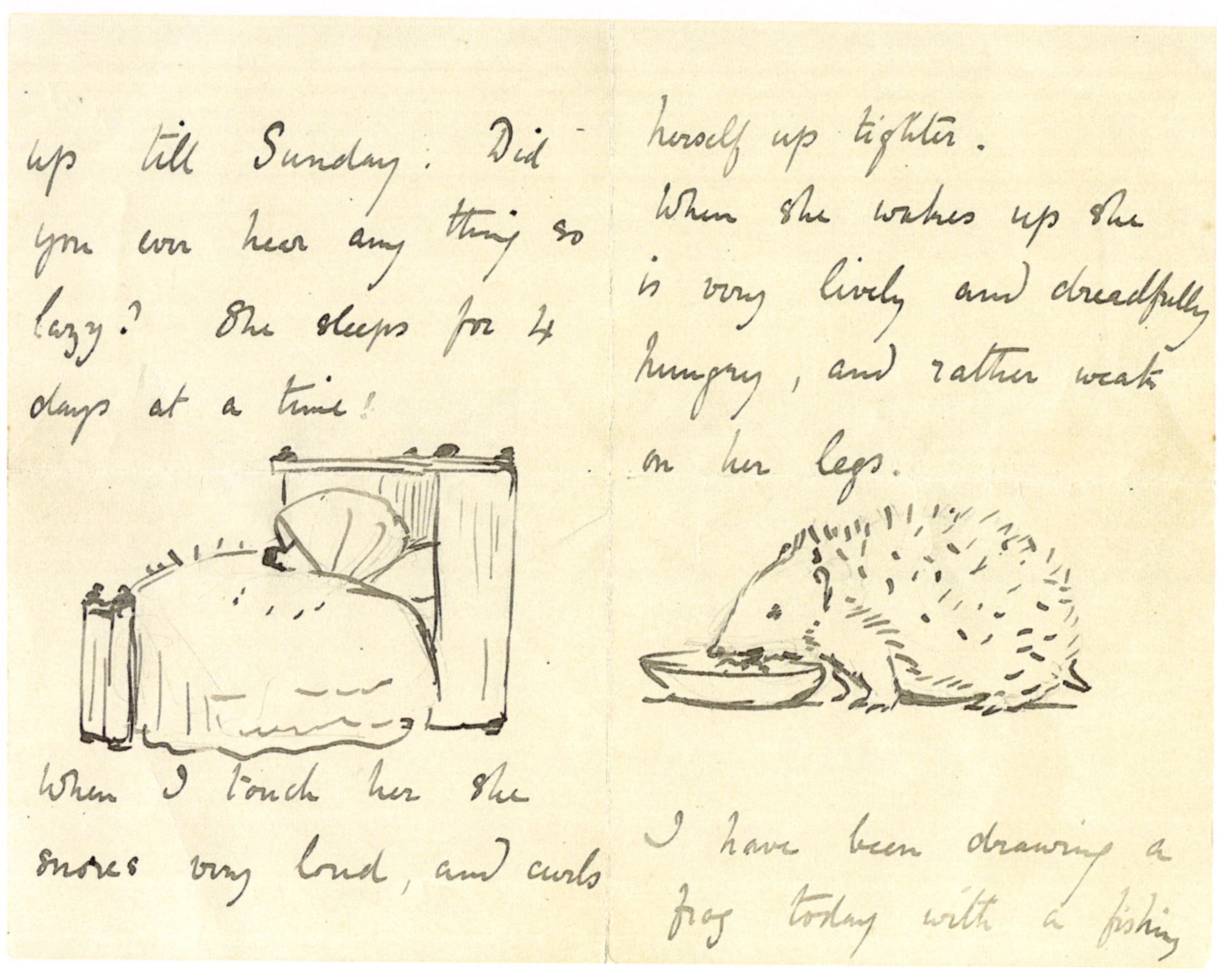

up till Sunday. Did you ever hear any thing so lazy? She sleeps for 4 days at a time!

When I touch her she snores very loud, and curls herself up tighter.

When she wakes up she is very lively and dreadfully hungry, and rather weak on her legs.

I have been drawing a frog today with a fishing

41.
Picture letter by Beatrix Potter sent to Winifred Warne, 15 December 1905
Ink on paper
Private collection

bell and drumming on a tambourine', although in company, 'Peter Rabbit…flatly refused to perform'.[7]

More conventionally, the Potter family owned dogs and the spaniel Spot was a constant in their lives from the early 1880s until 1892 (no.47).[8] Ponies and horses, although ostensibly kept for transport, were also regarded affectionately: 'Poor' Snowdrop 'was rather lazy, could scarcely be induced to pass… grandmother's' in nearby Palace Gardens, Bobby the pony was her 'one satisfaction' while Phyllis was 'a pleasure to watch…going, her tail whisking with satisfaction'.[9]

Bertram's taste in pets appears to have tended towards the wilder side. Even Beatrix, with her own eccentric preferences, was driven to describe a purchase of his as 'a pair of hideous little beasties';

42.
Picture letter by Beatrix Potter sent to Angela, Denis and Clare Mackail from 2 Bolton Gardens, London, 1 January 1903
Ink on paper
University of Leeds, Angela Thirkell Archive, BC Ms 20c Thirkell

I call him Twinkleberry; I think he will soon be tame, but at present he is a great deal too lively when I let him out; he rushes round the room on the tops of the picture frames, and jumps off the top of the bookcase in a way that alarms me. I have another squirrel called Nutkin, but he is unpleasant. He has

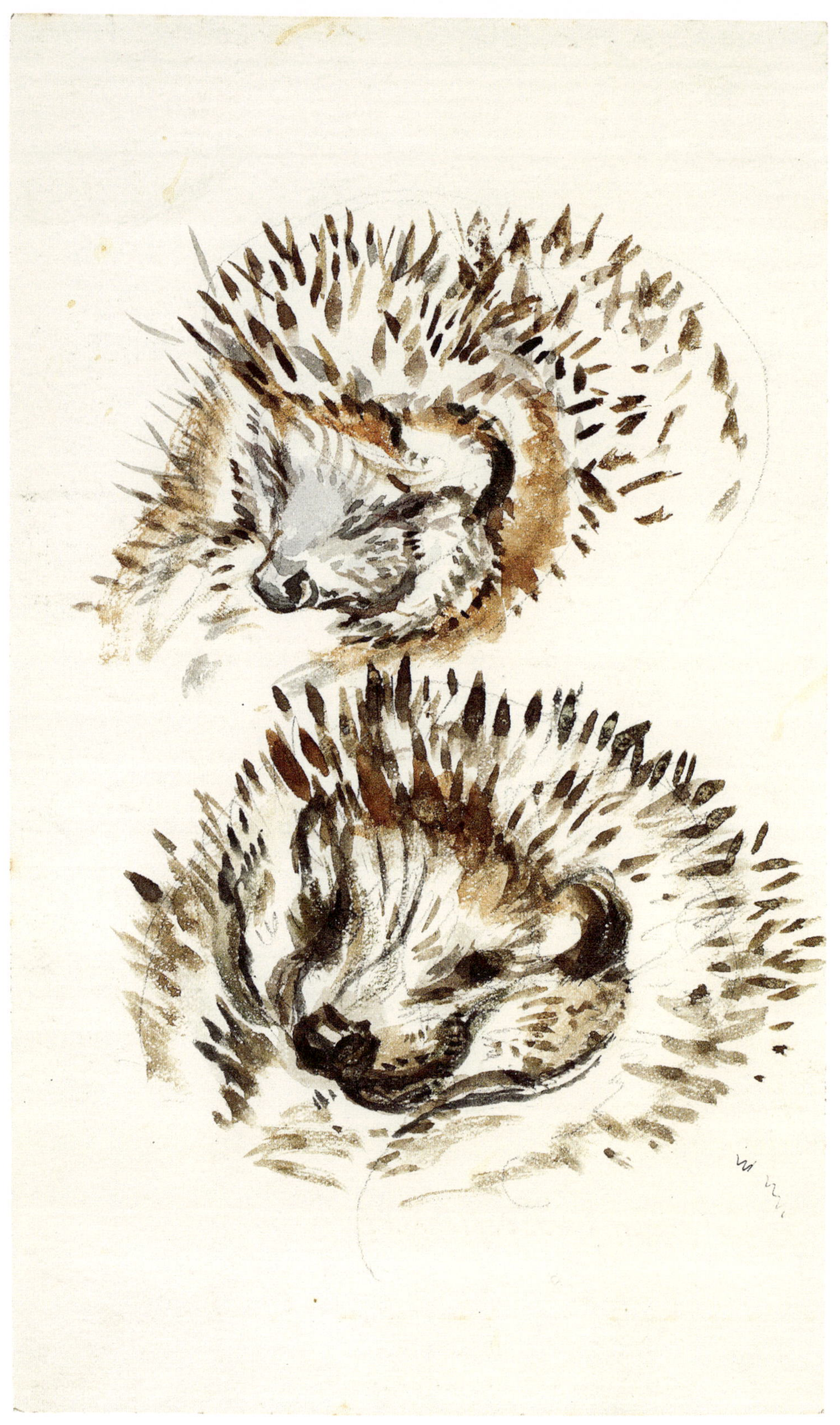

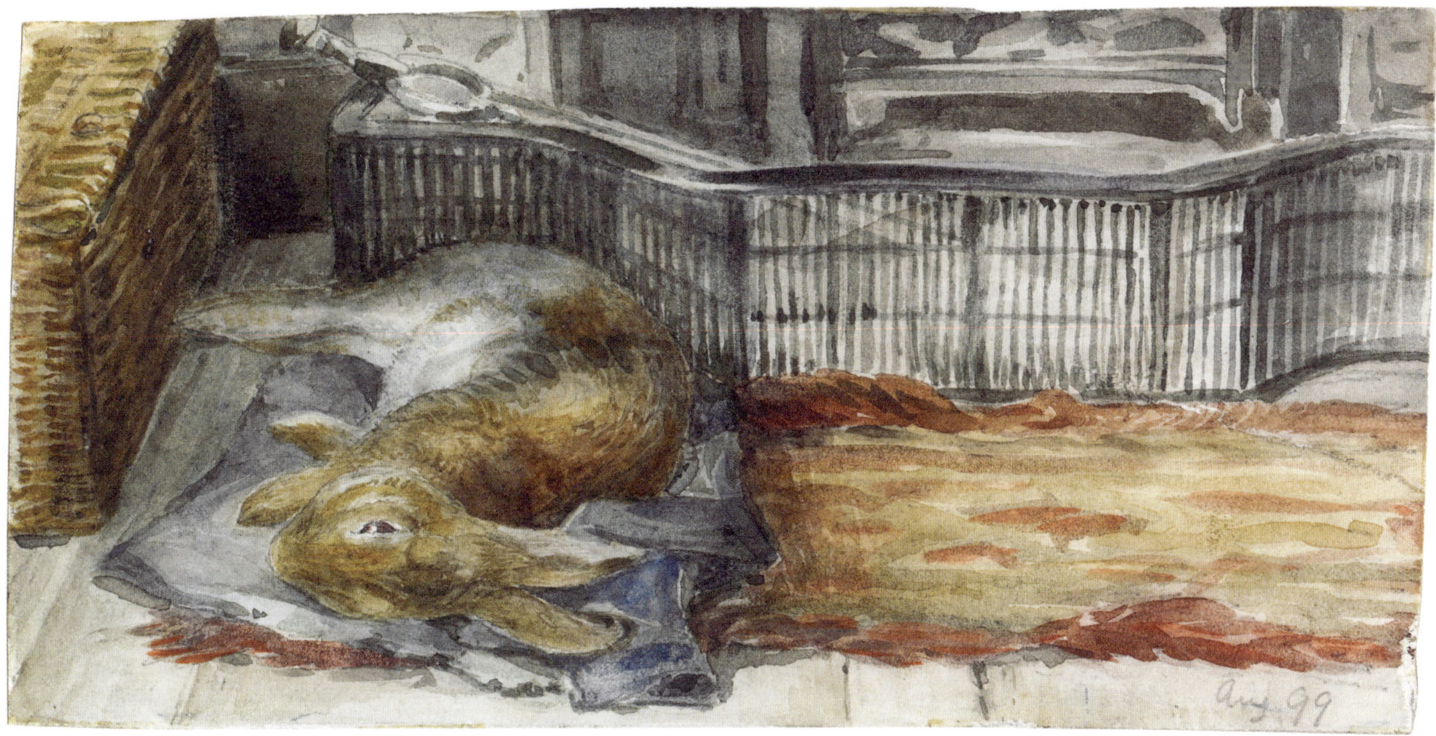

43. Opposite
Drawing of a hedgehog, assumed to be Mrs Tiggy, c.1904
Watercolour over pencil on paper
V&A: BP.495, Linder Bequest LB 866

44. Above
Peter Piper lying on his blanket at Lingholm, near Derwentwater, 1899
Watercolour over pencil on paper
V&A: LC 18/A/3, given by the Linder Collection

he named them Sally and Mandar, so presumably they were salamanders.[10] In 1884 Bertram also had a bat, which he left in Beatrix's care when he went to school, 'a charming little creature, quite tame and apparently happy as long as it has sufficient flies and raw meat'.[11] By March 1896 the now adult Bertram preferred the company of birds, 'a jay and a kestrel', then in 1897 an owl that hooted all night, and in 1899 a Barbary falcon.[12]

In around 1883 both children sustained quite an interest in reptiles and amphibians. Beatrix had already owned for 'five or six years' a pet frog called Punch when he died in March 1884.[13] With her brother she caught a 'small scaly' wild lizard, close to where they were staying at Woodfield, near Hatfield in Hertfordshire, on 18 September of that year, and three days later Bertram's pet Sally (the salamander), along with four black newts, escaped from their room. By then they had at least two more lizards, named Toby and Judy, which they had picked up at Ilfracombe the previous spring (no.48).[14] On 19 September they purchased from a shop a ringneck snake ('so pretty').[15]

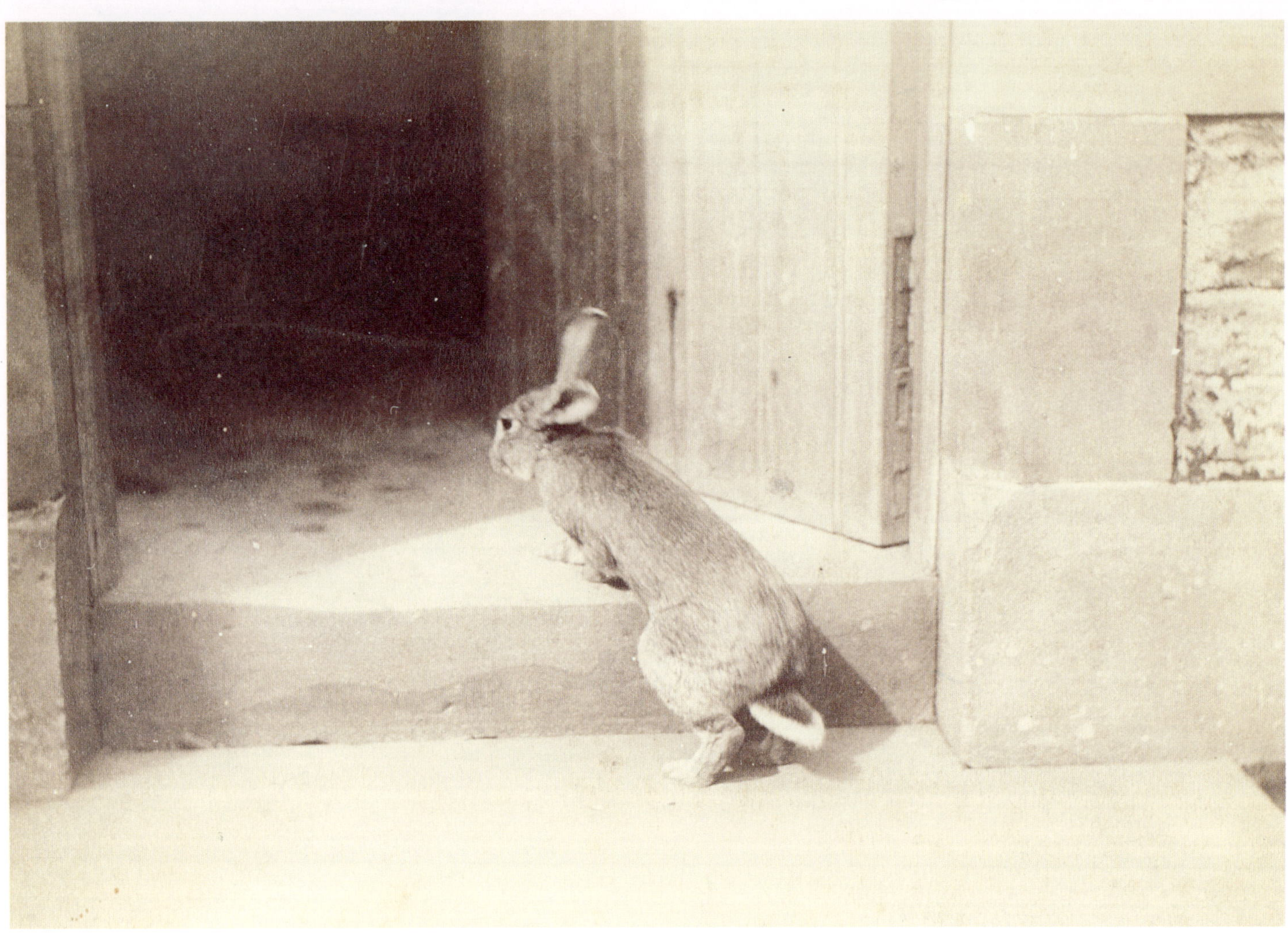

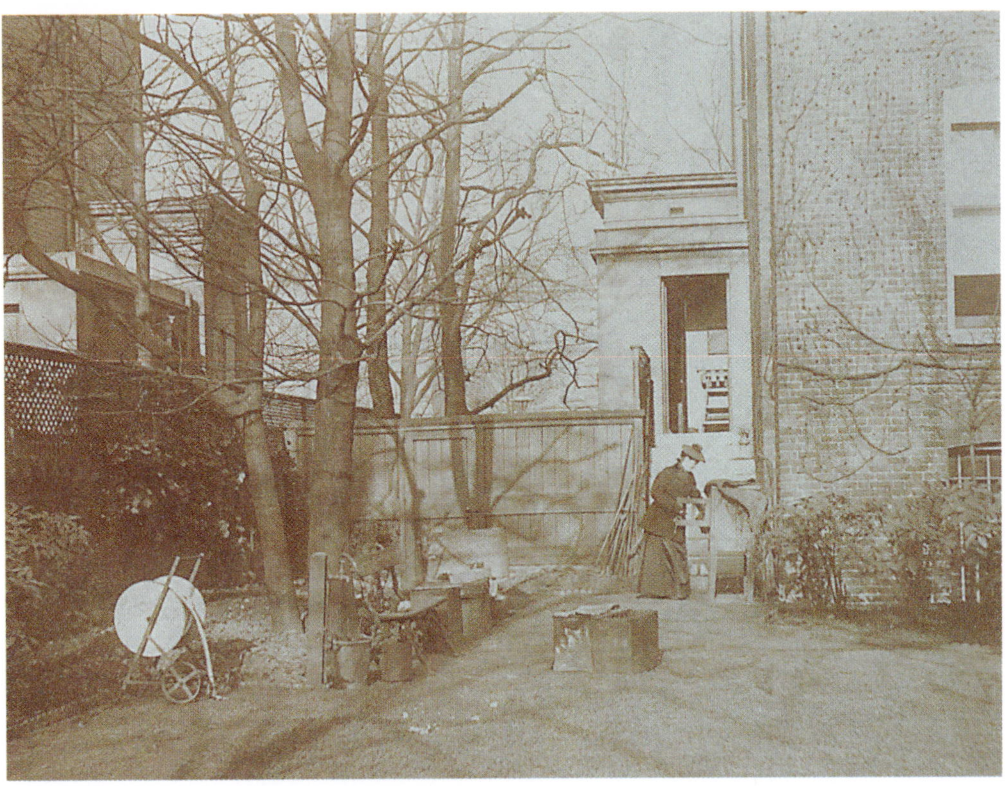

45. Opposite
Benjamin Bouncer ('Bounce'), photographed by Beatrix Potter, 1885–92
Albumen print on paper, mounted
National Trust, 242551

46. Above
Rupert Potter (1832–1914)
Beatrix Potter tending her rabbits, 2 Bolton Gardens, London, c.1895
Photograph in an album, albumen print on paper
Cotsen Children's Library, Special Collections, Princeton University Library, 10005.163

For her part, Potter seems to have been particularly fond of mice and dormice. The death of Xarifa, '*Poor Miss Mouse*', on 18 October 1886 moved her to lament on the manner of her passing: 'she had been so sensible about taking medicine and I thought she would get through, but the asthma got over her one night, and she laid herself out in my hand and died.'[16] Potter sometimes rescued mice caught in traps, including the famous pair Tom Thumb and Hunca Munca, who were later immortalized in *The Tale of Two Bad Mice* (1904).[17]

Xarifa aside, Potter was unsentimental about her animals and their deaths were usually recorded in a matter-of-fact way, even when they were accidental. Her duck, the Duc d'Orleans, 'began to smell suspicious...and has been eaten. Couldn't make out what had come to him...Sara had taken the opportunity of arranging him as if for dinner.'[18] She was 'very much put out', however, by the loss of a whole 'Bill' family of snails in 1883; each had 'a surprising difference of character' and included the Old, Mrs and Little Bills, Grimes and his 'wife' Sextus, Lord and Lady Salisbury, Mr and Mrs Camfield, Mars and Venus.[19]

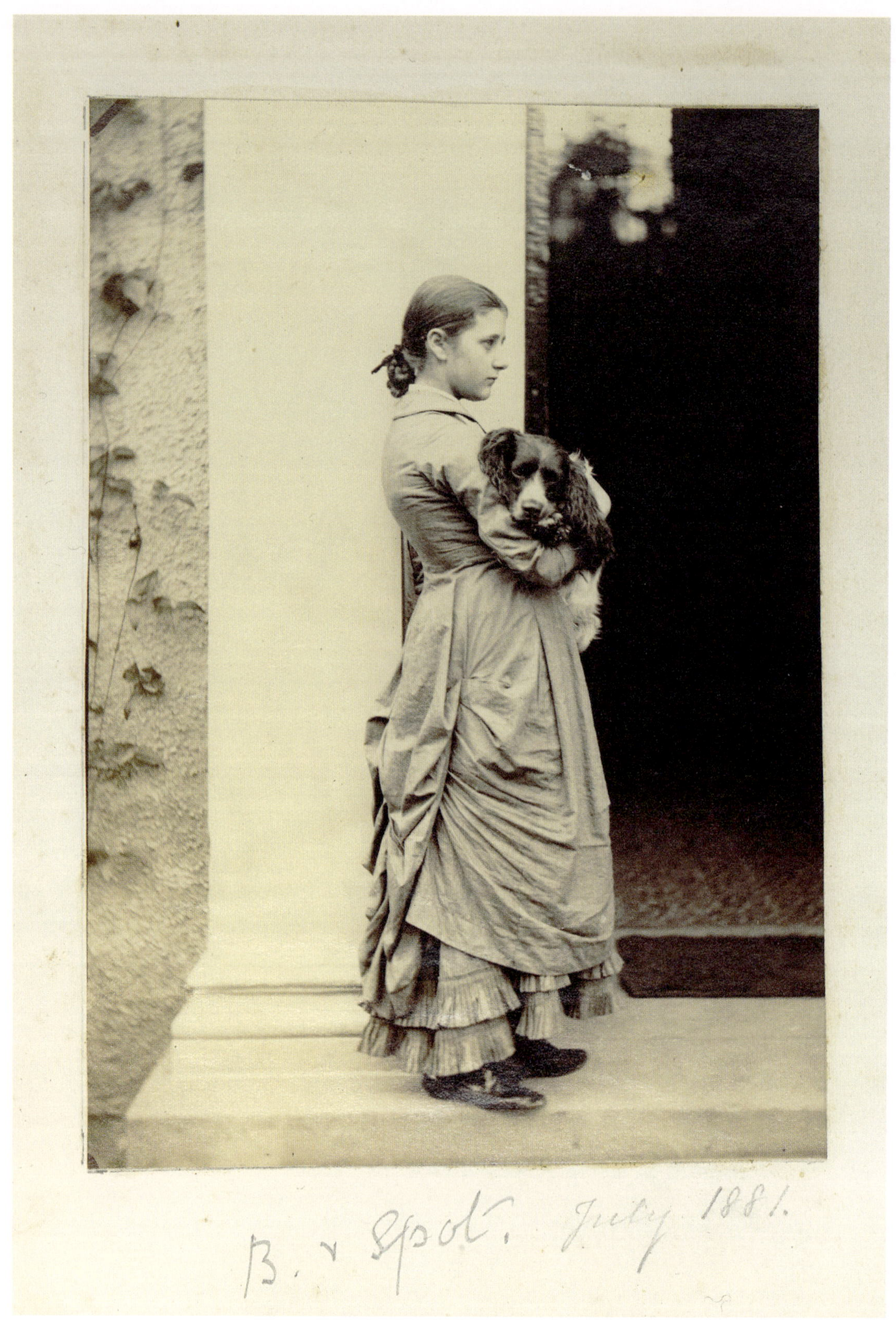
B. & Spot. July 1881.

47. Opposite
Rupert Potter (1832–1914)
Beatrix Potter with her dog, Spot, c.1880–1
Albumen print on paper
V&A: BP.1425, Linder Bequest LB 2110

48. Below
Beatrix Potter's lizard, Judy, February 1884
Watercolour and ink over pencil on paper
V&A: BP.405, Linder Bequest LB 378

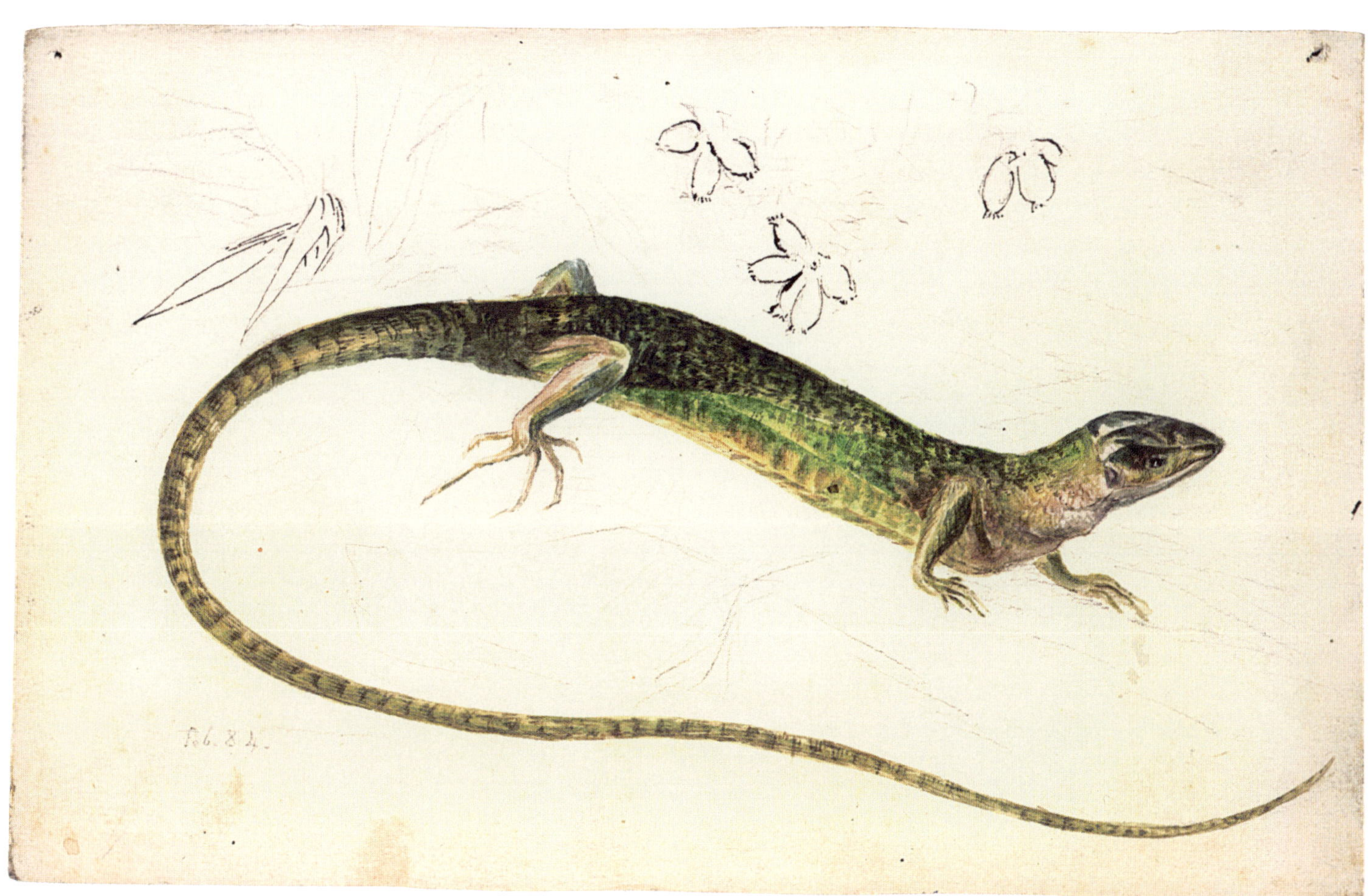

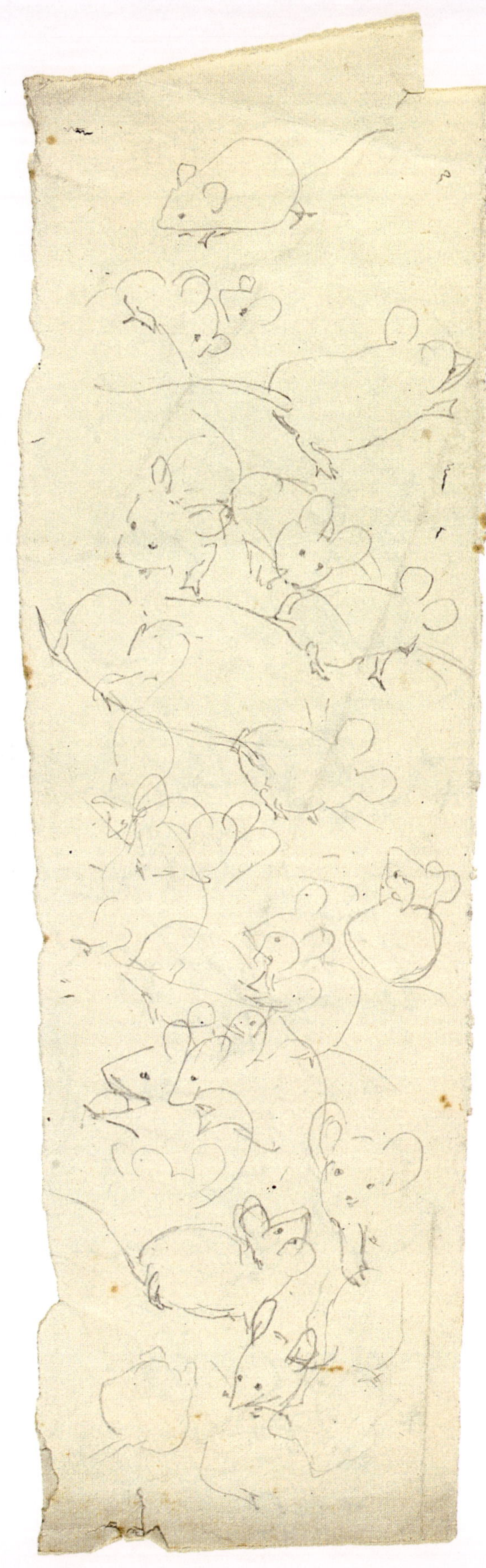

49.
Sketches of mice, c.1890s
Pencil on paper
V&A: BP.1015(II), Linder Bequest LB 320

What a strange thing force is… I sometimes reflect what may happen when Peter Rabbit stamps, which is one of the most energetic manifestations of insignificance which has come under my notice.

(BEATRIX POTTER, *JOURNAL*, 27 AND 30 APRIL 1896)[20]

Potter enjoyed observing animal habits and behaviour and made numerous pencil studies of them from every angle and sometimes in motion. Occasionally, her sketches look like exercises in speed drawing. One, on a torn strip of paper, starts with a conventional-looking mouse, which becomes gradually distilled into sketchier outlines as it moves around the page until it appears almost cartoon-like: a hint of nose and ear, and a dot for an eye (no.49).

An exceptional affinity with, and interest in, animals sometimes led Potter to contemplate aspects of their character and physiology. One day, out on a heath near Lennel, close to Coldstream on the Scottish Borders, she was conducting an experiment about sight by stalking a deer to see how soon and in what position it would spot her:

> I often consider what an important factor the arrangement of the eyes must be in determining… intellect in different animals…[In] a considerable proportion of animals, the two spheres of sight do not overlap at all, and in certain species, such as bats and rabbits, there is an absolute gap between the two planes of vision.[21]

In August 1883 at Woodfield, following a day fishing with her brother and having caught some newts, she speculated on the differences in breathing processes between frogs, toads, newts and salamanders, clearly basing her theories on what she had observed.[22] When Judy, her pet lizard, laid an egg that year, she was fascinated by the unborn lizard's appearance inside its transparent shell.[23] In 1888 she drafted a letter to

50.
Bertram Potter (1872–1918)
Still-life study of a preserved fish and snake, and a human skull, April 1889
Watercolour and pencil on paper
V&A: AAD/2006/4/406, given by Joan Duke

a newspaper discussing the feeding habits of hawfinches seen near her grandparents' home, Camfield Place, having noticed how they ate the holly seeds left behind by blackbirds.[24] Later in life she also remembered watching her albino rat, Sammy, that 'Representative of a Persecuted (but Irrepressible) Race', carry off numerous 'stolen articles' and even rolling a hard-boiled egg along a corridor.[25]

Occasionally, when their animals died, Beatrix and Bertram pickled them in jars, stuffed or anatomized them and made drawings of their skeletons, a practice that was not unusual in families where the study of natural history was encouraged (nos 50, 51).[26] A teenage Bertram's detailed instruction to Beatrix regarding his pet bat is matter-of-fact:

> If he cannot be kept alive...you had better kill him, + stuff him as well as you can. Be sure to take his measurements most carefully...the length of head, body, tail, Humerus, Radius, Femoris, Tibia, pollex + claw, + also the fingers...to keep the wings stretched out, perhaps if you pinned them out like the bat you got at Edinburgh...[27]

They kept and organized their animals' bones by type and may have practiced taxidermy. Beatrix recorded in 1895 that while 'dusting and mending our little bone-cupboards ... that containing the collection of British mice' fell on her head 'amidst a shower of glass eyes'; she just managed to catch 'the skeleton of a favourite dormouse'.[28] The Potter family must have appeared quite eccentric when they travelled by train, with rabbits on leads, hutches, cages and boxes of snails, shells and bone specimens. One of Beatrix's packing and 'to do' lists survives and provides an insight into how she occupied herself while away from home. Besides an object of sentimental value (such as a miniature portrait of her grandmother), the list includes customary mending and knitting tasks and Latin reading, but also a couple of bird skeletons and a painting of a stoat to finish:

> PACKING LIST
> March '89
> Haste 'haste' post haste.
>
> Slippers
> Miniature, grandmother P.
> 2 Pr. flannel drs. drs. to alter White petticoat }
> Cape to re-band, bag to mend
> To alter brown jacket.
> To look over papers that of G
> New sponge bag (*mend*)
> To see about old dresses
> Something for Miss M.
> Scrap book to buy
> To buy box
> Timothy box, mend
> Dentist
> Spirit bottles
> Virgil
> 2 bird's [sic] skeletons
> Paint stoat's eyes
> Dress scraps
> Knitting[29]

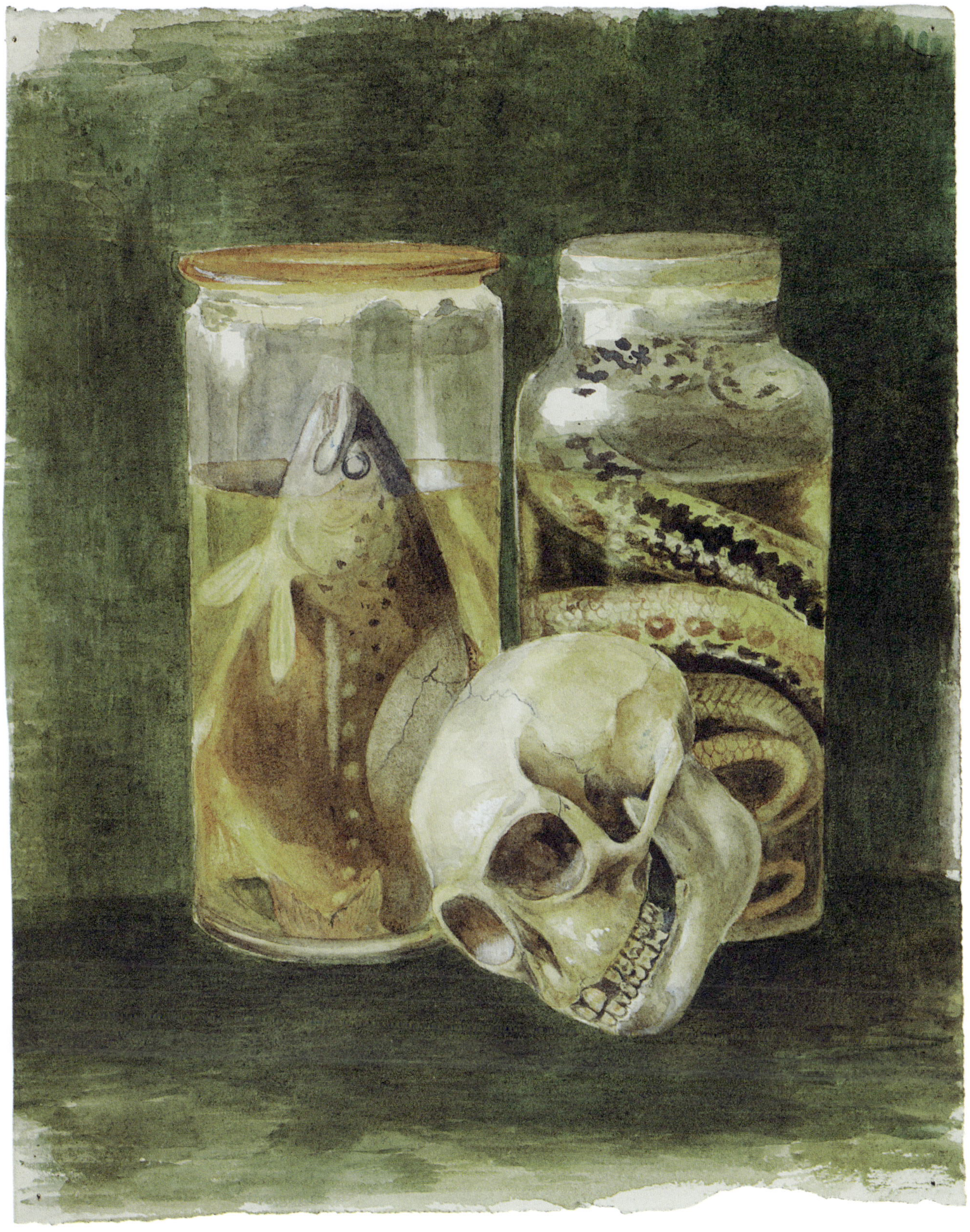

51.
Studies of a bat and its skeleton, 8 April 1887
Watercolour, ink and pencil on card
V&A: BP.250, Linder Bequest LB 109

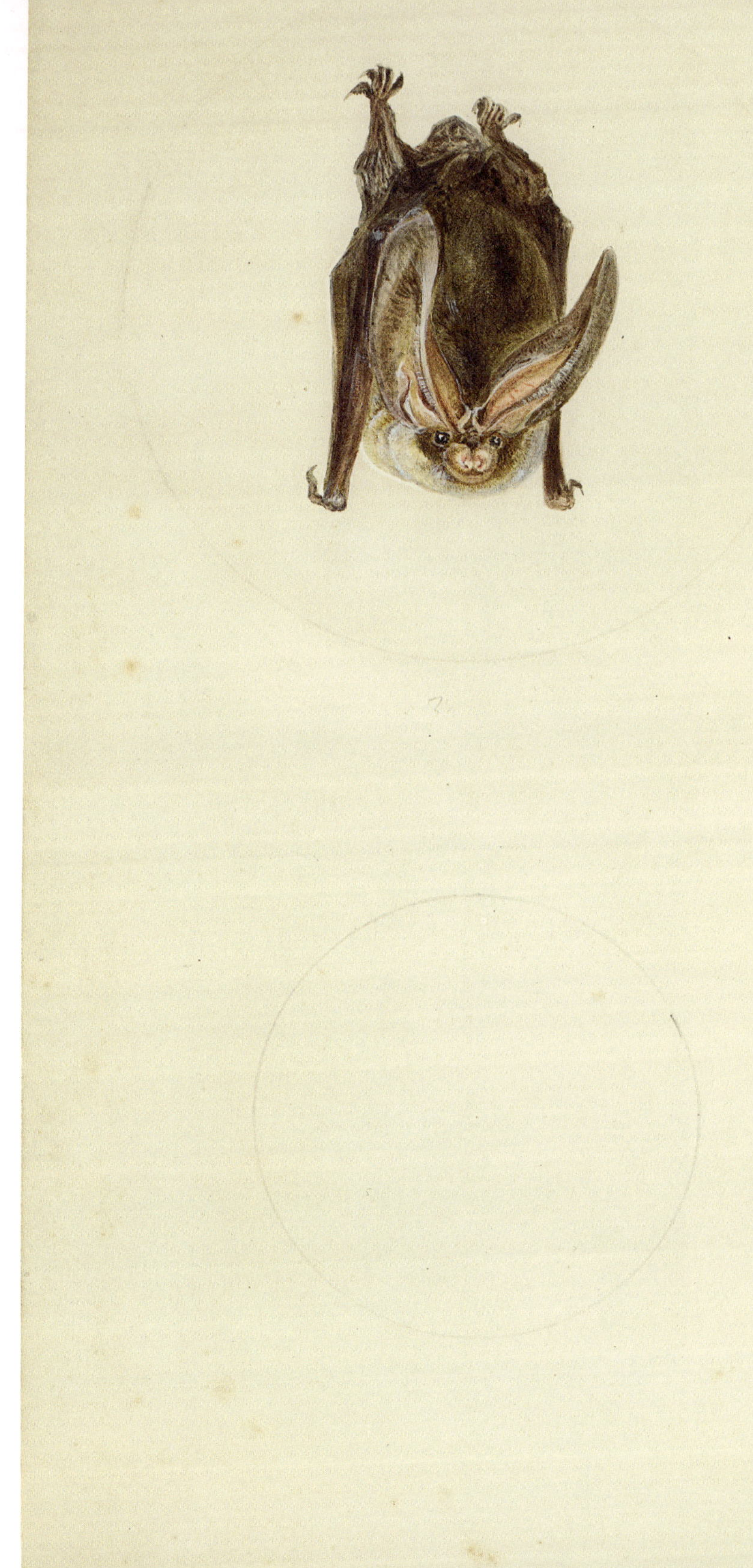

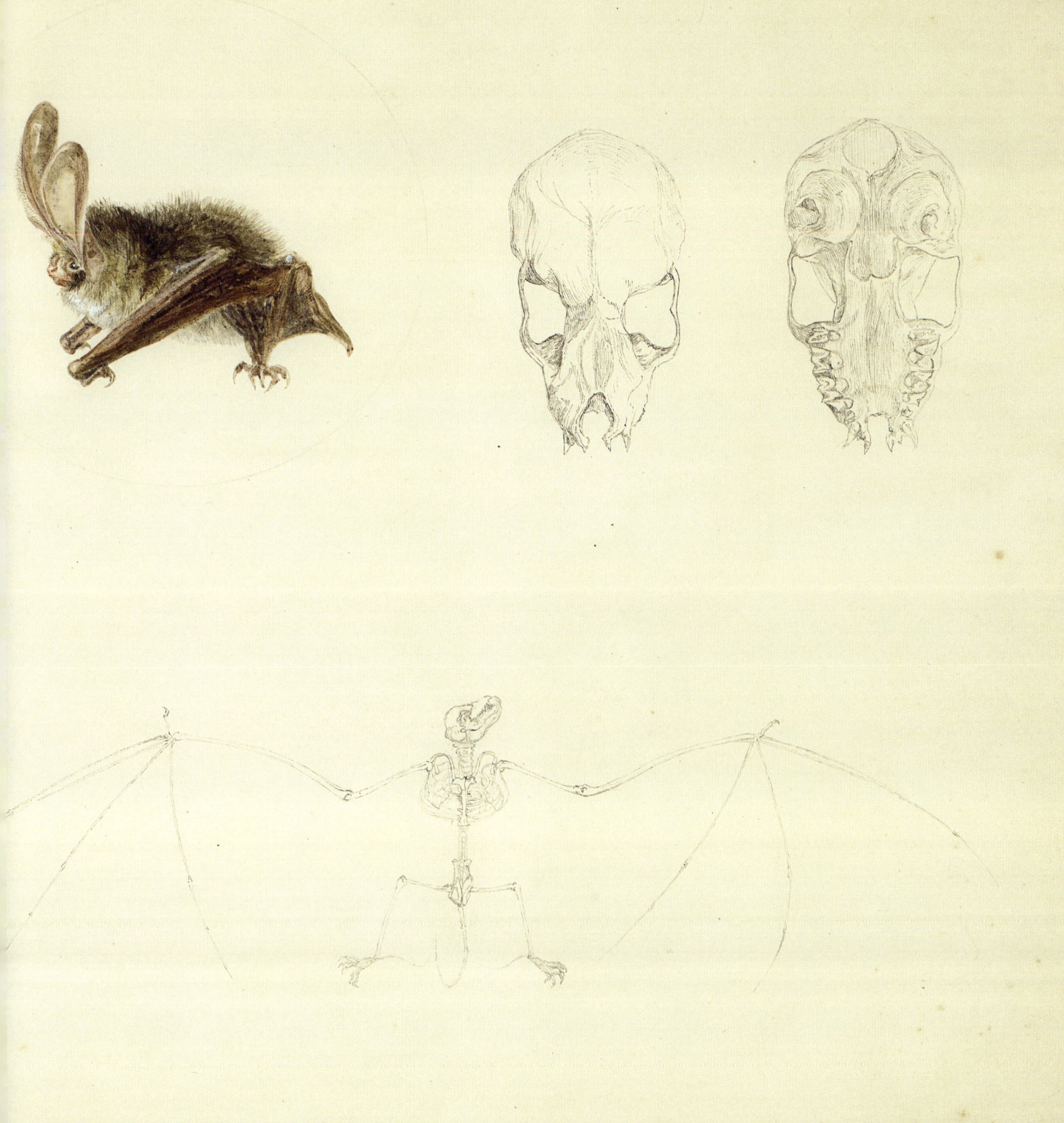

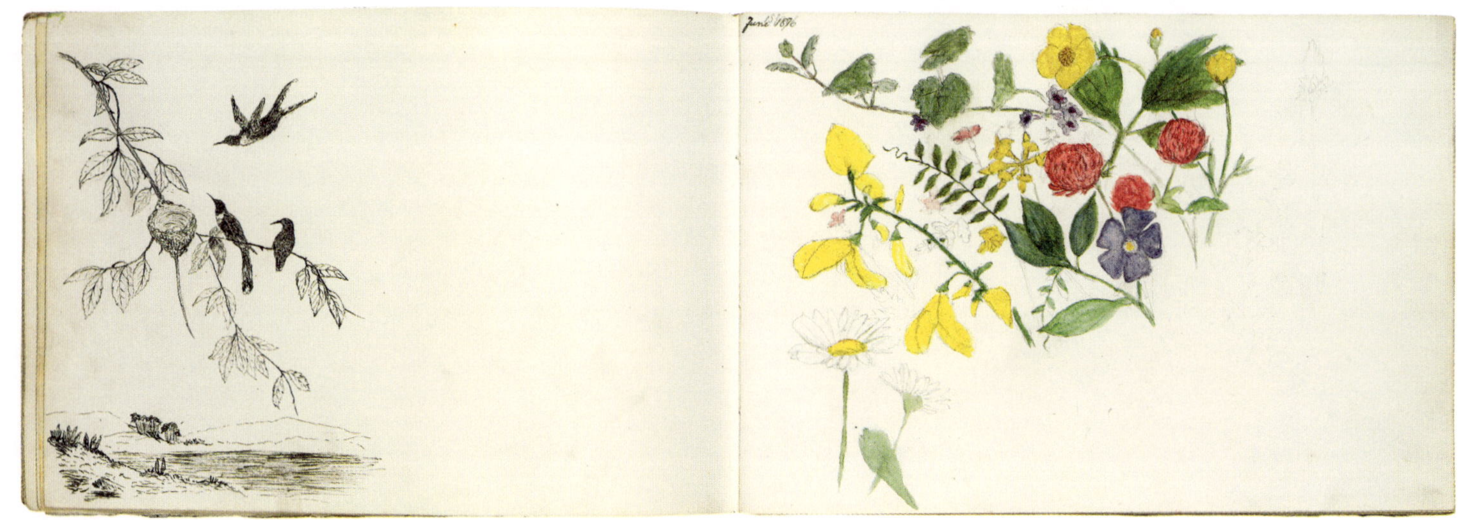

I remember so clearly…the morning I was ten years old – and my father gave me Mrs. Blackburn's book of birds, drawn from nature… I remember the dancing expectation and knocking at their bedroom door, it was a Sunday morning, before breakfast.

(BEATRIX POTTER, *JOURNAL*, 5 JUNE 1891)[30]

The sense of excitement at the prospect of a special present is palpable in Potter's description of her tenth birthday, which reads like a scene from any modern household. The Scottish naturalist, writer and illustrator Jemima Blackburn had a lasting impact on Potter, who traced and copied imagery from her books from a young age (no.13; pp.25, 32). Consequently, the occasion on which she first met her, at the age of 25, inspired a detailed diary entry. Blackburn, by then almost 70 years old, was still active on her family's estate. Potter had 'not been so much struck with anyone for a long time' and found her:

> a broad, intelligent observer with a keen eye for the beautiful in nature, particularly in plant-world life, as well as for the humorous, indeed I see no reason why common-sense should not foster a healthier appreciation of beauty than morbid sentimentality…[31]

It is instructive that an eye for beauty and a matter-of-fact approach to life (and death) should so strike her, as these qualities typify Potter's own life and her mode of illustration and storytelling.

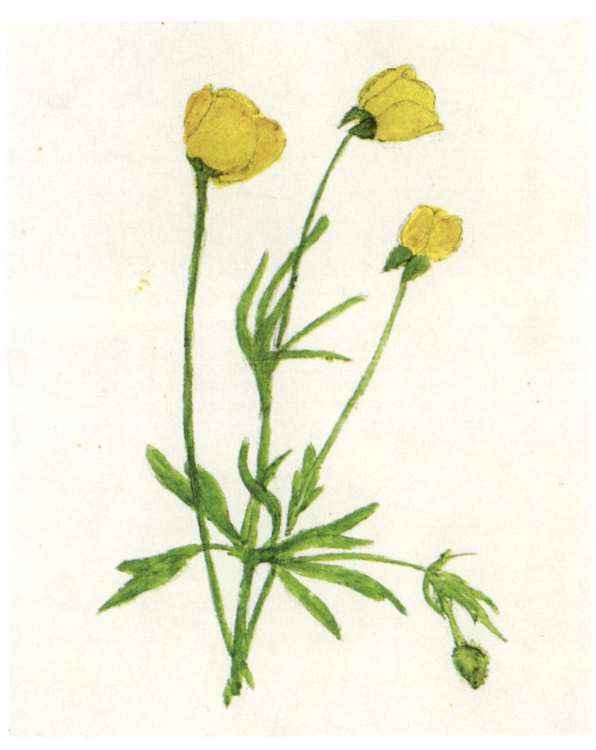

52. Opposite
Pages from a sketchbook, c.1876
Ink and watercolour over pencil on paper
V&A: BP.743, Linder Bequest LB 1093

53. Left above
Buttercups, c.1877
Watercolour over pencil on notepaper
V&A: BP.762, Linder Bequest LB 26

54. Left below
Bertram Potter (1872–1918)
Unfinished drawing of sweet pea blossoms, August 1888
Watercolour and pencil on paper
V&A: AAD/2006/4/407, given by Joan Duke

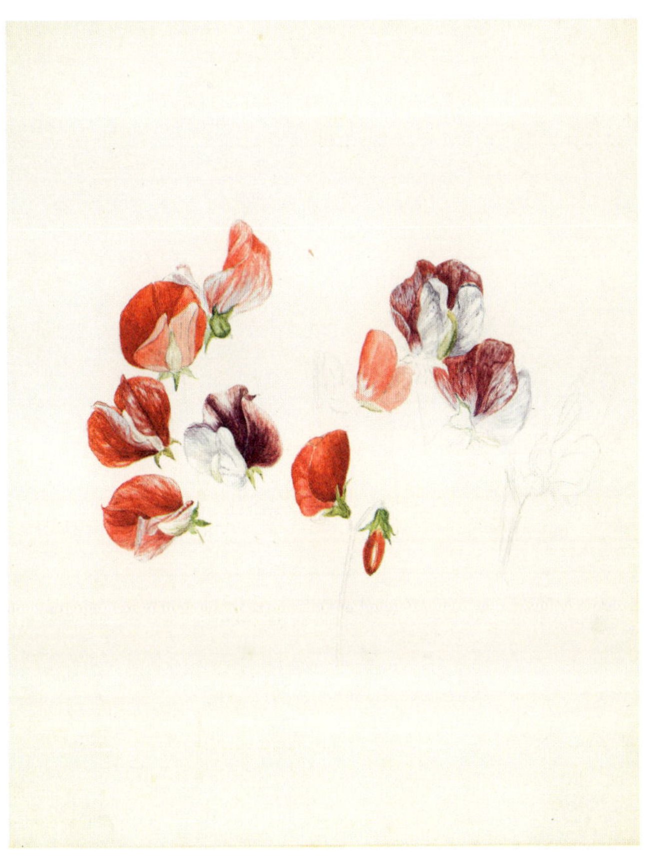

Besides having had the opportunity to observe animals since early childhood, Potter copied and recorded imagery of various kinds in her sketchbooks and collected examples; one of her schoolbooks still preserved pressed ferns (no.57). Her first sketchbook includes drawings of flowers, caterpillars (no.14) and birds' eggs, with texts describing some of them, suggesting that they relate to homeschooling. Beatrix (Bertram too) also copied from published illustrations, such as exotic birds and animals from engravings (no.52). While a number of their flower sketches are drawn in the round, others appear flat and stylized, showing an awareness of the style of presentation in botanical illustrations or herbals (nos 53, 54). Beatrix continued to draw flowers throughout her life (no.55). By the time of her death there was still a much-used copy of James Andrews' *Art of Flower Painting* (1842) as well as John Sowerby's *British Wild Flowers* (1858) in her library. From an early age she certainly copied from Vere Foster's drawing books and *The Instructive Picture Book* (1862) by Adam White; even in the 1890s, she presented some of her moss and fern drawings in a schematic way reminiscent of Sowerby (no.56).[32]

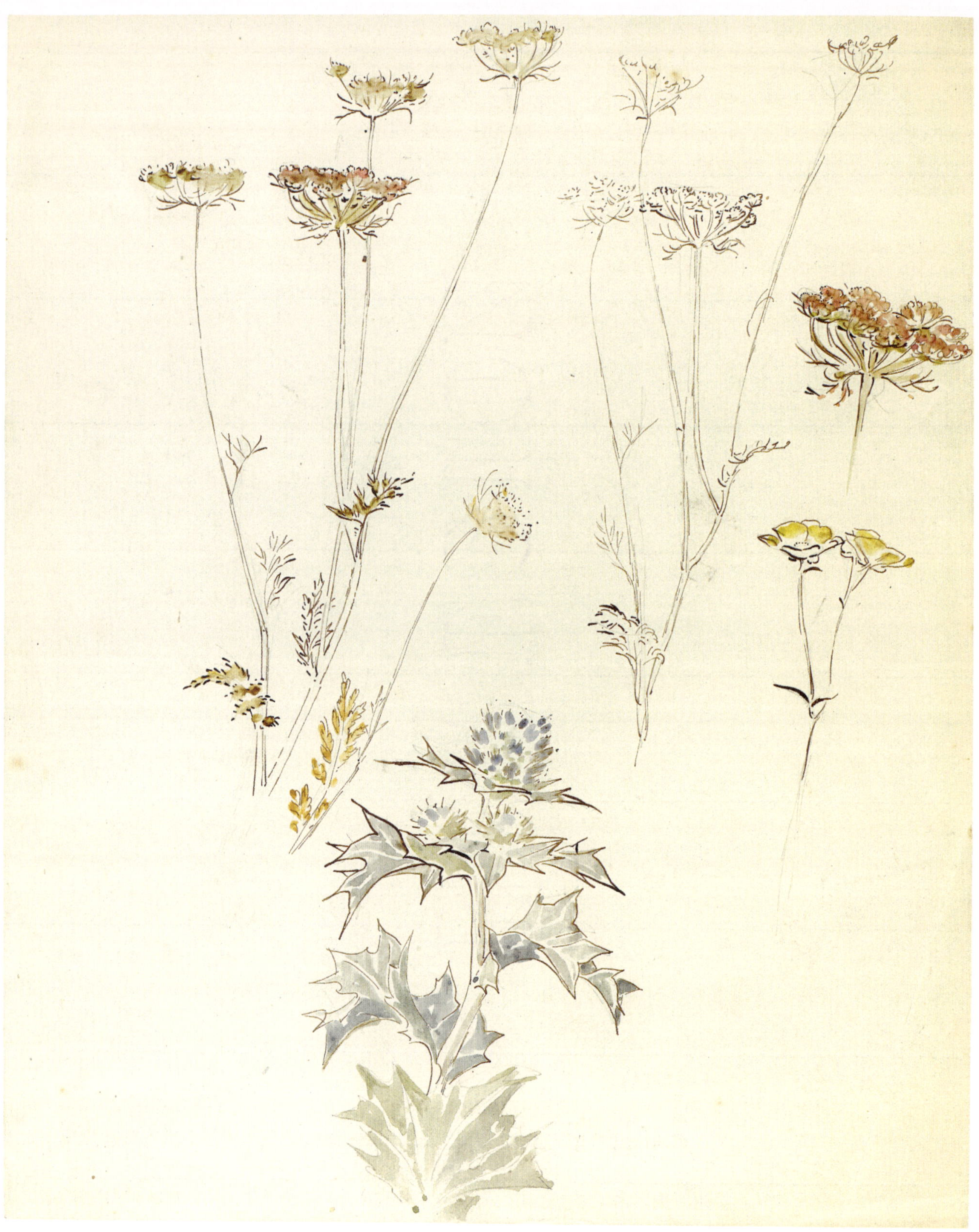

55. Opposite
Eryngium maritimum, 'Sea Holly', *Daucus carota*, 'Wild Carrot' and *Ranunculus*, 'Buttercup', c.1890–1905
Watercolour and ink over pencil on paper
V&A: BP.920, Linder Bequest LB 253

56. Right
Hypnum proliferum ('Herb Smith' moss), c.1890s
Watercolour on paper
Armitt Museum and Library, AMATL:ALMC 1958.6045

57. Below
Page from Beatrix Potter's history exercise book, 10 January 1879
Ink on paper, pressed fern
National Trust, 242301

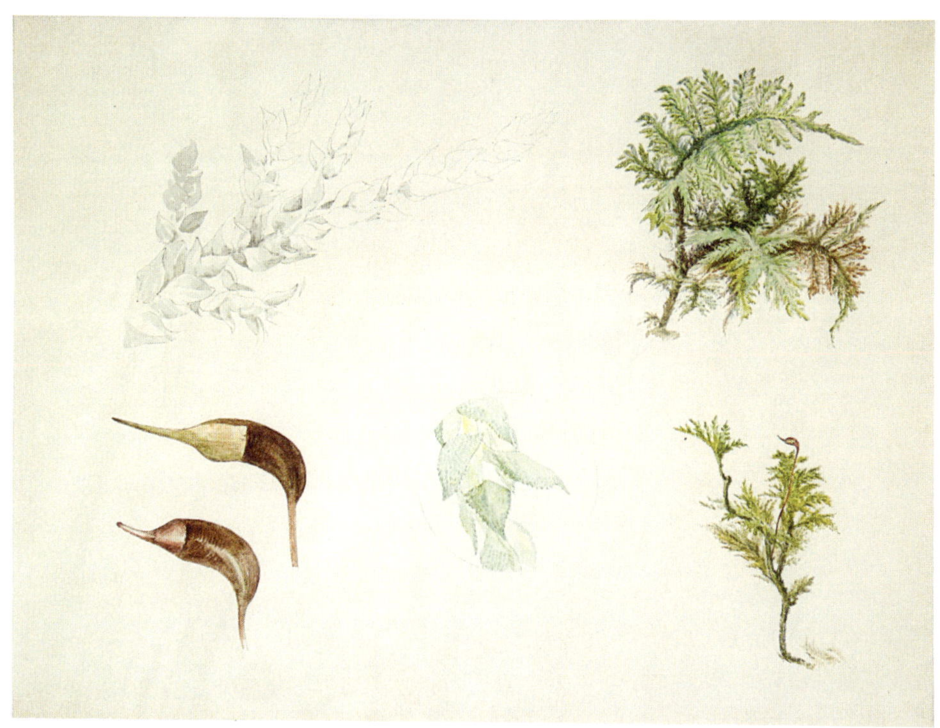

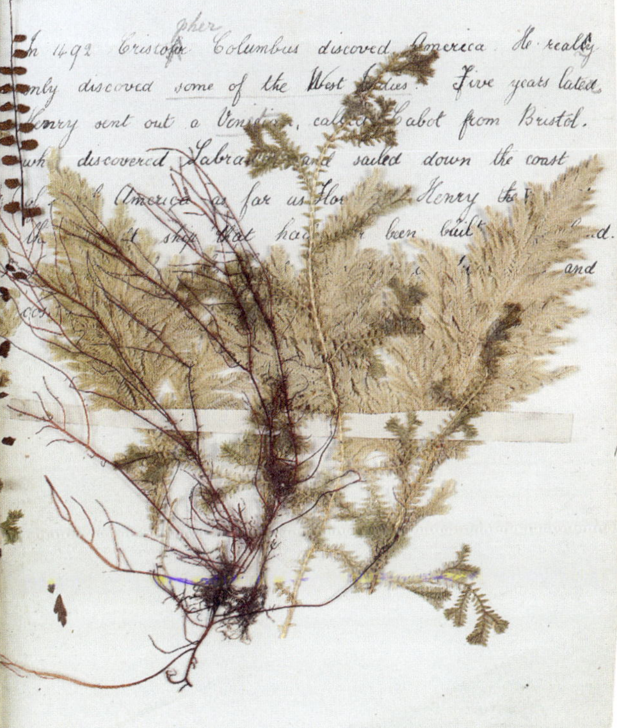

His men were defeated, some were hung and the rest sent home. His wife was kindly treated and ~~placed~~ made an attendant on the Queen and called the White Rose. Perkin Warbeck was taken prisoner and placed in the Tower, he was found to be plotting an escape with the Earl of Warwick and he was hung and the Earl executed. Henry VII suffered from gout, which injured his health and he died in 1509 of consumption. Queen ~~Anne~~ Elizabeth died six years before him. He had four children. Arthur who died before him; and Henry afterwards Henry VIII. Margaret, married James IV of Scotland; and Mary who was first married to Louis XII and afterwards to the Duke of Suffolk.

The three great ~~peculiarities~~ characteristics of the Tudors, were these; ~~they were very selfwilled~~, they understood the English people so well that they had great power over them. They had great courage, and Henry VII was very avaricious.

In 1492 Cristopher Columbus discovered America. He really only discovered some of the West Indies. Five years later Henry sent out a Venetian, called Cabot from Bristol, who discovered Labra[illegible] and sailed down the coast [illegible] America as far as Flo[illegible] Henry the [illegible] ship that ha[illegible] been built [illegible] and

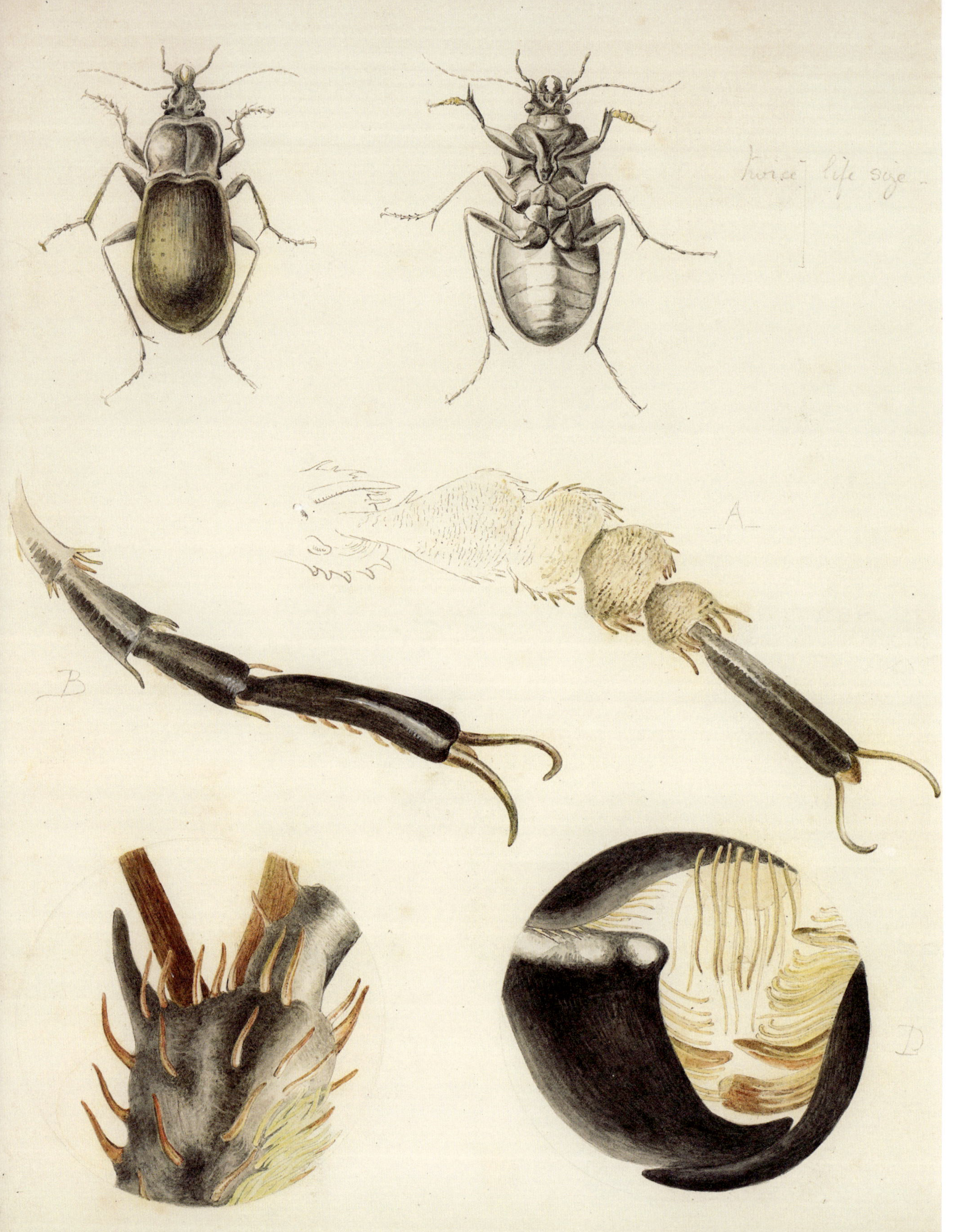
twice life size
A
B
D

58. *Opposite*
Magnified studies of a ground beetle, c.1887
Watercolour, ink and pencil on paper
V&A: BP.257, Linder Bequest LB 333

[Mr Lucy] seems to think it positively improper to collect fossils all over the country…I beg to state I intend to pick up everything I find which is not too heavy. 'A black ousel, cousin Shallow, a black ousel.'

(BEATRIX POTTER, *JOURNAL*, 9 JULY 1895)[33]

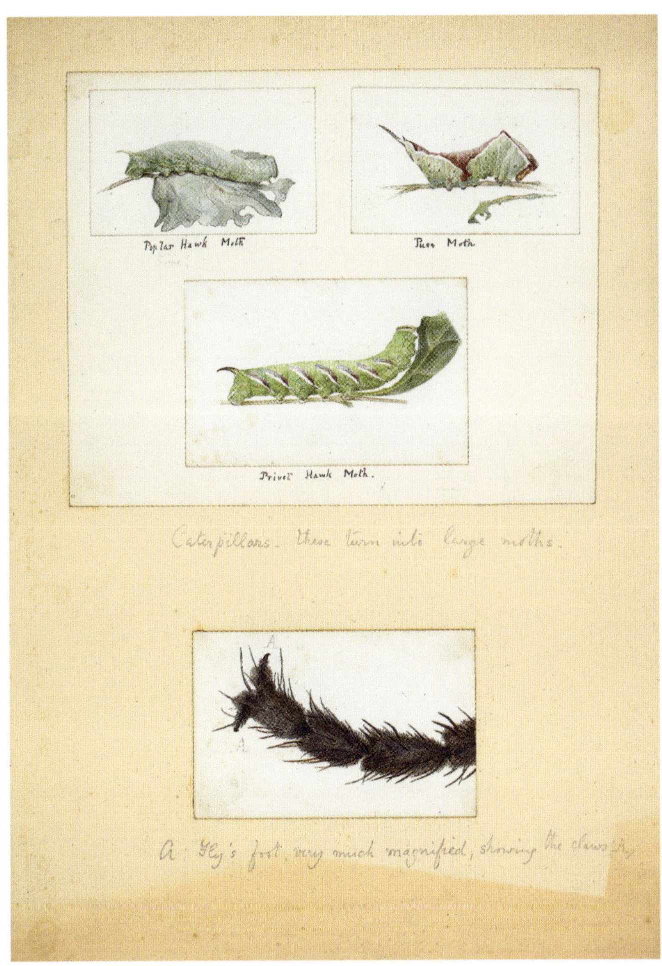

59.
Studies of caterpillars and a magnified fly's foot, one dated 5 February 1886
Watercolour and ink on paper, mounted on card annotated in ink
V&A: BP.248, Linder Bequest LB 341

Just as Potter had varied influences (see 'Town and Country', pp.20–47), she was also eclectic in her interests. In some ways she was a typical Victorian middle-class amateur, engrossed in collecting, and the archaeological and scientific study of the world around her. The Potter family also owned scientific books and took the journal *Hardwicke's Science-Gossip*, which was aimed at families of amateurs and collectors.[34] Beatrix was scathing of those, like her mother's friend Ada Smallfield, who pretended to collect but in fact bought their 'finds' from fishmongers.[35] She was also critical of experts too, considering it a weakness that they were too focused on one specialism and appeared to be 'less well informed than an ordinary person on any subject outside their own'.[36]

In her own activities Potter nevertheless honed in on detail, in some cases quite literally, for she became interested in microscopy. She bought a microscope in 1892 from a shop in Dunkeld, Perthshire, which she used to aid her drawing of insect anatomy, and she took advantage of the Natural History branch of the British Museum on her doorstep in London to learn more about insect taxonomy, although she found its '"Index" collection' frustratingly organized, 'nothing but labels and contrasts…without method'.[37]

The purpose of some of Potter's microscopic drawing was to make some lithographic plates illustrating the life cycle of insects for 'Miss Martineau' (thought to be Caroline Martineau [1844–1902], Principal of Morley College), perhaps for her science lectures (no.59).[38] In her drawing Potter may have taken inspiration from a friend, Gertrude Woodward (1854–1939),

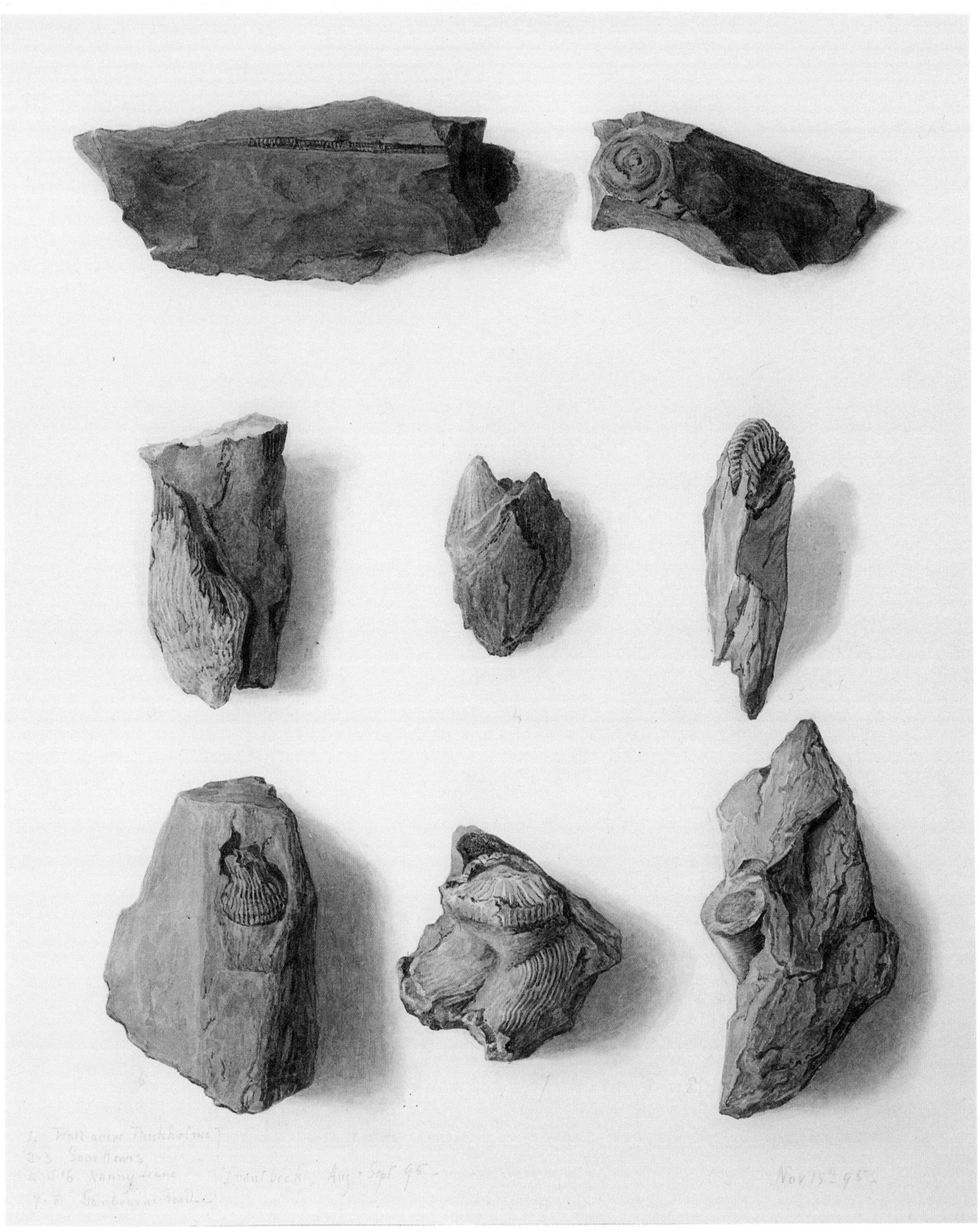

60. Opposite
Fossils found near Troutbeck, August–November 1895
Watercolour over pencil on paper
National Trust, 242758

61. Below
Roman archaeological finds from Bucklersbury, London, c.1894
Watercolour and pencil on paper
Armitt Museum and Library, AMATL:ALMC 1958.1152

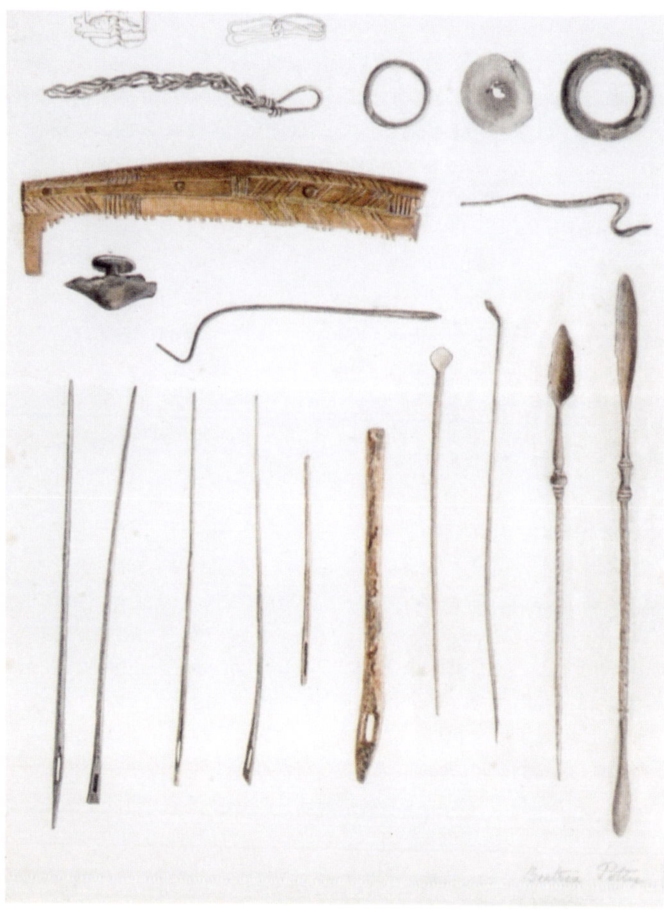

whom she sometimes met at the Natural History Museum. Gertrude's father was a Keeper there and edited the *Geological Magazine*, for which Gertrude worked as a scientific illustrator in the mid-1890s.[39] Whether Potter ever considered taking up such an occupation professionally herself is unclear, but she was undertaking several different activities at this time as though she were trying to find an outlet for her talents.

While preserved specimens interested Potter, between 1894 and 1895 she also collected fossils wherever the opportunity arose, whether in the park at Gwaynynog, Denbighshire, in the woods behind the back of Harescombe Grange, Gloucestershire, around the fells of Troutbeck in the Lake District, or 'grubbing' at Huddinknoll quarries; at Lennel she 'found out which stones to split and how to use a cold chisel' (no.60).[40] She made meticulous, lifelike illustrations of some of these finds, mostly marine invertebrates, especially brachiopods and trilobites.[41] She copied images in pen and ink of fossils from scientific publications, but her watercolours are in great contrast to the monochrome outline lithographs or engravings common in such journals; perhaps this explains why she did not take up scientific illustration professionally.[42] During the same period, back in London, Potter made scale drawings of archaeological artefacts, including Roman red-glazed pottery and metal implements, found during the construction of the National Safe Deposit Company building near Bucklersbury and Walbrook in the City (borrowed from 'the squire', probably the building's architect, John Whichcord), and sandals from Pickle Herring Street, found on the south bank of the River Thames (no.61).[43]

[Charlie's] judgement speaking to their accuracy in minute botanical points gave me infinitely more pleasure than that of critics who assume more, and know less...

(BEATRIX POTTER, *JOURNAL*, 29 OCTOBER 1892)[44]

Potter may have thought experts too limited in focus, but what is most striking about her various scientific pastimes is how often she approached them for encouragement or advice on her illustrations. At the London exhibition of finds from Old Sarum (Silchester), she expected to bump into 'the old gentleman', the archaeologist 'Mr [William] St. John Hope I suppose', to ask about Roman red-glazed pottery; two fragments, 'a stag-pattern and a running-scroll were almost identical with ones found at Bucklersbury which I borrowed from the squire to draw.' She even took her drawings with her when she went to the exhibition again the following year, hoping that archaeologist 'Mr. [George E.] Fox...might be struck' with them.[45] Potter took her studies of spiders, made with the aid of a microscope, to show the entomologist Reginald Innes Pocock (1863–1947) at the Natural History Museum, where she later met geologist William Charles Lucy (1822–1898) to look at the fossils, having previously sought his opinion on her photographs of fossils and her archaeological drawings.[46] Then, when she was experimenting with fungi, she visited the physiology and natural history lecturer at Morley College, Mrs Rose, for advice on cross-fertilization.[47] For Potter, with her awareness of propriety, it is easy to see the benefit of having learned women to speak to when she needed advice. By contrast, she found curators at the Natural History Museum somewhat exasperating:

> I worked into indignation about that august Institution. It is the quietest place I know – and the most awkward. They have reached such a pitch of propriety that one cannot ask the simplest question. The other Museum [South Kensington Museum, now V&A] is most disagreeable with the students, but if I want to find out anything at the library there is not the slightest difficulty...At the Natural History Museum the clerks seem to be all gentlemen and one must not speak to them. If people are forward I can manage them, but if they take the line of being shocked it is perfectly awful to a shy person.[48]

This did not stop her from asking, and she frightened the museum staff with searching questions about lichens, algae and their views on Schwendener's theory ('I should like to have heard more but he [George Murray] fled, so did Miss [Annie] Smith the Librarian').[49]

Potter's most fruitful connection was with Charles McIntosh (1839–1922, no.62), a postman working around Dunkeld and an expert in ferns and mosses whom she had met on holiday as a young girl; she remembered that she had played a game following his strides, jumping from puddle to puddle down the driveway.[50] The 'Perthshire Naturalist', as he became known, was also interested in mycology: the study of fungi.[51] Potter may have been familiar with his expertise through her parents. In any case, she seized the chance during a holiday in Dunkeld in 1892 to orchestrate a meeting with him. Although naturally shy, he was animated when talking on the subject of fungi, and 'spoke with quite poetical feeling about their exquisite colours.'[52]

Potter had started drawing fungi from around 1885 but knew little of the science behind them. She began exchanging letters with McIntosh; he dispatched

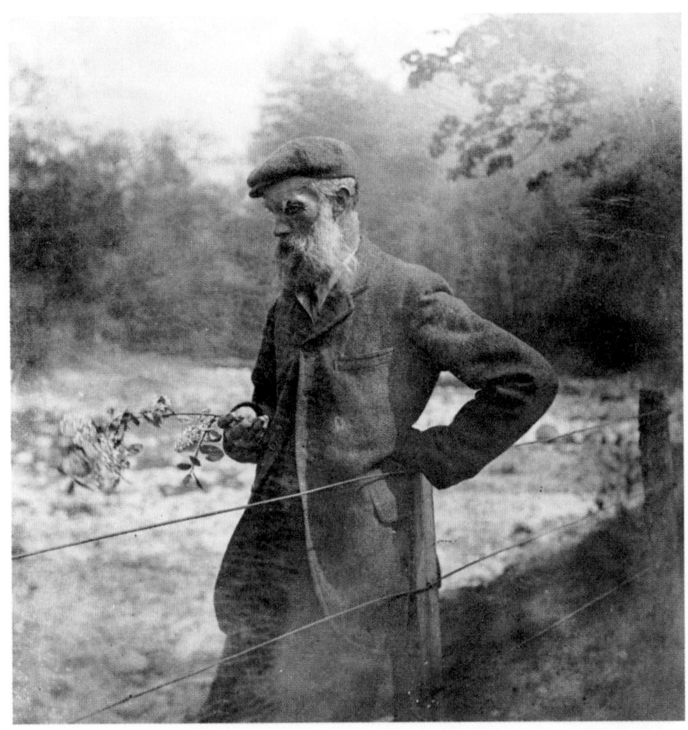

62.
Henry Coates (1859–1935)
Charles McIntosh, 22 May 1897
Albumen print on paper
Perth Museum and Art Gallery, MJ3188

samples and she made two drawings, sending him one and keeping the other for herself (nos 69, 70). She would describe specimens by their appearance, 'spluttered candle' (no.67), or smell, 'exactly like a dead sheep!', and it was McIntosh who directed her to appropriate reading matter and suggested she might better present her drawings scientifically by showing the gills and cross sections (nos 63, 64).[53]

As Potter grew more knowledgeable, she planned a scientific paper, encouraged by her 'Uncle Harry', the chemist Sir Henry Roscoe (1833–1915) (no.170). Through her uncle she met 'five different gentlemen' at the Royal Botanical Gardens at Kew, including the 'cynical' director William Thiselton-Dyer and 'very pleasant, kind' curator George Massee, but not without ruffling feathers.[54] Ultimately, the Linnean Society said her paper required more work, but surviving drawings show that Potter continued with her microscopic experiments at least until 1898 while her drawings in a scientific mode are dated as late as 1907.[55]

Inevitably, mushrooms also made their way into Potter's landscape sketches and, from there, into backgrounds for her Tales (nos 65, 66, 147). The exquisite detail in her watercolours shows how she relished recording the minutiae of nature, a characteristic that enriched her later illustrative work and appealed greatly to children.

Her delighted curiosity in animals' behaviour and knowledge of their anatomy gave her characters, even while standing upright and clothed, a credible unsentimental anthropomorphism (no.1). Just as Potter was a master of bringing the real world into the imaginative one, she also took fantasy into real life, whether she was explaining the miniature pony tracks seen in the 'green & blue hills' above her sheep farm at Troutbeck with reference to fairies, or describing 'the myriads of fairy fungi that start into life in autumn woods' at the same time as engaging in a scientific study of mycelium.[56]

Annemarie Bilclough

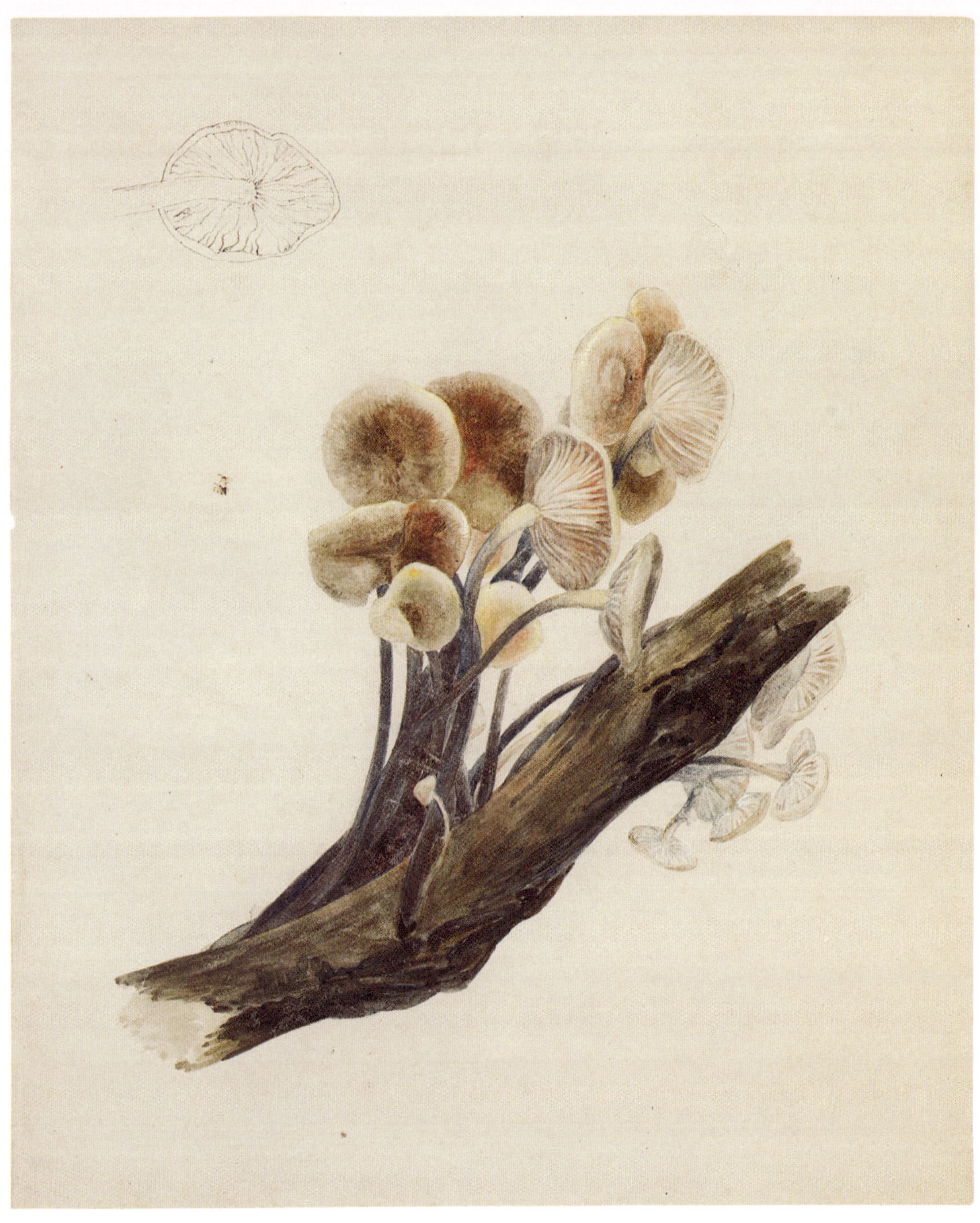

63. Above
Flammulina velutipes, 'Velvet Shank',
November 1892
Watercolour and pencil on paper
Perth Museum and Art Gallery,
FA 107/79.10

64. Opposite
Amanita excelsa, 'Grey Spotted Amanita',
Lennel, 22 July 1894
Watercolour and pencil on paper
Armitt Museum and Library,
AMATL:ALMC 1958.488

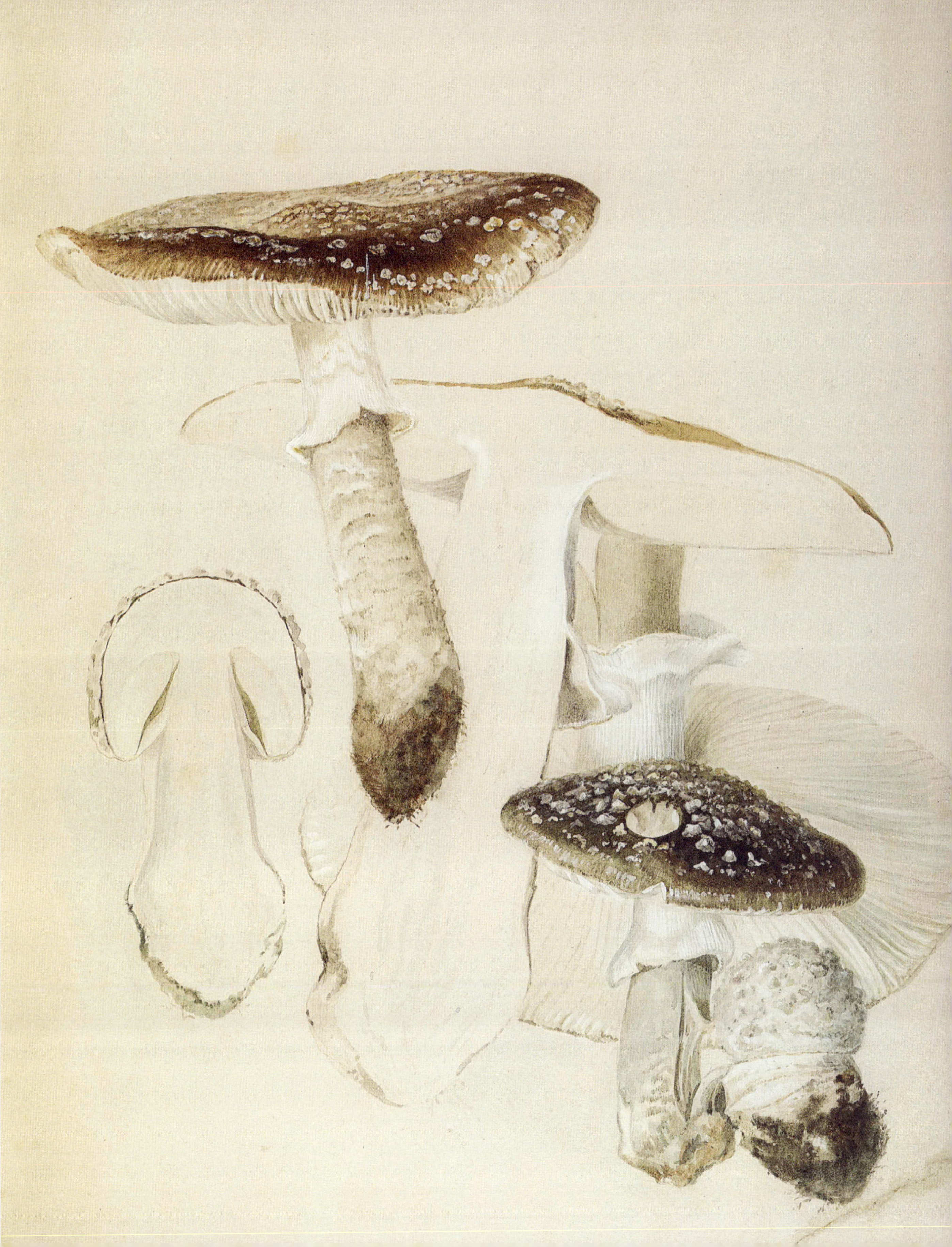

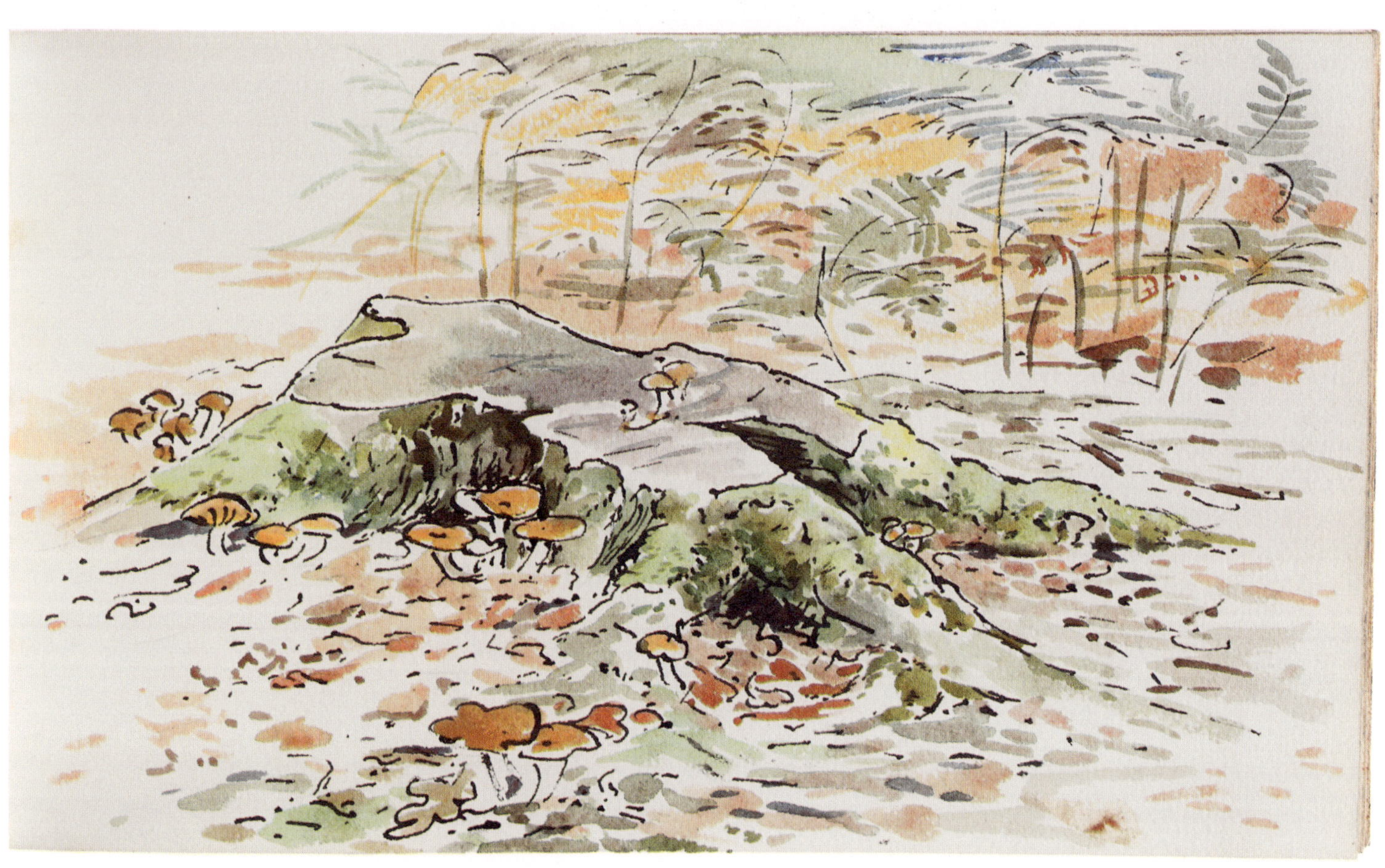

65. Above
Page from a sketchbook, 1901
Watercolour over pencil on paper
National Trust, 242740

66. Opposite
Fomitopsis betulinus (formerly called *Piptoporus betulinus*), 'Birch Polypore', on a tree trunk, early 1890s
Watercolour and gouache on paper
V&A: BP.243, Linder Bequest LB 291

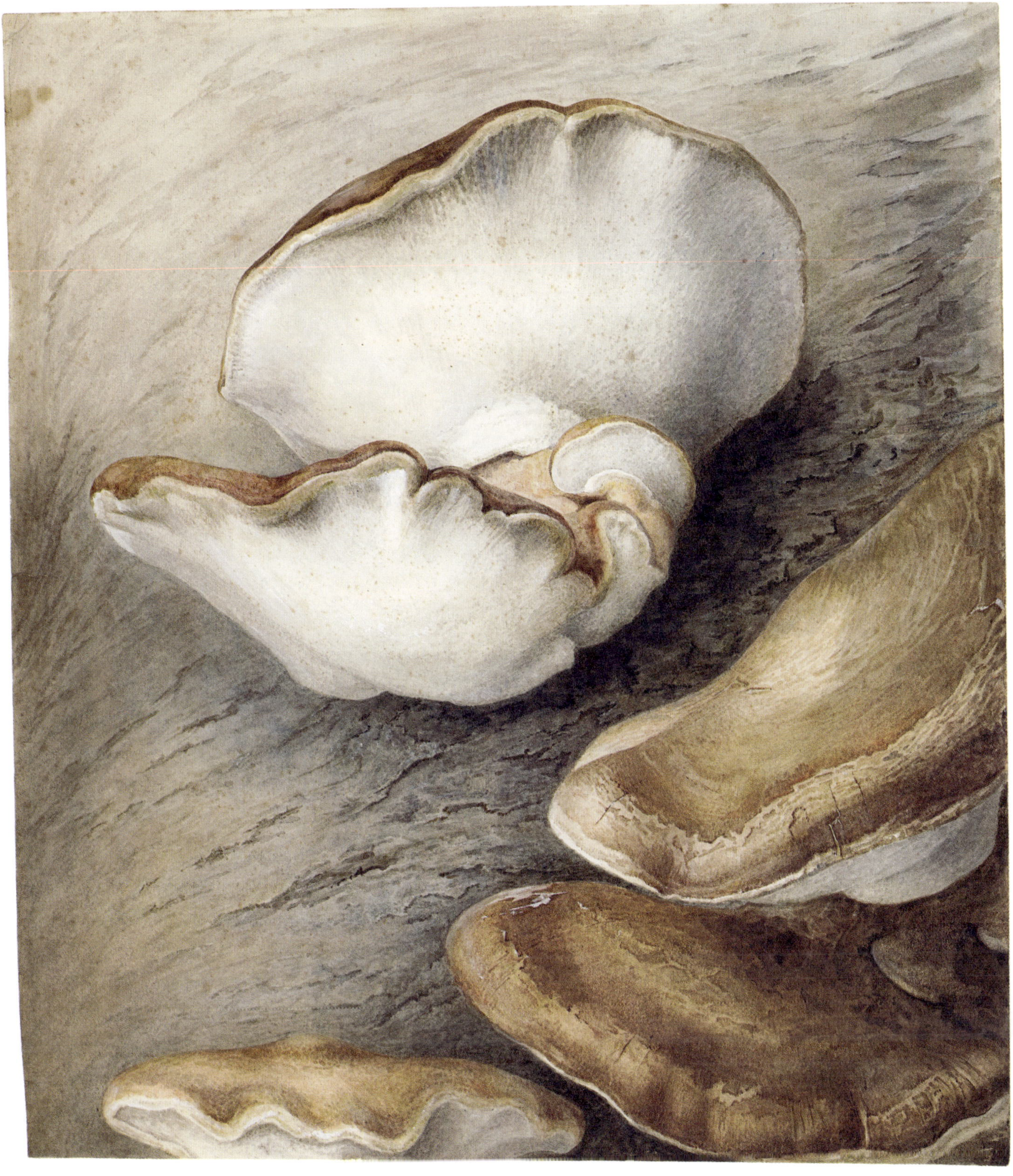

Miss Potter, the Mycologist

Beatrix Potter might well have become a scientist. More exactly, she was briefly set on course to become a mycologist: an expert on fungi. She made dozens of watercolour drawings of mushrooms and toadstools from when she was about 20 years old, clearly fascinated by the astonishing variety of shapes and colours that fungi display (see, for example, nos 67–9). She may have felt that these strange organisms, which could appear so quickly and decay so fast, had been comparatively neglected among the welter of illustrations of flowering plants favoured by Victorian ladies with a talent for drawing. The fungi deserved equal attention. Linnaeus – the great Swedish systematist of nature – had neglected the fungi when he classified flowers, even though fungi were mistakenly regarded as part of botany during the eighteenth century. Fungi presented challenges in identifying species that stimulated the young Potter. Their mode of reproduction was a matter of discussion in scientific circles.[1] At the same time, the technology of the microscope was improving, allowing closer observation of ever smaller objects. Potter wanted to gain an understanding of the fundamentals as well as portray mushrooms and toadstools in all their exotic profusion.

Fungi reproduce by means of spores – like the brown 'dust' expelled from a puffball – and it was hard to believe that entities only a few thousandths of a millimetre long could be their 'seeds'. For many years organisms that we now know depend on spores for propagation were called 'cryptogams' (meaning 'hidden reproduction'). Potter was among the first to demonstrate correctly how spores worked.
She set out to observe their germination under the microscope. Her drawings show the emergence of the feeding threads from the spores she selected. One of her most skilful drawings was made from a species with unusually large spores (thrice the usual size) now known as *Aleurodiscus amorphus* (no.68). She had written to her Scottish fungus guru Charles McIntosh in 1897 specifically to request him to find this particular species, which is rare in England. Her microscope drawings place the identification beyond doubt, even though there was apparently a muddle with the original labelling. They could be used in a modern textbook. She was critical of those working with herbarium material, who 'make theories out of dried specimens without the least experience of the way things grow.'[2]

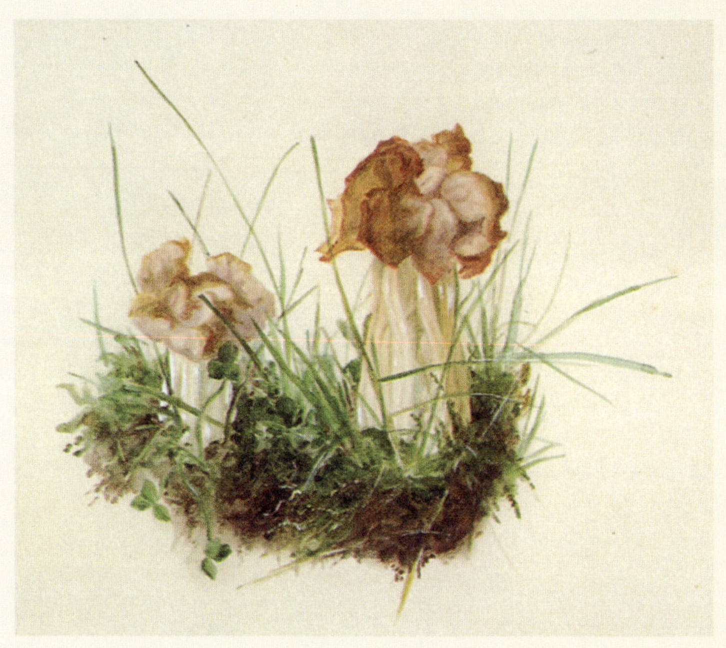

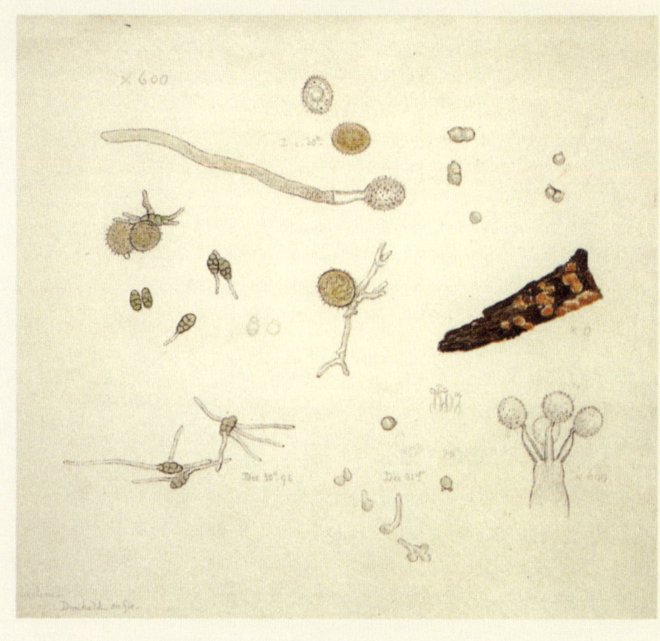

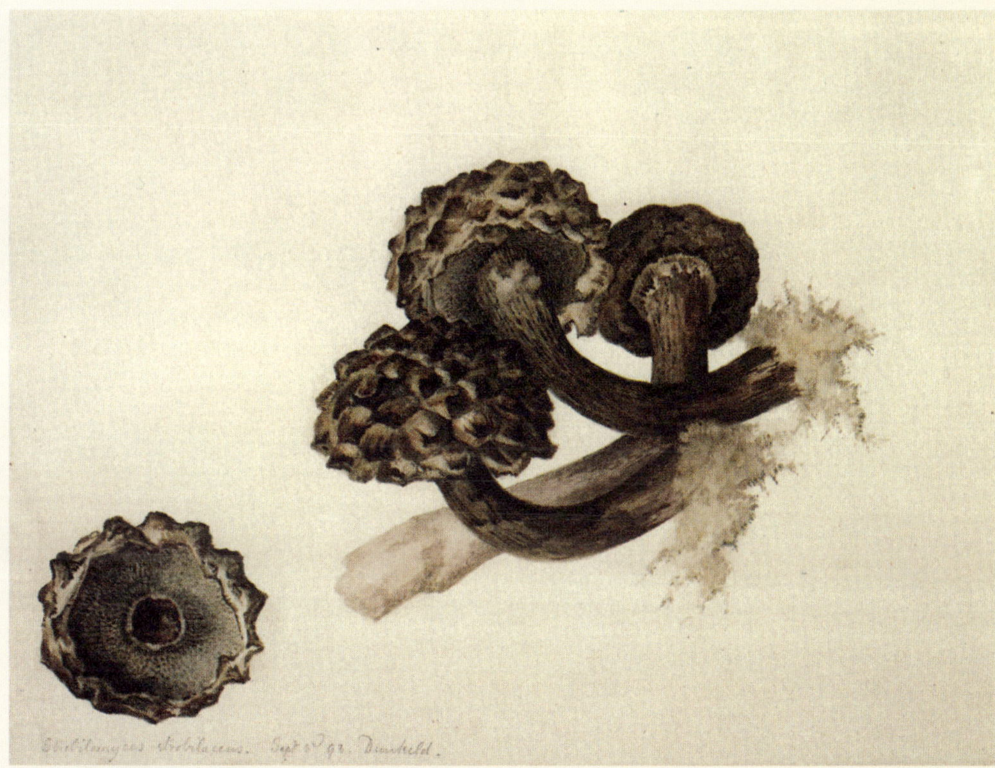

67. Above left
Helvella crispa, 'White Saddle' (the 'spluttered candle'), found at Derwentwater, 1888
Watercolour and pencil on paper
Armitt Museum and Library, AMATL:ALMC 1958.633

68. Above right
Microscopic drawing of *Aleurodiscus amorphus*, 30 December 1896, found on fir at Dunkeld
Watercolour and pencil on paper
Armitt Museum and Library, AMATL:ALMC 1958.4694

69. Left
Strobilomyces strobilaceus, 'Old Man of the Woods', drawn in situ at Eastwood, Dunkeld, 3 September 1893
Watercolour on paper
Armitt Museum and Library, AMATL:ALMC 1958.515

It is perhaps unsurprising that the forthright Potter did not enjoy good relations with several of the 'professionals' at the Royal Botanical Gardens at Kew or the British Museum (Natural History), now the Natural History Museum, in South Kensington. Thanks to her uncle, Sir Henry Roscoe, in 1896 she secured a precious ticket to Kew that allowed her access to literature and collections. By the end of the year she had fallen foul of the director, William Thiselton-Dyer, whose manner she described as 'on the outside edge of civil'. (She added: 'I took it philosophically.'[3]) She was on much better terms with the mycologist, George Massee, who admired her drawings. The illustrations in Massee's own *British Fungi* (1911) singularly lack the delicate touch of Potter's own. But it was Massee who read out her scientific paper at the Linnean Society of London on 1 April 1897, forbiddingly entitled 'On the germination of the spores of Agaricineae'. Women were not at that time permitted to present their work in person at the Linnean. The Society turned down the paper for publication, which must have been mortifying for Potter. It is worth speculating that had her paper been accepted, and had there been a career for a professional female scientist as the nineteenth century drew to a close, Potter might have spent the rest of her life as a pioneer mycologist. Although her observations from life were cast-iron, some of the inferences she drew from them have proved erroneous. For example, her concept of 'hybridization' between various fungi as a source of producing major different fungal groups was naïve. Her formal scientific career was curtailed.

What we still have are her wonderful drawings. Their accuracy is in debt to the knowledgeable 'Perthshire Naturalist' Charles McIntosh, who notably suggested

2

canister & forgotten, and now another
species of fungus has sprung up.
It is a pale straw colour, grown
entirely in the dark, and there are
nearly 100 'fingers',
the longest measure
1¼ inch - Miss Potter
wonders whether it
grows out of doors at
this season or whether it is brought
out by the heat of the room? It was

about this size when first observed
but being moved into a hot cupboard
near the kitchen chimney, it puffed
out in a very odd shape.
The last shoots that have grown
are the same size all the way up.
Miss Potter supposes the plants are
over for this season, judging by the
weather reported in the Perthshire paper,
but when Mr McIntosh can get any
more she will be glad to draw them.

Acc. 9757

cross sections through mushrooms and microscopic details (nos.64 and 68). Much correspondence survives between Potter and McIntosh; particularly appealing is a sketch of what must surely be immature winter agaric grown in the dark: the source of the popular Japanese delicacy enoki (no.70). She also drew subjects other than mushrooms, such as cup fungi (complete with illustrations of their spore apparatus) and what appears to be a pin mould of the type that grows on animal droppings (no.72). Her watercolours are so detailed that they can still be used to identify her subjects, even if the scientific names have changed in the interim. Her painting of what she called *Lepiota konradii* can be confidently identified now as *Macrolepiota mastoidea* (no.71). No matter, her art surpassed the mere bidding of nomenclature.

Richard Fortey

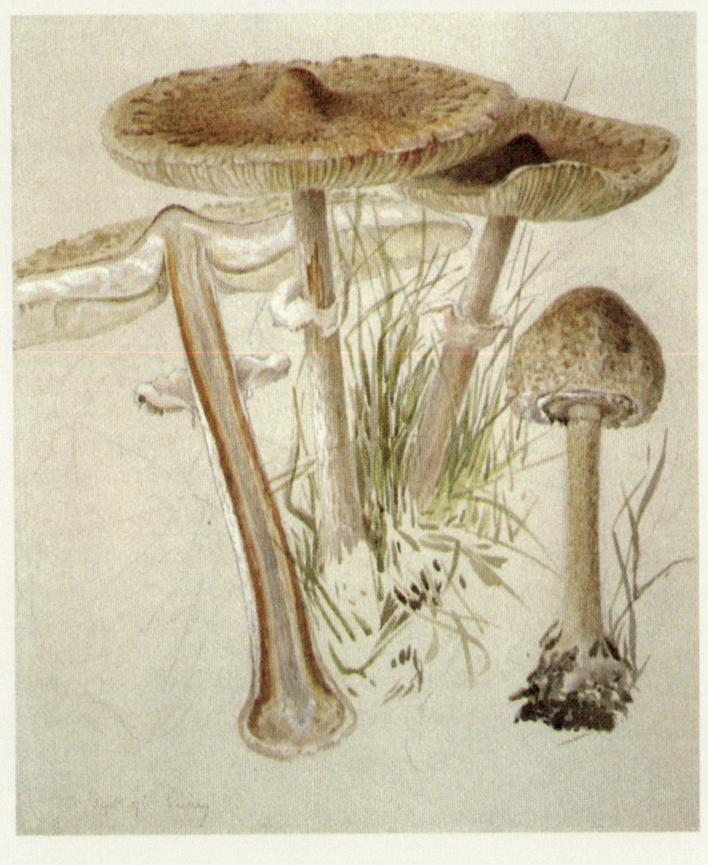

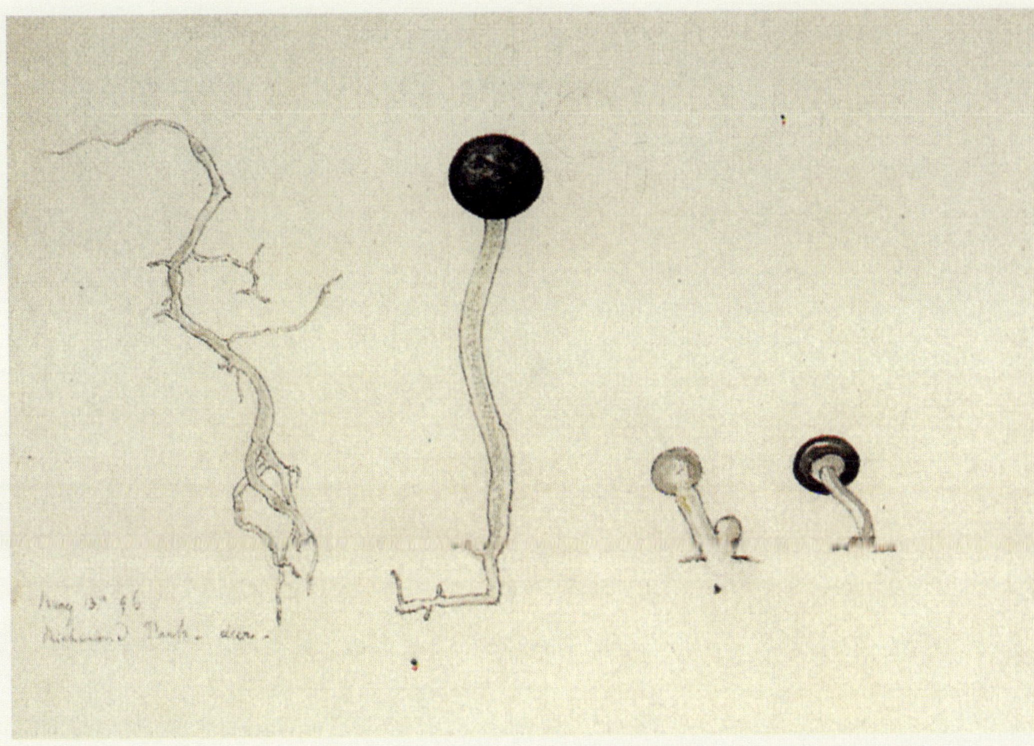

70. Opposite
Letter by Beatrix Potter sent to Charles McIntosh from 2 Bolton Gardens, London, 10 December 1892
Ink on paper
National Library, Edinburgh, Acc.9757

71. Above
Macrolepiota mastoidea (formally called *Lepiota konradii*), 'Slender Parasol', Sawrey, September 1896
Watercolour and pencil on paper
Armitt Museum and Library, AMATL:ALMC 1958.548

72. Left
One of the 'Pin Moulds', *Mucorales*, 13 May 1896, found on deer droppings in Richmond Park, London
Watercolour and pencil on paper
Armitt Museum and Library, AMATL:ALMC 1958.4758

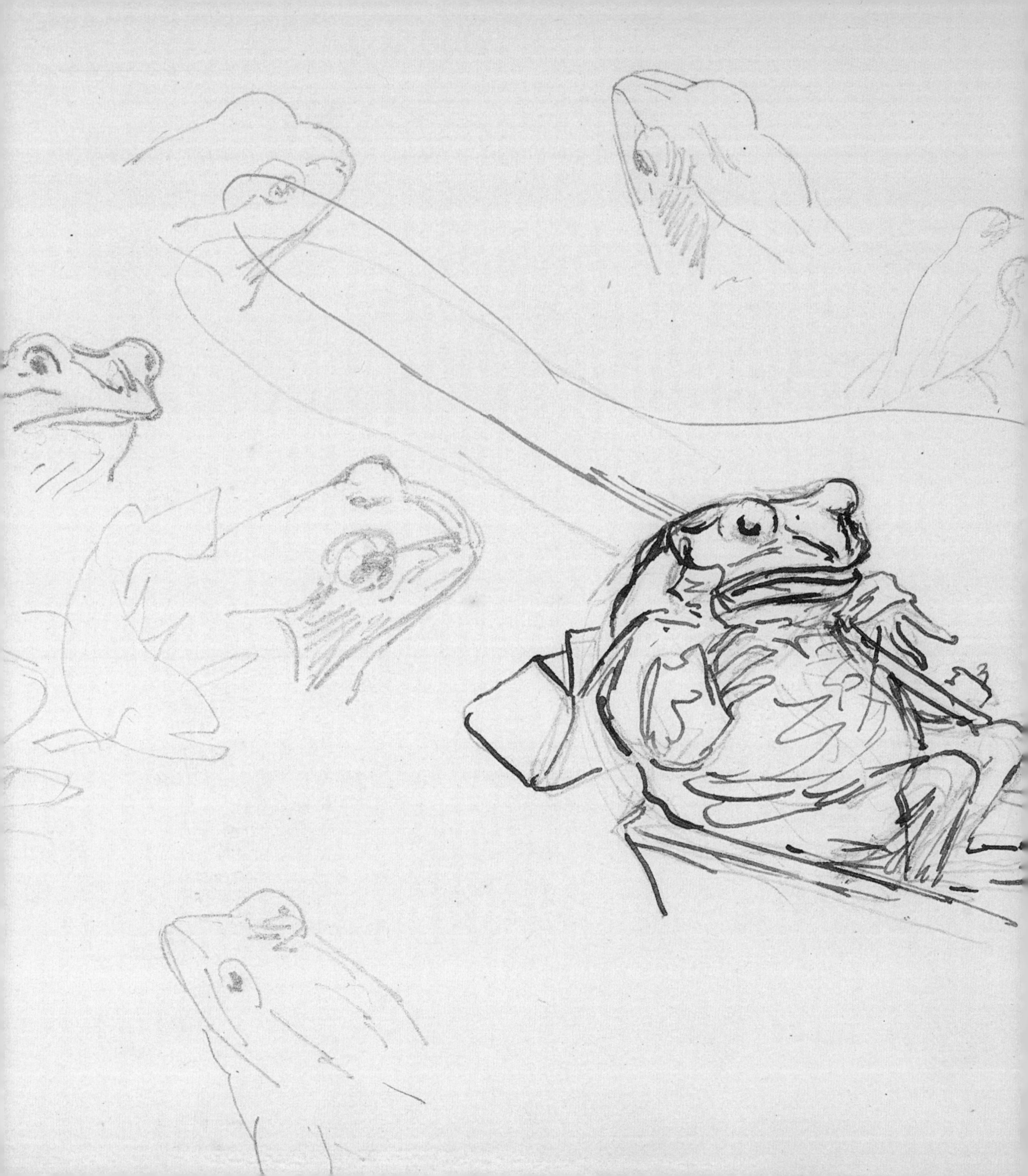

A Natural Storyteller

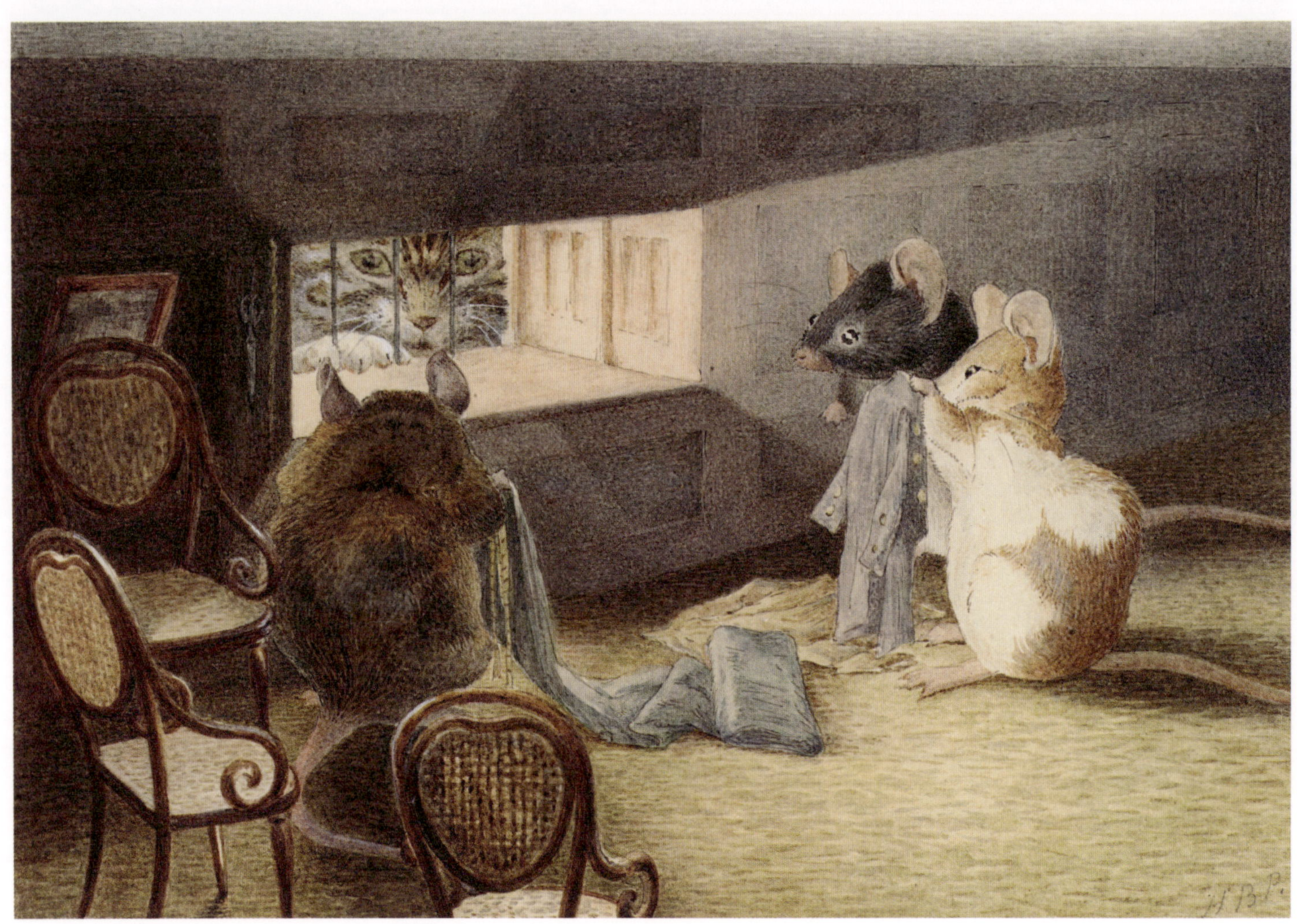

73.
Three Little Mice Sat Down to Spin,
one of a set of six, c.1892
Watercolour and ink on paper
V&A: BP.634(11), Linder Bequest LB 1069

We decided that I should make a grand effort in the way of Christmas cards.

(BEATRIX POTTER, *JOURNAL*, MAY 1890)

Beatrix Potter celebrated her first commercial success on 14 May 1890. The evening post delivered a 'fat letter' from publishers Hildesheimer & Faulkner, containing a cheque for £6: payment for six Christmas card designs featuring her pet rabbit Benjamin, a 'charming rascal' (no.105). Anticipation kept her 'awake chuckling till 2 in the morning'. Benjamin's reward for his part in the 'happy business' was a cup of hemp seeds; he had proved 'an investment…in spite of the hutches'.

Potter recounted her 'grand' publishing venture in her journal. She recalled trying out her designs on an audience at home, placing them under the plates set out on the breakfast table. The home-made cards proved a 'five minutes wonder' and her uncle, Sir Henry Roscoe, suggested that 'any publisher would snap at them'.[1] The reality was not quite as encouraging. Marcus Ward rejected them by return of post and even Frederick Warne would later claim that such designs were no longer of use to them, but that if she were ever to 'have any ideas & drawings in book form' they would be happy to consider them.[2]

Hildesheimer & Faulkner, however, were in the business of publishing greetings cards and requested to see more of Potter's designs. Sir Henry accompanied his niece to the firm's office, a journey that would take her geographically further into the City than she had ever ventured, and emotionally well beyond her comfort zone, 'just like going to the dentist'.[3] In fact, as an aspiring female artist Potter was following a well-trodden path. Twenty years earlier, Kate Greenaway had embarked on her career in a similar way.

From the outset, Potter determined not to 'invent to order'.[4] Despite the heady thrill of success, she held firmly to her beliefs about illustration and concluded that Mr Faulkner was not 'a person with much taste' when he suggested that 'humour' signified more than 'likeness'.[5] Instead, she submitted new designs featuring carefully drawn mice and guinea pigs. Later in 1890 the publisher reissued her rabbit card designs alongside verses by Frederic E. Weatherly in a little booklet, *A Happy Pair*:

My name's Mister Benjamin Bunny,
And I travel about without money,
There are lots I could name,
Do precisely the same,
It's convenient, but certainly funny![6]

Potter's early attempts at storytelling were almost entirely visual; best known are several unpublished drawings from around 1892, collectively referred to as 'The Rabbits' Christmas Party', featuring elegantly dressed rabbits dancing, eating and playing blind man's buff (no.1). Potter observed her pet rabbit intensely using a fine dry brush for detail but without the subtle irony that distinguishes her mature book illustrations. Another narrative sequence, 'Three Little Mice Sat Down to Spin', also remained unpublished, except for one drawing that reappeared in *The Tailor of Gloucester* (1903) (no.73). Her energetic drawings of a frog fishing, however, were purchased by the children's publisher Ernest Nister in June 1894 and matched with unremarkable verses by Clifton Bingham (no.94).

I don't know what to write to you, so I shall tell you a story.

(BEATRIX POTTER, LETTER TO NOEL MOORE, 4 SEPTEMBER 1893)[7]

By 1892 Potter was already a mature writer, though not yet of fiction. Towards the end of her life she recalled, 'When I was young I already had the itch to write, without having any material to write about'.[8] Her early efforts included hymns and romantic descriptions of scenery until in 1881 she began to write a journal, documenting holidays, impressions of people and pets, and snippets of overheard conversations. The earliest entries comprise somewhat incongruent observations of everyday life – verbal sketches equivalent to her careful drawing of the 'swill bucket' (see 'Town and Country', p.38): 'The proper way to clean unpolished slate chimney-pieces is to wash them with milk'; likewise, Benjamin Bunny decides the 'proper way to get in [to Mr. McGregor's garden], is to climb down a pear tree'.[9] Potter's 'irresistible desire to copy any beautiful object' extended beyond modelling, drawing and painting; in her journal, too, she reported on the world around her while rehearsing her distinctive narrative voice.[10]

As a young child, Potter recorded the natural world in a sketchbook, drawing pictures of caterpillars and writing descriptions of their habitats (no.14). Only in letters to children, however, did she combine words and pictures in any real sense. In her journal on 20 August 1892 she noted Benjamin Bunny's encounter with a wild rabbit:

> After breakfast taking Mr. Benjamin Bunny to pasture at the edge of the cabbage bed with his leather dog-lead, I heard a rustling, and out came a little wild rabbit to talk to him, it crept half across the cabbage bed and then sat up on its hind legs...but the stupid Benjamin did nothing but stuff cabbage.

The following day she recounted the incident in a letter to four-year-old Noel Moore, the son of her former governess, this time, however, incorporating a charming pen and ink sketch of the two rabbits. She was beginning to construct compelling narratives in text and image (no.74).

By the time Benjamin Bunny had come 'to a premature end through persistent devotion to peppermints',[11] Potter had already acquired another rabbit. Despite an initial outlay of 'the exorbitant sum of 4/6', Peter Piper was to prove an even sounder investment and by 1893 he had replaced Benjamin as the model for Potter's imaginative work.[12]

Potter conceived her story of Peter Rabbit on 4 September 1893 in a letter to Noel. He was a frail child and often unwell, but she knew just the thing to cheer him up: 'I shall tell you a story' (nos 76–9).

Annie Moore was Potter's live-in governess from 1883 to 1885 and remained a lifelong friend. Her first child, Noel, was born on Christmas Eve 1887; a brother, Eric, was born 11 months later, followed by six sisters, Marjorie, Winifrede, Norah, Joan, Hilda and Beatrix. Potter visited the family often, sometimes with a basket of excited mice, or perhaps a naughty rabbit, to entertain the children. She probably began writing to them in early 1892, although the impetus may well have come from the children. Her earliest extant letter, addressed to Noel and dated 11 March 1892, begins, 'Thank you for your very interesting letter, which you sent me a long time ago'.

I think Mr Bunny likes this place because there is so much green stuff for him to eat, but there is no wall round the garden, like your garden wall, so I have to lead him with a strap for fear he should run away into the fields. When he is sleepy, he digs a hole in the soil & lies down.

Yesterday I took him into the garden to eat his breakfast, & presently I heard something rustling amongst the leaves & a little wild rabbit came out to talk to Mr Bunny. It sat up on its hind legs and made a little grunting noise. but Mr Bunny was eating so fast he did not take any notice until it came quite close to him & then he was so much surprised that

74.
Picture letter by Beatrix Potter sent to Noel Moore from Heath Park, Birnam, 21 August [1892]
Ink over pencil on paper
Cotsen Children's Library, Special Collections, Princeton University Library, 35887

Holidays to Scotland in the summer and to the West Country in the spring provided interesting material for letters to children. Potter's earliest letter to Noel describes a visit to Falmouth; she sketches the train, a group of fishermen catching crabs and a cat observing fish (no.39). Creatures of all sorts had been her closest childhood friends; now they formed the basis of her relationship with the Moore children. Potter bundled her pets into boxes and baskets to accompany her on holidays and invariably came home with new friends.

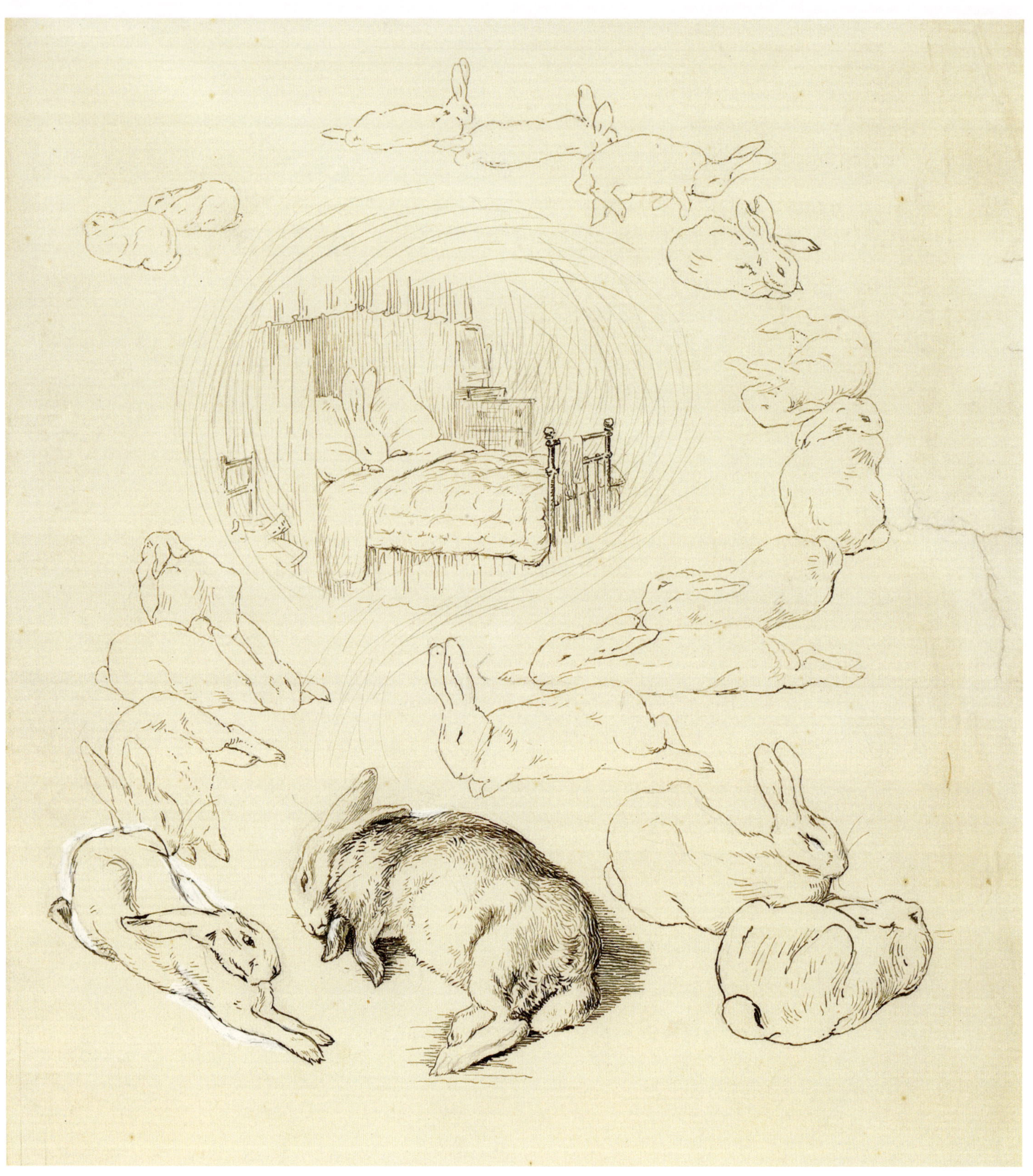

75.
'The Rabbit's Dream', c.1895–9
Ink on paper
V&A: BP.432, Linder Bequest LB 1002

She wrote to Eric from Perthshire in August 1892, 'Do you remember the little mouse which you saw at Bolton Gardens? I have got another one now'; the same day she wrote to Noel, 'I think you would like to hear about my rabbit' (see no.74).[13]

Potter's audience soon extended to the children of other friends and family. Her rabbit Peter Piper was the chief source of entertainment: he was 'good at tricks when hungry' and, in private, able to jump, ring a bell and drum on a tambourine.[14] He 'condescended to jump' for the children of her cousin, Edith Gaddum, and even provoked 'shrieks of amusement' from the usually very shy daughters of a Mrs Bruce.[15] In her letters, Potter conjured magic from the seemingly mundane details of everyday life, including even the clipping of Peter's claws: 'he was tickled, & kicked, very naughty'.[16] She illustrated such 'nonsense' with what she later described as 'scribbles': the seeds of ideas and drawings that she later incorporated in her little books.[17] A sketch for Eric of her brother's tame owl eating a mouse with the 'tail hanging out' reappeared in *The Tale of Squirrel Nutkin* (1903),[18] and another charming drawing of an old mouse teaching his children to read anticipated a similar scene in *The Tale of Two Bad Mice* (1904).

In 1912 Potter recalled, 'I was cram full of stories... when I was a small child...only I could not for the life of me get them out.'[19] Her brother Bertram's tiny book of stories, 'The stag and the dog or other tales', is held at the V&A,[20] but if the young Beatrix wrote and illustrated miniature books, none survive. Her picture letter to Noel of 4 September 1893 is her earliest extant story (nos 76–79). Remarkably, her tale of Peter Rabbit, written almost certainly on the spur of the moment and for pleasure rather than for publication, was to prove her most successful. Potter later maintained, 'it is much more satisfactory to address a real live child; I often think that that was the secret of the success of Peter Rabbit, it was written to a child – not made to order'.[21]

Elsewhere, Potter hints at another secret to her success: 'I have just made stories to please myself, because I never grew up.'[22] As a young adult, she was haunted by her childhood. She collected and preserved memories as she did the precious butterflies and birds' eggs in her specimen cabinet in the nursery at Bolton Gardens and feared returning to places she had loved as a child, in particular Dalguise House in Perthshire: 'the memory of that home is the only bit of childhood I have left'.[23] Yet, in her letters and drawings to children, Potter discovered a way to 'retain the spirit-world of childhood'.[24] She wrote both for children and, perhaps more importantly, for the 'fanciful' child within.[25]

Indeed, as each story was published, she began another, and another: 'I always feel very much lost when they are finished'.[26] Potter's enchanting drawing of Peter Rabbit asleep in a bed at Camfield Place, her grandparents' house in Hertfordshire, attests to the profound connection between the imaginative world of Peter Rabbit and her memories of childhood: 'To me all is bound up together in fact and fancy, my dear grandmother, the place I love best in the world... where I have been so happy as a child.' (no.75)[27]

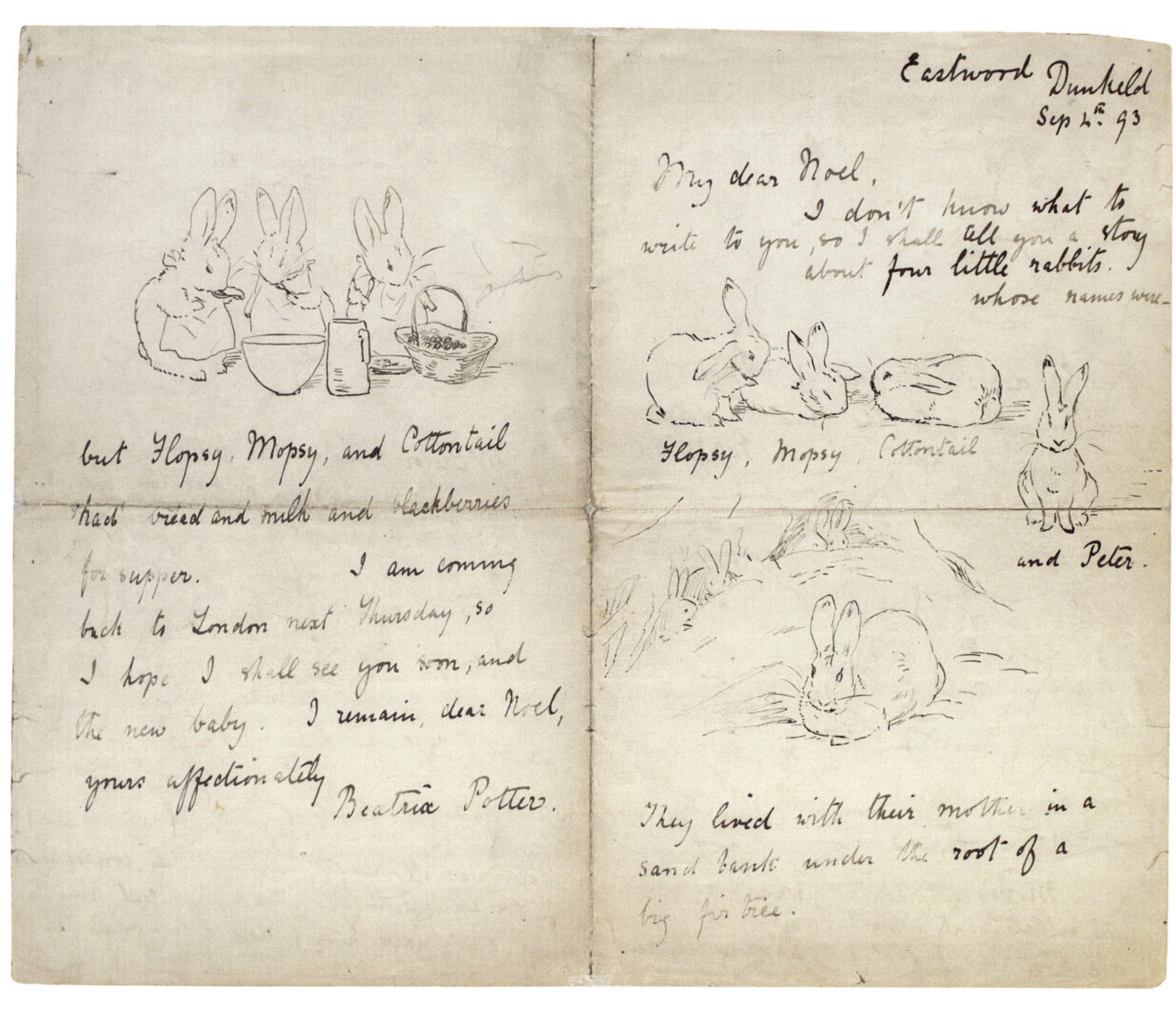

but Flopsy, Mopsy, and Cottontail had bread and milk and blackberries for supper. I am coming back to London next Thursday, so I hope I shall see you soon, and the new baby. I remain, dear Noel, yours affectionately Beatrix Potter.

Eastwood Dunkeld
Sep 4th 93

My dear Noel,
I don't know what to write to you, so I shall tell you a story about four little rabbits. whose names were—

Flopsy, Mopsy, Cottontail and Peter.

They lived with their mother in a sand bank under the root of a big fir tree.

76, 77, 78, 79. Above, Opposite and Overleaf
Picture letter by Beatrix Potter sent to Noel Moore from Eastwood, Dunkeld, containing the story of Peter Rabbit, 4 September 1893
Ink on paper
V&A: LOAN: PEARSON PLC.1–1991
76 shows p.8 of the story (left); p.1 (right)
77 shows p.2 of the story (left); p.7 (right)
78 shows p.6 of the story (left); p.3 (right)
79 shows p.4 of the story (left); p.5 (right)

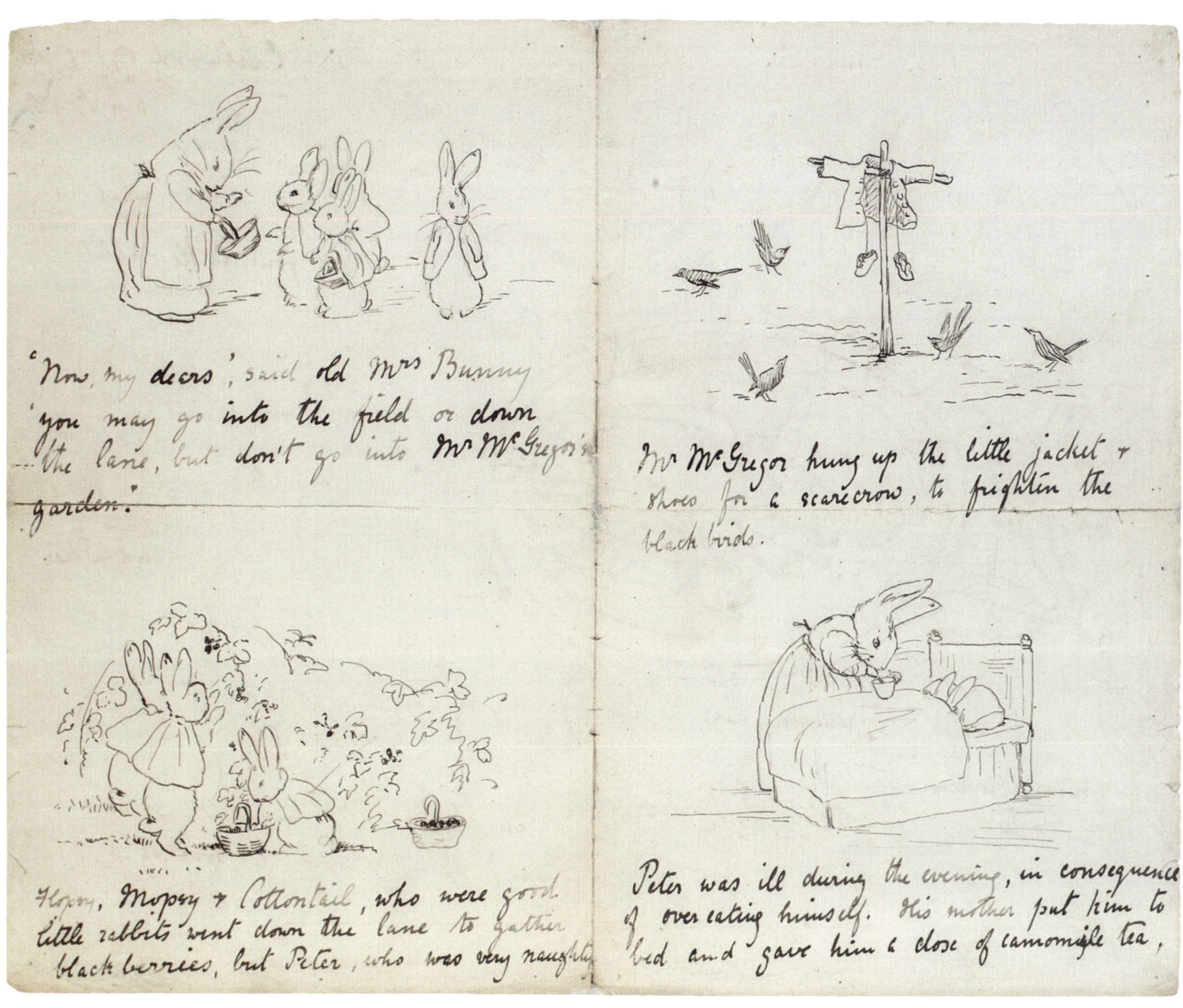
'Now, my dears', said old Mrs Bunny
'you may go into the field or down
the lane, but don't go into Mr McGregor's
garden.'

Mr McGregor hung up the little jacket +
shoes for a scarecrow, to frighten the
black birds.

Flopsy, Mopsy + Cottontail, who were good
little rabbits went down the lane to gather
black berries, but Peter, who was very naughty

Peter was ill during the evening, in consequence
of over eating himself. His mother put him to
bed and gave him a dose of camomile tea,

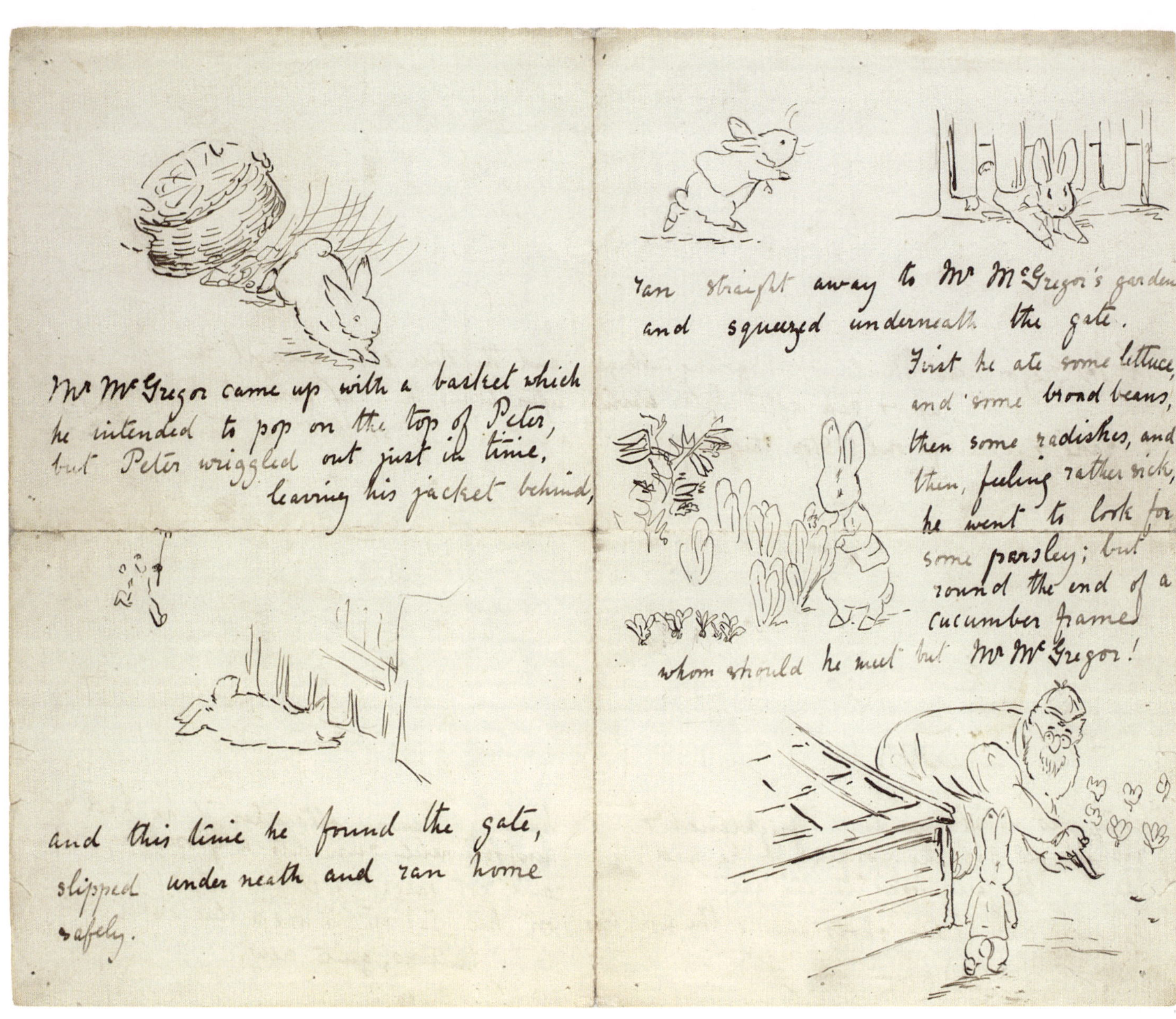

Mr McGregor came up with a basket which
he intended to pop on the top of Peter,
but Peter wriggled out just in time,
leaving his jacket behind,

and this time he found the gate,
slipped underneath and ran home
safely.

ran straight away to Mr McGregor's garden
and squeezed underneath the gate.
First he ate some lettuce,
and some broad beans,
then some radishes, and
then, feeling rather sick,
he went to look for
some parsley; but
round the end of a
cucumber frame
whom should he meet but Mr McGregor!

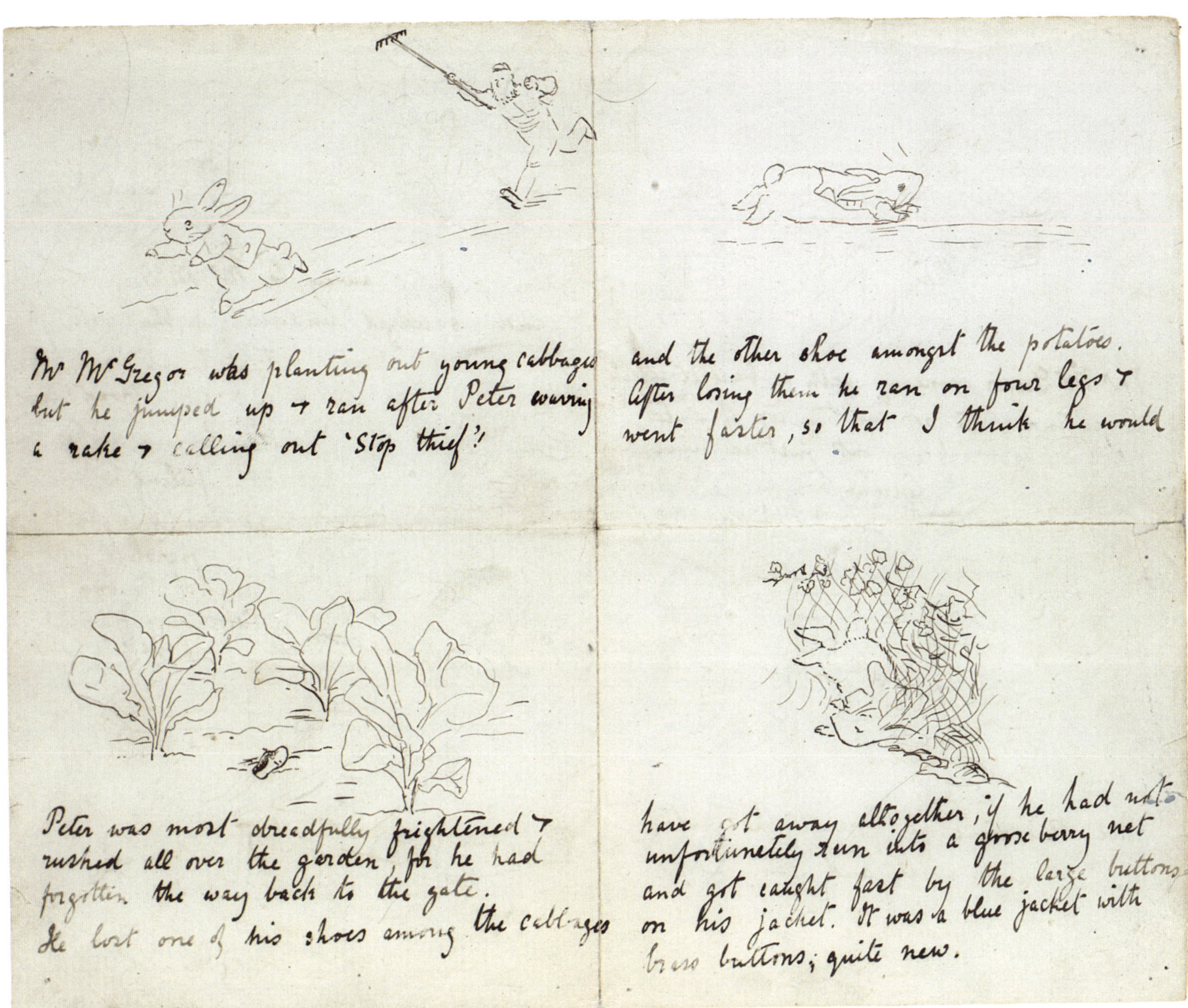

Mr McGregor was planting out young cabbages
but he jumped up & ran after Peter waving
a rake & calling out 'Stop thief'!

Peter was most dreadfully frightened &
rushed all over the garden for he had
forgotten the way back to the gate.
He lost one of his shoes among the cabbages

and the other shoe amongst the potatoes.
After losing them he ran on four legs &
went faster, so that I think he would

have got away altogether, if he had not
unfortunately run into a goose berry net
and got caught fast by the large buttons
on his jacket. It was a blue jacket with
brass buttons, quite new.

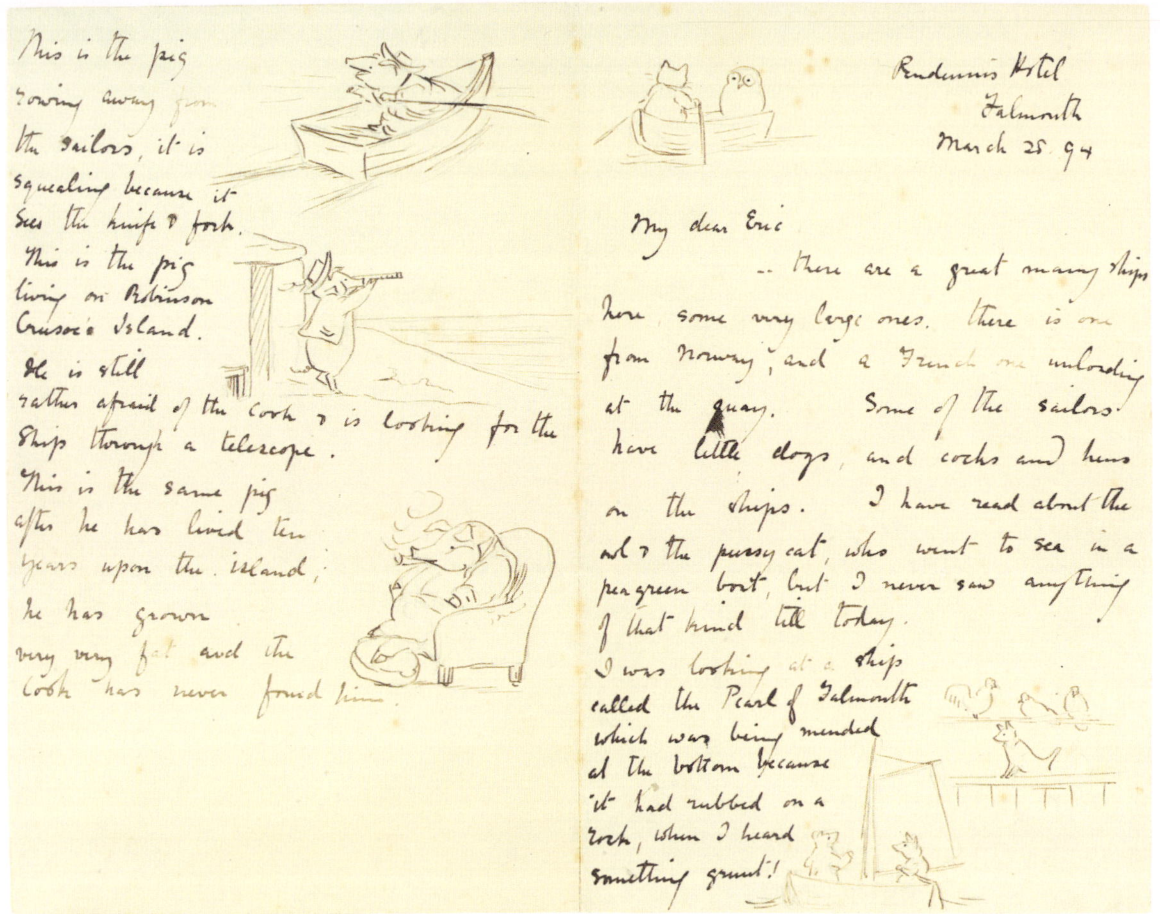

Rendennis Hotel
Falmouth
March 25. 94

My dear Eric

.. there are a great many ships here, some very large ones. there is one from Norway, and a French one unloading at the quay. Some of the sailors have little dogs, and cocks and hens on the ships. I have read about the owl & the pussy cat, who went to sea in a pea green boat, but I never saw anything of that kind till today.

I was looking at a ship called the Pearl of Falmouth which was being mended at the bottom because it had rubbed on a rock, when I heard something grunt!

This is the pig rowing away from the sailors, it is squealing because it sees the knife & fork.

This is the pig living on Robinson Crusoe's Island. He is still rather afraid of the cook & is looking for the ships through a telescope.

This is the same pig after he has lived ten years upon the island; he has grown very very fat and the cook has never found him.

I will manage to make a nice book somehow.

(BEATRIX POTTER, LETTER TO NORMAN WARNE, 12 FEBRUARY 1904)[28]

Potter continued writing stories to the Moore children throughout the 1890s. On 5 September 1893 she wrote to Eric about a gentleman frog called Mr. Jeremy Fisher, who eats a dinner of 'roasted grass-hopper with lady-bird sauce'. The following March she wrote to Eric again about a little stowaway pig at risk of being made into sausages (no.80); another picture letter to Noel contained a story about Benjamin Bunny.

In 1900 Annie Moore suggested to Potter that her letters might contain ideas for several children's books. Fortunately, the children had treasured them; Potter copied them and chose to work first on Noel's story of Peter Rabbit, editing and extending the narrative to fill a small book. The road to publication was hampered by Potter's stubborn attitude towards the format of her book: she wanted it to be small, cheap and abundantly illustrated. One publisher after another returned her manuscript, 'with or without thanks';

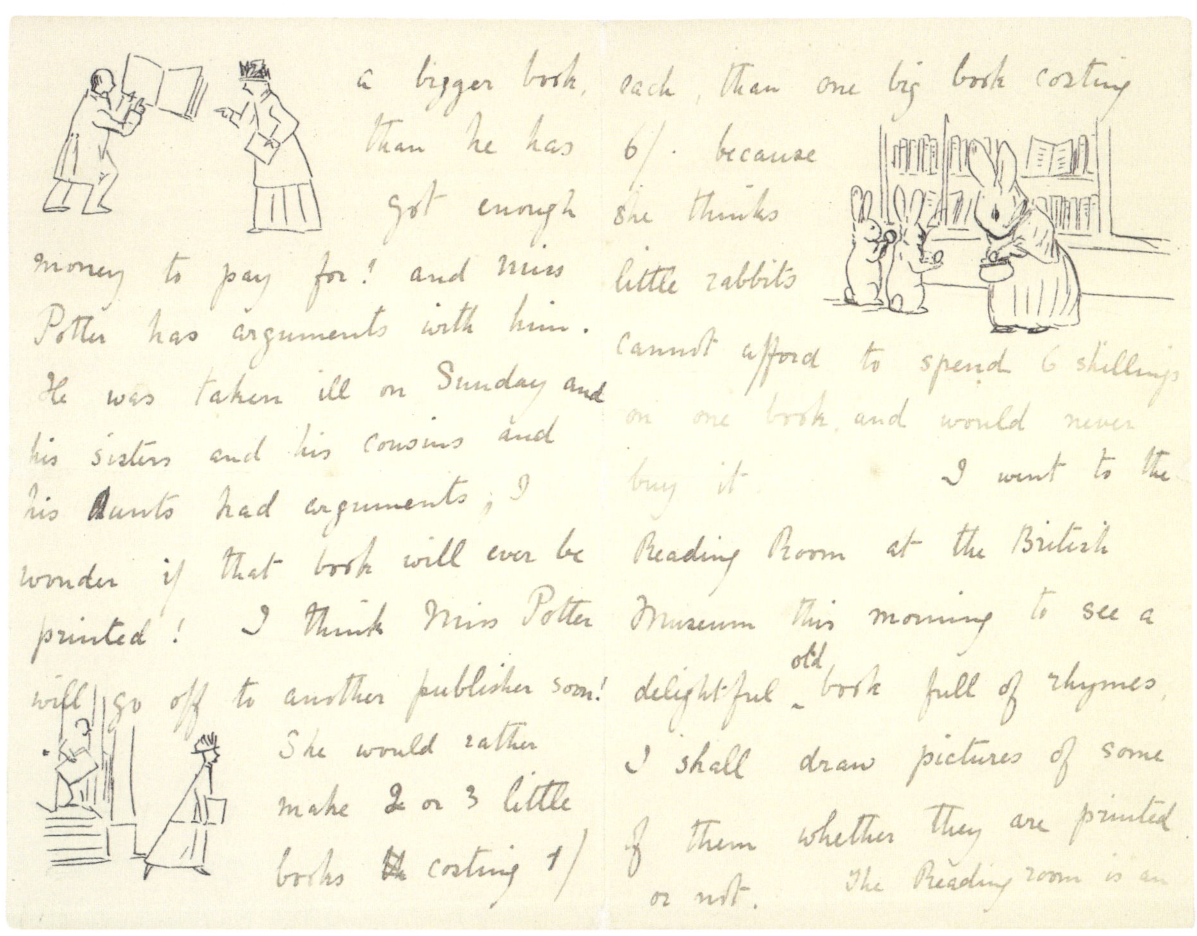

a bigger book, than he has got enough money to pay for! and Miss Potter has arguments with him. He was taken ill on Sunday and his sisters and his cousins and his Aunts had arguments; I wonder if that book will ever be printed! I think Miss Potter will go off to another publisher soon! She would rather make 2 or 3 little books ~~costing~~ costing 1/ each, than one big book costing 6/. because she thinks little rabbits cannot afford to spend 6 shillings on one book, and would never buy it. I went to the Reading Room at the British Museum this morning to see a delightful old book full of rhymes, I shall draw pictures of some of them whether they are printed or not. The Reading room is an

80. Opposite
Picture letter by Beatrix Potter sent to Eric Moore from Pendennis Hotel, Falmouth, 28 March 1894
Ink on paper
V&A: BP.877, Linder Bequest LB 1463

81. Above
Picture letter by Beatrix Potter sent to Marjorie Moore from 2 Bolton Gardens, London, 13 March 1900
Ink on paper
Morgan Collection

they preferred larger and more expensive books printed in colour.[29] Potter explained her dilemma to Marjorie Moore (no.81):

> The publisher is a gentleman who prints books, and he wants a bigger book than he has got enough money to pay for! and Miss Potter has arguments with him...She would rather make 2 or 3 little books costing 1/each, than one big book costing 6/ because she thinks little rabbits cannot afford to spend 6 shillings on one book, and would never buy it.[30]

Eventually, Potter published the book herself with black-and-white illustrations and a colour frontispiece. The first edition of 250 copies was printed by Strangeways & Sons in December 1901 followed by a second edition in February 1902. Meanwhile, Frederick Warne & Co. had expressed an interest in publishing

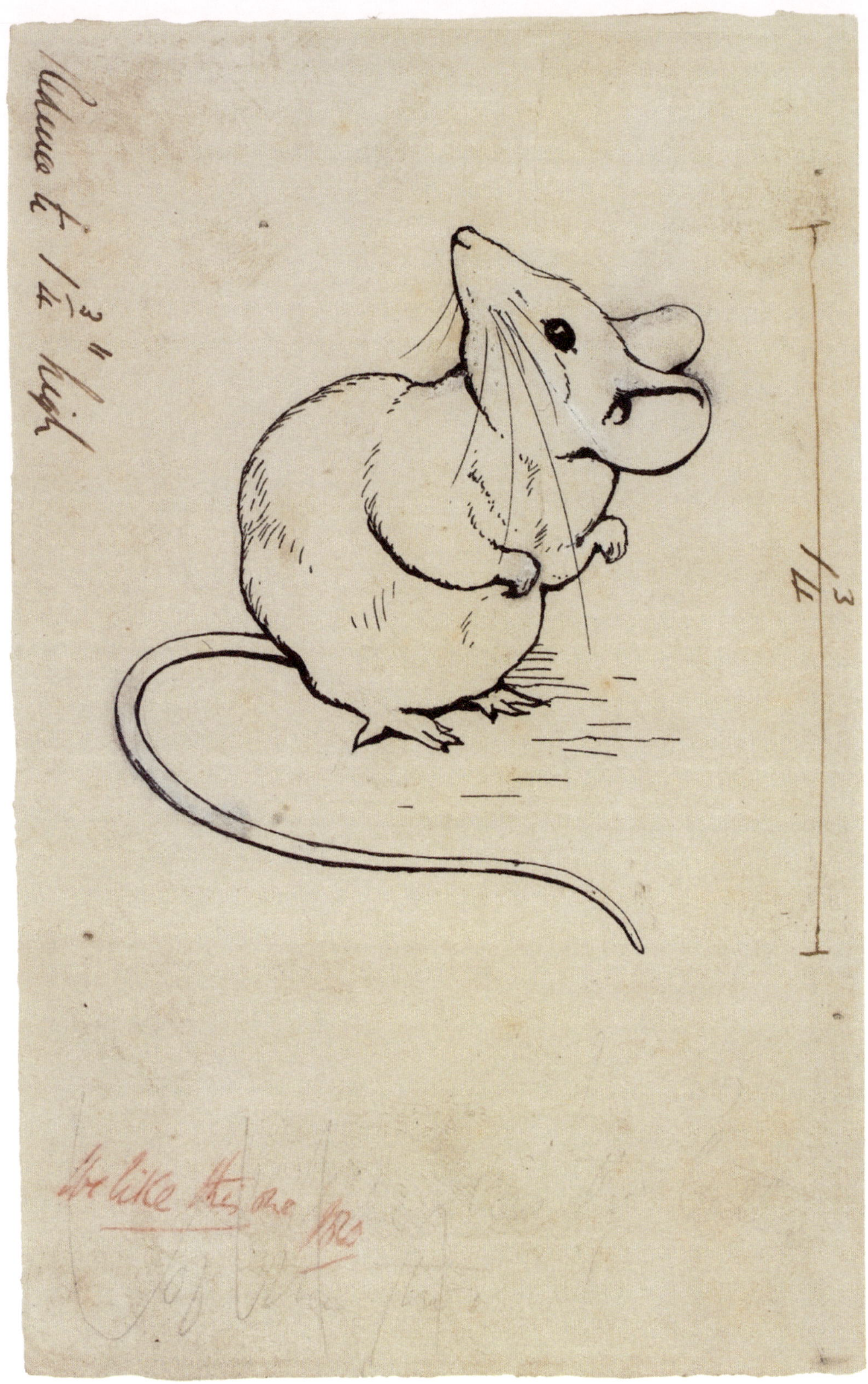

82.
The Tale of Two Bad Mice title-page design, 1903–4
Ink and pencil on paper
V&A: LC 25/A/1, given by the Linder Collection

an abridged version with fewer illustrations, printed in colour using Potter's preferred method, the new three-colour process. Since she had now published her book the way she wanted it she was prepared to compromise, even agreeing to forgo royalties on the first edition. The book was ready by October 1902 and within a year Frederick Warne & Co. had published a fifth edition: 'The public must be fond of rabbits! what an appalling quantity of Peter.'[31]

Potter paid meticulous attention to every aspect of the production of her books, inspecting proofs of the illustrations and text and designing the covers, title pages and endpapers (no.82). Frederick Warne & Co. supplied dummy books so she could arrange the text and illustrations in a cohesive page design. For example, in the first edition of *The Pie and the Patty-Pan* (1905) the vignettes of Ribby and Duchess at the table face each other as if in conversation. Sadly, in modern editions the vignettes do not even appear on the same double-page spread (no.84).

Potter was fascinated by the art and design of books. Notably, what she recalled most about a tenth birthday present, Jemima Blackburn's *Birds Drawn from Nature* (1862), was that it was 'bound in scarlet with a gilt edge': she washed her 'grimy little hands' before retrieving it from the drawing-room cupboard.[32]

Covers, she believed, should be 'strong and distinct', endpapers 'something to rest the eye between the cover and the contents of the book; like a plain mount for a framed drawing.'[33] She objected to, but finally accepted, the 'idiotic prancing rabbit' chosen for the cover of *The Tale of Peter Rabbit* (1902) and the 'rather heavy' endpaper design featuring characters from her books, introduced for *The Tailor of Gloucester* in December 1903 (no.83).[34] Later, she experimented with different book sizes and formats. The panoramic structures of *The Story of Miss Moppet* (1906) and *The Story of a Fierce Bad Rabbit* (1906), while beguiling to a very young audience, were not robust (no.158). *The Pie and the Patty-Pan* and *The Roly-Poly Pudding* (1908, published in 1926 as *The Tale of Samuel Whiskers*) were issued in a larger format, imitating the picture books of Randolph Caldecott, with sepia line drawings within the text and full-page colour plates (no.84).

Eventually Frederick Warne & Co. issued all 23 tales in uniform bindings as *The Original Peter Rabbit Books*.

Potter continued writing for real children, even as an established author-illustrator. In 1903 she visited Melford Hall, the home of her little cousin, Stephanie Hyde Parker, to 'try the new stories on the children there';[35] she had composed an early version of *The Tale of Mrs. Tiggy-Winkle* for Stephanie two years previously. She wrote to Norah Moore about an 'excessively impertinent' squirrel called Nutkin (no.85),[36] and her manuscripts of *The Tailor of Gloucester* and *The Roly-Poly Pudding* were Christmas presents, the former to Winifrede Moore, 'Because you are fond of fairy-tales and have been ill',[37] and the latter to another Winifred, the daughter of her publisher, Fruing Warne. Just as the stories existed in Potter's imagination long before publication, so they continued to develop beyond the parameters of the published tales. When six-year-old Harold Botcherby wrote to ask how the fight between Mr. Tod and Tommy Brock was resolved, Potter replied at some length:

> I have inquired about Mr Tod & Tommy Brock, & I am sorry to tell you they are still quarrelling... As for the end of the fight – Mr Tod had nearly half the hair pulled out of his brush (= tail) and 5 bad bites, especially one ear, which is scrumpled up... The only misfortune to Tommy Brock – he had his jacket torn & lost one of his boots.[38]

Some of Potter's best-loved stories begin and end in letters to children. For the children closest to her, she devised miniature letters, written as if from one character to another, offering a glimpse of the next chapter in their lives (no.86). When Peter Rabbit is feeling better after his terrifying ordeal in Mr. McGregor's garden, he writes an impertinent letter to Mr. McGregor to enquire whether his 'spring cabbages are ready'. Mrs. McGregor informs him that she has recently bought a very large pie dish but foolishly lets slip that her husband is in bed with a cold. Peter writes immediately to Benjamin Bunny to arrange to meet later that evening at the edge of the wood for yet another adventure in Mr. McGregor's garden.[39]

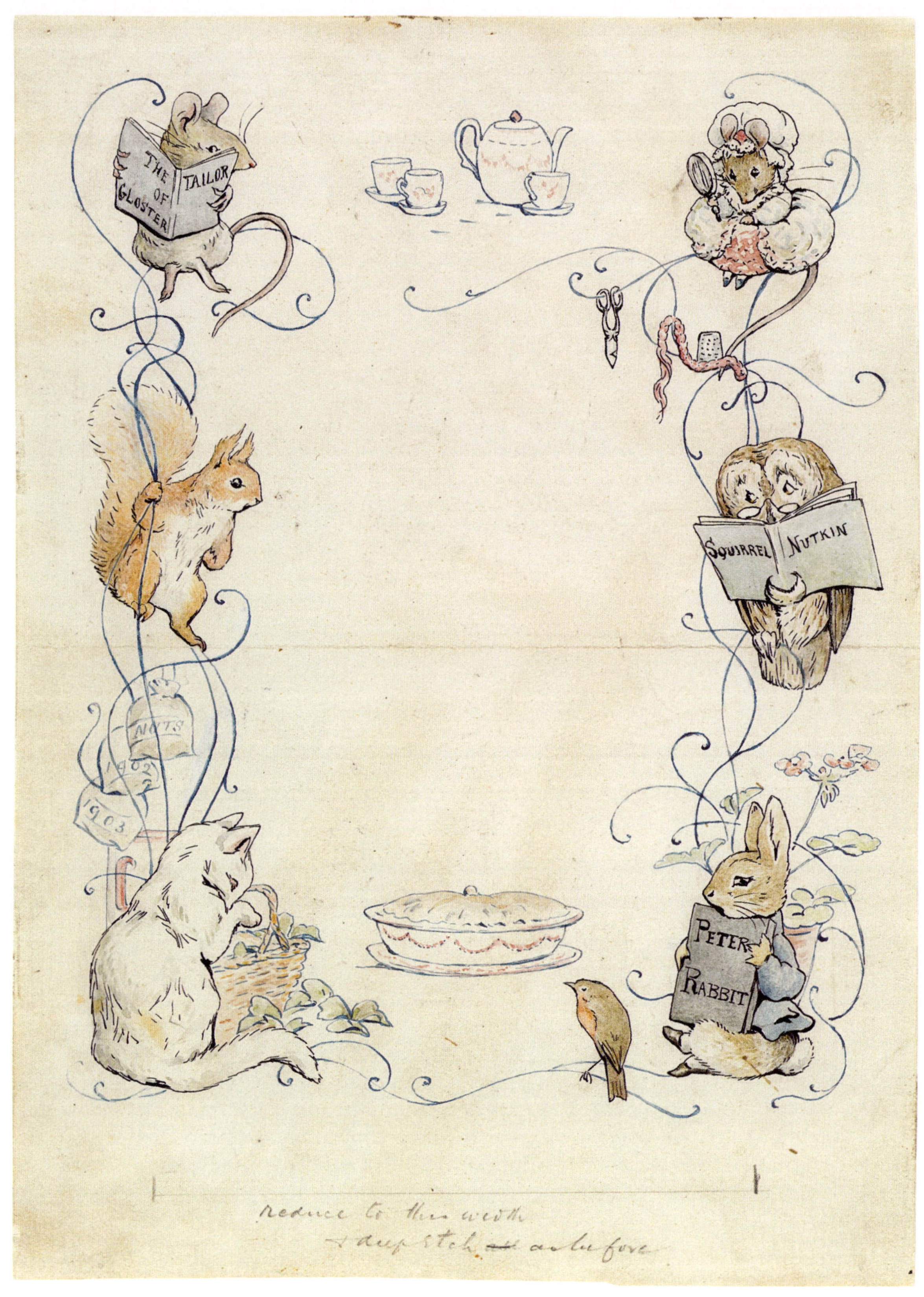
THE TAILOR OF GLOSTER
SQUIRREL NUTKIN
NUTS
1902
1903
PETER RABBIT
reduce to this width
+ deep etch as before

THE PIE AND THE PATTY-PAN.

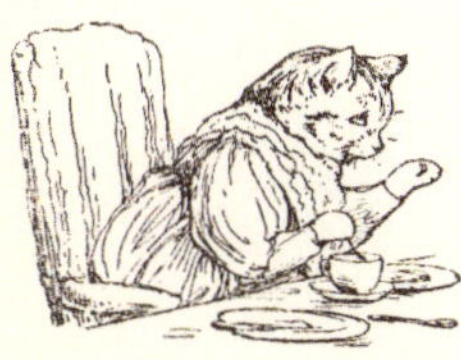

Duchess looked very much alarmed, and continued to scoop the inside of the pie-dish.

"My Great-aunt Squintina (grand-mother of Cousin Tabitha Twitchit)—died of a thimble in a Christmas plum-pudding. *I* never put any article of metal in *my* puddings or pies."

Duchess looked aghast, and tilted up the pie-dish.

"I have only four patty-pans, and they are all in the cupboard."

Duchess set up a howl.

"I shall die! I shall die! I have swallowed a patty-pan! Oh, my dear Ribby, I do feel so ill!"

"It is impossible, my dear Duchess; there was not a patty-pan."

40

THE PIE AND THE PATTY-PAN.

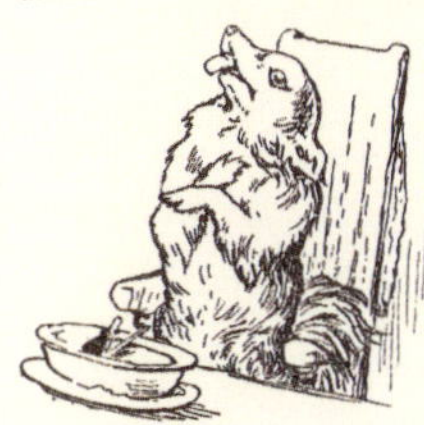

Duchess moaned and whined and rocked herself about.

"Oh I feel so dreadful, I have swallowed a patty-pan!"

"There was *nothing* in the pie," said Ribby severely.

"Yes there *was*, my dear Ribby, I am sure I have swallowed it!"

"Let me prop you up with a pillow, my dear Duchess; where do you think you feel it?"

"Oh I do feel so ill *all over* me, my dear Ribby; I have swallowed a large tin patty-pan with a sharp scalloped edge!"

"Shall I run for the Doctor? I will just lock up the spoons!"

"Oh yes, yes! fetch Dr. Maggotty, my dear Ribby; he is a Pie himself, he will certainly understand."

D 41

83. Opposite
The Tailor of Gloucester endpaper, December 1903
Watercolour, ink and pencil on paper
V&A: BP.460, Linder Bequest LB 943

84. Above
Pages from *The Pie and the Patty-Pan*, 1905,
from a later edition
V&A: BP.156, Linder Bequest LB 1545

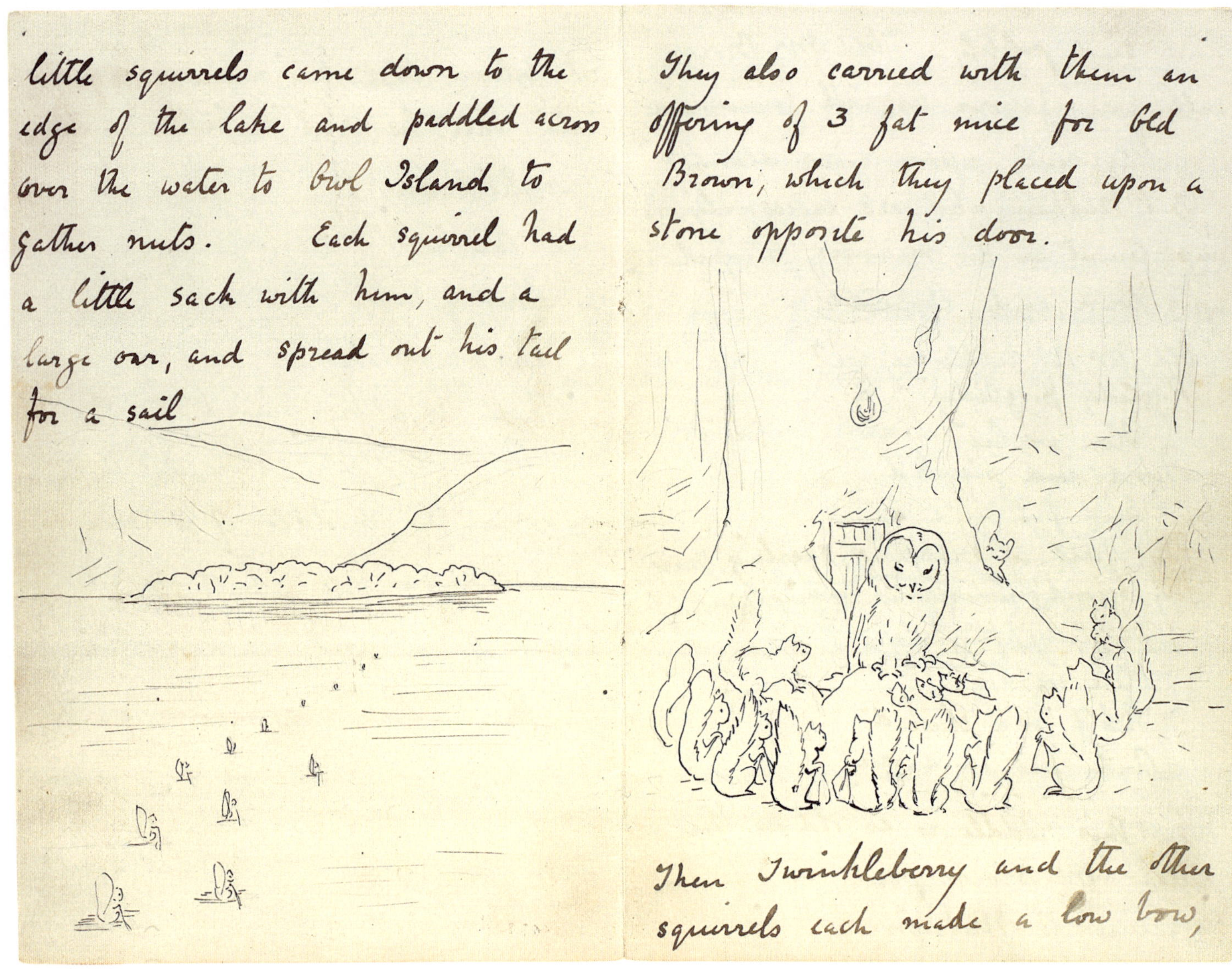
little squirrels came down to the edge of the lake and paddled across over the water to Owl Island to gather nuts. Each squirrel had a little sack with him, and a large oar, and spread out his tail for a sail

They also carried with them an offering of 3 fat mice for Old Brown, which they placed upon a stone opposite his door.

Then Twinkleberry and the other squirrels each made a low bow,

85. Above
Picture letter by Beatrix Potter sent to Norah Moore from Lingholm, Keswick, containing the story of Squirrel Nutkin, 25 September 1901
Ink on paper
V&A: BP.880, Linder Bequest LB 1468

86. Opposite
Miniature letters between Squirrel Nutkin and Twinkleberry Squirrel of Derwent Bay Wood, and Rt Hon. O. Brown Esq. MP (Old Mr. Brown) of Owl Island, c.1903–5
Ink on paper
V&A: AAD/1996/12/2/v-viii, given by Lucie Carr

An answer will oblige

Dear Sir,
I should esteem it a favour if you will let me have back my tail, as I miss it very much. I would pay postage.
yrs truly
Squirrel Nutkin

Dear Sir, I should be exceedingly obliged if you could kindly send back a tail which you have had for some time. It is fluffy brown with a white tip. I wrote before but I am afraid I did not direct my letter right. I will pay postage.
yrs respectfully
Sqr. Nutkin.

Dear Sir,
I write on behalf of my brother Nutkin to beg that as a great favour you would send him back his tail, for which he will gladly pay three bags of nuts. He never asks riddles now and he is truly sorry that he was so rude.
Trusting that you continue to enjoy good health
I remain yrs obediently
Twinkleberry Squirrel.

Mr Brown writes to say that he cannot reply to letters as he is asleep.

Mr Brown cannot return the tail.

He ate it some time ago; it nearly choked him.

Mr Brown requests Nutkin not to write again, as his repeated letters are a nuisance.

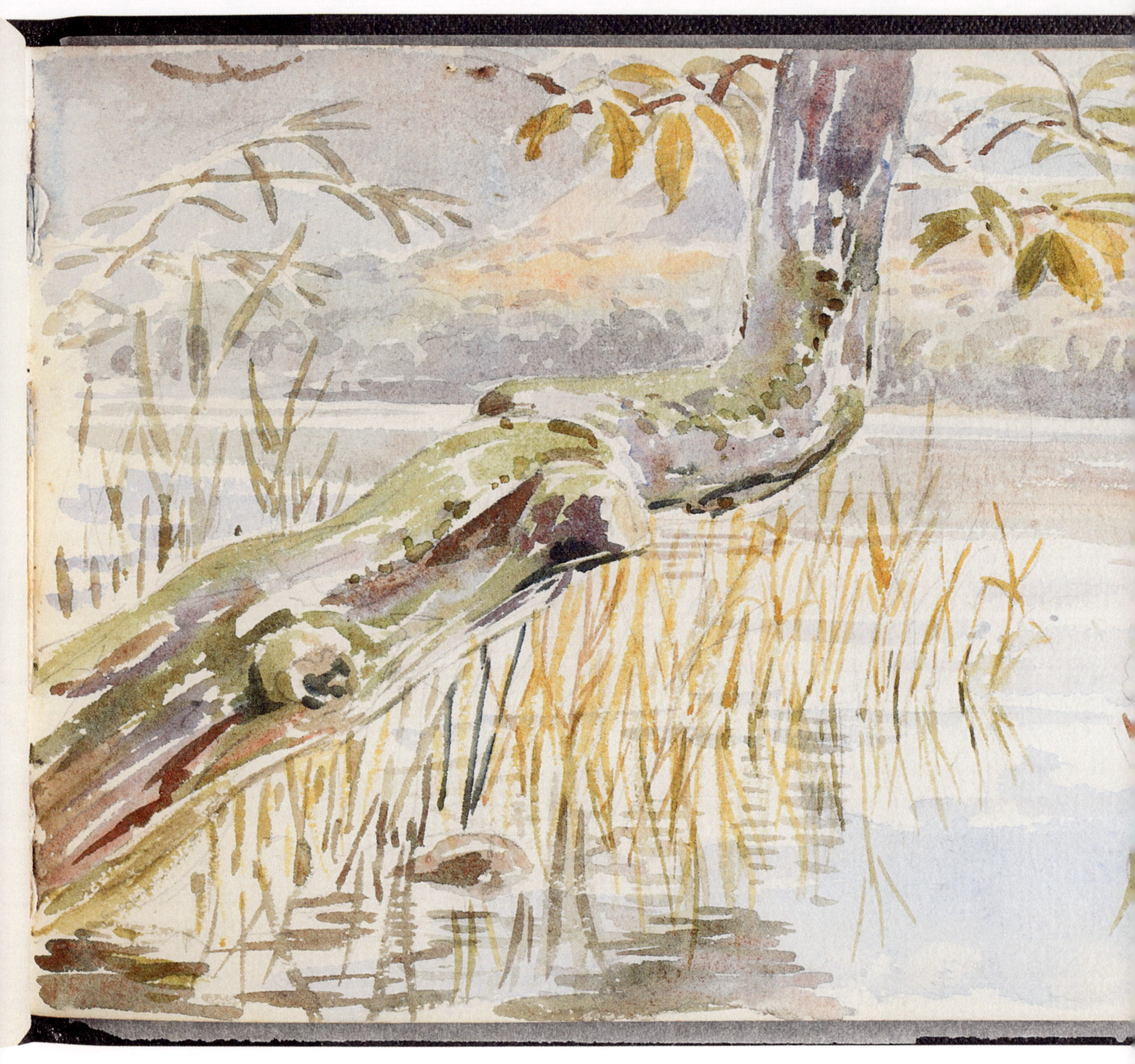

87.
Page from a sketchbook, Derwentwater, 1901
Watercolour over pencil on paper
National Trust, 242740

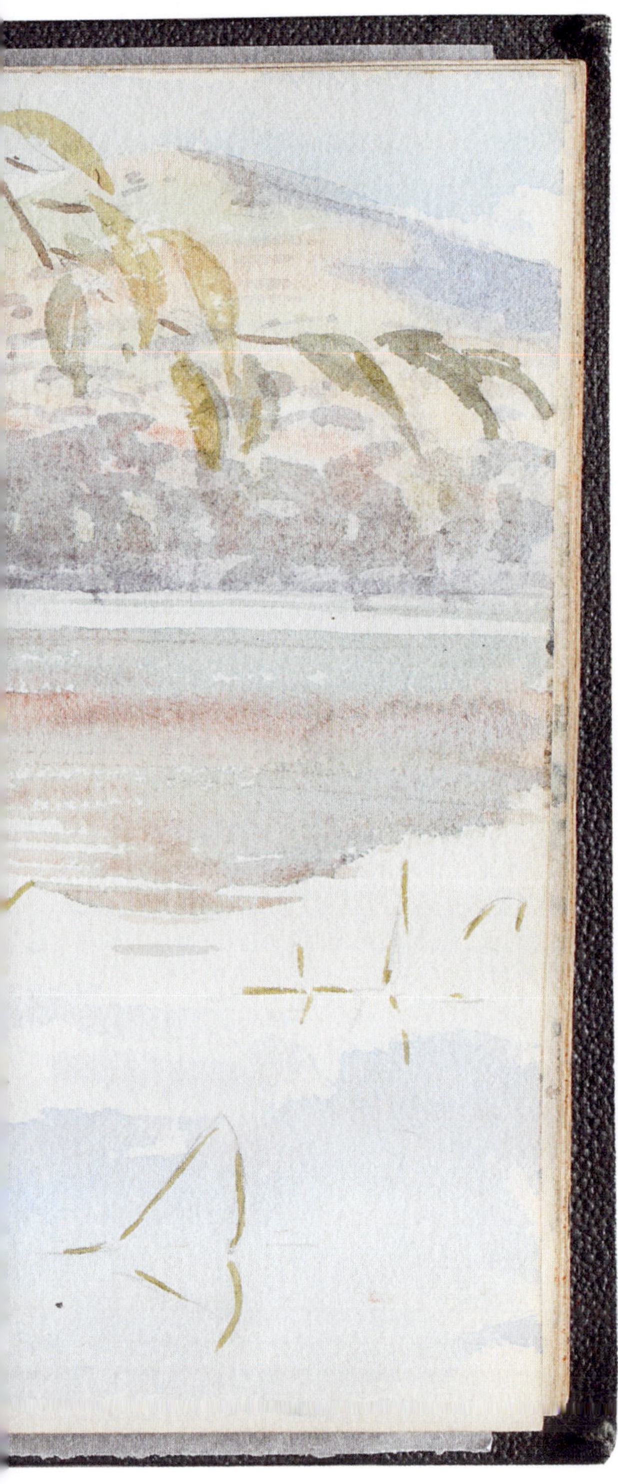

I do not remember a time when I did not try to...make for myself a fairyland.

(BEATRIX POTTER, LETTER TO BERTHA MAHONY MILLER, 25 NOVEMBER 1940)[40]

In January 1900 Potter stayed in Derwent Cottage, a 'funny old cottage' in Winchelsea, Sussex:

> I am sure it is a mouse-house, for Mrs Cooke, the landlady, and her family go to bed up a sort of ladder stair-case, and I can hear them scuffling about...upon the rafters just above my head![41]

Reality and fantasy coalesced in Potter's imagination. Every detail of the world around her was a potential playground for her characters: a broad area of grass could be 'just right for a picnic – or for rabbits to dance on'.[42] As a child, Potter used to 'half believe and wholly play with fairies' but they had little in common with the fairies of Victorian imagination.[43] Potter's fairyland was 'amongst the wild flowers, the animals, fungi, mosses, woods and streams, all the thousand objects of the countryside', and her fairies were 'tiny fungus people singing and bobbing and dancing in the grass... that start into life in autumn woods'.[44]

While on holiday, or when visiting family and friends, Potter collected fragments of landscapes, buildings and interiors to put in her books. Her aunt and uncle's garden at Gwaynynog in Denbighshire is home to the Flopsy Bunnies (see no.28), Squirrel Nutkin lives on the shore of Derwentwater (nos 97, 148), Mrs. Tiggy Winkle in the Newlands Valley (nos 88, 89) and Jemima Puddle-Duck, Tom Kitten and Samuel Whiskers in the village of Sawrey (nos 161, 162, 165). Duchess's house in *The Pie and the Patty-Pan* is the village post office, the path to it strewn with tiger lilies, poppies and snapdragons (no.91). *The Tale of Ginger and Pickles* (1909) caused considerable amusement among

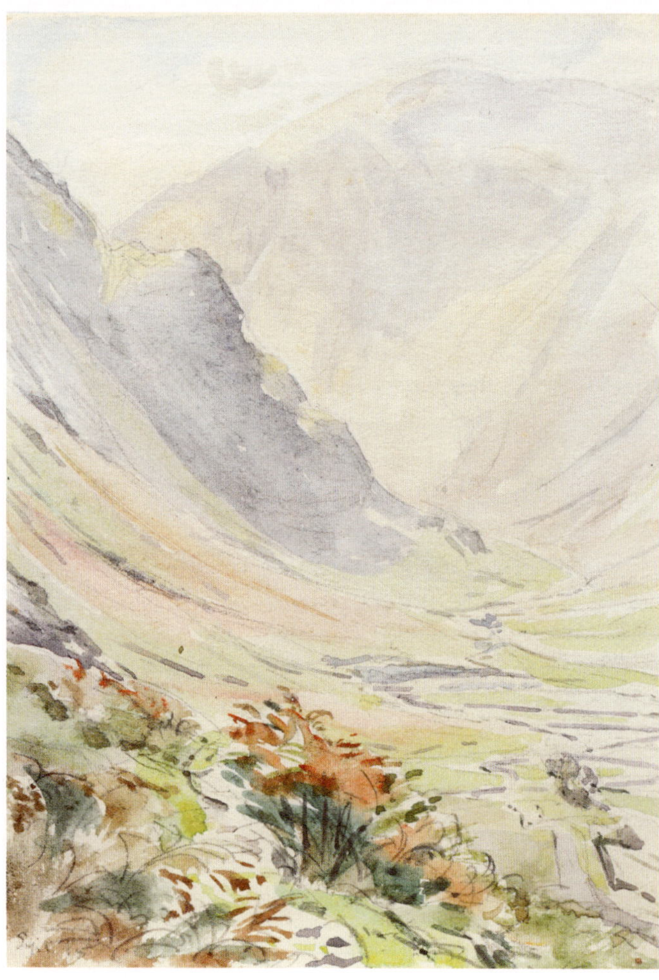

88. Above
Page from a sketchbook, Newlands Valley, near Derwentwater, 1903
Watercolour over pencil on paper
National Trust, 242727

89. Opposite
The Tale of Mrs. Tiggy-Winkle artwork, November 1904–July 1905
Watercolour and ink over pencil on paper
National Trust, 243291

Potter's neighbours: 'they are all quite jealous of each others *[sic]* houses & cats getting into a book'.[45] Mr. Jeremy Fisher and Peter Rabbit are part-Scottish in origin, although Jeremy Fisher eventually took up residence on Esthwaite Water (no.100) and *The Tale of Peter Rabbit* amalgamates several of Potter's favourite locations, including Tenby (see no.27) and the gardens and woods around Keswick. Fawe Park, an estate overlooking Derwentwater, is the setting for *The Tale of Benjamin Bunny* (1904); Potter visited in 1903 and reported to Norman Warne, 'I think I have done every imaginable rabbit background...I hope you will like them, though rather scribbled.'[46] She knew instinctively what a little rabbit might find interesting: slate borders, a water butt, baskets, flowerpots, and plank walks winding through the vegetable patches (nos 92, 93).

Potter was less acquainted with people than she was with animals. In fact, she often perceived people as animals: her Aunt Harriet as a 'weasel', Betty Harris's aunt as 'an elderly sheep' and Mr Cutter, a shopkeeper near the British Museum, as 'a wood-louse diving in and out of a rotten log'.[47] When writing her story of Mrs. Tiggy-Winkle, Potter was reminded of Kitty MacDonald, the family's washerwoman on holidays in Scotland: 'She is a comical, round little woman, as brown as a berry and wears a multitude of petticoats and a white mutch'.[48] Potter never learned to draw the human figure; Lucie makes a rather unconvincing portrait in *The Tale of Mrs. Tiggy-Winkle* (1905) but Potter's original drawing of Mrs. McGregor for *The Tale of Peter Rabbit* is, arguably, a masterful character study. Unfortunately, Frederick Warne & Co. asked her to redraw it but she would eventually develop a more forthright attitude towards her publisher: 'If it were not impertinent to lecture ones publisher – you are a great deal too much afraid of the public for whom I have never cared one tuppeny-button'.[49]

Inevitably, Potter filled her books with the little creatures that she smuggled upstairs in her childhood home in Bolton Gardens: rabbits, mice, frogs, newts, hedgehogs, squirrels and all sorts of 'creepy-crawly people',[50] from spiders and snails to beetles and bumblebees. She viewed animals scientifically and often with little sentiment. She could play with Peter Rabbit in the morning and kill a snake in the

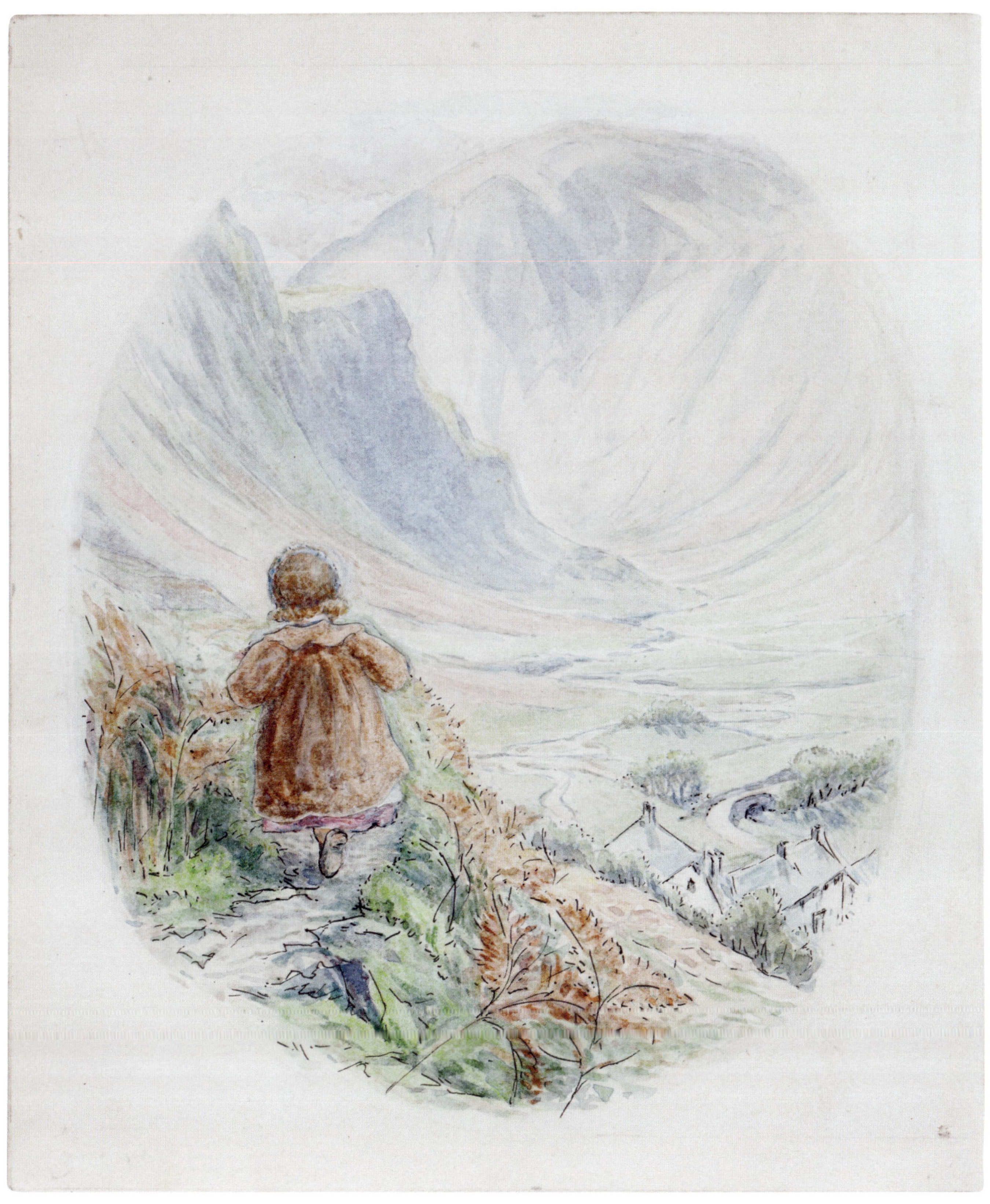

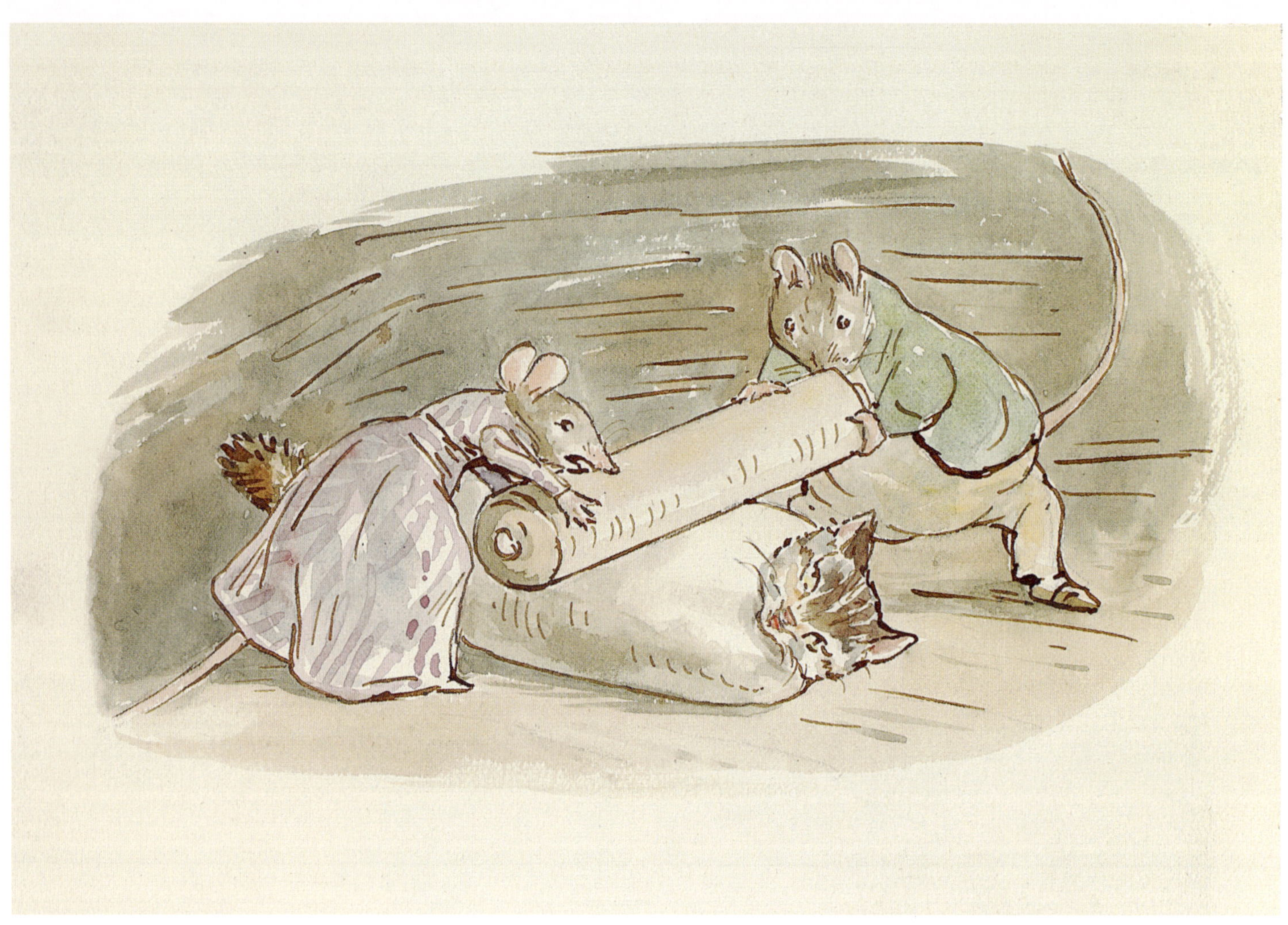

90.
The Roly-Poly Pudding; later renamed
The Tale of Samuel Whiskers
Pages from a manuscript, c.1906
Watercolour and ink on paper
V&A: BP.596, Linder Bequest LB 1162

91. Below
The Pie and the Patty-Pan artwork, March–June 1905
Watercolour and ink over pencil on paper
National Trust, 243463

92. Overleaf left
Corner of the garden at Fawe Park,
near Derwentwater, September 1903
Watercolour and ink over pencil on paper
V&A: LC 24/A/2, given by the Linder Collection

93. Overleaf right
Garden at Fawe Park, July–September 1903
Watercolour and ink over pencil on paper
V&A: LC 24/A/4, given by the Linder Collection

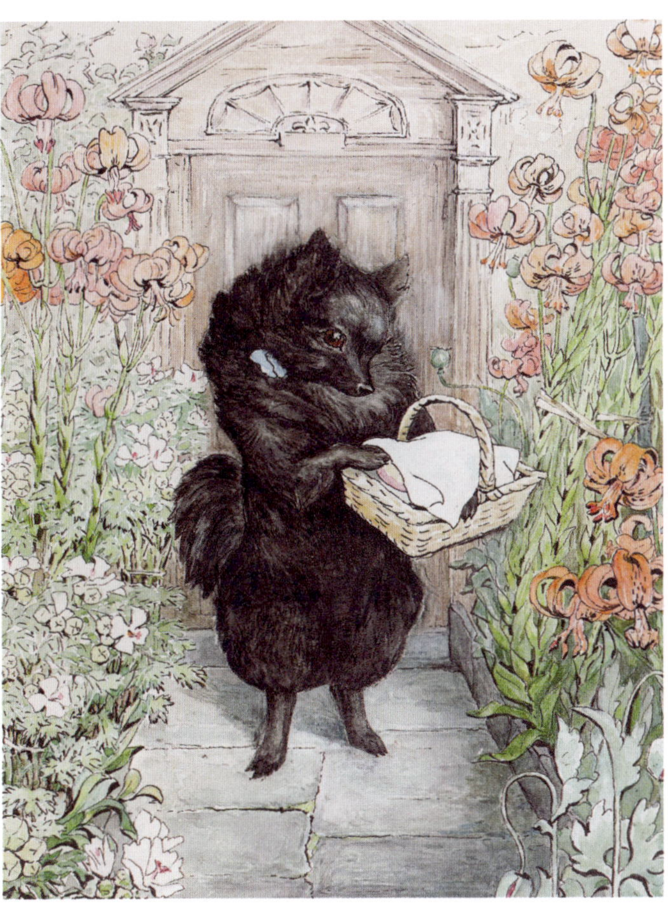

afternoon,[51] and her techniques for catching wild animals were rather perilous: 'had great fun with the frogs. I caught one old frog four times during the afternoon...You can't lift frogs out of the water on the string, they're too heavy. Newts you can swing about'.[52]

The enduring appeal of her fictional characters, however, owes something to the fact that underneath their clothes they are real animals. Potter copied rather than invented them. A page of preliminary sketches for 'A Frog He Would A-Fishing Go' reveals her seemingly effortless creative process. She draws her frog from every angle as it moves around in front of her, and finally adds the little details that will extend her real-life frog into a fictional character: the faint outline of a boat and a hint of facial expression (no.95). When her publishers asked her to verify details within her illustrations, Potter was usually able to produce the live specimen as proof: 'I was asked to pass a message... about the *tail* of the cat [in *The Tale of Benjamin Bunny*], its owner wants you to be assured that the real tail is even larger'.[53]

Potter's careful copying of the natural world inevitably commanded her storytelling and humour. Towards the end of her life she reflected, 'nature, though never consciously wicked, has always been ruthless'.[54] In her stories, scientific cause and effect replaces human morality; animals kill other animals – a harsh reality of life. Potter casually punctuates her stories with humorous understatements of violence and death: Dorcas and Porcas led 'prosperous uneventful lives, and their end was bacon'; Anna Maria, while preparing to bake Tom Kitten alive in a pudding, wished he 'would hold his head still, as it disarranged the pastry' (no.90); and Pickles observes to Ginger, 'it would never do to eat our customers; they would leave us and go to Tabitha Twitchit's'.[55]

Unsentimental, dispassionate and dark, this is gallows humour; but it is palatable in an animal story and, in any case, children 'take things seriously; at least the old fashioned ones did'.[56]

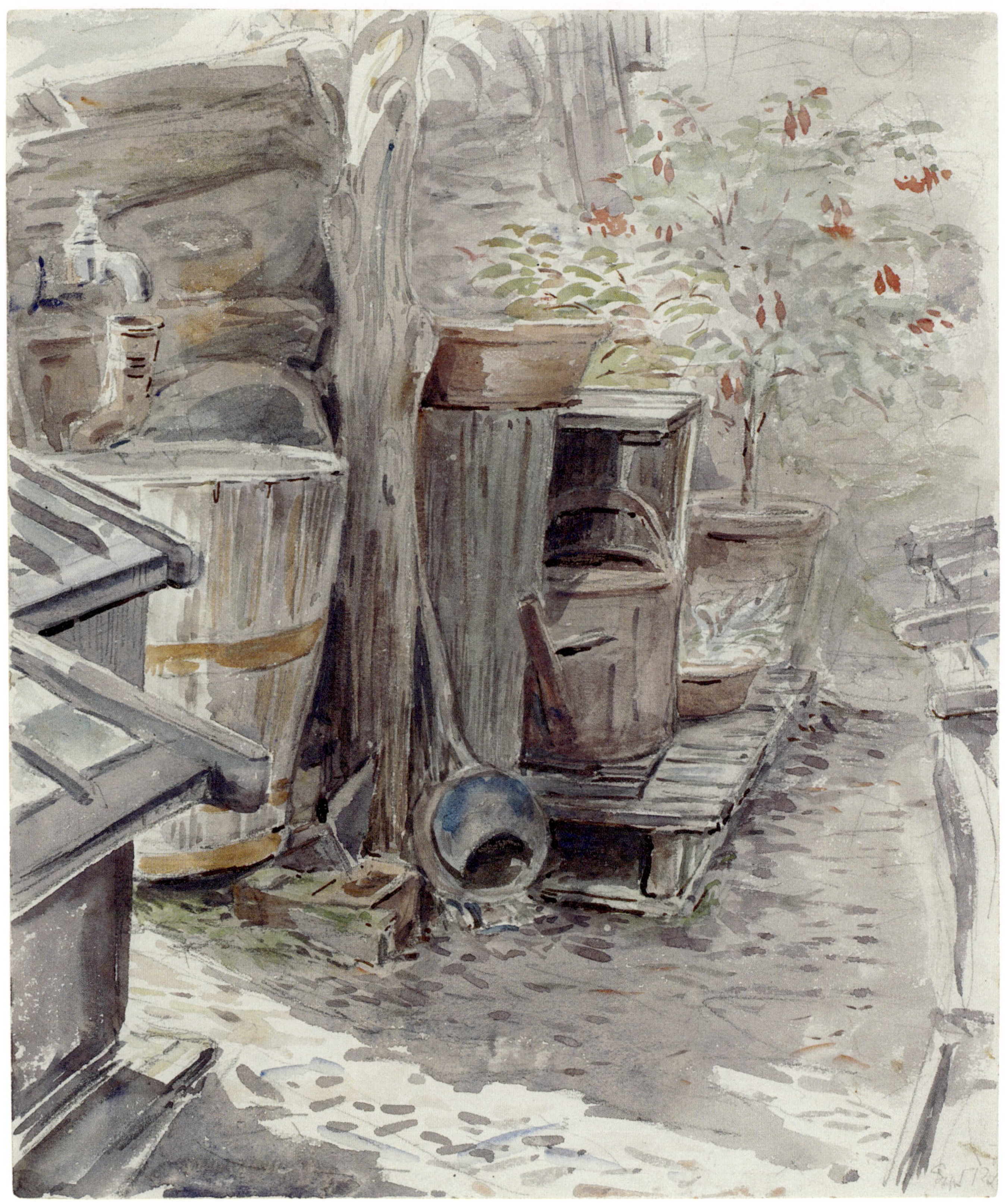

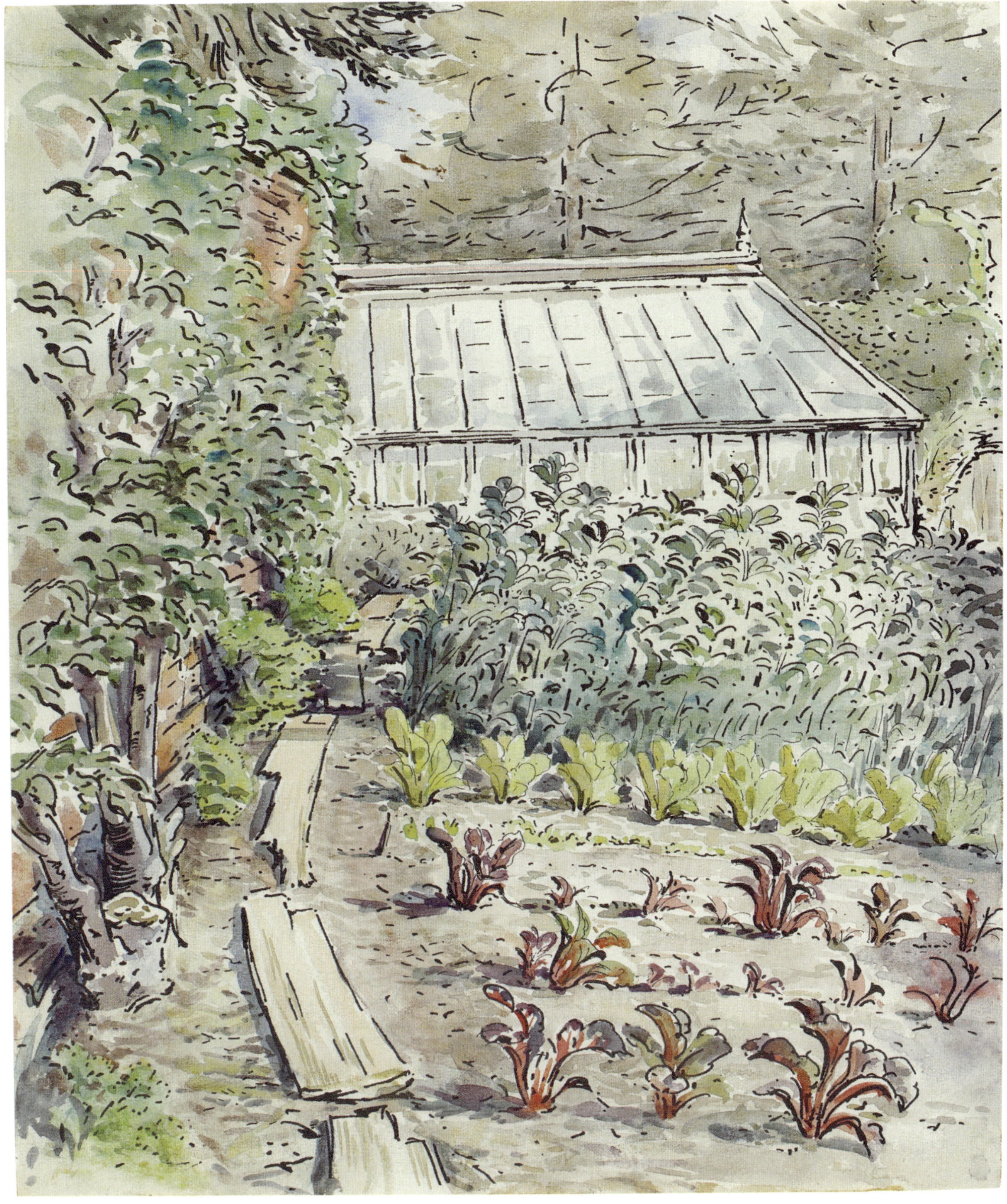

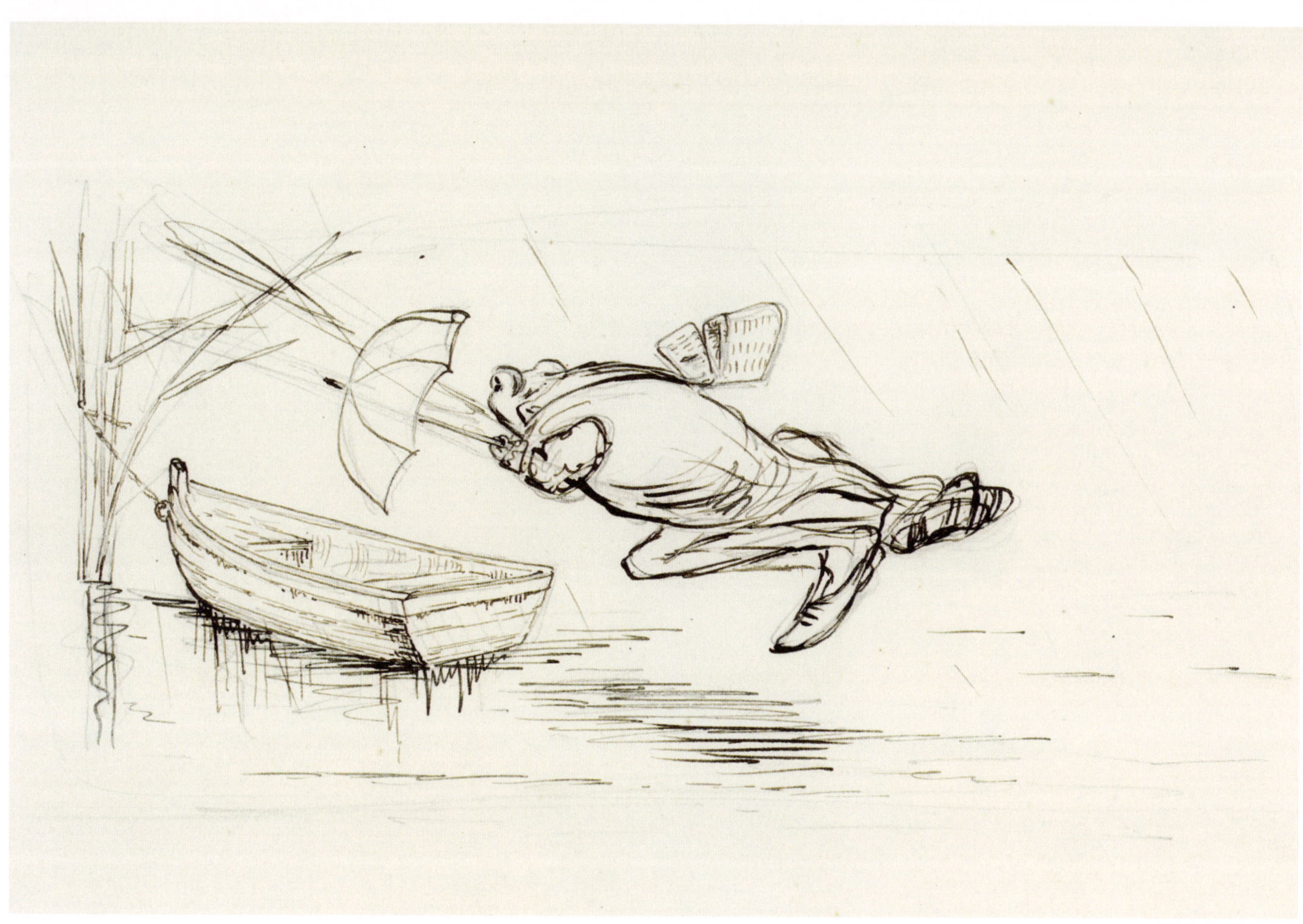

I polish! polish! polish! – to the last revise.

(BEATRIX POTTER, LETTER TO BERTHA MAHONY MILLER, 18 FEBRUARY 1942)[57]

Potter's letters to children reveal an instinct for visual and verbal storytelling. At the heart of her stories is her relationship with a young family – the Moores. Her narrative voice is intimate and familiar: after all, she is addressing real children, not writing for publication. In her story of Peter Rabbit she speaks directly to Noel, 'I think he would have got away altogether, if he had not unfortunately run into a gooseberry net'; further on, she confides in him, 'It was a blue jacket with brass buttons; quite new'.[58] These conspiratorial asides, although incidental to the action, invite Noel into the storytelling. In the published tale the invitation extends to the young child, snuggled, perhaps, on a grown-up's lap, 'reading' the pictures while listening to the story.

Evidently, Potter intended her stories to be read aloud. Sound effects, or onomatopoeias, animate her

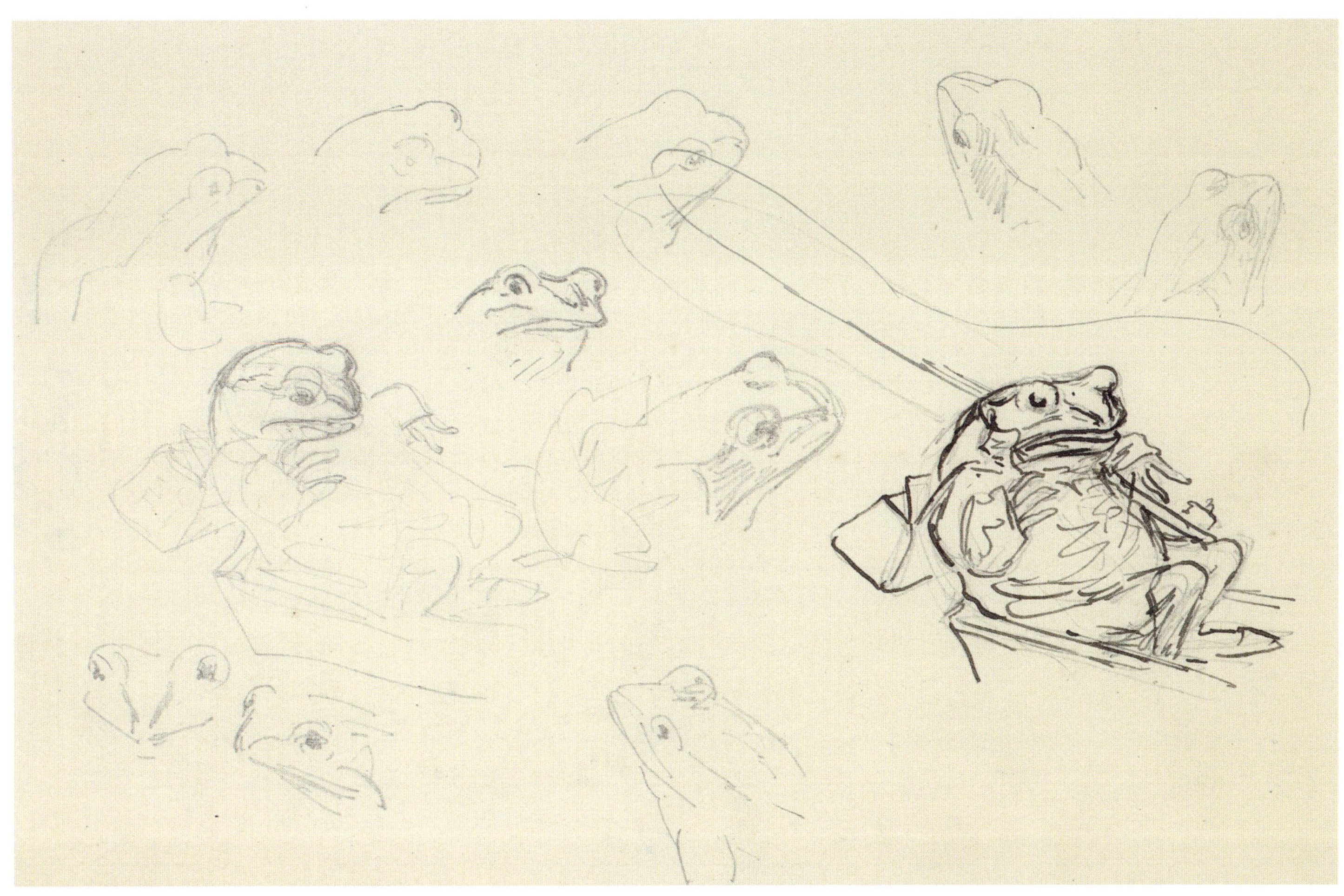

94. Opposite
Sketch, c.1894, to accompany the verse 'A Frog He Would A-Fishing Go', published in Ernest Nister's *Comical Customers*, 1896
Ink over pencil on paper
V&A: BP.507(b), Linder Bequest LB 1030

95. Above
Studies of frogs relating to 'A Frog He Would A-Fishing Go', c.1894
Pencil and ink on paper
V&A: BP.1263(iii), Linder Bequest LB 1047

prose and prompt the reader to perform the story: 'Kertyschoo', 'Ker-pflop-p-p-p', 'Squeak!', 'bang, bang, smash, smash', and 'scr-r-ritch scratch, scratch, scritch'.[59] Italics and capital letters, too, are clues to reading aloud: *'But Nutkin was in his waist-coat pocket!'*.[60] Potter had a fascination with dialect and archaic words; several characters, including Mrs. McGregor, speak with a hint of 'common Lancashire': 'She said that Mr. McGregor had "done it a purpose".'[61] Dialogue energizes Potter's stories and distinguishes the characters; 'children like conversations' but it is the reader, however, who must impersonate the characters and convey her gentle satire: 'My Great-aunt Squintina...died of a thimble in a Christmas plum-pudding. *I* never put any article of metal in *my* puddings or pies.'[62]

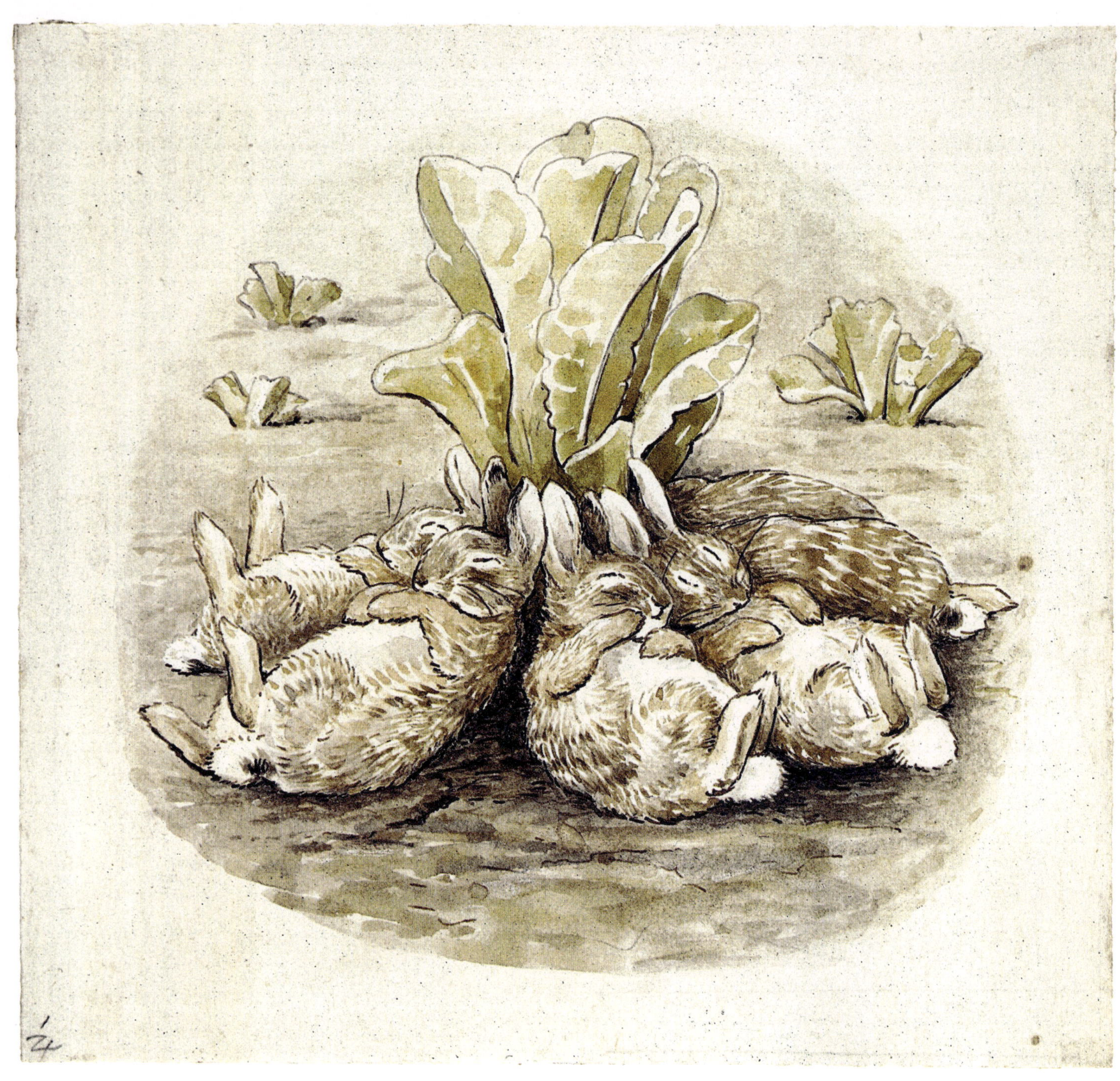

96.
The Tale of the Flopsy Bunnies artwork, 1909
Watercolour and ink on paper
British Museum, 1946,1121.3

At its best, Potter's prose has the sound and rhythm of poetry; alliteration and assonance add a touch of elegance: 'hot buttered toast', 'little live lady mouse', 'little twittering tunes', 'spread out his tail for a sail', 'terribly tidy particular little mouse' and 'Mr. McGregor came up with a sieve, which he intended to pop upon the top of Peter'.[59]

Such phrases are a delight to read aloud and Potter took pleasure in writing them: 'I think I write carefully because I enjoy my writing, and enjoy taking pains over it'.[60] Her grammar and punctuation are purposeful. In *The Tale of Peter Rabbit* sentences extend across several pages, protracting the action from one gripping page-turn to another. Potter piles sentence upon sentence, often beginning them with 'And' or 'But' to intensify the pace of the storytelling. In *The Tale of Squirrel Nutkin*, however, punctuation slows the action and creates suspense: 'There was Old Brown sitting on his door-step, quite still, with his eyes closed, as if nothing had happened'.[61]

Potter was a fastidious line-editor, even asking her publisher to reduce the exclamation marks in *The Tale of Jemima Puddle-Duck* (1908): 'the fox is not meant to be excited in manner'.[62] Her humour, in particular, owes much to the semicolon, which she uses effusively to pair seemingly incongruent phrases: 'Your father had an accident there; he was put in a pie by Mrs. McGregor'.[63] Here, the semicolon, like a musical pause, elevates dramatic tension; what follows is a brilliant understatement of complete catastrophe. To be 'put in a pie' can hardly be considered an 'accident'. Here, and elsewhere in her stories, Potter's pragmatic and highly ironic storytelling is reinforced by a wonderful economy of words. She described her 'usual way of writing' as the 'shorter and plainer the better. And [I] read the Bible...if I feel my style wants chastening.'[64]

Potter indulges children's innate love of language with delightful made-up words – 'a snippeting of scissors, and snappeting of thread' and 'a flutterment and a scufflement' – while 'piled up adjectives' parody their limited language experience: 'the most beautifullest coat', 'great big enormous trout' and 'fatter and fatter and fatterer'.[65] She explained to her publisher, 'children like a fine word occasionally';[66] the meaning of difficult words – 'excessively impertinent', 'affronted', 'improvident', 'impertinent', 'incurably indolent', 'alacrity', 'disconsolately' and 'implored' – can be communicated in the performance but, when necessary to the story, Potter explains them within the narrative: 'It is said that the effect of eating too much lettuce is "soporific" (no.96). *I* have never felt sleepy after eating lettuces; but then *I* am not a rabbit.'[67] Some words, however, are purely atmospheric. In *The Tailor of Gloucester*, Potter paints a rich tapestry in velvety language to convey the expense of the clothing (nos 26, 145):

> full-skirted coats with flowered lappets...ruffles, and gold-laced waistcoats of paduasoy and taffeta...a coat of cherry-coloured corded silk embroidered with pansies and roses, and a cream-coloured satin waistcoat.[68]

Sophisticated illustrations complement her elegant prose. In *The Tale of Mrs Tittlemouse* (1910) Potter resists drawing the butterfly as a child might imagine it, with wings outstretched; instead, she observes it scientifically and offers an unusual view of the legs and the underside of the upright wings (no.98).

As an author-illustrator, Potter could use pictures in place of words. In her letter to Noel she describes Peter Rabbit visually rather than verbally; he faces away from his mother and sisters, hands deep in his pockets. Potter reworked the drawing several times for the published tale, eventually settling on a diagonal composition that identifies Peter as the protagonist of the story (no.97).

Potter appreciated, too, that children learn to read pictures long before words. In *The Tale of Mr Jeremy Fisher* (1906) she directs the child's attention to the minutiae of the fishing tackle: a 'dearest little red float', a rod made from a 'tough stalk of grass', a line from 'a fine long white horse-hair' and a 'little wriggling worm' tied at the end (no.100).[69] Eagle-eyed children may notice tiny details that develop the stories beyond the text: for example, Mrs Tittlemouse tickling the ear of one of the Flopsy Bunnies to keep it from falling asleep. Potter's illustrations are often unexpected but always appropriate. Peter is 'dreadfully frightened'[70] and rushes all over the garden yet she depicts only the aftermath of terror: one lonely shoe

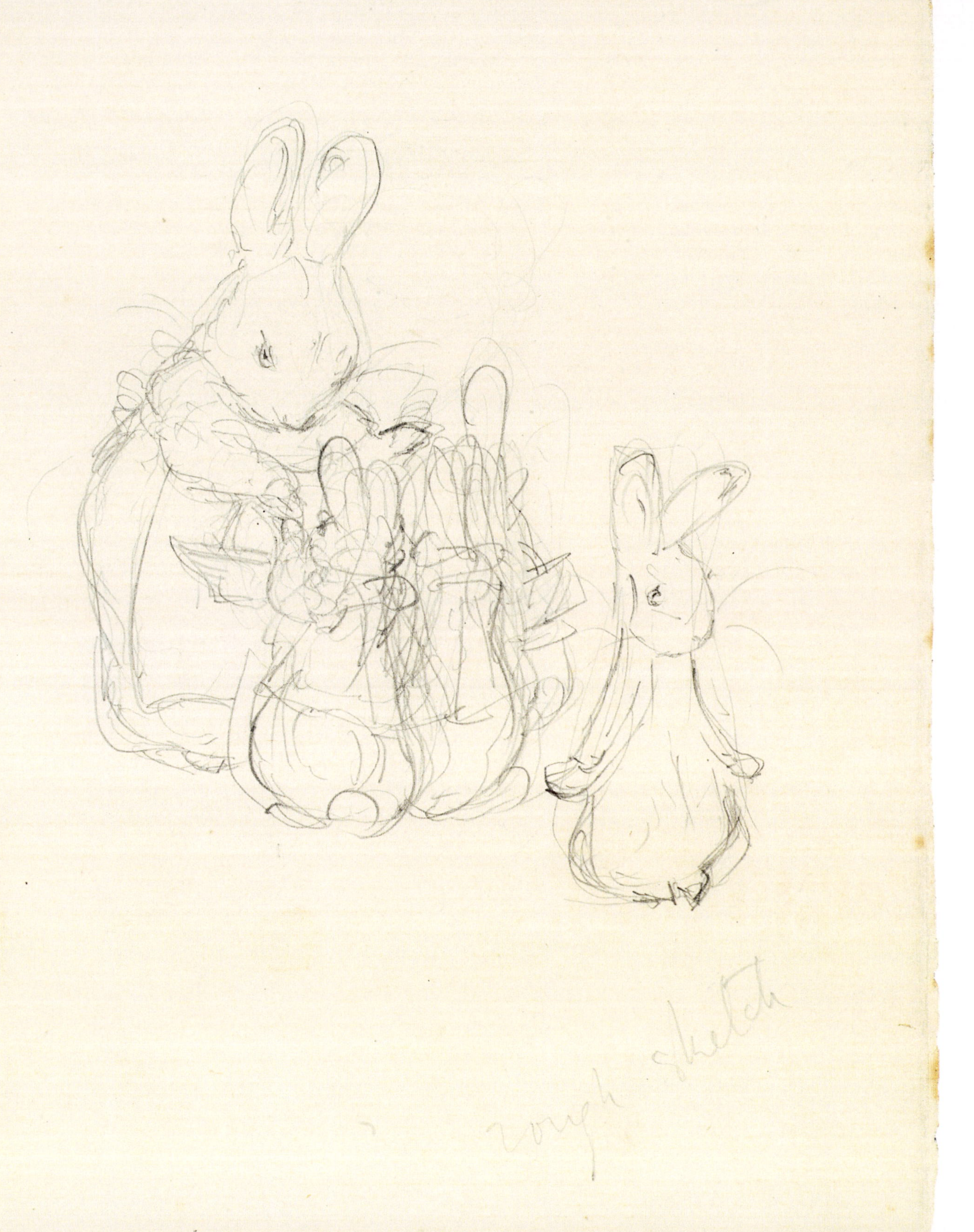
rough sketch

97. Opposite
Sketch for the privately printed edition of *The Tale of Peter Rabbit*, 1901
Pencil on paper
V&A: BP.583(5), Linder Bequest LB 889

among the cabbages and the other among the potatoes (no.99). For very young children there are no nasty surprises. In *The Tale of Mr. Jeremy Fisher* Potter forewarns the reader of the 'really *frightful* thing': out of sight of Mr. Jeremy Fisher, the enormous trout is already in view, wide-eyed and mouth open, ready to seize him 'with a snap'.[75]

Young children may not have heard of irony but they can certainly sense when an illustration does not match the text: the blackbirds are not, in fact, frightened of Mr. McGregor's scarecrow in *The Tale of Peter Rabbit*, and in *The Tale of Two Bad Mice* the nurse's mousetrap is shown to be utterly ineffective. Incongruity between the illustrations and the text creates dramatic irony, a clever narrative device that draws the reader into the creative process.

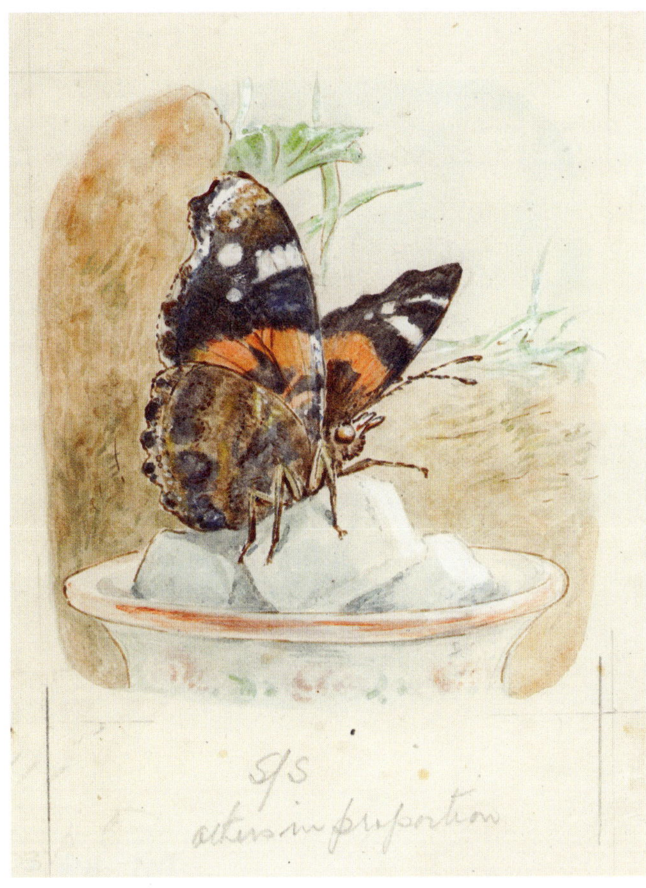

98.
The Tale of Mrs. Tittlemouse artwork, January–June 1910
Watercolour and ink on paper
National Trust, 243065

In *The Tale of Jemima Puddle-Duck*, for example, the 'foxy-whiskered' gentleman offers Jemima the use of his woodshed as a comfortable nesting-place. The text states, 'The gentleman opened the door, and showed Jemima in'; the illustration, however, tells an entirely different story. Potter lets very young children, 'reading' the pictures while listening to the story, in on a secret: they perceive Jemima's predicament before she does.[76]

Not everything in the stories is for children, however. While there is plenty of slapstick humour to amuse young readers, only adults will perceive the irony in Potter's description of Benjamin and Flopsy's large family: 'they were very improvident and cheerful' (no.101).[77] Potter's writing is deeply satirical; she exposes the disingenuous village gossips and laughs at the absurdity of social etiquette in *The Pie and the Patty-Pan*: 'They only bowed to one another; they did not speak, because they were going to have a party'.[78]

Similarly, she makes fun of the characters' preoccupation with domestic one-upmanship, even in the midst of a crisis: while searching for Tom Kitten, Ribby's attention is diverted by the presence of soot in Tabitha Twichit's fender.

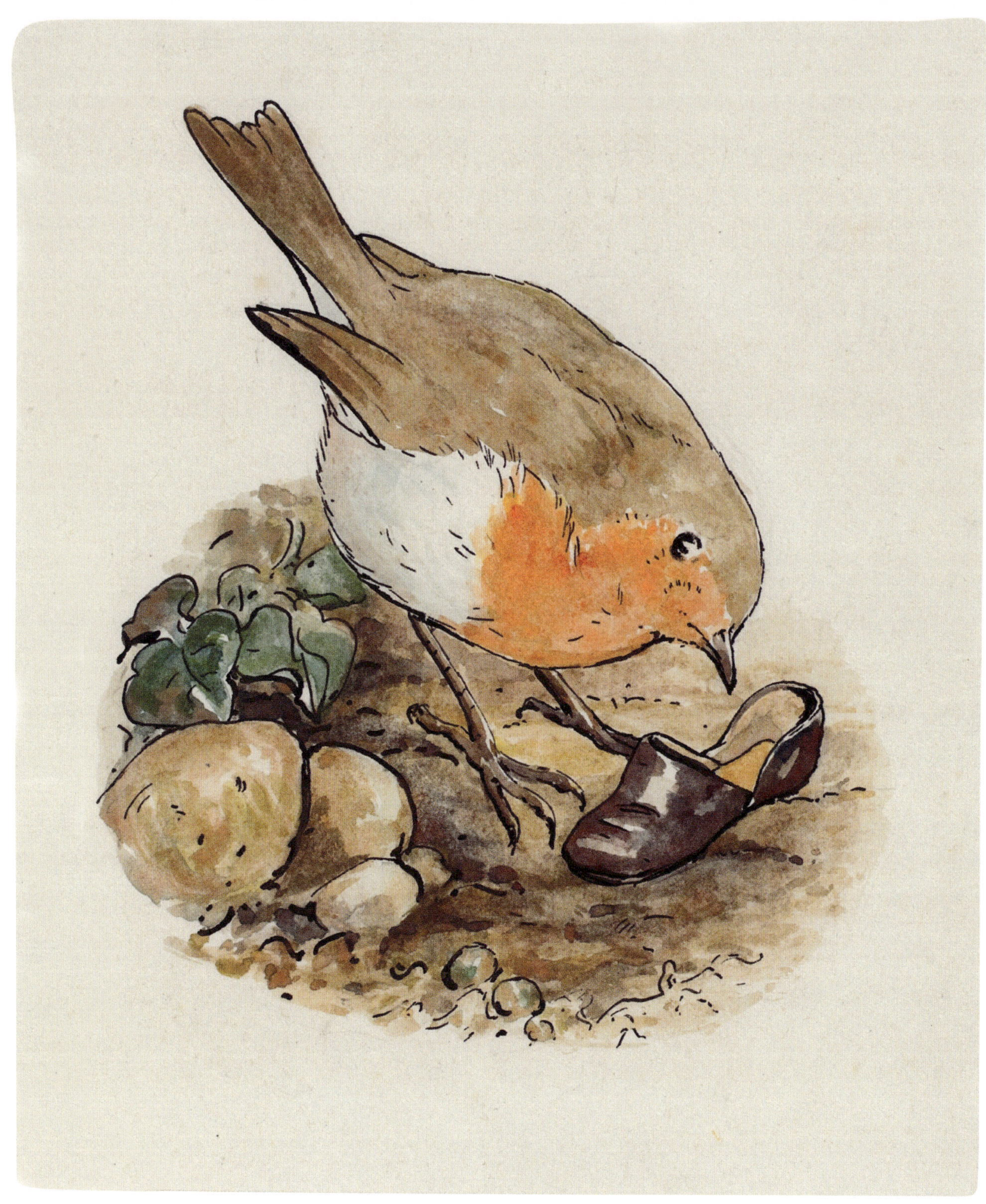

99. Opposite
The Tale of Peter Rabbit artwork, 1902
Watercolour and pen and ink over pencil on paper
V&A: LC 22/A/2, given by the Linder Collection

100. Below
Pages from *The Tale of Mr. Jeremy Fisher*, 1906
V&A: BP.91, Linder Bequest, LB.1601

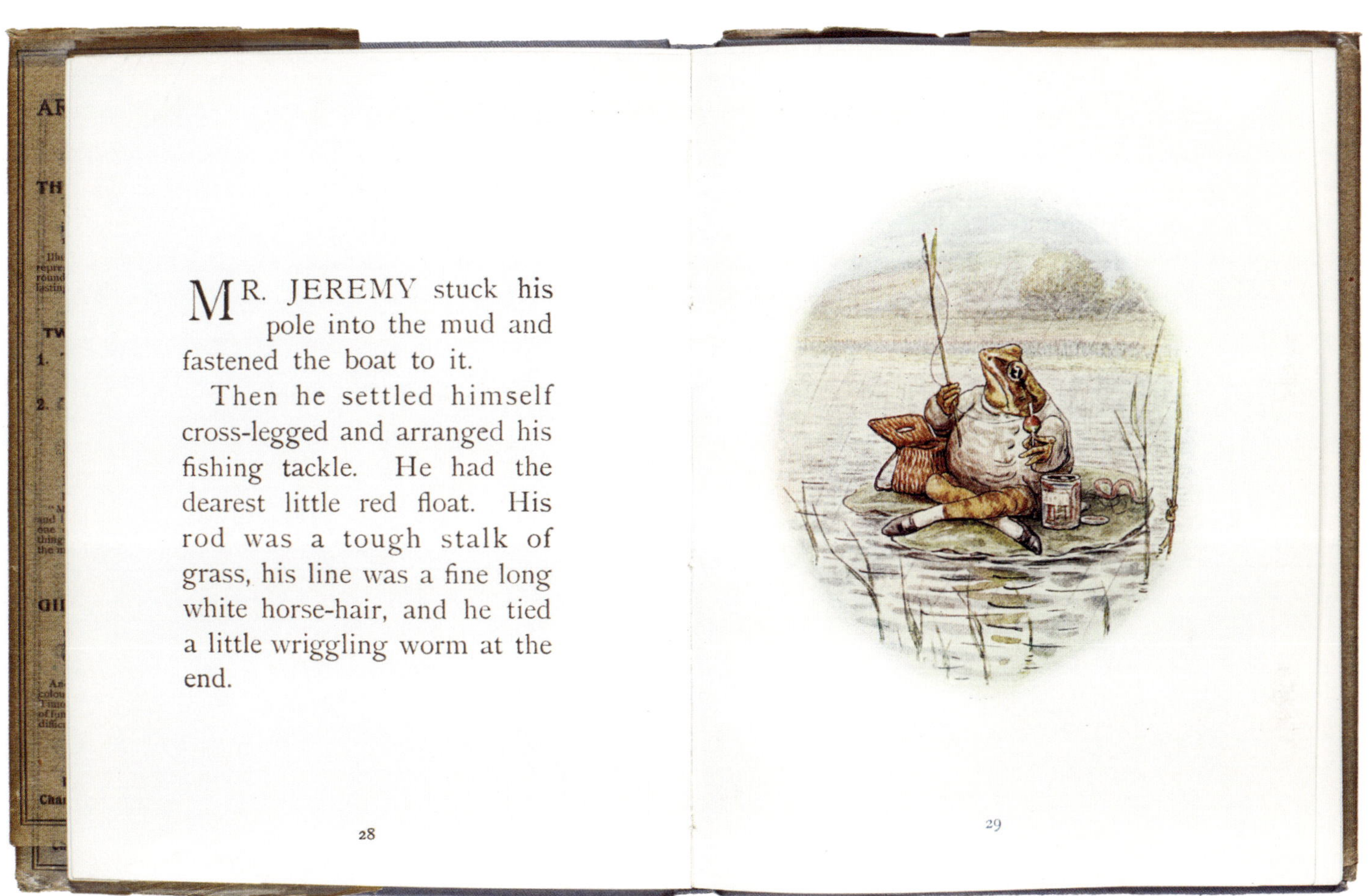

MR. JEREMY stuck his pole into the mud and fastened the boat to it.

Then he settled himself cross-legged and arranged his fishing tackle. He had the dearest little red float. His rod was a tough stalk of grass, his line was a fine long white horse-hair, and he tied a little wriggling worm at the end.

28

29

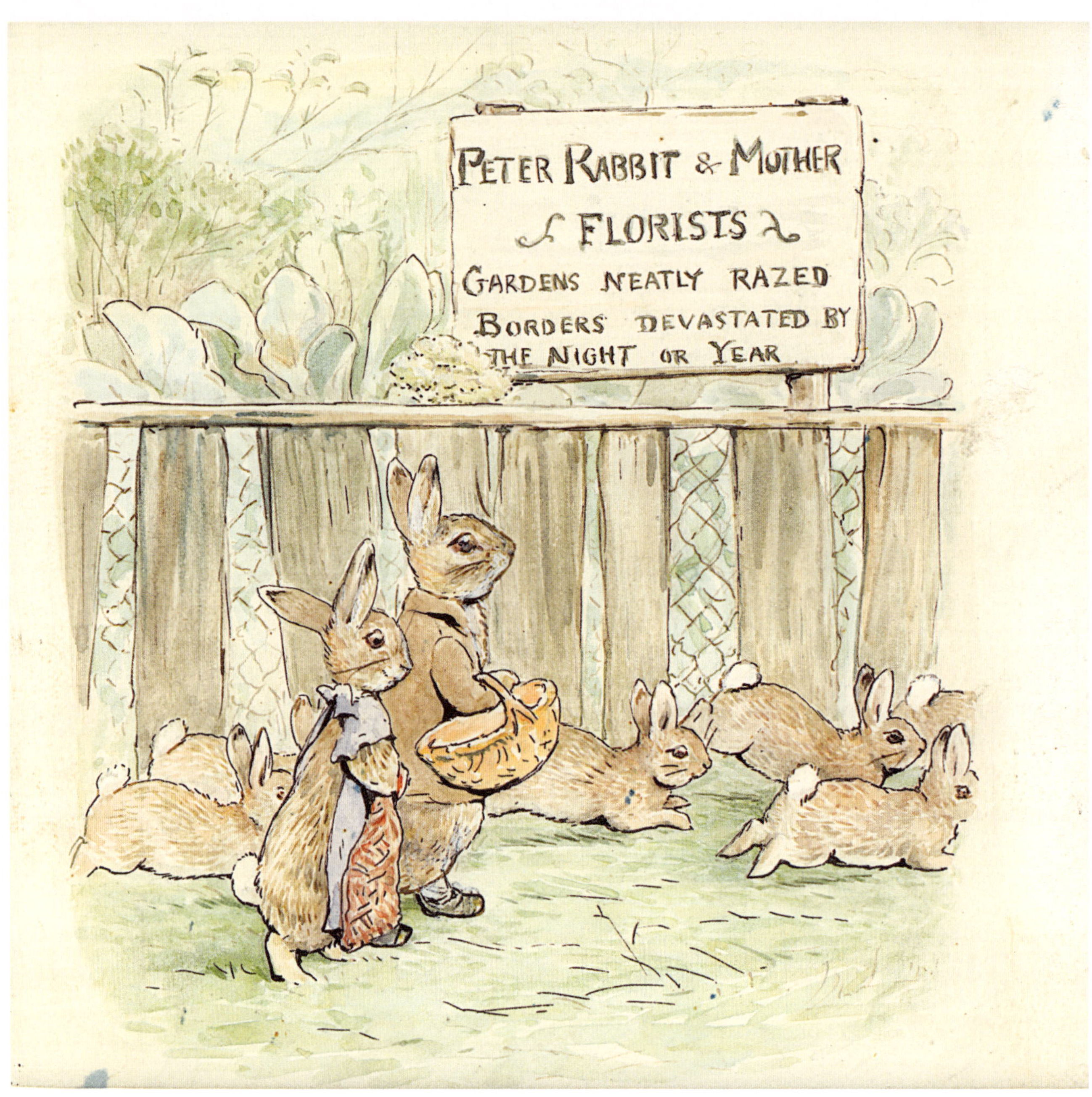

101. Above
The Tale of the Flopsy Bunnies artwork, 1909
Watercolour and ink on paper
Warne Archive

102. Opposite
Pumpkin carriage drawn by three pairs of rabbits, c.1890s
Ink and wash on paper
V&A: BP.452, Linder Bequest LB 974

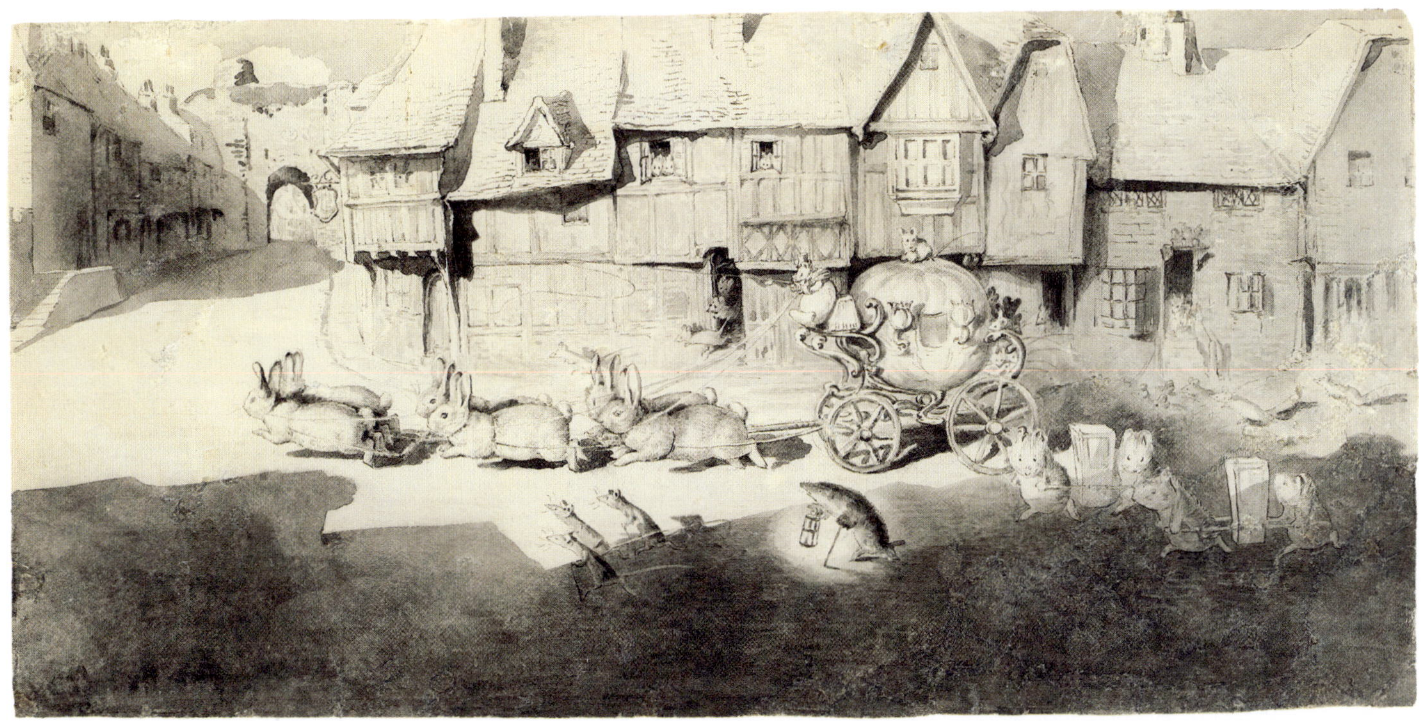

There is nothing new under the sun; and in the making of many books there are bound to be coincidences.

(BEATRIX POTTER, LETTER TO HELEN DEAN FISH, 19 SEPTEMBER 1930)[79]

Potter had a childlike appetite for fairy tales. In the mid-1890s she reimagined scenes from Cinderella (no.102), Sleeping Beauty and Puss-in-Boots, and included a lively drawing of Tom Thumb riding a mouse in a letter to Noel. Although her stories of 'Once upon a time' are fairy tales in the broadest sense, *The Tailor of Gloucester* (based on a rumour fabricated by a real tailor, Mr Prichard) is a sumptuous retelling of the Grimm brothers' *The Elves and the Shoemaker*, set in 'the time of swords and periwigs'.[80] In 1902 Potter privately printed an early version of the story, crammed with nursery rhymes. The story of Mrs. Tiggy-Winkle owes something to the 'fairy-tale' *Alice's Adventures in Wonderland*: just as Alice wakes from her dream to exclaim, 'You're nothing but a pack of cards!', so, in Potter's story, Lucie finally realizes, 'Why! Mrs. Tiggy-Winkle was nothing but a HEDGEHOG'.[81] However, the story perhaps owes even more to another fairy tale, the Grimms' *Little Red Riding Hood*: 'And *how* small she had grown – and *how* brown – and covered with PRICKLES!'[82]

Songs, rhymes and riddles abound in many of Potter's tales and their rhythms infuse her prose: just as Old King Cole 'called for his pipe and he called for his bowl',

103. Below
'The Amiable Guinea-Pig', 1917
Appley Dapply's Nursery Rhymes variant illustration,
Watercolour and ink on paper
V&A: BP.622, Linder Bequest LB 718

104. Opposite
Brer Rabbit rescuing the terrapin, May 1895
Pencil and ink on paper
V&A: LC 8/A/3, given by the Linder Collection

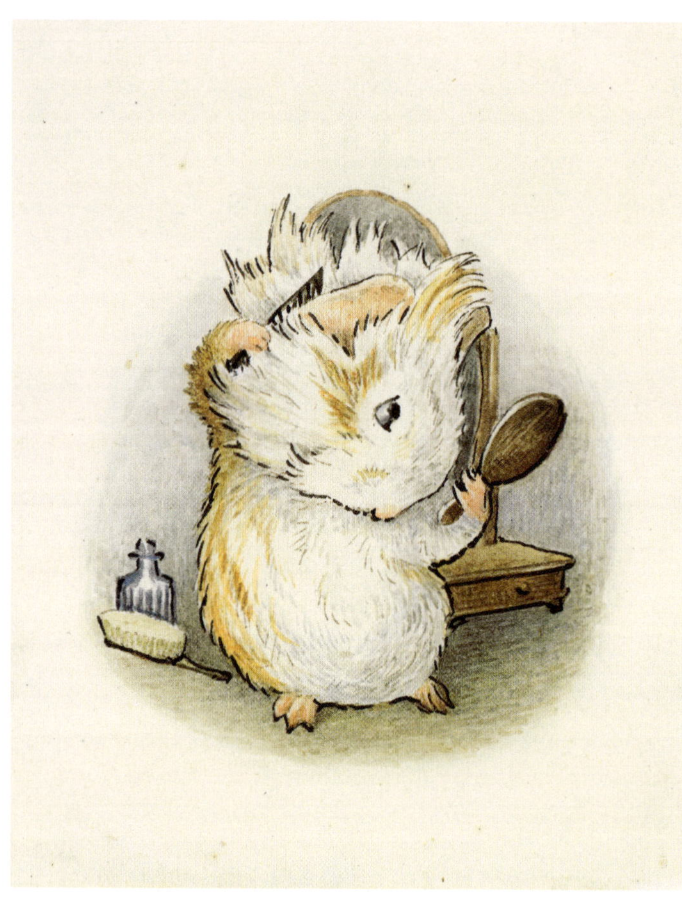

so the tailor of Gloucester 'grew quite stout, and he grew quite rich'.[83] Even the ships in *The Tale of Little Pig Robinson* (1929, a fusion of Edward Lear's nonsense poem, 'The Owl and the Pussy-Cat' [1871], and Daniel Defoe's *Robinson Crusoe* [1719]) are named 'Goldielocks', 'Little Bo Beep' and 'Margery Dawe'.[84] When her publisher and fiancé, Norman Warne, died suddenly in 1905, Potter put aside her plans to 'make a nice book' of 'extremely odd rhymes',[85] but in 1917, for the sake of the old firm, she agreed to cobble together a few verses and pictures in Appley Dapply's Nursery Rhymes, including a limerick in the style of Lear: 'There once was an amiable guinea-pig, Who brushed back his hair like a periwig' (no.103, see also pp.196–7).[86] Potter dismissed her later little books as 'pot-boilers' and described as 'atrocious' her retelling of Aesop's fable, *The Tale of Johnny Town-Mouse* (1918).[87]

Potter confessed that she wrote *The Tale of Mr. Tod* (1912) in 'imitation of "Uncle Remus"'.[88] Joel Chandler Harris's *Uncle Remus: His Songs and Sayings* (1880) and the sequel, *Nights with Uncle Remus* (1883), were favourite books. Harris's 'wonderful portrait' of Brer Rabbit inhabited Potter's imagination from the early 1890s; one of her watercolour studies of a rabbit even bears the inscription, 'Brer Rabbit in a garden'.[89] She illustrated several stories from *Uncle Remus* (no.104), including 'In some lady's garden' in which Brer Rabbit tricks his way into a garden to steal 'sparrer-grass' and green peas. The similarity to *The Tale of Peter Rabbit* is no coincidence; Potter even paid tribute to *Uncle Remus* in her manuscript, 'Uncle Remus says that rabbit tobacco is what we call lavender'.[90] She borrowed plots, names, words and phrases – 'clippity

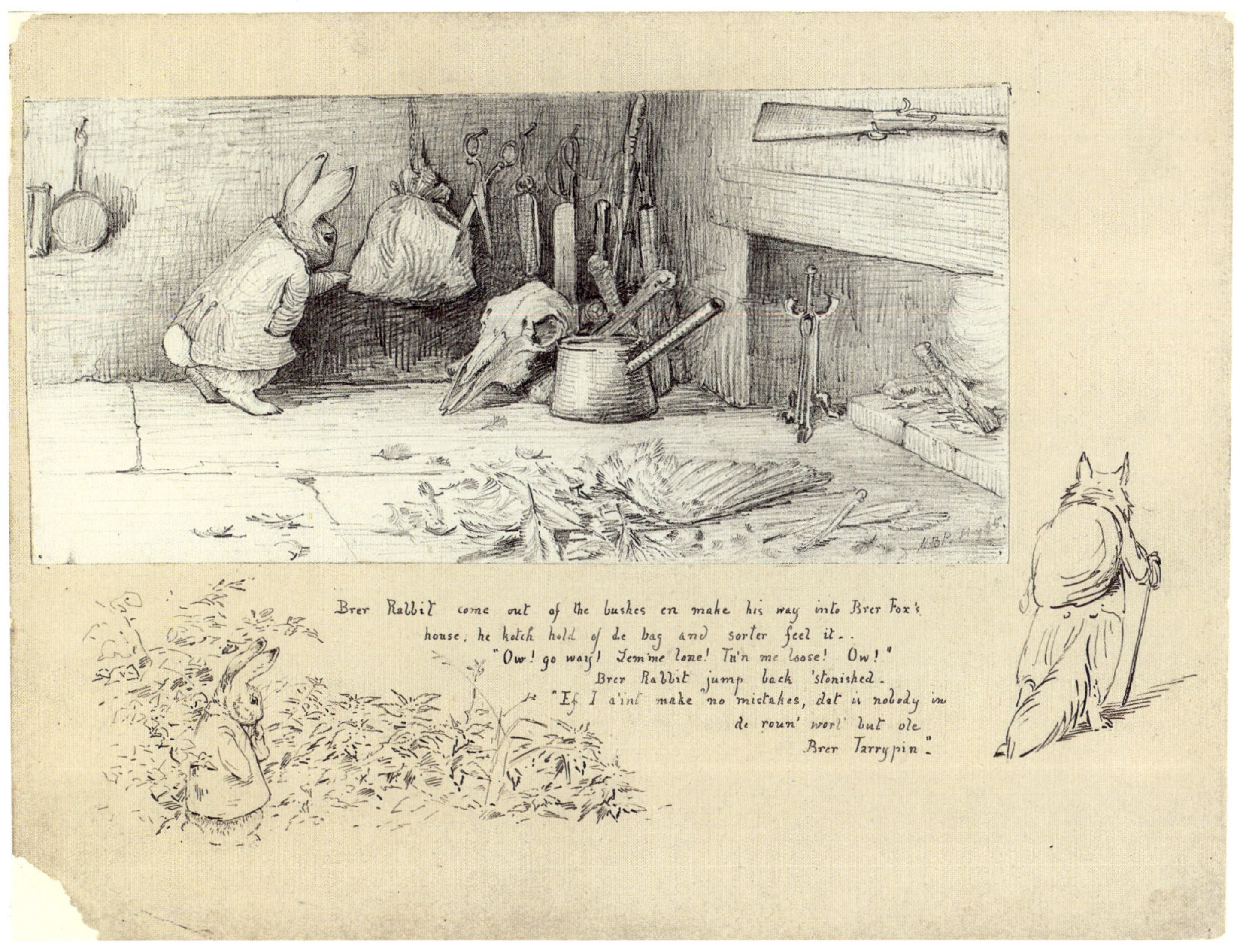

lippity', 'Cotton-tail', 'rabbit terbacker' and 'Miss Puddle-duck' – but her debt to *Uncle Remus* is more subtle and fundamental. She imbued her prose with the onomatopoeic rhythms of Uncle Remus's storytelling: '*Tip tap, tip tap, tip tap tip!*'; 'pit pat paddle pat! pit pat waddle pat!'; 'trit-trot, trit-trot of a pony'; 'pitter-patter, pitter-patter'; 'Tiddly, widdly, widdly! Pouff, pouff, puff!'; and 'They had stolen it out of a bumble bees' nest on the tippitty top of the hill'.[91] Potter's sprinkling of dialect probably owes something to Uncle Remus, and her matter-of-fact humour has much in common with his 'severe seriousness'.[92] Reflecting on her own work she said, 'there is more in the books than mere funniness'.[93]

Writing and illustrating stories ultimately occupied a brief period in Potter's life; marriage offered her the possibility to move permanently to the Lake District and to pursue other interests. She shunned publicity and to the end remained modest about her extraordinary success: 'If I have done anything – even a little – to help small children on the road to enjoy and appreciate honest simple pleasures…I have done a bit of good'.[94]

Emma Laws

Beatrix Potter, Entrepreneur

In 1890 Beatrix Potter took her first step into the male-dominated business world, at a time when ambitious women were rarely allowed to flourish outside the domestic environment. In order to contribute to a printing machine she and her brother Bertram wished to purchase, Beatrix decided to sell Christmas cards. She was encouraged by her uncle, Sir Henry Roscoe, who had admired the greetings cards she had made for the family the previous year.

Potter prepared six card designs and sent them to five publishers for consideration. After the first rejection, her brother decided to hand deliver the pictures to his preferred publisher, Hildesheimer & Faulkner. In her journal entry of May 1890, Potter records that on the following day an envelope arrived containing 'a cheque for £6...and a very civil letter under the misapprehension that I was a gentleman, requiring me to send more sketches'.[1] This was the first time she had received payment for her art and she was eager to take advantage of the opportunity. Potter created new designs and attended her first business meeting, accompanied by Sir Henry, at which she negotiated the deal by herself with Mr Faulkner, the owner of the publishing company. She was 24 when her designs were published, first as Christmas and New Year cards, and then as illustrations to a set of verses by Frederic E. Weatherly. Twelve years later, Potter had her next commercial success with the publication of *The Tale of Peter Rabbit* (1902), followed by 22 other tales. As the popularity of her little books grew, Potter, with the help and support of her publisher Frederick Warne & Co., initiated the development of related merchandise, including toys, wallpaper, tea sets, ceramic tiles and even slippers. Between 1903 and 1916 she was at the forefront of all creative and commercial details, with most of the best-known products being made to her design and often wholly administered by her.

After 1917 Frederick Warne & Co. became much more involved with the merchandise programme, while Potter concentrated on her work in the Lake District. However, she still actively commented on the items that were licensed, providing her thoughts on their appearance and quality. A true entrepreneur, with good business sense, Potter was one of the first artist-illustrators to initiate character licensing. Realizing the wider market appeal of her characters, she was always open to new ideas and opportunities, but never at the cost of their integrity.

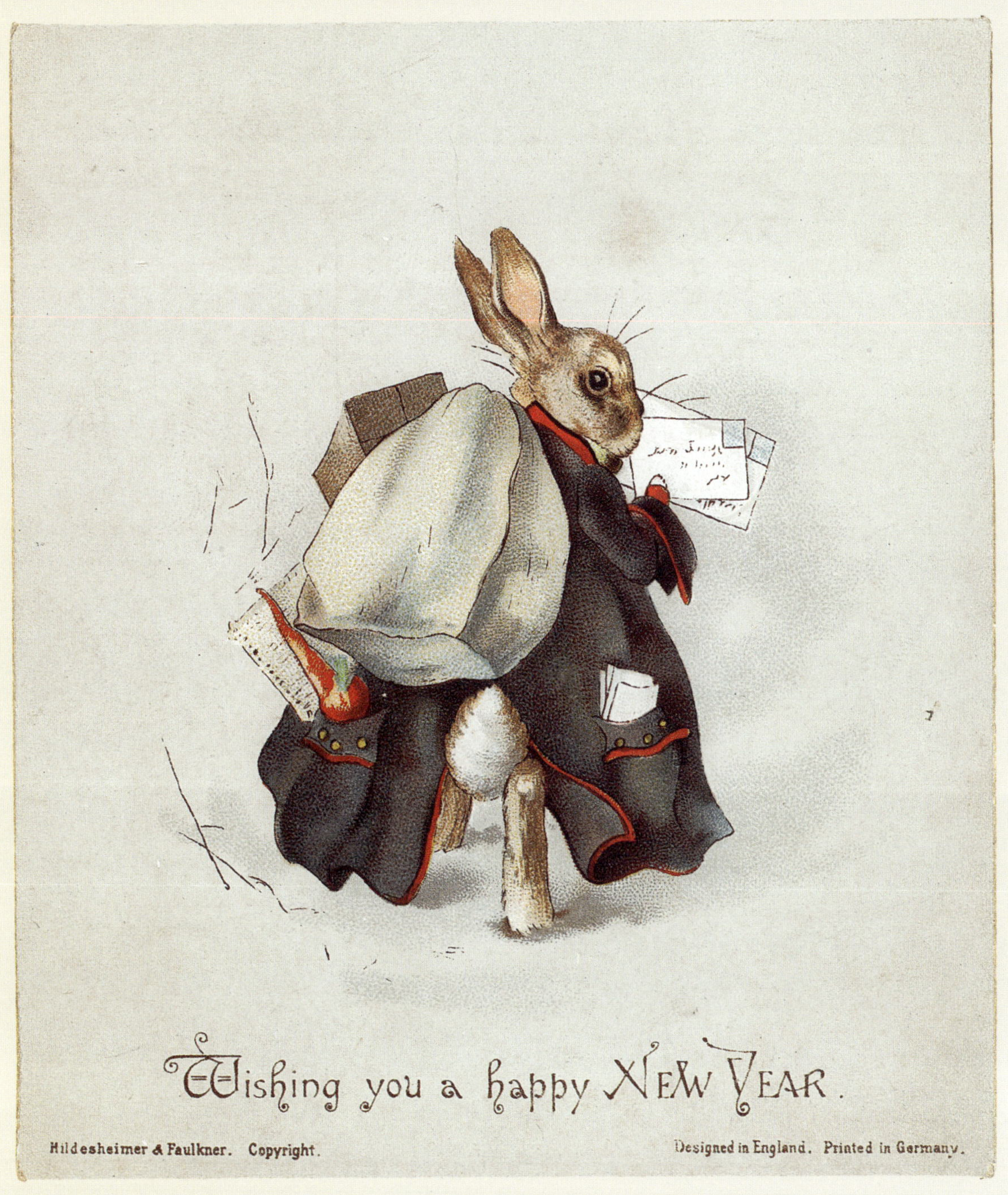

105.
'Postman' greetings card,
published by Hildesheimer & Faulkner, 1890
Chromolithograph on card
V&A: BP.569(A), Linder Bequest LB 1791

Potter's first card designs were inspired by her rabbit Benjamin Bouncer and took her two months to complete. Always keeping in mind the final product, she adapted her use of colour so that her designs could be reproduced well using the colour printing method, chromolithography. Even so, the results were not satisfactory and she reportedly never liked them.

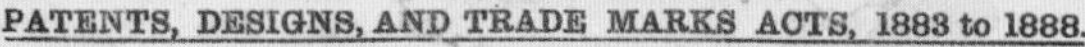

PATENTS, DESIGNS, AND TRADE MARKS ACTS, 1883 to 1888.

Certificate of Registration of Design.

Rd. No. 423888

THE PATENT OFFICE: DESIGNS BRANCH,
25, SOUTHAMPTON BUILDINGS,
CHANCERY LANE, LONDON, W.C.,

1903.

This is to certify that the Design, of which annexed is a Copy, was registered this 28th day of December, 1903, in respect of the application of such Design to articles comprised in Class Twelve in pursuance and subject to the provisions of the Patents, Designs, and Trade Marks Acts, 1883 to 1888.

C. N. DALTON.

Messs Fredk. Warne & Co.

EXTRACT FROM DESIGNS RULES, 1898.

Rule 5.—For Rule 32 of the Designs Rules, 1890, shall be substituted the following Rule:—

32. Before delivery on sale of any article to which a registered design has been applied, the proprietor of such design shall if such article is included in Class 13 or Class 14 in the Third Schedule hereto cause each such article to be marked with the abbreviation Regd., and shall, if such article is included in any of the Classes 1 to 12 in the Third Schedule hereto, cause each such article to be marked with the abbreviation Rd., and also, in the case of articles other than lace, with the number appearing on the certificate of registration.

W B & L (55Ds)—5677—10500-8-3
10946—10500-8-3

106.
The Peter Rabbit Doll made by Beatrix Potter, certificate of registration of design assigned to Frederick Warne & Co., 28 December 1903
Gelatin silver bromide print, ink, embossed paper seal attached with tape
Warne Archive

Following the immediate success of *The Tale of Peter Rabbit*, Potter created a prototype Peter Rabbit doll. Made from velveteen and fur, with brush bristles for the whiskers and lead shot in its feet for balance, the design was registered in 1903. However, this version was never produced commercially. A similar German toy rabbit appeared in the shops soon after and was sold as 'Peter', much to Potter's disdain.

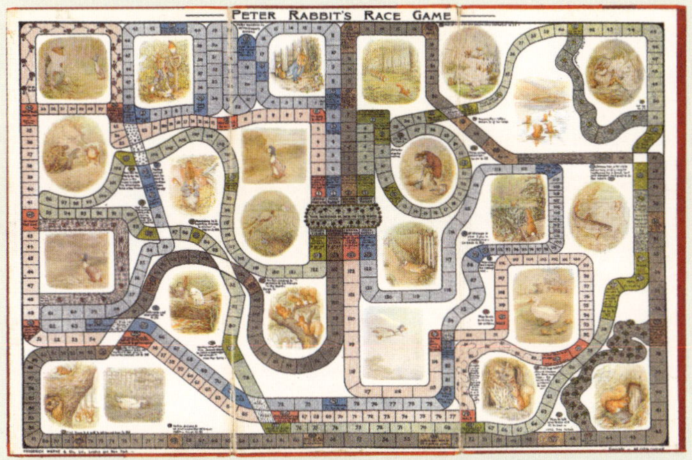

In 1904 Potter came up with a design for *The Game of Peter Rabbit*. It was overly complicated, however, so was never put into production. Fifteen years later, Mary Warne, the wife of Potter's publisher, developed a new board game that featured more of Potter's characters. Potter preferred her own earlier version 'because it is a game of skill and more like the book', but recognized that 'Mary's version might easily be the better seller'.[2] *The Peter Rabbit Race Game* went into production in 1919 and was a great success.

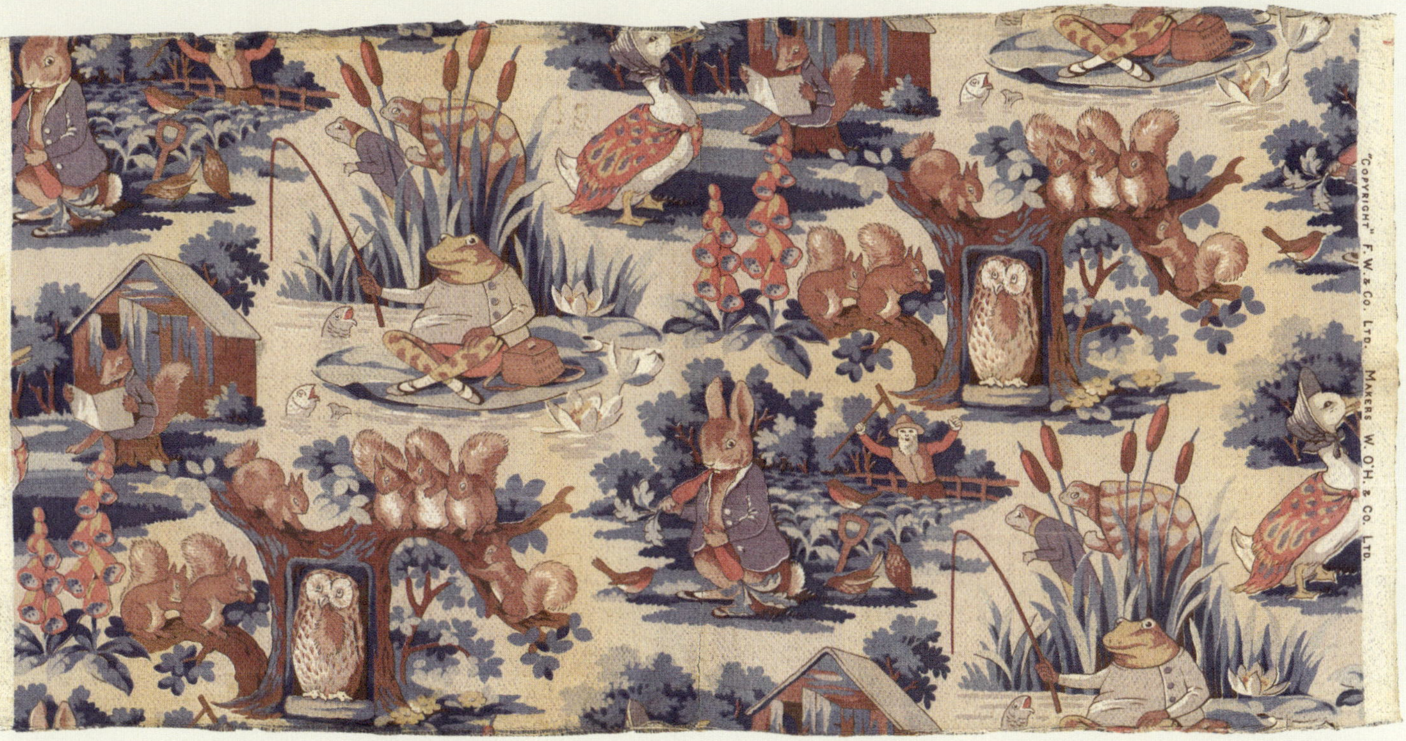

107. Top
Frederick Warne & Co.
The Peter Rabbit Race Game, Style II, c.1920
Chromolithograph on paper and card
Warne Archive

108. Above
O'Hanlon & Co.
Chintz, 1923
Printed cotton fabric
Warne Archive

Messrs O'Hanlon approached Frederick Warne & Co. in 1923 with a design for cretonne fabric. Warne submitted the design to Potter for her approval and she responded by saying, 'The chintz is rather crude, but well designed; well covered & repeats well. The animals are awful. The fact that they are sketchy does not explain the want of anatomy'.[3] Despite these comments, the cretonne was manufactured and O'Hanlon & Co. retained the license for three years.

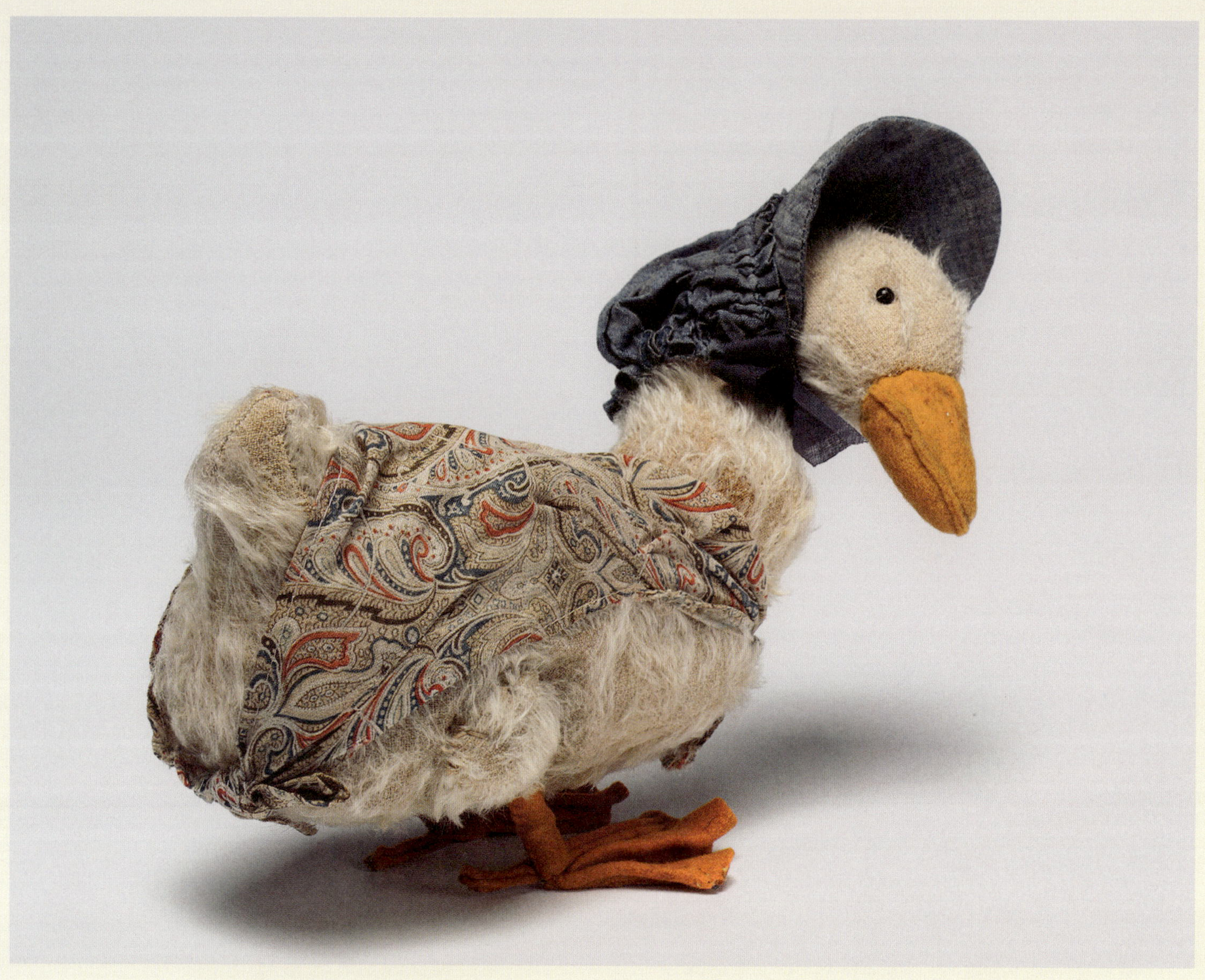

109.
J.K. Farnell
Jemima Puddle-Duck doll, c.1925
Mohair body, cotton hat and shawl, felt beak and feet, and glass eyes
Warne Archive

In 1910 Potter registered the design for a Jemima Puddle-Duck doll. She contacted the company J.K. Farnell to manufacture the doll, negotiated the agreement with them herself and visited their factory in Acton, west London, to collect the royalties. With mohair to imitate her feathers, Jemima wore a cotton hat and shawl and had movable parts, which made her extremely popular.

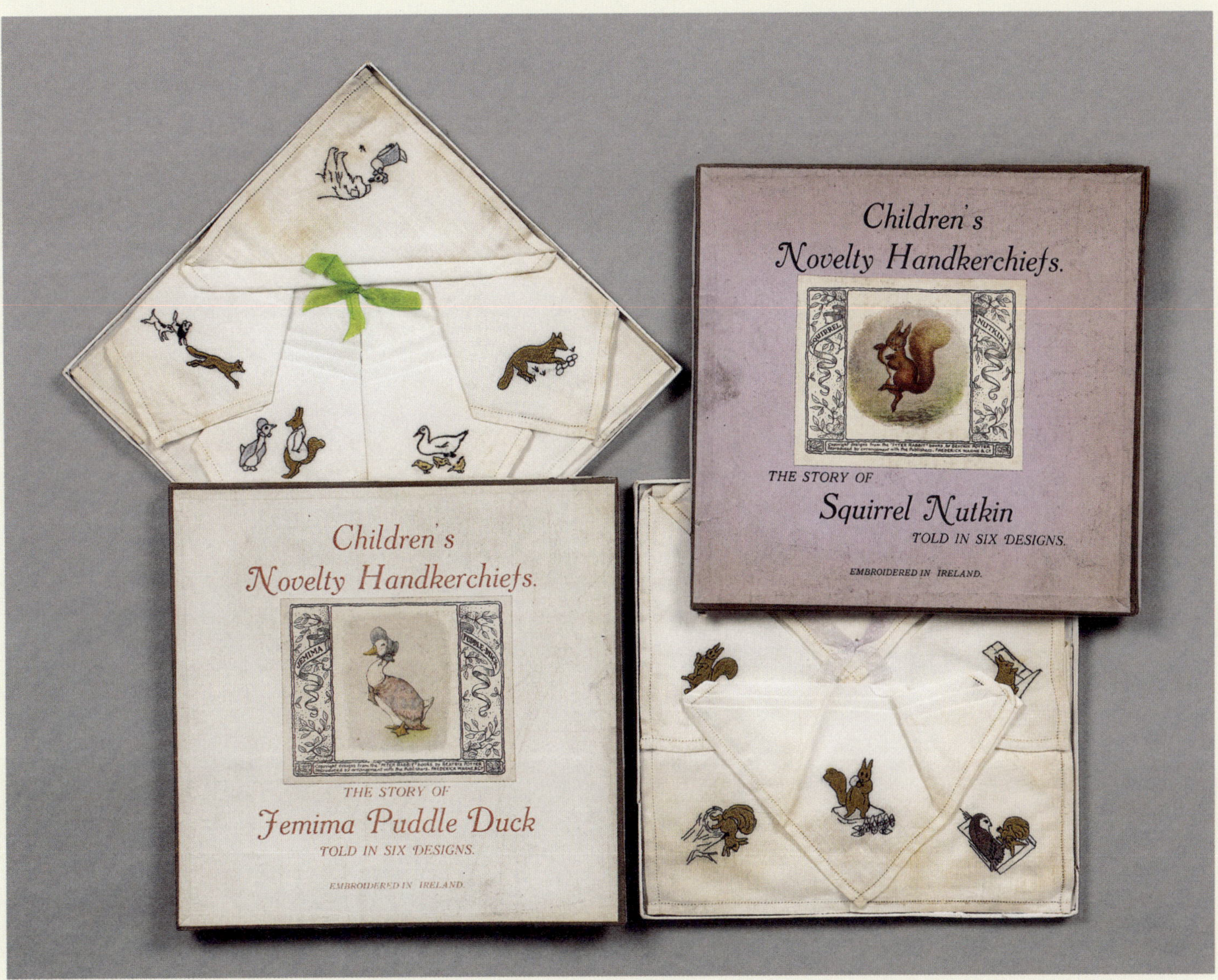

110.
John Brown & Co.
Embroidered handkerchief, 1917
Embroidered cotton fabric and chromolithograph on card box
Warne Archive

Embroidered cotton handkerchiefs featuring scenes from *The Tale of Squirrel Nutkin* (1903) and *The Tale of Jemima Puddle-Duck* (1908) were produced by John Brown & Co. in 1918. Potter was very pleased with them: 'The handkerchiefs are wonderful! I feel sure they will have a good sale – of course the stitching at that price of 6d each must have limitations, but the boxes alone are enough to sell it'.[4]

Sara Glenn

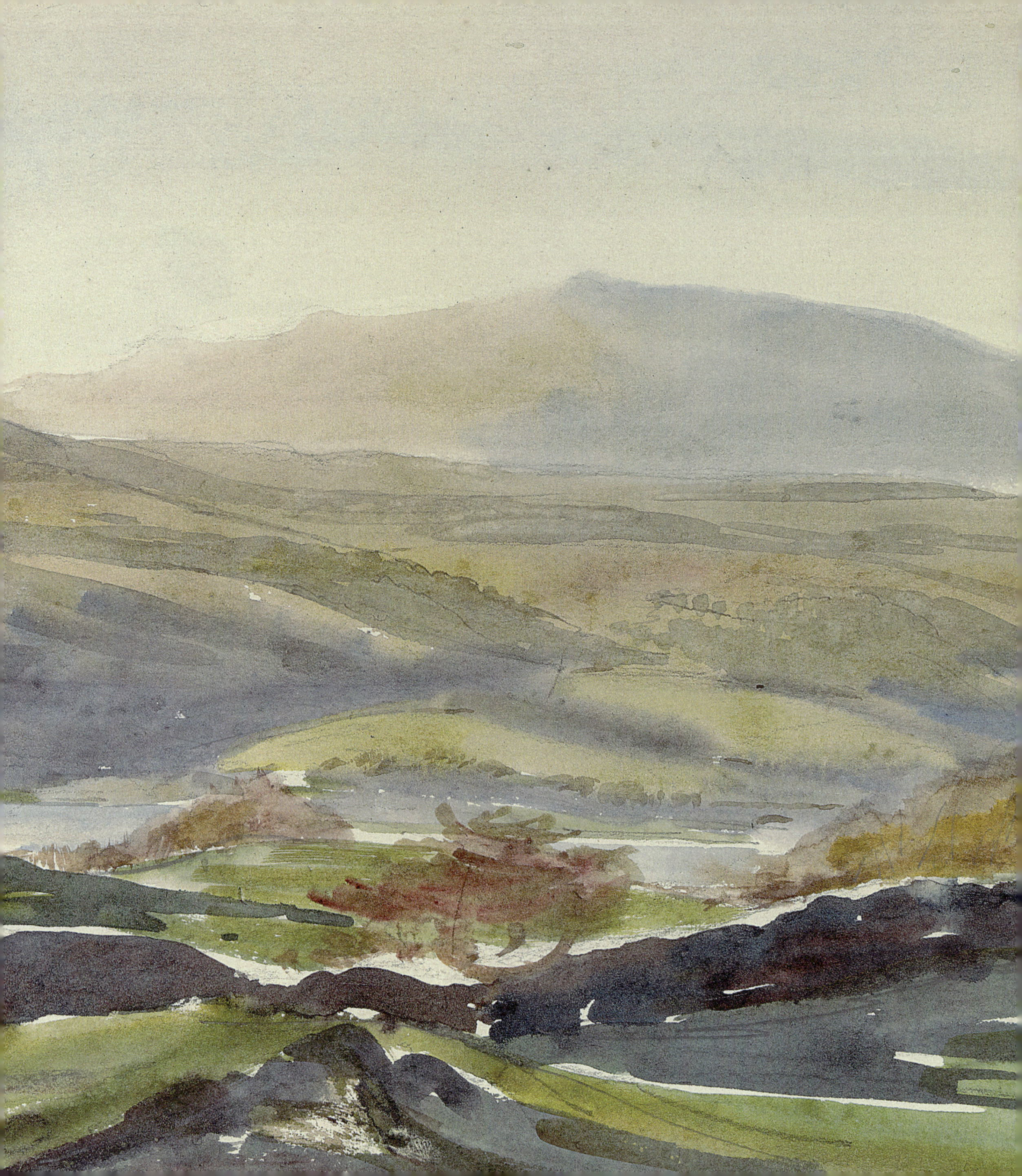

Living Nature

Beatrix Potter in the Lake District

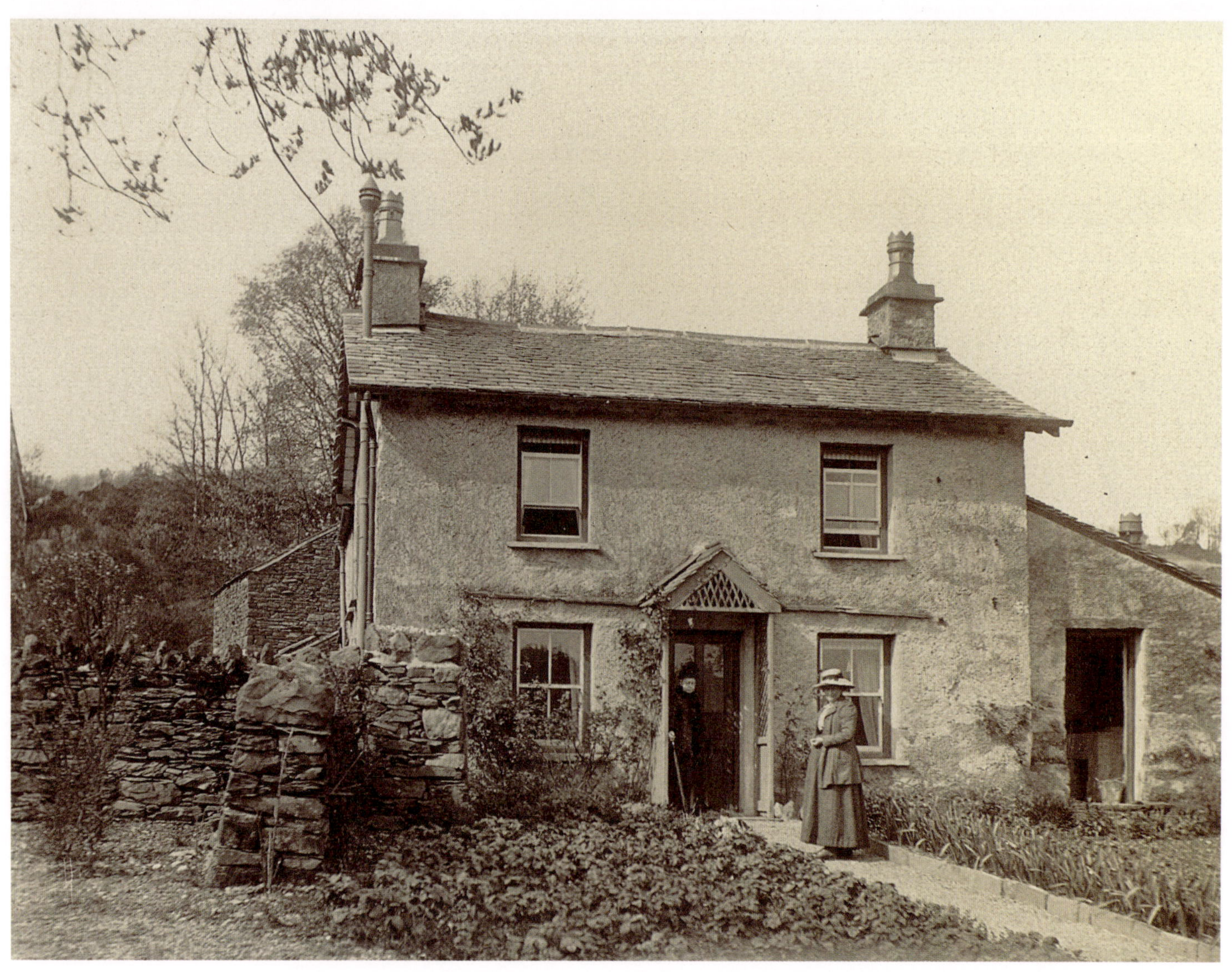

I do not remember a time when I did not try to invent pictures and make for myself a fairyland amongst the wild flowers, the animals, fungi, mosses, woods and streams, all the thousand objects of the countryside; that pleasant, unchanging world of realism and romance, which in our northern clime is stiffened by hard weather, a tough ancestry, and the strength that comes from the hills.

(BEATRIX POTTER, LETTER TO BERTHA MAHONY MILLER FOR *THE HORN BOOK*, 25 NOVEMBER 1940)[1]

111.
Rupert Potter (1832–1914)
Beatrix Potter and her mother, Helen, at Castle Cottage, Sawrey, 1909
Albumen print on paper
V&A: AAD/2006/4/529, given by Joan Duke

What we have loved,
Others will love, and we
will teach them how

(WILLIAM WORDSWORTH, *THE PRELUDE*, 1850)[4]

When, in 1943, the National Trust Secretary, Donald Matheson, described Beatrix Potter as a 'many-sided genius',[2] he summed up perfectly her multiple legacies. Her observations and recordings of the minutiae of the natural world were exquisitely rendered. Her little books demonstrated her consummate skill as both storyteller and illustrator. In the management of her farms she showed dedication and attention to detail as well as a determination to succeed in a notoriously closed and male-dominated world. As a landowner she recognized the need to conserve the inspirational landscapes of the Lake District, while ensuring they remained living, working spaces in which the people among whom she had settled could thrive. Through all these aspects of Potter's life runs a common thread: inspiration drawn from nature with a respect for the beauty, and sometimes harsh realities, of rural life.

AN ENGLISH ARCADIA

Potter followed in a long and distinguished line of artists and writers who had been captivated by the English Lake District. The idea of the Lake District as a symbol of the inspiring beauty and majesty of nature developed from the mid-eighteenth century onwards. Up until then, it had been a wild and virtually inaccessible place, which had slowly developed from dense woodland into grazed valleys and fells, providing its farmers with income sufficient to expand their dwellings into comfortable farmhouses containing handsome carved-oak furniture, although it continued to be an isolated region.[3] When the Napoleonic Wars (1800–15) put a halt to European excursions, British grand tourists looking for dramatic scenery ventured to the north-west corner of their own country. Earlier, the accounts of travellers such as Thomas Gray and Thomas West had been published, encouraging artists and poets to follow, keen to capture the scenery – Lake District tourism had begun. Further guides explained to the now steady stream of visitors what to look at and where to stand in order to appreciate the perfect views. William Wordsworth's romantic vision acknowledged the importance of people, specifically farmers, in the shaping of the Lake District landscape. He also advocated future development being in harmony with the land and its traditions.

The region started to be regarded as the peak of England's beauty and a symbol of national pride. Anything that might threaten this northern Arcadia was to be fiercely guarded against. So, from the mid-nineteenth century, as the flocks of tourists began to outnumber the sheep, the voices warning that both tourism and industry would despoil the area became louder.[5] Those, such as John Ruskin, who were passionate about the spiritual benefits to be gained by visiting the Lakes, also vigorously expounded the need for protection. This was part of an emerging broader environmentalist movement that articulated the risks of industrial development continuing unchecked.

Ruskin's campaigning inspired many, including a young Reverend Hardwicke Drummond Rawnsley. In turn Potter, like many, was influenced by Rawnsley's passion and enthusiasm for preserving the countryside and the rural way of life. She was, however, also furnished with the means to turn these thoughts and ideas into a 'splendid reality'.[6]

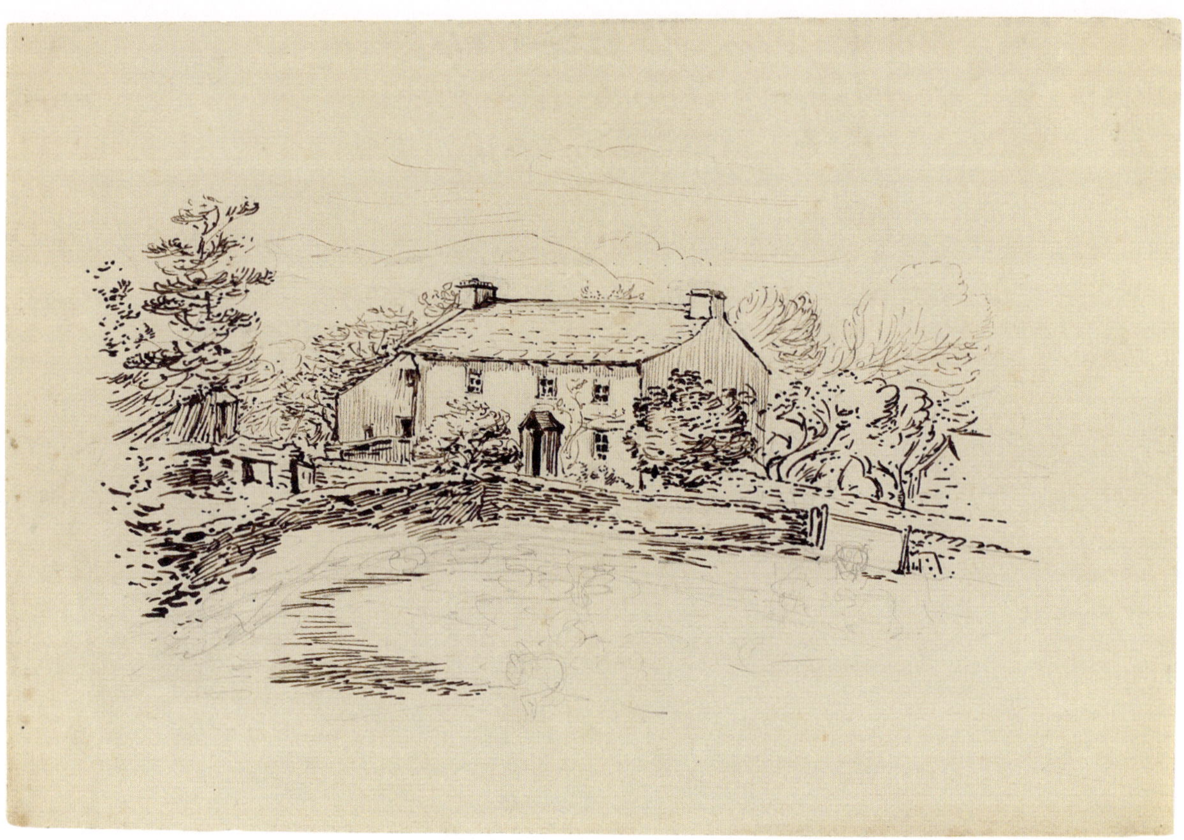

It is in here I go to be quiet and still with myself.

(BEATRIX POTTER TO ULLA HYDE PARKER, C.1940)[7]

A PLACE OF HER OWN

Beatrix Potter's introduction to the Lake District, starting in 1882, was by no means love at first sight but it was to have such an impression on her that, once she had the means, some 23 years later, she would purchase a small corner of it (nos 111–13), so she might escape her 'unloved birthplace' in London.[8] Her purchase of Hill Top farm was the first in a train of events that culminated in an astonishing achievement: the gift to the nation of a considerable swathe of the Lake District.

Potter's purchase was made possible through the success of her earliest books and a small legacy from her aunt, Harriet Burton. She was familiar with the village of Sawrey (no.114) from having spent holidays in the area and had determined to find somewhere of her own there as soon as she was able; Hill Top farm came up for sale in 1905 and by October it was hers. The sale could not have been concluded at a better time. Reeling as she was from the sudden loss of her

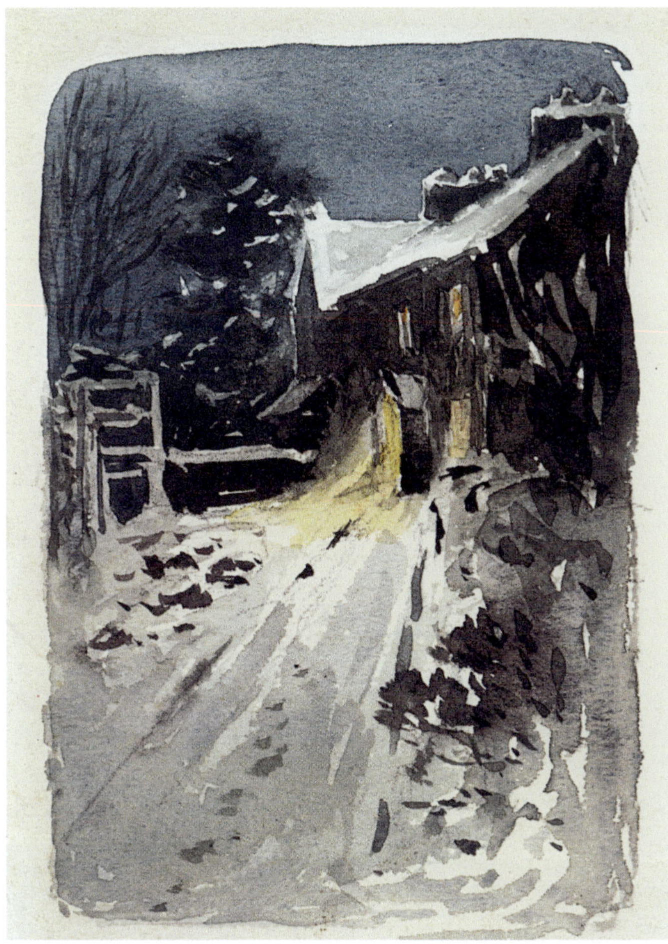

112. Opposite
Early sketch of Hill Top, Sawrey, 1905
Ink and pencil on paper
V&A: LC 15/A/1, given by the Linder Collection

113. Above
Hill Top by night, 1908–12,
possibly December 1912
Watercolour on paper
V&A: BP.294, Linder Bequest LB 445

fiancé Norman Warne and unable to grieve openly, Potter needed a bolthole. Hill Top offered peace and tranquillity and the distraction of planning and supervising alterations, as well as taking the garden in hand – it was a place where she could heal: 'The garden is very overgrown & untidy, I hope next time you come it will be straighter, I have got the quarryman making walks & beds.'[9]

As Potter settled into life in Sawrey, albeit in snatched breaks away from domestic obligations to her parents, her lack of conformity began to show. When she could negotiate a summer holiday home for the family nearby, she was freed from the constraints of her Kensington life, and was able to spend less time socializing and more time with her animals: 'I spent a very wet hour *inside* the pig stye drawing the pig. It tries to nibble my boots, which is interrupting.'[10]

The boots were soon replaced with clogs and accompanied by a heavy Herdwick wool tweed skirt, accessorized with a piece of sacking to keep off the rain. On more than one occasion she was mistaken for a pedlar, as far removed from the wealthy author as one could possibly imagine; this was a state of affairs that suited the publicity-shy Potter very well.

In contrast to the heavily stuffed Japanned furnishings that typified her Kensington home, Potter would be influenced by an altogether more vernacular style for the interiors at Hill Top (nos 115–16). This was not merely a case of appropriateness. She had been exposed to a wealth of artistic and design influences throughout her early life (see 'Town and Country', pp.32–8). A side effect of her crippling shyness was that she observed and absorbed with a critical eye. When it came to her own rural idyll, she demonstrated a rejection of urban contagion, perhaps inspired by her neighbours' efforts on display at the newly refurbished Coniston Institute. Following the death of Ruskin, the likes of furniture and textile designer Charles Francis Annesley Voysey (1857–1941), artist and local historian William Gershom Collingwood (1854–1932, also a friend of Rawnsley) and Kendal-based wood carver Arthur W. Simpson (1857–1922) passionately championed exhibitions of arts and crafts. Amateur artists and craftspeople were urged to bring a high degree of excellence and originality to their submissions.

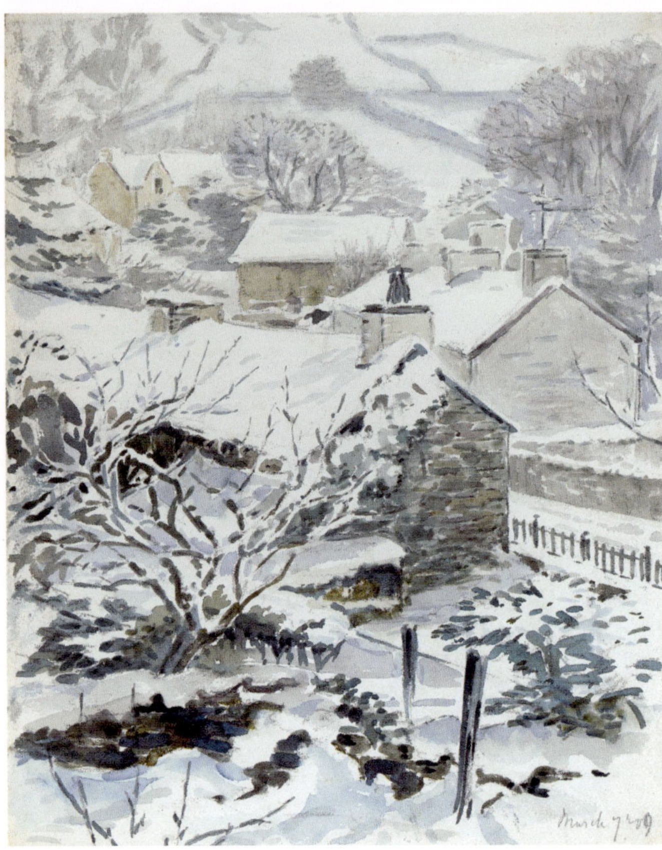

114.
A village in snow, probably Near Sawrey, 7 March 1909
Watercolour over pencil on paper
V&A: BP.1157, Linder Bequest LB 669

Potter indulged in a romantic and eclectic gathering and arranging of her possessions, an activity that she relished and which continued until her death.

As she bought more land and property, she was advised by William Heelis, partner in the local firm of solicitors, W.H. Heelis & Son. Heelis's advice extended to helping manage her affairs while she was away from the area. She began to rely on him, their relationship blossomed and in 1912 he proposed marriage. Potter accepted, despite her parent's misgivings, and she was finally able to make a permanent move and live among her beloved lakes and fells.

Within Hill Top there are rush-seated, ladder-backed chairs of the north-country style, a Lakeland court cupboard dated 1667, purchased at a nearby farm sale, and an Ulverston chest with carved tulip, pomegranate and vine patterns (no.118): 'This Ulverston chest has a running vine, a leaf and bunch of grapes design which occurs on Ulverston cupboards. I should be inclined to derive this pattern from the influence of Furness Abbey.'[11]

Potter enjoyed learning about the Lakeland vernacular furniture, seeking out examples and noting the variations she came across as well as theorizing over the influence of other 'off comers' on their development: 'I do think that some of the old joiners and carvers must have been familiar with such patterns as those on the Gosfirth Cross *[sic]*.'[12]

Many of the pieces were bought at farm sales locally. Alongside these were some personal items that Potter gathered and decided to keep at Hill Top: her grandmother's copper warming pan, bed hangings and a Thonet bentwood chair from the bedroom she used at her grandparents' Hertfordshire home (which featured in early illustrations; see, for example, no.73), joined by items sent by young fans from all over the world, such as a small grass bag, a green morocco leather writing box and a penholder. Later, she set large oil paintings by her brother Bertram into wall panels in an extension she had built, with husband William creating a carved lintel over the door.

This glorious mix of objects from rustic to genteel to the downright bizarre (there are three door knockers,

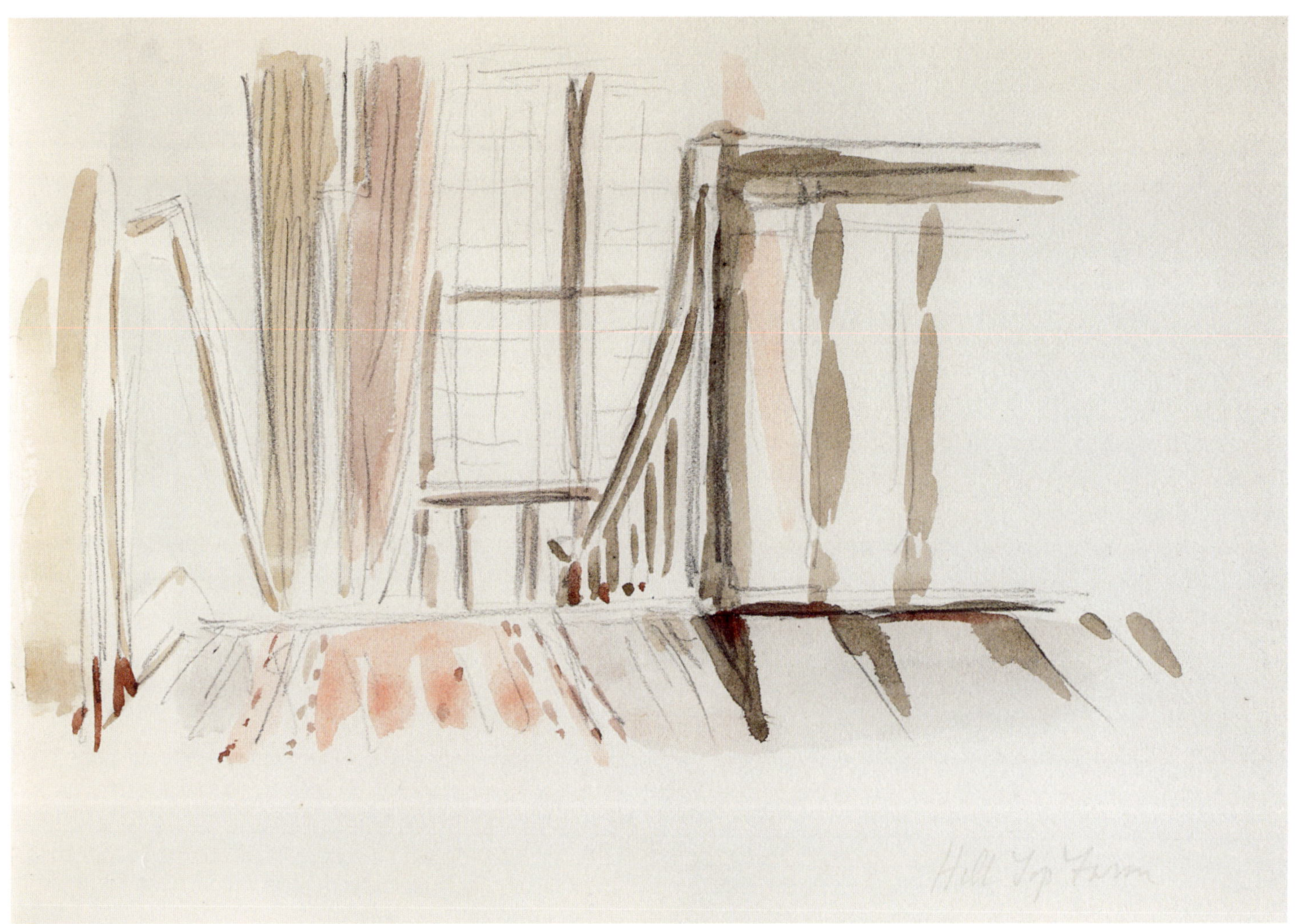

115.
Page from a sketchbook, first-floor landing of Hill Top, Sawrey, 1907
Watercolour over pencil on paper
National Trust, 242721

two of which are on internal doors) showed Potter's strong emotional connection to a place she could at last call her own. This was the place destined to become her memorial, the spiritual home of the characters that inhabited not just her books, but also her imagination. In a candid moment she shared her feelings for the cottage with her cousin, Ulla Hyde Parker:

> It is in here I go to be quiet and still with myself. This is me, the deepest me, the part one has to be alone with. So, you see, when [...] Willie asked me to marry him I said yes but I also said we cannot live here at Hill Top. We will live at Castle Cottage, as I must leave everything here as it is. So, after I married I just locked the door and left.[13]

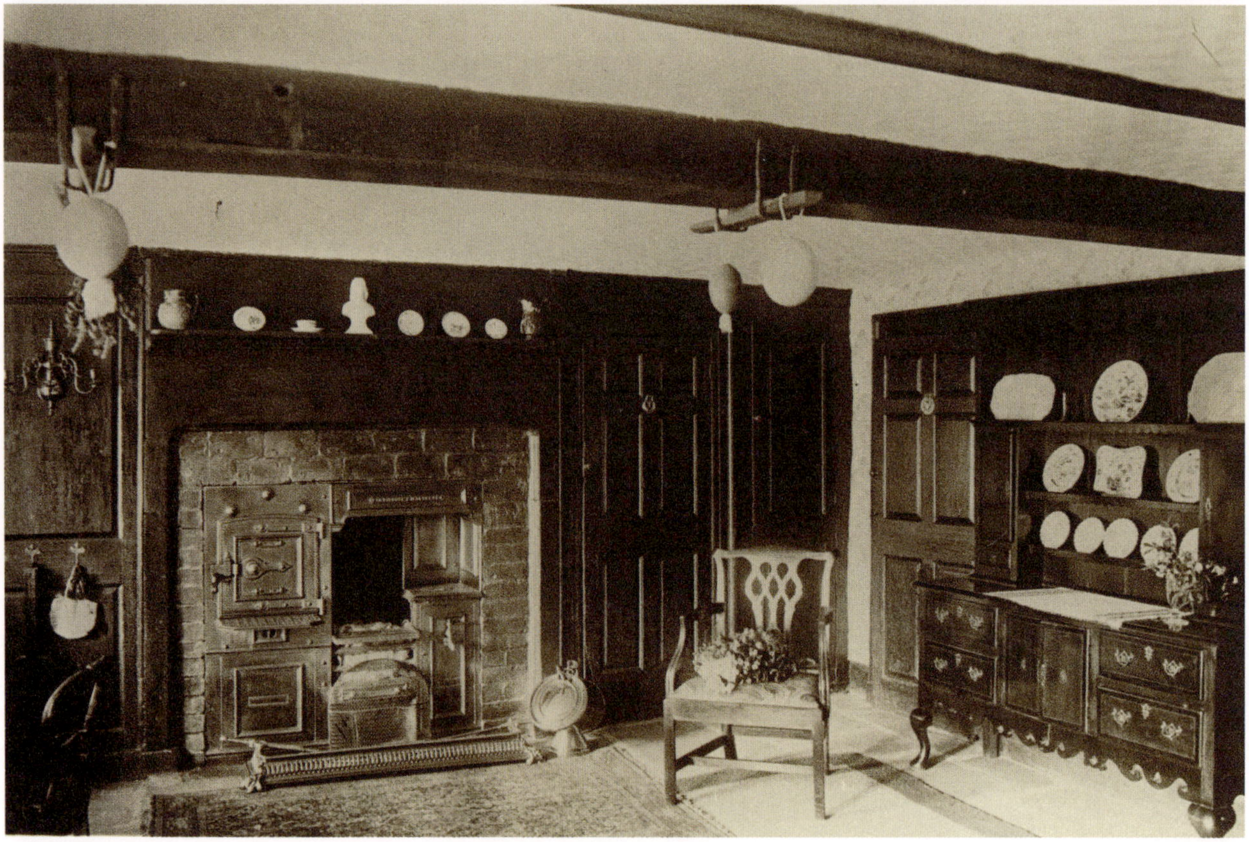

116. Above
Rupert Potter (1832–1914)
The firehouse of Hill Top, Sawrey, before alterations, c.1908
Albumen print on paper
V&A: BP.1296, Linder Bequest LB 2025

117. Right
The Roly-Poly Pudding; later renamed *The Tale of Samuel Whiskers*
Pages from a manuscript, c.1906
Watercolour and ink on paper
V&A: BP.596, Linder Bequest LB 1162

118. Opposite
Notes for a draft of a letter from Beatrix Heelis to Bertha Mahony Miller, 11 October 1940
Pencil on paper
National Trust, 242302

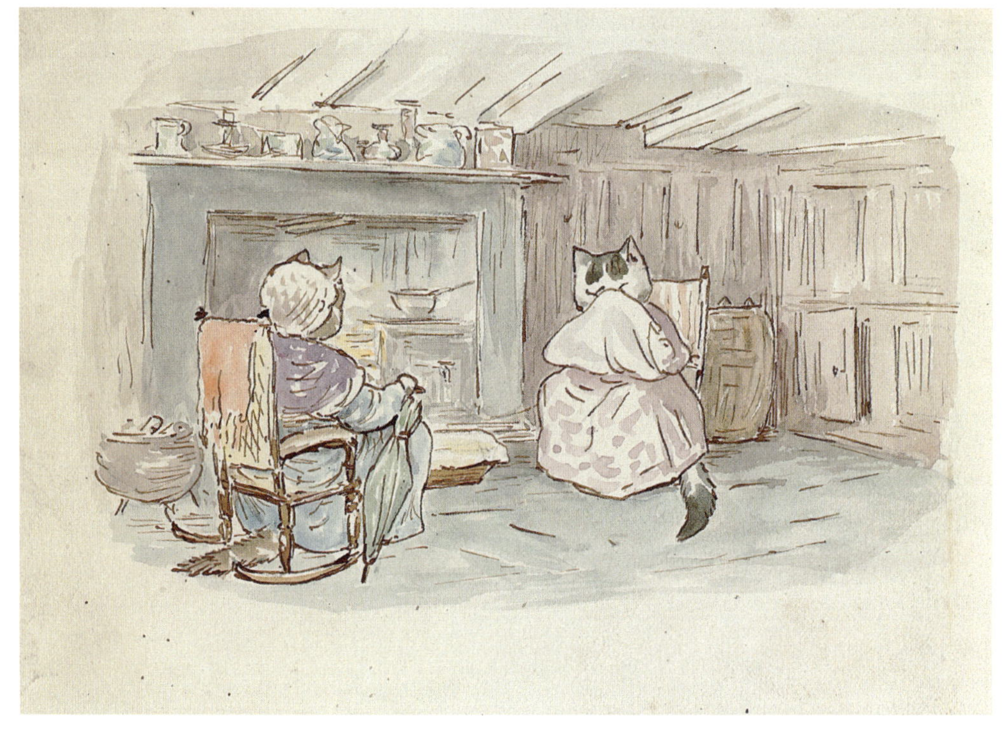

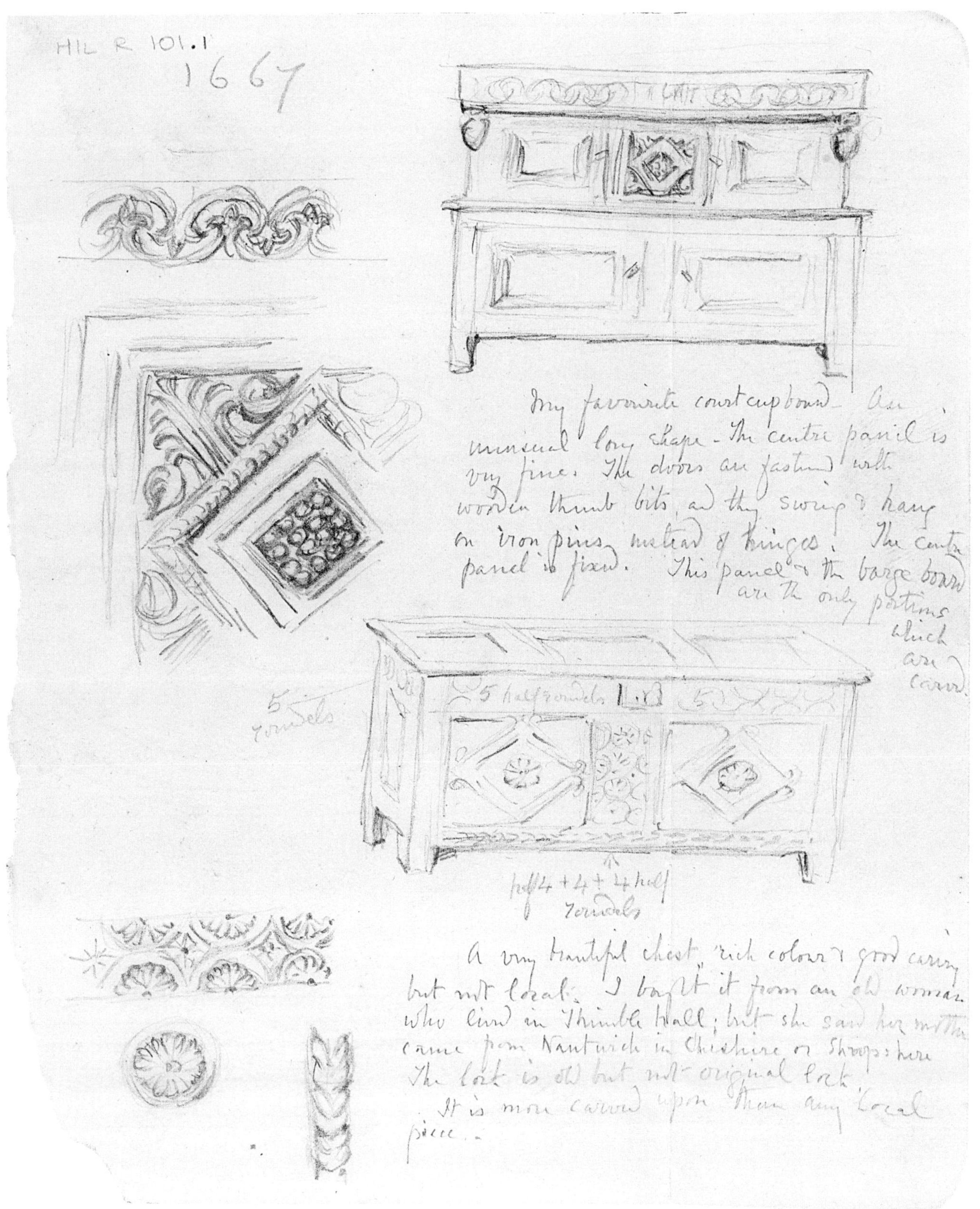
HIL R 101.1
1667
My favourite court cupboard. An unusual long shape. The centre panel is very fine. The doors are fastened with wooden thumb bits, and they swing & hang on iron pins instead of hinges. The centre panel is fixed. This panel & the barge board are the only portions which are carved.
5 rondels
5 half roundels
half 4 + 4 + 4 half roundels
A very beautiful chest, rich colour & good carving but not local. I bought it from an old woman who lived in Thimble Hall; but she said her mother came from Nantwich in Cheshire or Shropshire. The lock is old but not original lock.
It is more carved upon than any local piece.

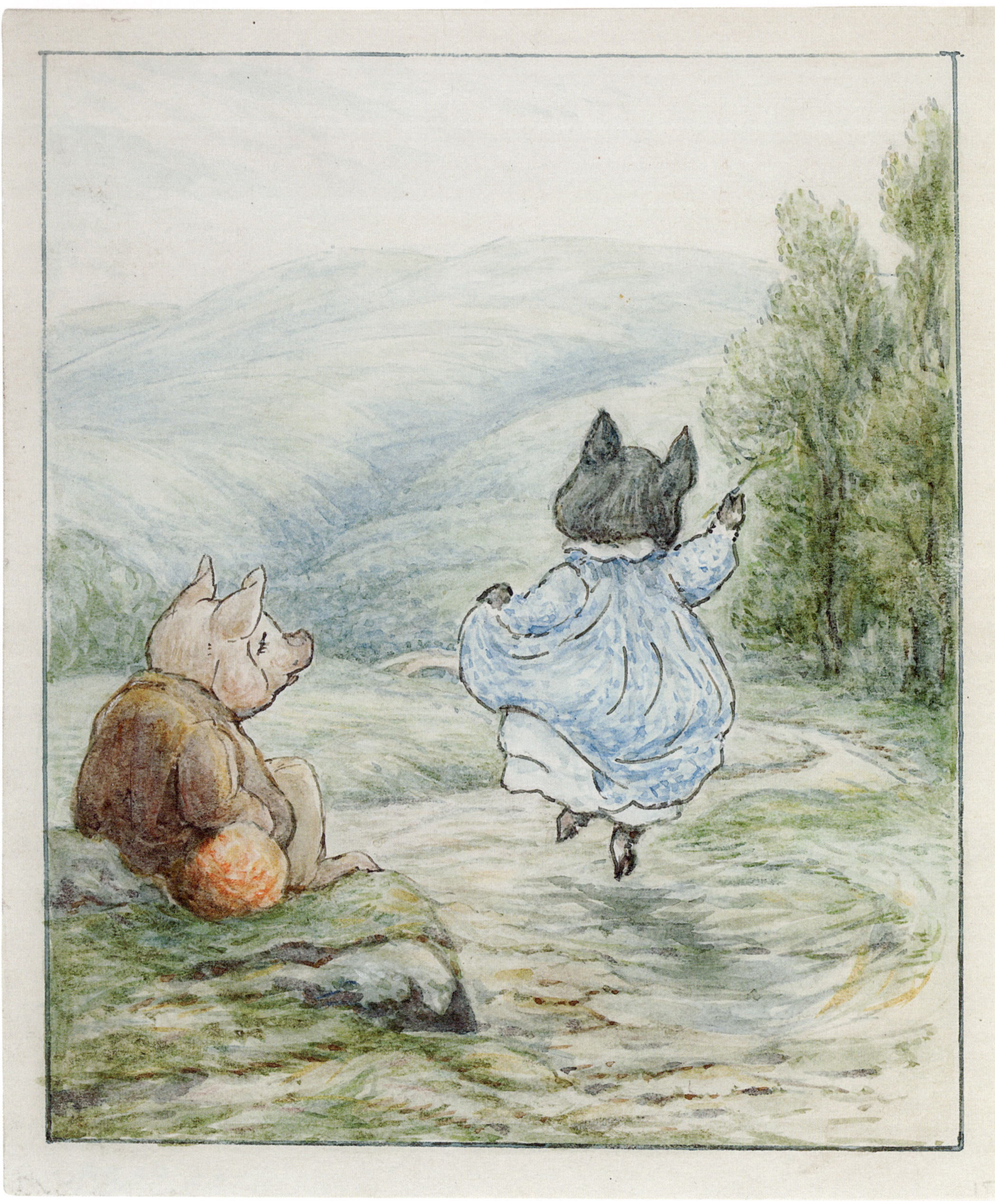

119. Opposite
The Tale of Pigling Bland artwork, May–September 1913
Watercolour and ink over pencil on paper
National Trust, 242792

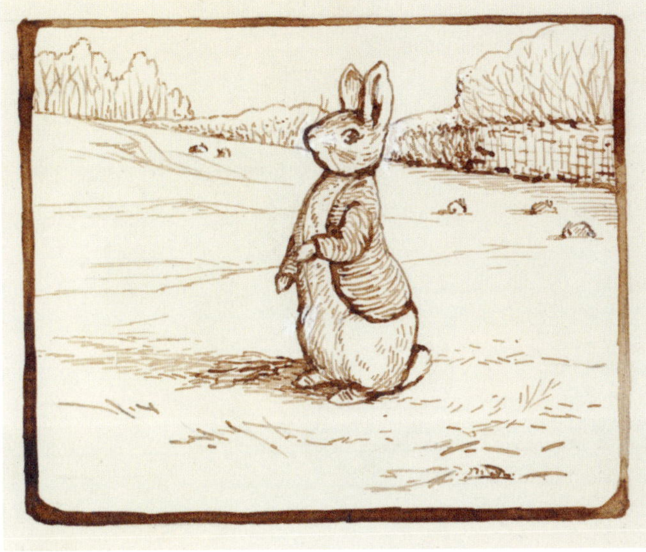

120. Above
The Tale of Mr. Tod artwork, 1912
Ink on paper
National Trust, 242860

Having offered Hill Top as a place for William Hyde Parker (her cousin Ulla's husband) to recuperate after a wartime accident, Beatrix and William were invited to join them at Hill Top for a Christmas party. Hoping to delight her host, Ulla had decorated a tree, complete with candles, which she lit just as Beatrix arrived. To Ulla's dismay Beatrix's response was one of horror: 'Put the candles out! Put them out at once; the house will catch fire.'[14] The thought that a fire might consume her beloved Hill Top was more than she could bear.

Already immortalized in Sawrey-based tales such as *The Tale of Tom Kitten* (1907), *The Roly-Poly Pudding* (1908, no.117) and others, the house also features in a sentimental description in a draft sequel to her later book, *The Fairy Caravan* (1929):

> First there is the porch made of great slabs of Brathay slate, on either side a slate 6 foot high, with two smaller slates for the roof, and honeysuckle and cabbage roses hanging over. The flowers love the house, they try to come in and do not willingly stay outside the porch.[15]

Hill Top, and the surrounding landscape of Near Sawrey (no.120), were so steeped in Potter's personality that it was inconceivable to her that it might become home to anyone else. In 1913, Beatrix and William achieved their own happy ending together (just like Pigling Bland and Pig-wig, created that same year; no.119) and moved into Castle Cottage, a farmhouse she had purchased with land, adjacent to Hill Top (nos 122–3). In a 1940 letter to a journalist Potter stated that she hoped: 'Some day the National Trust might care to preserve [Hill Top] along with my land.'[16]

Ill health and the advent of the Second World War prevented Beatrix from fully creating what William termed her 'memorial museum',[17] but thanks to a small notebook in the V&A collection, there is a record of some of the couple's discussions.

Aware that the success of her little books would make Hill Top a place of pilgrimage, Beatrix had planned that the house be opened to the public and should pay for itself.

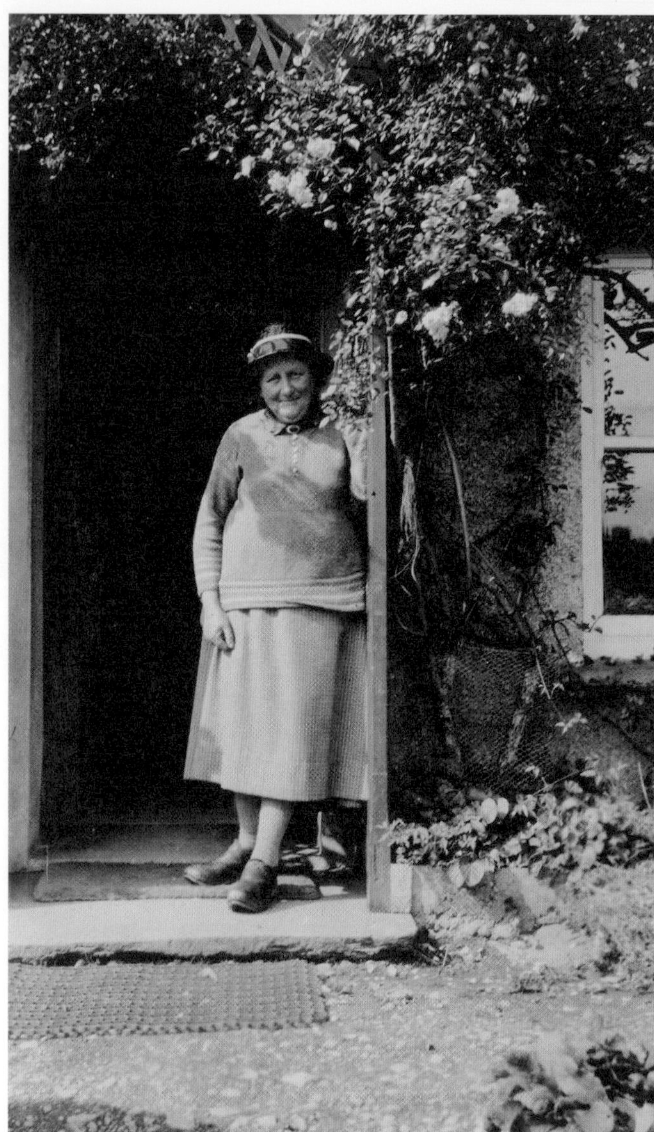

122. Below
Clarence Edmund Fry & Son (active 1893–1916)
Studio portrait of Beatrix and William Heelis,
15 October 1913
Sepia toned photographic print
V&A: AAD/2006/4/462, given by Joan Duke

123. Opposite
Picture letter by Beatrix Heelis sent to June Steel,
from Castle Cottage, Sawrey, Autumn 1926
Ink on paper
Toronto Public Library, Lillian H Smith Collection

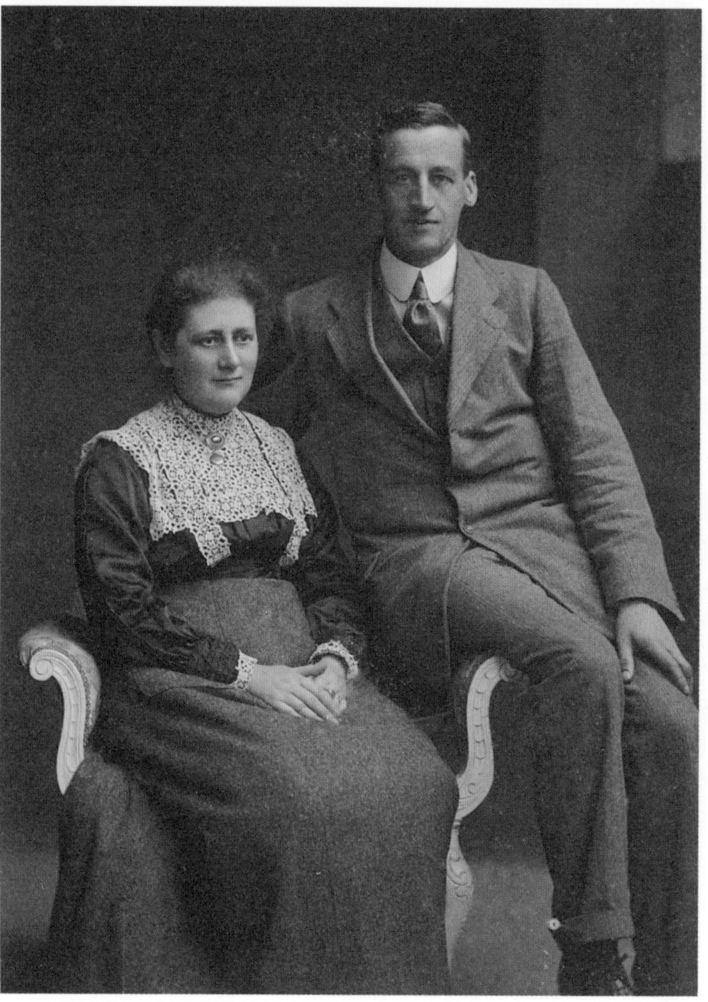

121. Above
Beatrix Heelis at Hill Top, Sawrey,
c.1940
Photographic print on paper in an album
Cotsen Children's Library, Special Collections,
Princeton University Library, 10005.144

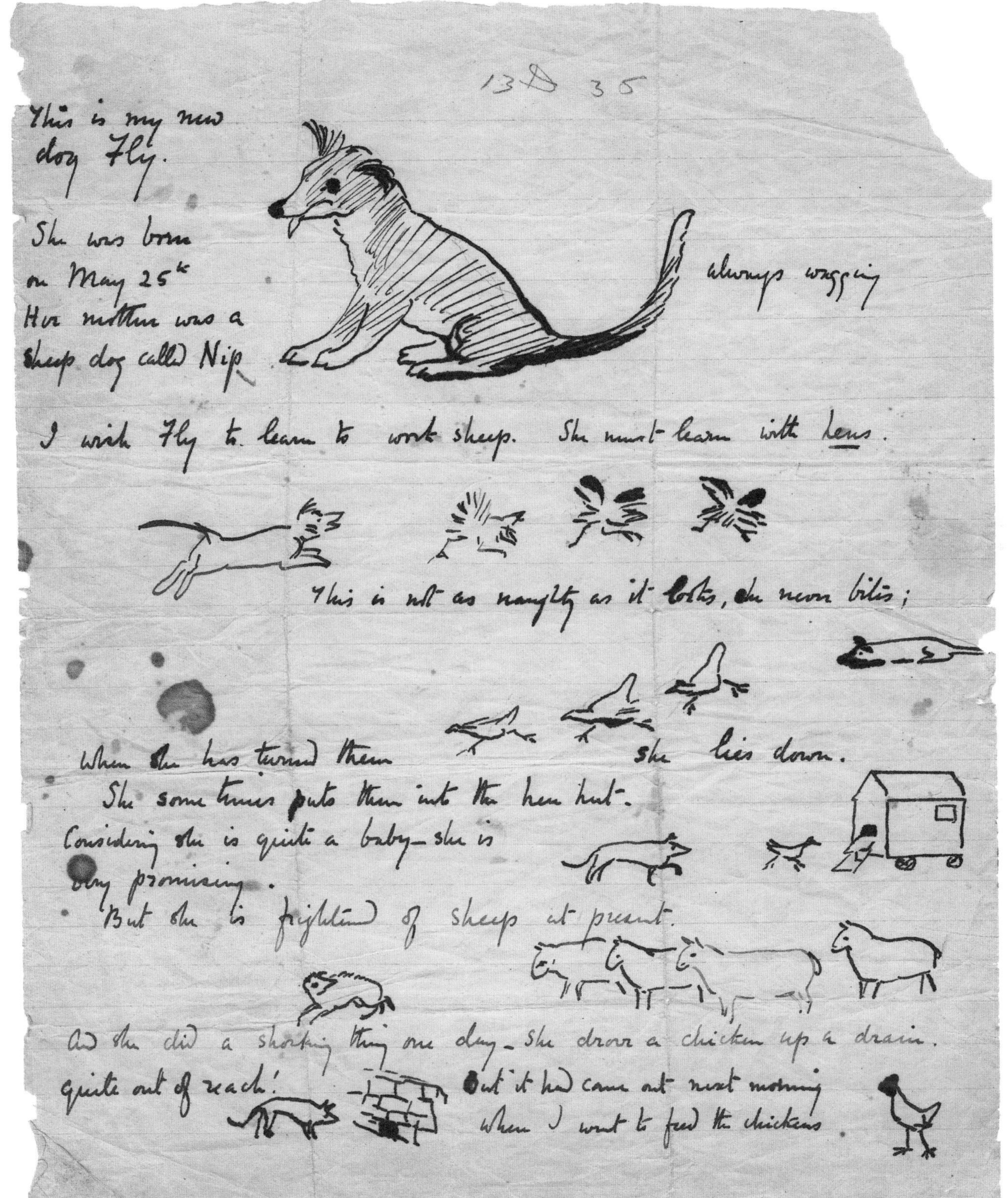

13 D 35

This is my new dog Fly.

She was born on May 25th
Her mother was a sheep dog called Nip.

always wagging

I wish Fly to learn to work sheep. She must learn with hens.

This is not as naughty as it looks, she never bites;

When she has turned them she lies down.

She sometimes puts them into the hen hut.

Considering she is quite a baby – she is very promising.

But she is frightened of sheep at present.

And she did a shocking thing one day – she drove a chicken up a drain. quite out of reach! But it had come out next morning when I went to feed the chickens.

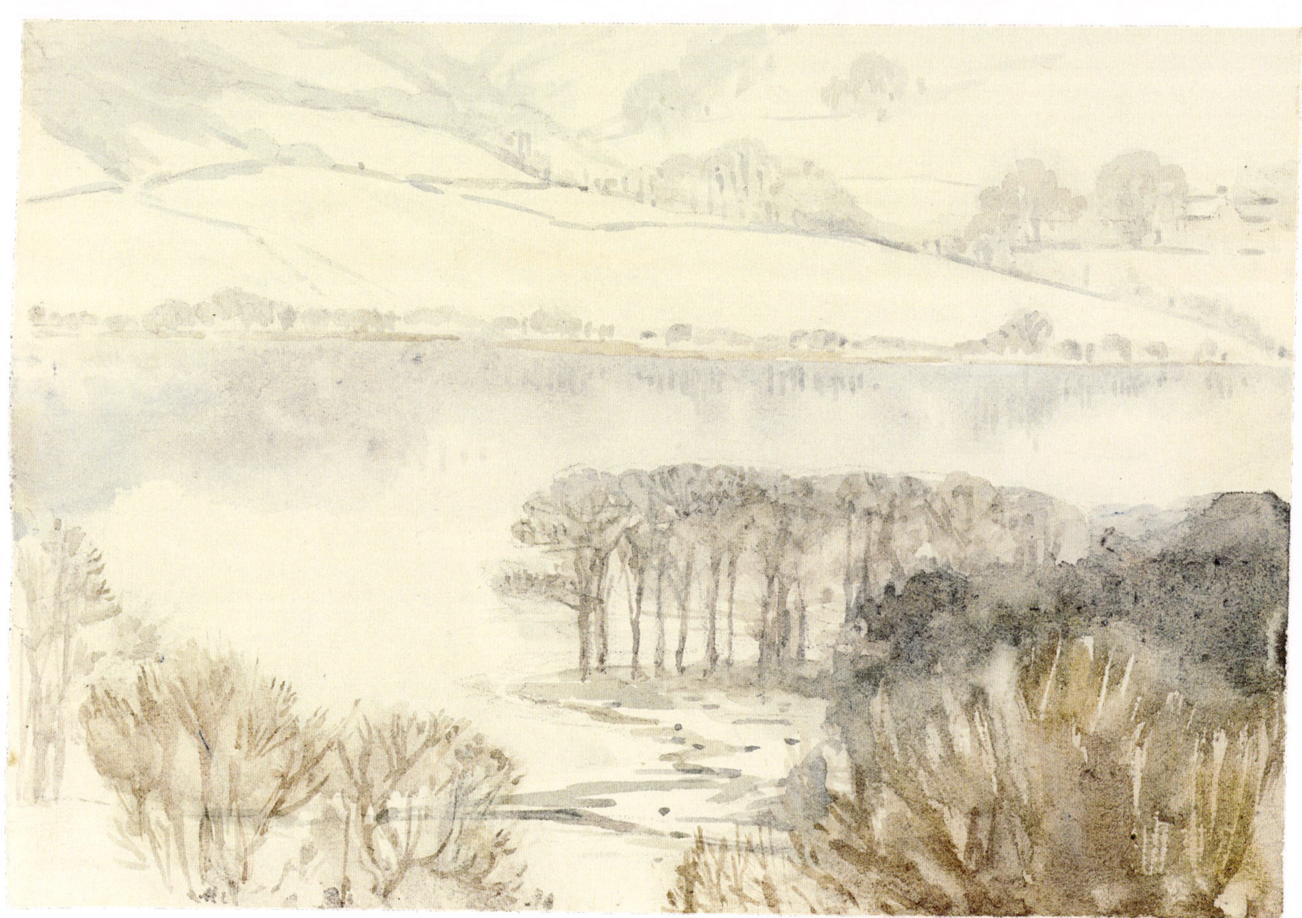

No one can now travel through the more frequented tracts, without being offended, at almost every turn, by an introduction of discordant objects, disturbing that peaceful harmony of form and colour, which had been through a long lapse of ages most happily preserved.

(WILLIAM WORDSWORTH, *A GUIDE TO THE LAKES*, 1835)[18]

PROTECTING THE LAKES

Although it is the most famous of her properties, Hill Top, close to Esthwaite Water, was the first of many Potter came to own and it was where she began to learn how to be a farmer. She spent as much time as possible on the farm, absorbed in helping with lambing and haymaking, gathering bracken for animal bedding and discovering the myriad tasks required in the upkeep of a small farm. The actions of her storybook characters echo the knowledge she was gaining about the way of life she was so keen to pursue herself. Whether they were engaged in village gossip or going off to market, they infuse her whimsical tales with a sense of reality.

From her earliest visits to the Lakes Potter had been made aware of the need to protect this special landscape (nos 124, 125). Shaped by a farming heritage that stretched back for a thousand years,

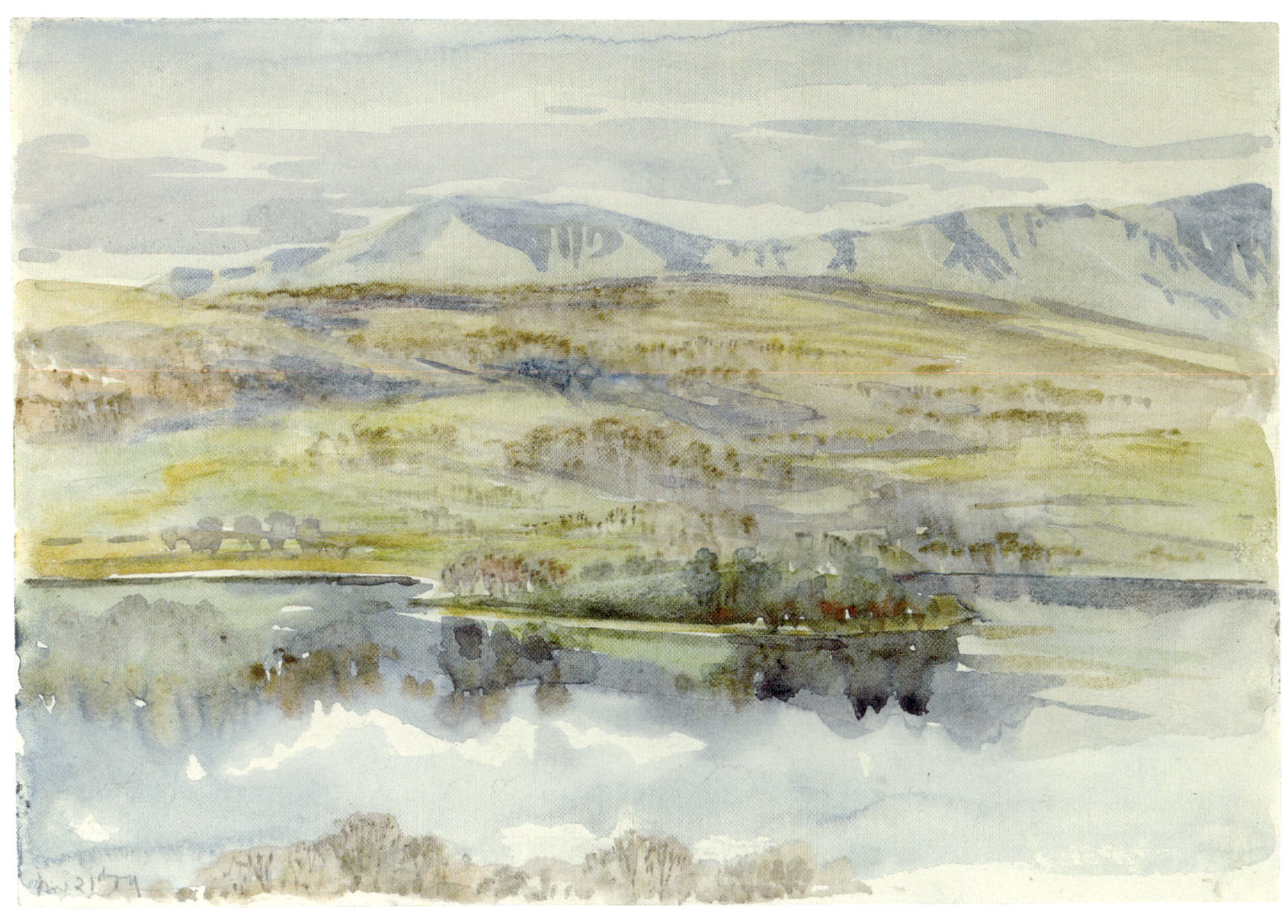

124. Opposite
Esthwaite Water and snow-covered hills, December 1913
Watercolour over pencil on paper
V&A: BP.340, Linder Bequest LB 538

125. Above
View across Esthwaite Water, 21 November 1909
Watercolour over pencil on paper
V&A: BP.1079, Linder Bequest LB 542

126. Overleaf
Rupert Potter (1832–1914)
Beatrix Potter and Canon Hardwick Rawnsley at Broad Leys, Bowness-on-Windermere, 29 July 1912
Albumen print on paper
National Trust, 242454

the area with its lush valleys, woodlands and grazing sheep and cattle had become threatened by its own popularity with those who sought its beauty, peace and tranquillity. Potter's awakening to the vulnerability of the Lake District was thanks to Canon Hardwicke Rawnsley, who had been the vicar at Wray when the Potters had holidayed there in 1882 (no.126).

Already a prolific author, Rawnsley had been impressed by Potter's artistic talent and they shared an interest in the natural world, archaeology and geology. They would maintain their friendship for the next 38 years, with the Potters calling on Rawnsley during holidays to the Lakes. When Potter was taking her first steps into publishing, it was Rawnsley she approached for advice. His assertion that *The Tale of Peter Rabbit* (1902) would be improved by being set into rhyme was one that thankfully she decided against. She did, however, follow his suggestion to approach the firm Frederick Warne & Co. to publish her tales.

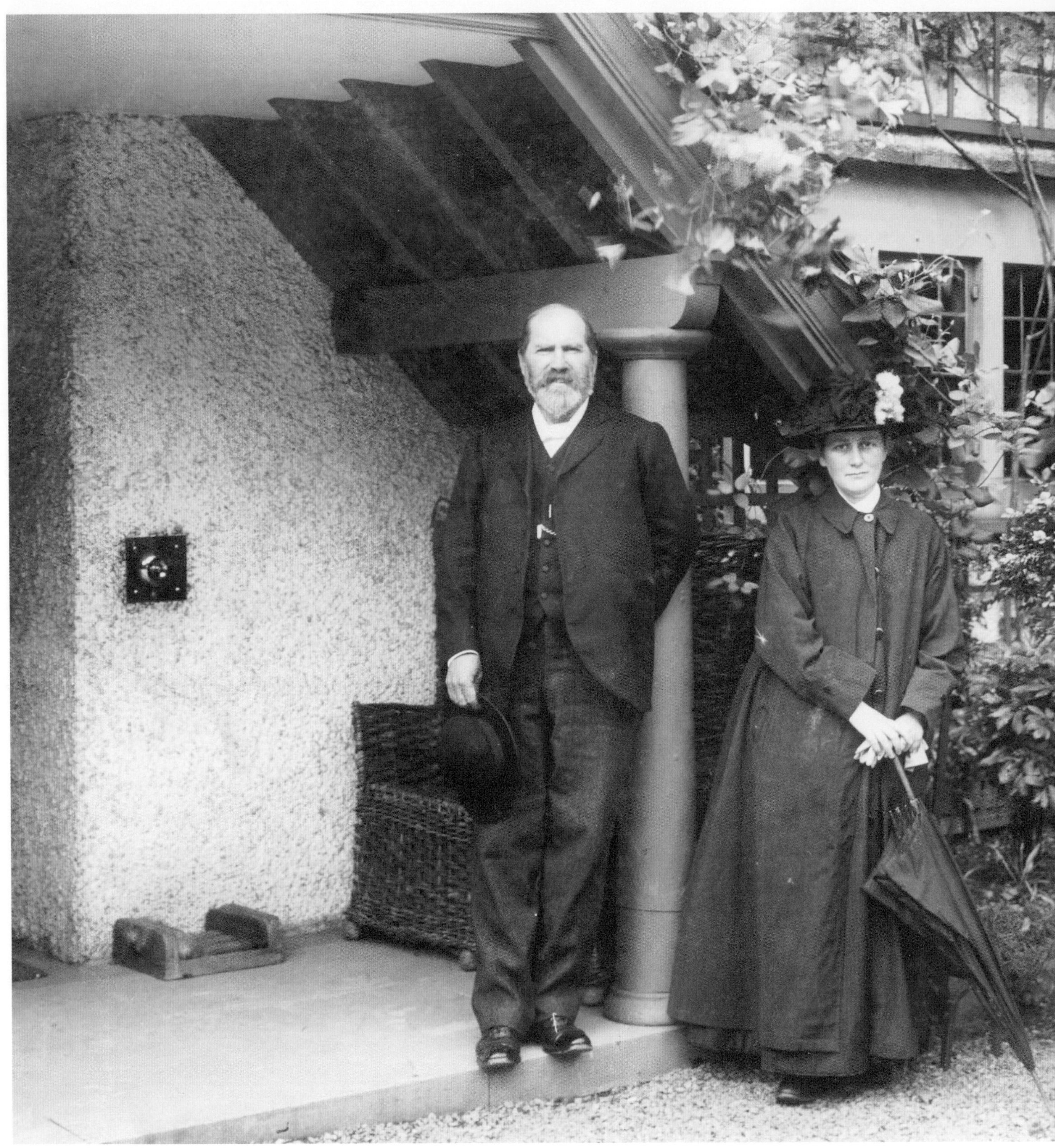

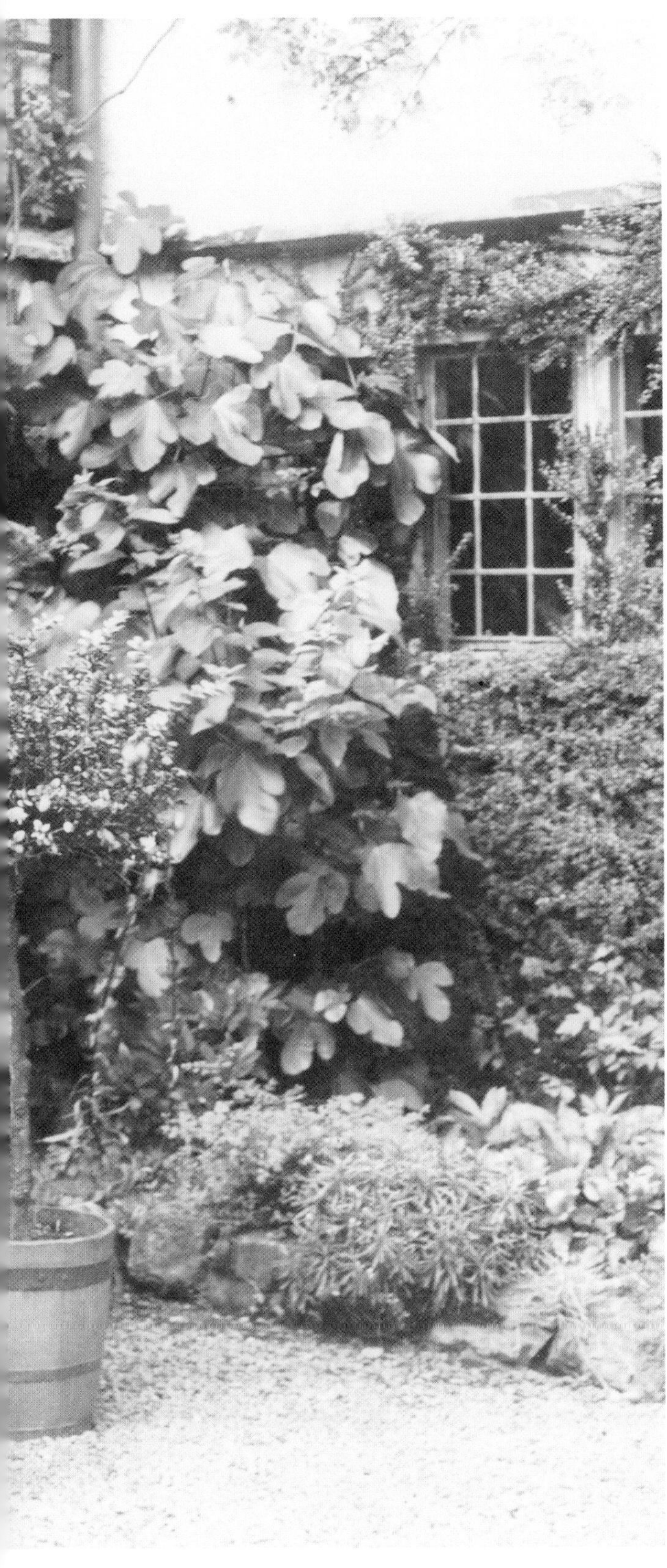

A charismatic clergyman, Rawnsley was also fervent in his defence of the Lake District against the Victorian enthusiasm for railways and new buildings. Fearing the effect this would have on life in the dales, any threat to his beloved Lake country resulted in a slew of letters urging his many contacts to express their support. Influenced by Ruskin while still at Oxford University, Rawnsley had also maintained links in artistic circles, one of a number of common interests with the Potters. He actively campaigned for the protection of the countryside, in particular against the encroachment of the railways into the heart of the area.

The passion with which Rawnsley threw himself into campaigns elicited support from prominent figures, including Ruskin who lent his name to a protest against a proposed railway to transport slate through the Lakes and towards Lancashire, although he was sceptical of what good it might do: 'You may use my name... It's all of no use – you will soon have a Cook's Tourist Railway up Scafell, and another up Helvellyn – and another up Skiddaw – and then a connecting line all round.'[19]

Realizing that only through land ownership could real protection be afforded to these precious valleys and lakes, Rawnsley joined forces with solicitor Sir Robert Hunter and social reformer Octavia Hill to form a new organization: 'The National Trust for Places of Historic Interest or Natural Beauty', which came into being on 12 January 1895. With only eight members and little in the way of funds, the fledgling organization relied solely on the talents and enthusiasm of its members for its success. The Trust was quickly besieged with requests for help to save buildings or places of natural beauty threatened with desecration, and not just in the Lake District but also across the whole of the United Kingdom. It is a testament to the tenacity of its founders that, by 1899, the Trust was becoming established and had acquired several properties. The Potter family had responded to its rallying call immediately; Beatrix paid her membership subscription every year as well as contributing to various appeals, and her father Rupert was one of the very first life members. The Trust's focus was on people and the benefits of beauty and open spaces for all. The National Trust Act of 1907 granted the Trust the ability to declare land inalienable, thus offering lasting protection.

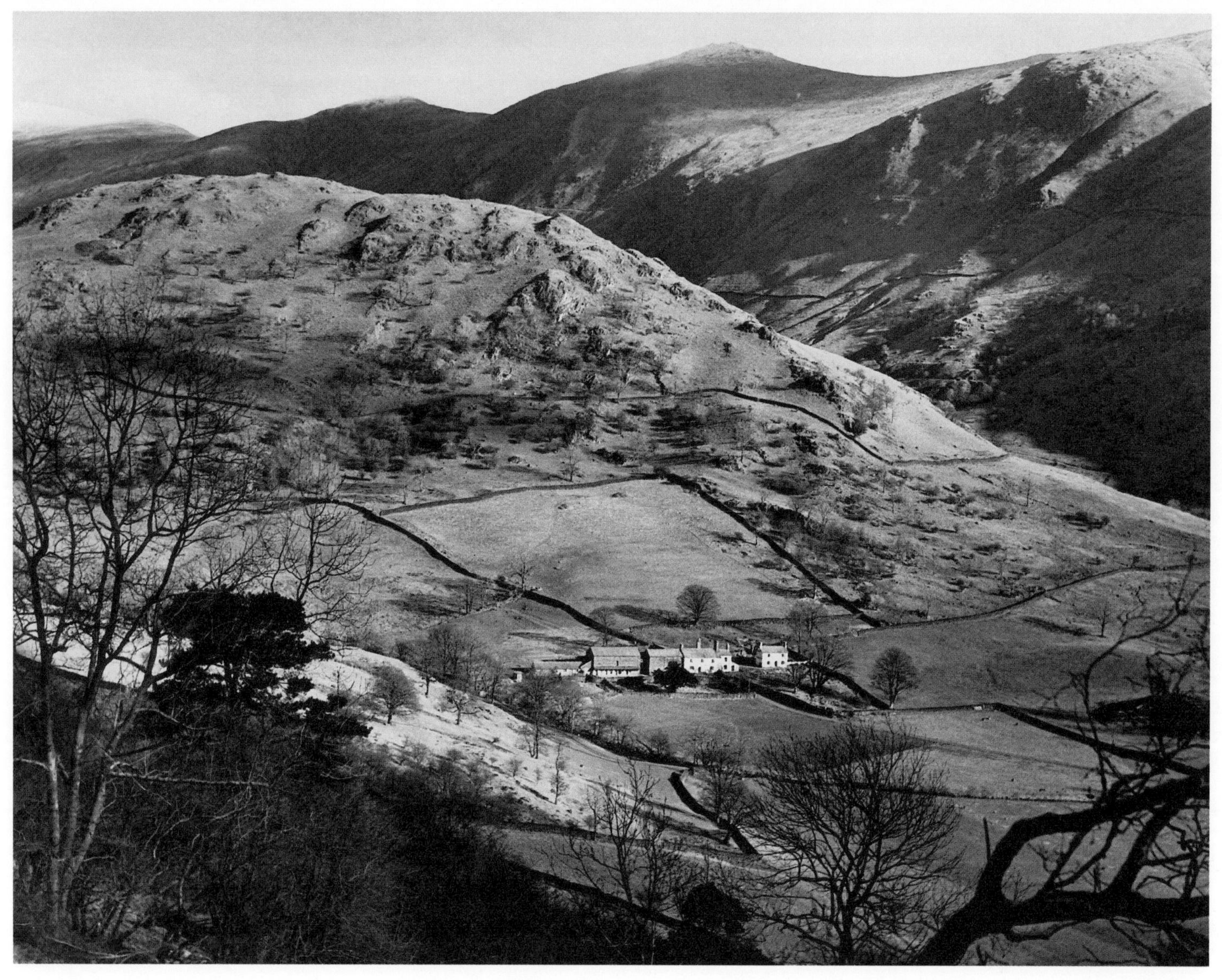

We stopped at the wonderful view over Troutbeck Tongue, and blue shadows creeping up the head of the den. The Troutbeck valley is exquisite when it is fine, which is but seldom.

(BEATRIX POTTER, *JOURNAL*, 17 AUGUST 1895)

127.
Joseph Hardman (1893–1972)
Troutbeck Park Farm from the high fell at Townend, 1948
Photographic print
National Trust, 234729

LANDOWNER

As Potter settled in the Lake District she became more deeply involved in the Trust's efforts. Initially she focused on increasing her land in Sawrey, with a smallholding, adjoining parcels of land, meadows and cottages being added to Hill Top. Later she began to see opportunities to buy buildings at risk of demolition or land being eyed up by developers. She and William were regular attendees at property auctions and farm sales.

Potter had long been in love with the Troutbeck fells (no.127). They had a wild and dramatic beauty, altogether different from the pastoral, gentle landscape around Sawrey. They captivated her, and held an almost mystical power, reigniting her poetic and storytelling tendencies:

> Mist is beautiful I think, though troublesome for sheep gathering. It takes strange shapes when it rises at sunset. During storms it rushes down the valleys like a black curtain billowing before the wind, while the Troutbeck river thunders over the cauldron. Memories of 'old unhappy far-off things and battles long ago'; sorrows of yesterday and today and tomorrow – the vastness of the fells covers all with a mantle of peace.[20]

In 1924 a substantial fell farm on the opposite side of Windermere to Sawrey came onto the market. Troutbeck Park Farm, strategically placed at the head of the Troutbeck valley, was exactly the type of land in demand by developers looking to build villa and mansion properties. Although it was ailing, it had an extensive area of grazing land on the fell that was especially suited to the hardy Herdwick breed of sheep. Perhaps influenced by memories from almost 30 years earlier, of watching an 'ancient shepherd' on the steep hillside calling to his dog across the Troutbeck valley (see 'Town and Country', p.47),[21] Potter decided to buy the farm with the express intention of protecting it, increasing the hefted flock and leaving it to the Trust on her death.[22] This was coupled with a determination to purchase further parcels of adjoining land to create a larger block and to prevent it from being used for building projects. Rather than letting the farm to a new tenant, she assumed its management herself and her life took on a new dimension.

Having secured the farm, Potter created a comfortable study to use during her visits and set about restoring both the buildings and the health of the stock, which was riddled with parasitic sheep fluke. She needed a skilled local shepherd and placed an advertisement in the *Westmorland Gazette*, but she also asked around. Discovering that a Tom Storey was thinking of leaving his employment at the Greggs' farm at Townend, Potter offered to double his wages. Together they set to work on improving the farm, and Potter turned her meticulous attention to detail towards the health of her sheep.

She took a practical and scientific interest in the problem. She dusted off her microscope and began to examine samples of sheep faeces, looking for evidence of parasites. Storey recalled Potter securing the latest medicines to treat the sheep fluke: 'She believed in

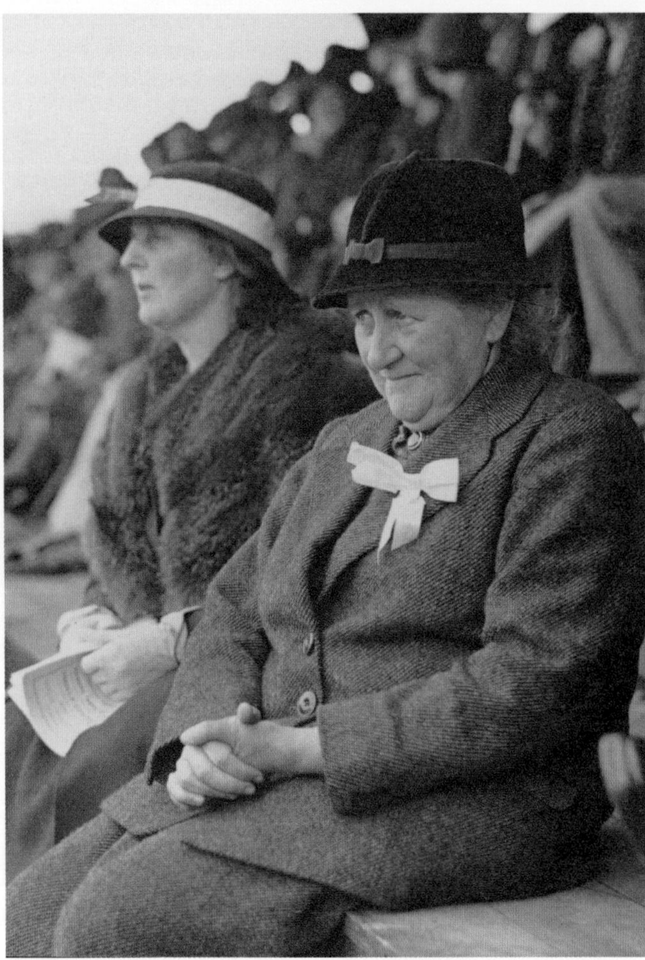

128.
Unknown photographer
Beatrix Heelis (show president) and Mrs Charlton (a judge) in the stands at the Keswick Show, September 1935
Photographic print
V&A: AAD/2006/4/533, given by Joan Duke

modern medicine. She was good that way. If you saw anything that was doing a sheep any good, she'd write up and send for it.'[23]

The treatment she had obtained was successful and the following spring Potter was delighted: 'I have a ewe stock of about 1100 herdwicks, very healthy, since we have got rid of fluke.'[24] She had other plans in mind for Storey, however; offering another one pound to his wages, she asked if he would move to Hill Top and manage the farm there. Storey recalled that his wife, Hilda, had guessed the reason behind the request: 'I told the missus. I remember her saying "by gum, she'll bribe you into anything". So we decided to come – the wife said "she wants you there to show sheep".'[25]

It was another shrewd decision by Potter: under Storey's watchful eye, her sheep would go on to win cups and trophies for Herdwick ewes at most of the local agricultural shows until the outbreak of the Second World War (nos 128, 130).

Alongside the day-to-day management of her farms Potter still found time to write for publication when the 'scribbling fit' took her.[26] In addition to giving her opinions on topics as wide-ranging as hedgehogs, farm practices and the shortage of horses, encouragement from her American friends led her to develop a series of short stories into a longer book for older children.

Yet again past interests would seep into her work when, in *The Fairy Caravan*, Paddy Pig becomes unwell after eating 'toadstool tartlets' in Pringle Wood. Potter demonstrates her awareness of the hallucinogenic effects of consuming what appear to be *Gymnopilus purpuratus* (a species of fungi found on hardwoods and pig dung). How she came about this knowledge, however, is a matter of conjecture!

Intensely personal and with recognizable place names and characters, Potter intended the book to be published only in America (no.129). In order to register copyright in the UK, she had 100 copies bound by a local printer and shyly handed one to Storey, which she had inscribed: 'To Tom Storey, In memory of "Queeny" and the sheep dogs.' Potter had sketched the sheep dogs in his copy and cared more about the opinion of her shepherd than anyone else.

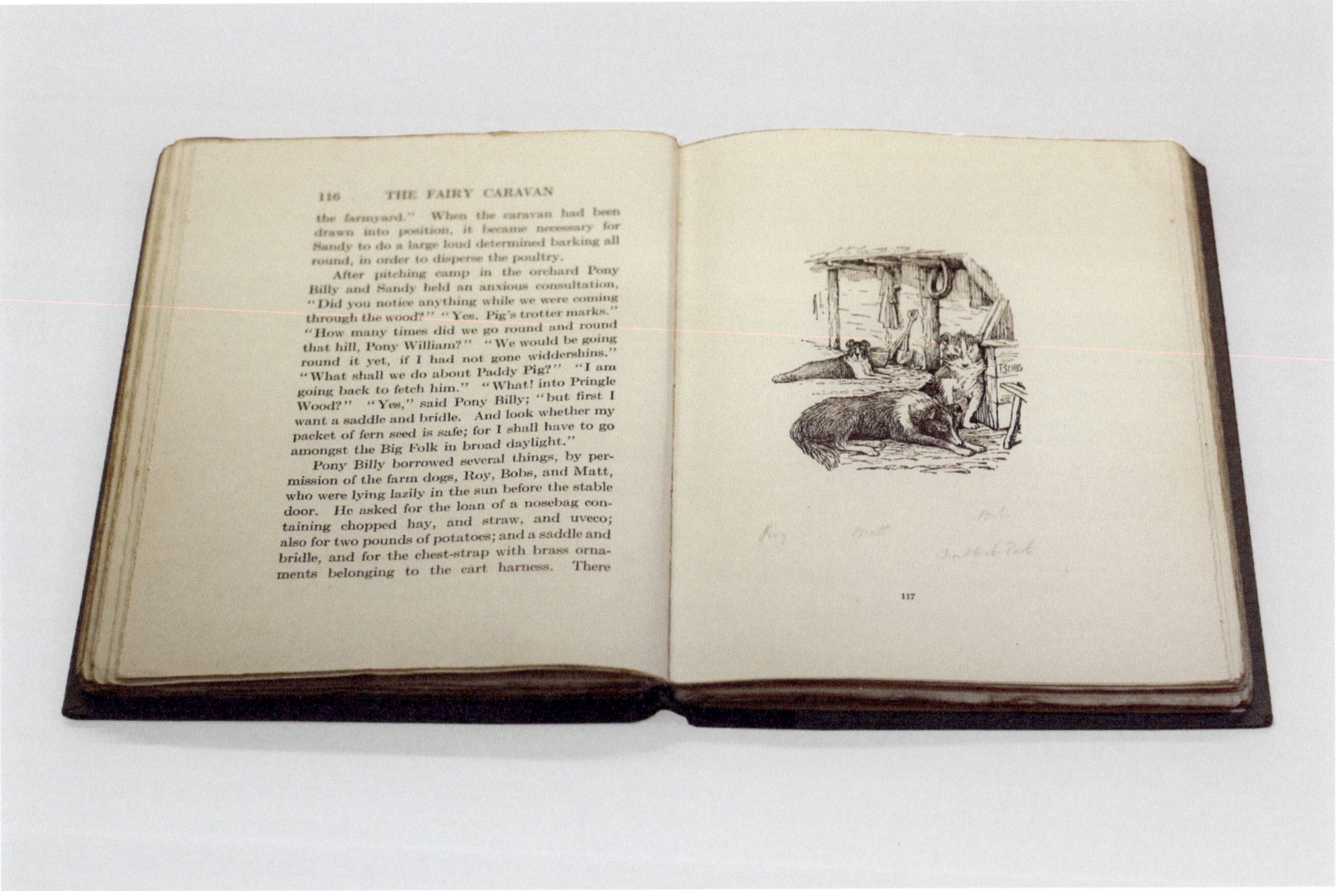

116 THE FAIRY CARAVAN

the farmyard." When the caravan had been drawn into position, it became necessary for Sandy to do a large loud determined barking all round, in order to disperse the poultry.

After pitching camp in the orchard Pony Billy and Sandy held an anxious consultation, "Did you notice anything while we were coming through the wood?" "Yes. Pig's trotter marks." "How many times did we go round and round that hill, Pony William?" "We would be going round it yet, if I had not gone widdershins." "What shall we do about Paddy Pig?" "I am going back to fetch him." "What! into Pringle Wood?" "Yes," said Pony Billy; "but first I want a saddle and bridle. And look whether my packet of fern seed is safe; for I shall have to go amongst the Big Folk in broad daylight."

Pony Billy borrowed several things, by permission of the farm dogs, Roy, Bobs, and Matt, who were lying lazily in the sun before the stable door. He asked for the loan of a nosebag containing chopped hay, and straw, and uveco; also for two pounds of potatoes; and a saddle and bridle, and for the chest-strap with brass ornaments belonging to the cart harness. There

117

129. Above
Page from Beatrix Potter's copy of *The Fairy Caravan*, published by Alexander McKay, Philadelphia, 1929, annotated with the names of three sheepdogs from Troutbeck Park Farm: Roy, Matt and Bobs, p.117
National Trust, 242447

130. Right
Certificate from the Loweswater and Brackenthwaite Agricultural Show, 1931
National Trust, 252367.2

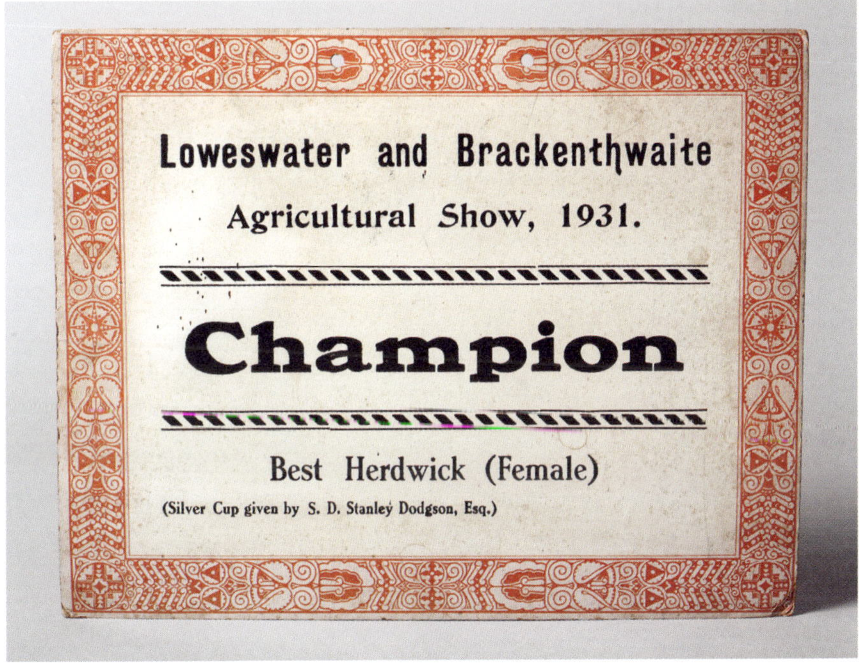

131. Below
Mrs. Rabbit, artwork, drawn for sale through *The Horn Book* magazine to raise funds to purchase Cockshott Point at Lake Windermere, September 1927
Watercolour and ink on paper
V&A: BP.548, Linder Bequest LB 1832

132. Opposite
Landscape of Tarn Hows, near Coniston, c.1905
Watercolour and ink on paper
V&A: BP.1154, Linder Bequest LB 687

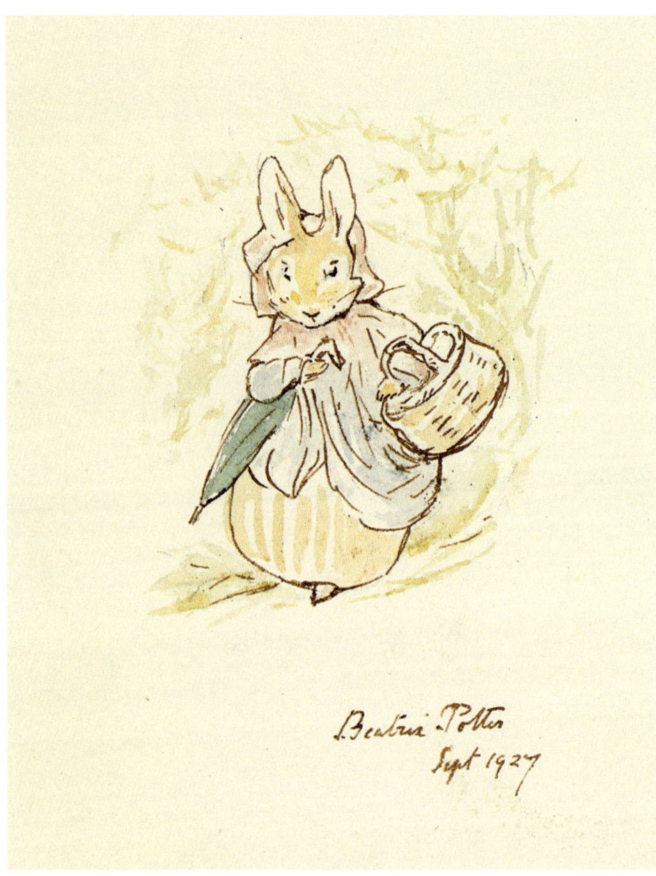

AMERICAN FRIENDS

At this time, Potter had begun corresponding with Bertha Mahony Miller, who ran a children's bookshop in Boston, Massachusetts, and was also the editor of *The Horn Book*, a magazine devoted to children's books. Potter's friendship with Miller was to be a fruitful one. Following the First World War the threat from housing developers became ever greater and Potter was keen to point this out to her American friend, who was an enthusiastic admirer of both Potter's books and the English countryside.

Never one to miss an opportunity, Potter saw that the enthusiasm for her books might also generate an interest in, and income for, her campaigns to protect vulnerable pieces of land, such as Cockshott Point, a strip of lakeshore on the east side of Windermere. She sent Miller a series of original drawings, asking if she would use them to raise funds. To Potter's delight, she accumulated £104 for the National Trust: a significant contribution towards the purchase of Cockshott Point (no.131).

A VERY BIG THING

By 1930 the world was in recession and Potter was well into her sixties, but she was yet to realize her most ambitious project. James Marshall's Monk Coniston estate (no.133), 5,000 acres of prime Lakeland landscape, including several farms and the famed beauty spot Tarn Hows, came up for sale (no.132). As farmland, the estate would not attract a high price but by selling it piecemeal for housing development

It seems that we have done a big thing; without premeditation; suddenly, inevitably – what else could one do?

(BEATRIX POTTER, LETTER TO JOHN BAILEY, 15 FEBRUARY 1930)[27]

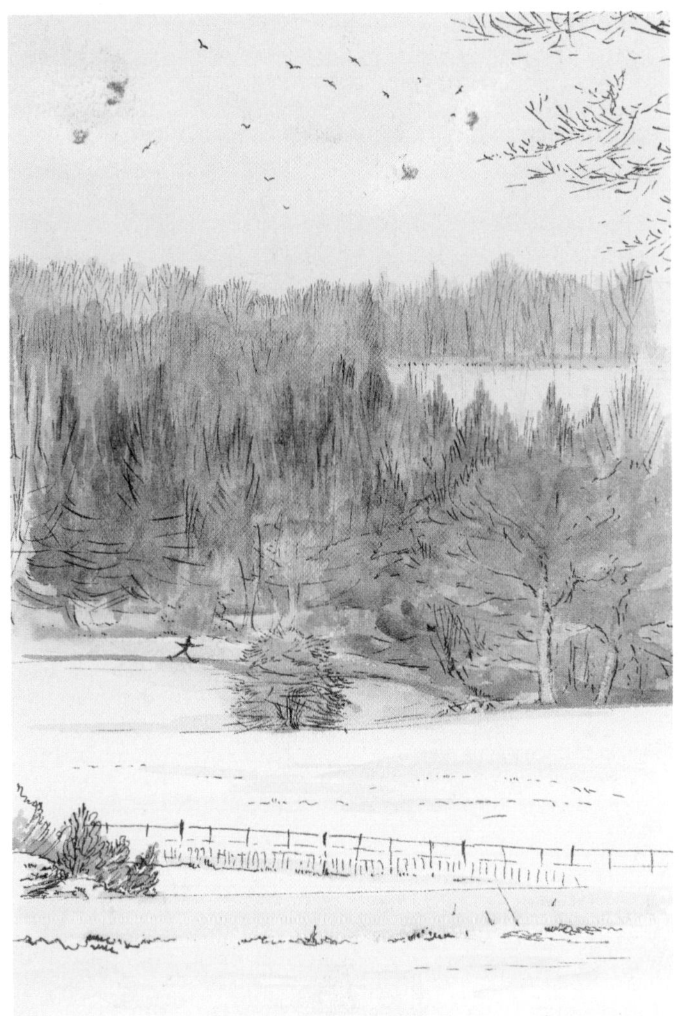

Marshall could expect to raise a significant sum. In addition, the Forestry Commission was looking to acquire the land, to get rid of the farms and create vast plantations of conifers and larch. Potter understood the urgency of protecting and keeping the estate together and began negotiating with the Trust's Secretary, Samuel Hamer:

> Could you see it – spare a weekend? But if it is as wild and misty as today, it might take more than two days to go over. What about Mr Baillie *[sic]*? It is a very big thing, and worth looking at. Yesterday was a cloudless autumn day, and the panorama from Tarn Hows was bewildering.[28]

In addition to the 'bewildering' landscape, Potter wanted to ensure the future of the fell farms; one in particular had personal resonance. Holme Ground at Tilberthwaite had once belonged to her great-grandfather, Abraham Crompton, and this inspired her to make the Trust a generous offer: she would purchase the estate whole, but offer half of it to the Trust, at cost, as soon as the money could be raised by them to buy it. The remainder of the estate she would leave to the Trust in her will. While her husband undertook the delicate negotiations with Marshall, Potter was gleefully reporting back on the proceedings. She was clearly enjoying herself: 'I was listening behind the dining room door...'.[29]

When the Trust appealed to the nation to raise the funds to purchase 2,600 acres of the estate, the enormity of her actions hit home:

> Those of us who have felt the spirit of the fells reckon little of passing praise; but I do value the esteem of those who have understanding. It seems that we have done a big thing; without premeditation; suddenly, inevitably – what else could one do? It will be a happy consummation if the Trust is able to turn this quixotic venture into a splendid reality.[30]

This was a pivotal moment in the conservation of a valley that defines the character of the Lake District landscape. Potter had indeed accomplished a very big thing.

Liz Hunter MacFarlane

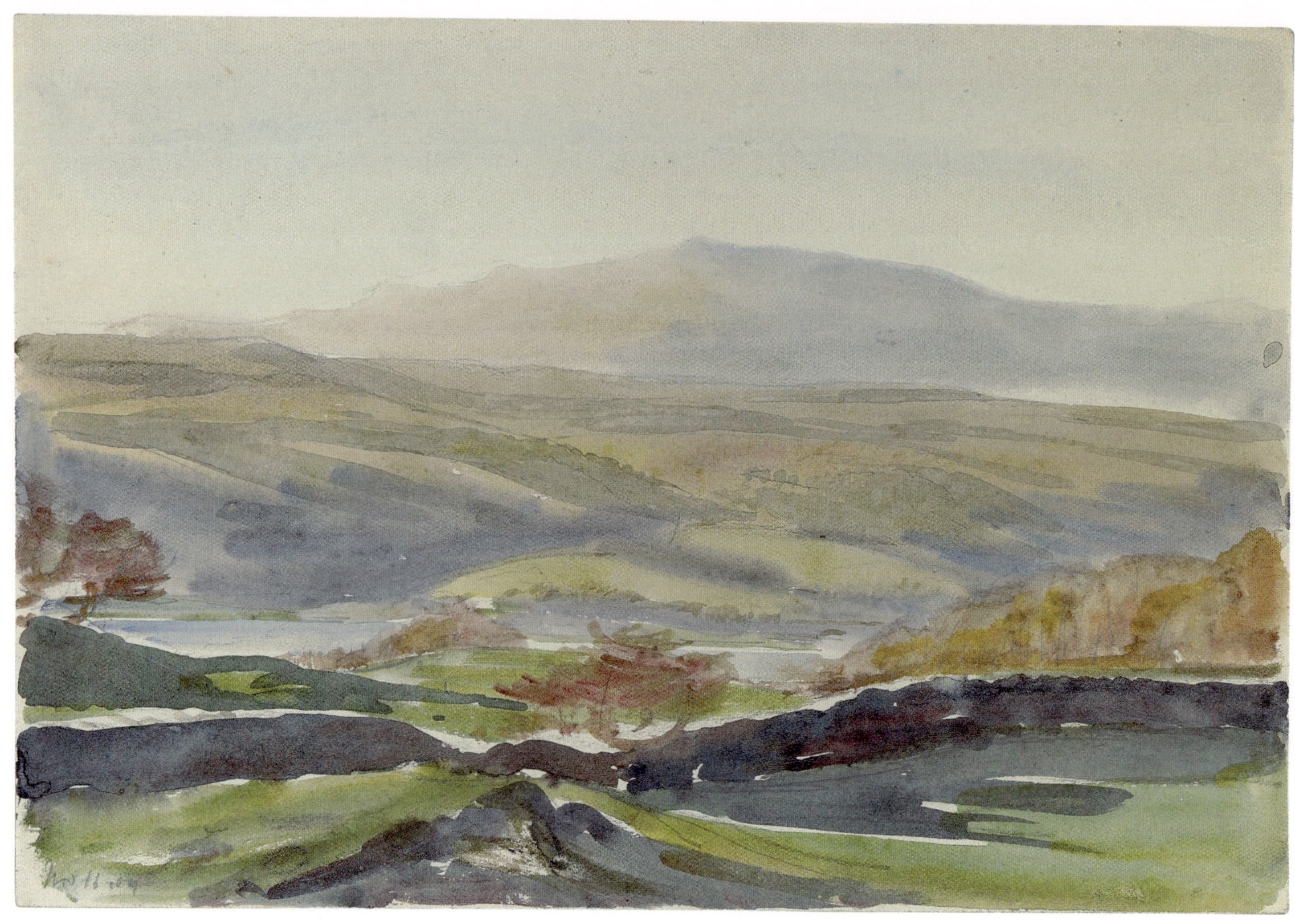

Your first agent should be a superior man with more than a merely local outlook, a clear head, a good presence, presentable in London; honourably independent above local politics and squabbles.

(BEATRIX POTTER, LETTER TO SAMUEL. H. HAMER, 20 OCTOBER 1929)[31]

STAYING ON

Realizing that an expert with local knowledge and experience was needed to manage the estate, the Trust asked Potter if she would continue to do so on its behalf. She agreed and carried out this role until 1936. She had a huge task on her hands: the Great Depression and years of neglect by previous tenants had left the farms in a sorry state. Potter took a pragmatic approach to the job. While she felt that the Lake District should evolve to remain a living, working landscape, she believed this could be achieved with sensitivity to the architectural heritage and made great efforts to ensure that repairs, alterations

133.
Monk Coniston moor, 16 November 1909 (7am)
Watercolour over pencil on paper
V&A: BP.1057, Linder Bequest LB 541

and even new building work would be carried out in a way that complemented the existing structures. With her artist's eye, perhaps this attention to detail came naturally to Potter. She understood the need to preserve the character of the countryside: 'Our pretty old white-washed farm houses in the sheltered valleys are a feature of the district.'[32]

Potter was not averse to change if she felt it would enhance the life of the community. In the wake of the 1918 influenza pandemic, she was instrumental in setting up the District Nursing Association for the parishes of Sawrey, Hawkshead and Wray. Having witnessed the suffering caused by illness and lack of medical assistance during childbirth, she was determined to help improve access to affordable healthcare for those in the more remote areas. For a payment of two shillings and sixpence, subscribers could sign up and gain access to a Queen's Nurse. In addition to acting as treasurer for the association and keeping the nurse updated with who needed visiting, Potter supplied a cottage and a car for use by the nurse. She was also supportive of those tenants who saw the need to diversify in order to make their farms viable: 'There is a very fine old house Yew Tree Farm near Coniston belonging to the Trust. We fitted up a tearoom with good furniture and pictures. Unluckily the woman has been ill; it was a great success the first summer it was open.'[33]

With such detailed knowledge of local farming, tenants and the Lake District way of life, Potter held a formidable position in the community and kept herself informed through her work on various committees. She had always striven for perfection, so when she decided to step aside and the Trust sought a replacement, it was unlikely that anyone coming into the role would be able to match up to her exacting standards.

Bruce Thompson had the unenviable task of taking over and Potter made sure to remain on hand, offering guidance and pointing out when things did not proceed as she felt appropriate. This 'guidance' often came in the form of acerbic letters sent either to Thompson directly, or to the Trust's head office in London. In one such communication Potter is incensed by the Trust's approach to felling woodland.

Her decisions had always been based on aesthetic considerations and a desire to preserve the picturesque character of the area. Her response was a personal attack on Thompson: 'I am writing about your agent Mr Bruce Thompson. There is a keen demand for all sorts of wood, and he may do irreparable damage. It is useless for me to talk to him. A man cannot help having been born dull. Thompson is supercilious as well.'[34] Thompson frequently bore the brunt of Potter's more irascible moments but in fact was held in high regard by most in the community.

Despite her outbursts, Potter remained a staunch supporter of the Trust, believing it to be the best guardian of the Lake District with its unique ability to protect the way of life she loved.

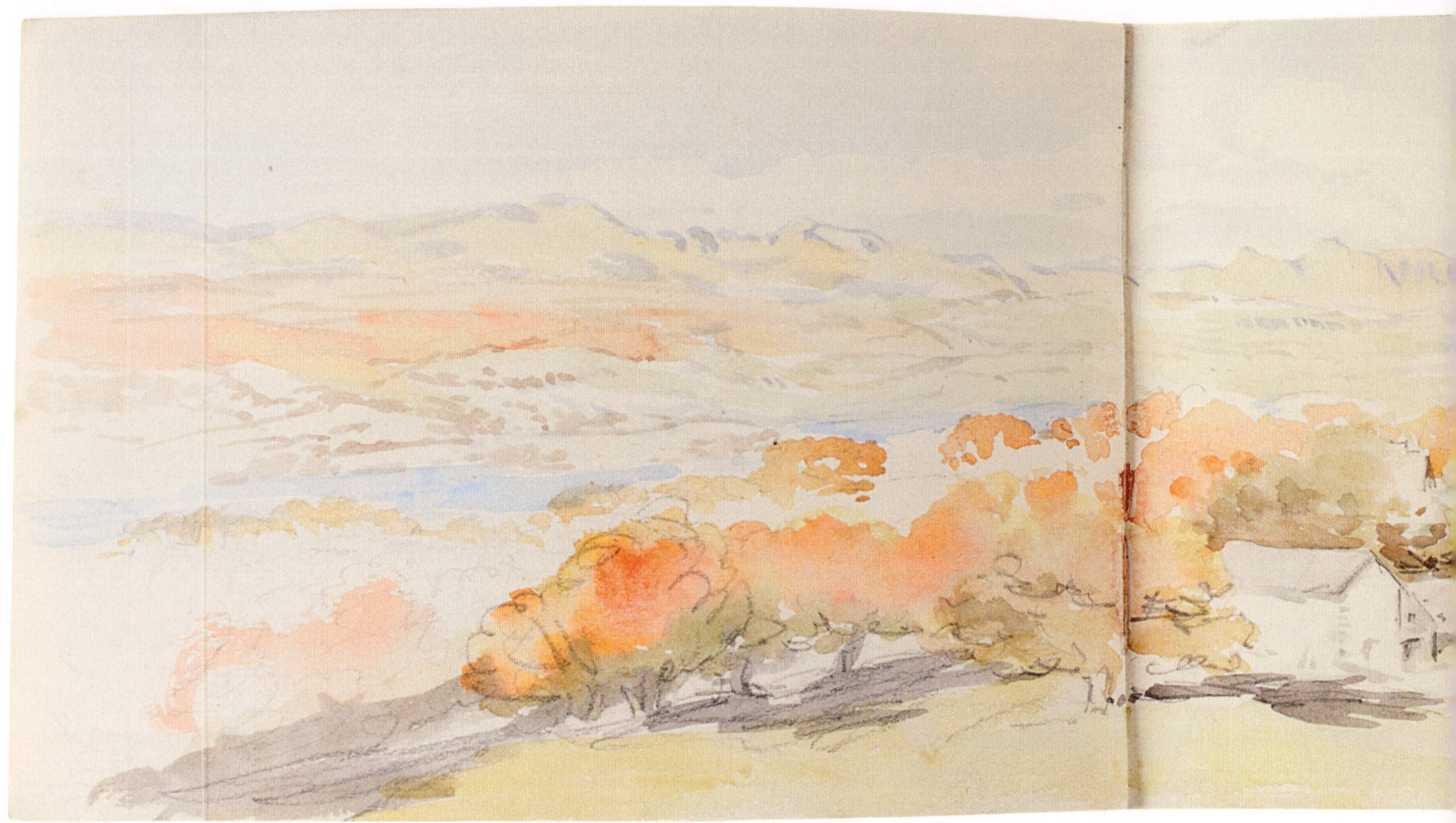

I have tried to do my humble bit of preservation in this district…

(BEATRIX POTTER, LETTER TO JOHN STONE, 5 JUNE 1940)[35]

A LASTING LEGACY

The Second World War brought further trials as, despite ailing health, a lack of available labour meant Potter had to take on more direct control of her own farms. She was exasperated by officialdom, in particular the Ministry of Agriculture's insistence that she should grow what she felt to be unsuitable crops: 'It's perfectly absurd and wrong to force hill sheep farms to grow acres and acres of potatoes without manure or suitable land.'[36]

Potter continued to offer her advice and opinions, but as she slowed down and bouts of influenza and bronchitis frequently interrupted her work, she spent more time indoors, with her two faithful Pekinese dogs: Chuleh and Tsuzee. She relied on her imagination to take her onto the fells: 'Thank God I have the seeing eye, that is to say, as I lie in bed I walk step by step on the fells and rough lands seeing every stone and

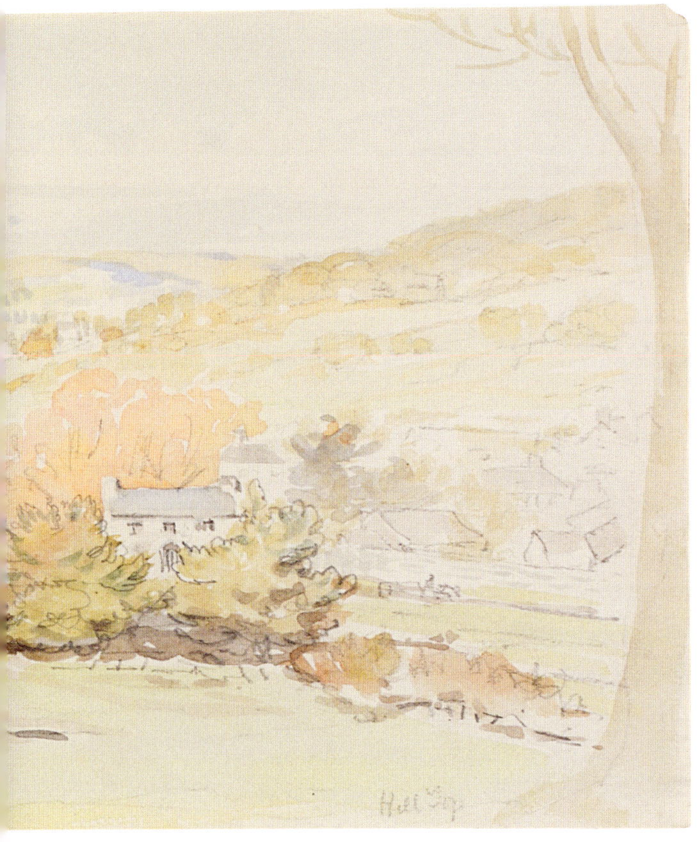

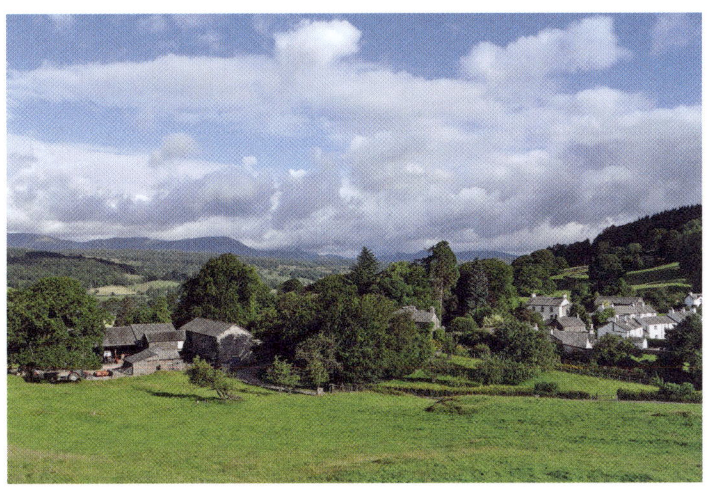

134. Left
Pages from a sketchbook, view from fields above Hill Top across Sawrey and Esthwaite, 1905
Watercolour over pencil on paper
National Trust, 242722

135. Above
Val Corbett (b. 1948)
Near Sawrey, c.2015
Photographic print
National Trust, 1163804

flower and patch of bog and cotton grass where my old legs will never take me again.'[37] Beatrix Potter died on 22 December 1943. Far better known in the Lake District as a farmer, landowner and Herdwick sheep breeder than as an author and illustrator, what many believe to be her greatest achievement was about to be revealed to the nation: a bequest of over 4,000 acres of land, farms and cottages to the National Trust. The Heelis bequest remains its largest and most significant acquisition in the Lake District. The support it displayed for the organization substantially reinforced the message that the Trust was uniquely able to protect the Lakes by the virtue of its 1907 Act of Parliament.

Thus, many of the scenes immortalized in Potter's artwork are little changed (nos 134, 135), a factor that contributed to the decision by UNESCO to inscribe the Lake District as a World Heritage Site in 2017. Potter's talent as an artist gave her the ability to capture the beauty of the natural world. From her very first visits to the Lake District as a shy teenager, she was motivated its the flora and fauna and dramatic lakes and fells. The farms and villages, with their rich source of characters, inspired her to create tales that would continue to delight for generations and provide her with an income that enabled her to take the positive action which would safeguard her much-loved adoptive home.

Beatrix Potter was the right person, in the right place, at the right time. Inspired by nature, she took a vision that began with Wordsworth's desire for a 'sort of national property, in which every man has a right and interest who has an eye to perceive and a heart to enjoy',[38] and turned Ruskin's and Rawnsley's 'quixotic venture into a splendid reality'.[39]

Mrs Heelis, Farmer

The old shepherds still called her 'Mrs Heelis' when I was a boy. She was a kind of ghostly memory, some strange woman that had come among them. She was not exactly felt to be 'one of us', but she had achieved the rare thing indeed of being an outsider who had made a mark in the Lake District farming world – she had earned our respect.

Beatrix Potter had known about the Lakeland shepherds since she was a child. She knew about them not just because of her family's summer holidays in the Lake District, but because the adults in her childhood took shepherds and farming seriously. William Wordsworth had written of there being a 'perfect republic of shepherds' in the Lake District: an egalitarian counterpoint to the feudal landscapes of much of the rest of England.[1] This northern radical idea was very much alive in the Potter household, not least because of their friendship with Canon Rawnsley, who wrote about the farming of these valleys. When as an adult Potter bought Herdwick farms in the Lake District, it was not on a sudden whim: she had long loved the place and been fascinated by its people.

The Lake District in which Potter farmed has more in common with parts of Norway than with southern England. The hardy Herdwick sheep were basically Norse sheep, something claimed then and largely proven by DNA testing recently. They are just about the toughest out-wintering sheep on the planet, able to survive snowdrifts and terrible mountain vegetation through hungry winters, protected by their thick, grey fleeces. They are also fiercely independent and proud matriarchs – something that seemed to appeal to Potter. The Lakeland flocks travelled to and from their 'heaf' (their traditional place of grazing learnt from their mothers) on the fells several times a year, which was made possible only because of the sheepdogs (no.137). 'Sheepdogs' were sometimes Border Collies, like 'Kep' (no.136), and sometimes more mongrel-like creatures bred for the unique work in the crags and steep fell sides. From time to time sheep would get stuck on rocky crags, 'crag fast', and men would lower themselves down on ropes to rescue them. The way the farms operated, with their 'common' grazing lands on the fells, their privately owned and farmed intakes and allotments, and 'in-bye' land, was more akin to Scandinavian farmsteads than anything in the English lowlands. Even the dialect words were from the Old Norse: 'beck', 'fell', 'lig', 'laik', 'ga'an' and 'lowp'. This was 'dog and stick' farming, mostly unchanged from centuries earlier: small farms carving a living from

136. Right
'Kep', 5 March 1909
Watercolour and pencil on paper, mounted on card
V&A: BP.297, Linder Bequest LB 178

137. Below left
Beatrix Potter with a young smooth-haired collie at Castle Cottage, Sawrey, after 1914
Photographic print on paper in an album
Cotsen Children's Library, Special Collections, Princeton University Library, 10005.167

138. Below right
The Fairy Caravan artwork, c.1929
Watercolour and ink over pencil on paper
National Trust, 243180

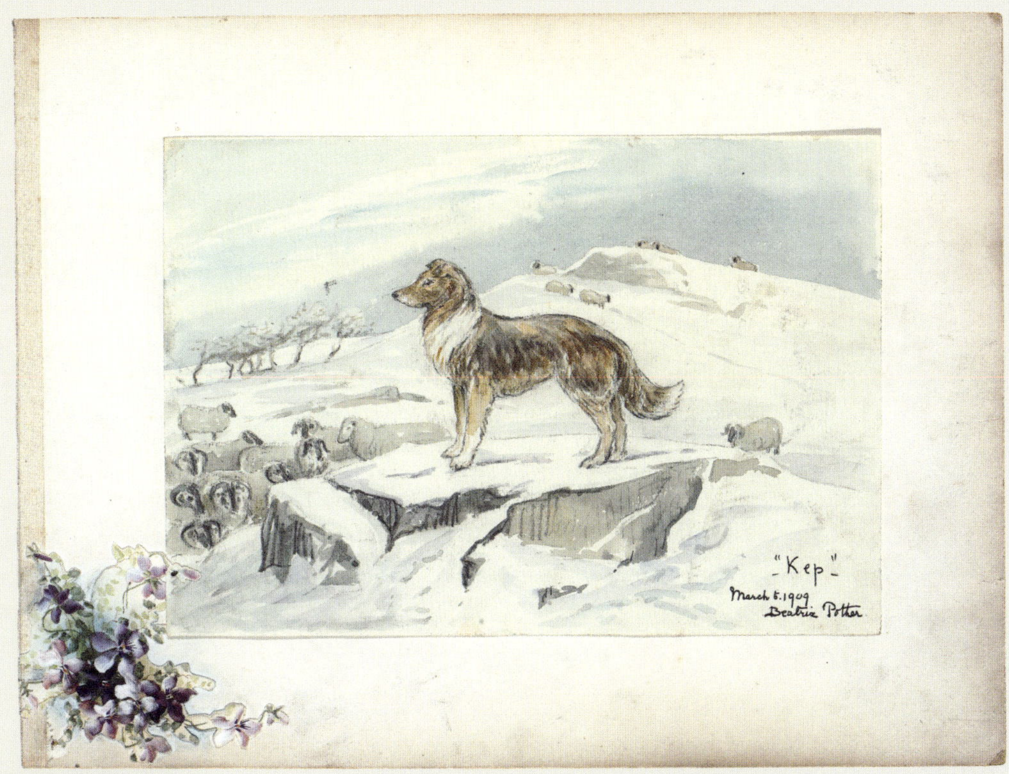

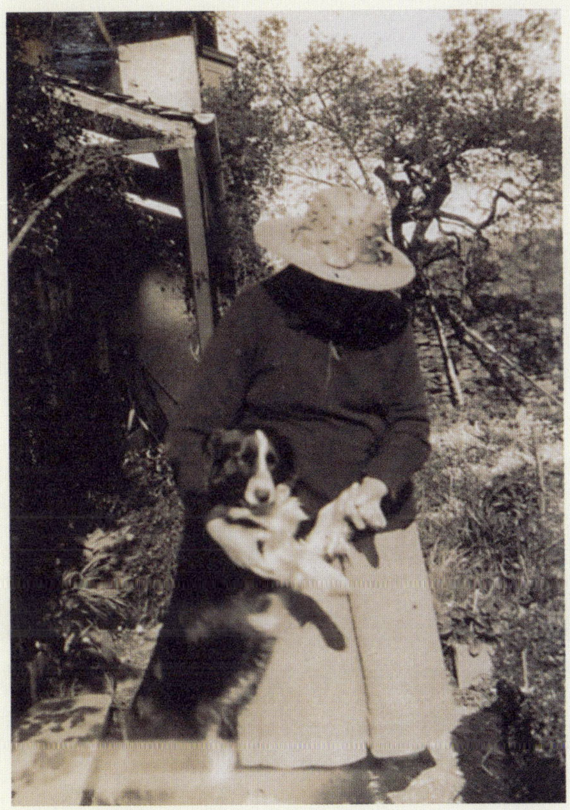

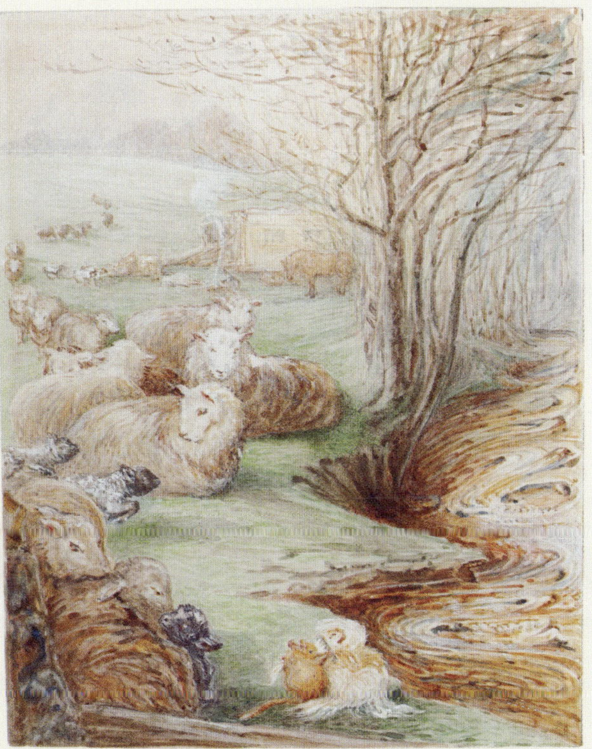

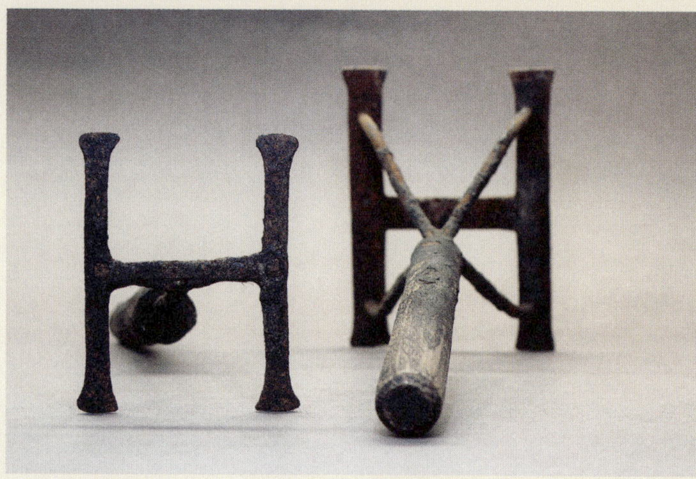

139.
Maker unknown
Smit markers for Beatrix Heelis's flock, c.1930–40,
Iron
National Trust, 642286

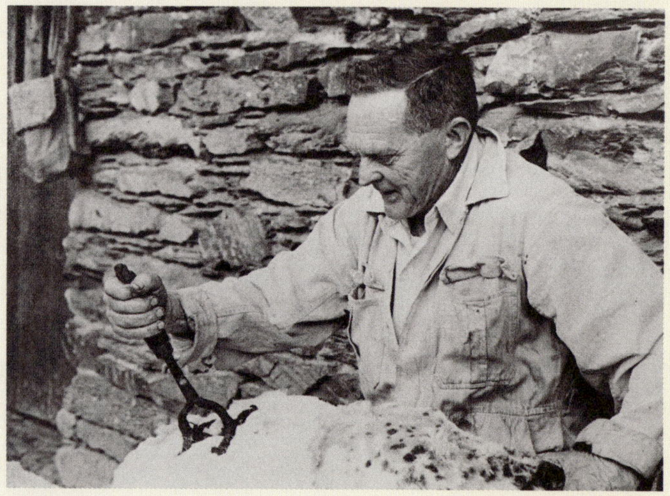

140.
George Rodger (1908–1995)
Tom Storey using smit markers for Beatrix Heelis' flock,
7 October 1946
Photographic print
National Trust: 243517. Gift of Hilary Ainsworth

the hard, thin soil and pastures. It was a tough and unforgiving place to be a sheep, sheepdog or shepherd. Potter's letters to Joseph Moscrop, her extra lambing-time shepherd and long-time friend, are full of the struggles of such a farming life.

The letters between Potter and Moscrop contain some of the nicest words she ever wrote. They are often seen as evidence of how close she became to the Lake District farming folk, but this is not quite the whole truth. Moscrop was by all accounts a decent man and a good farm worker, but he was not a Lake District native. He was a hired lambing shepherd from the Scottish borders, and therefore as much of an outsider as Potter was, and therein lies the root of their bond. They both had one foot in the life of these dales, and yet were destined never to be fully accepted as part of that world. Once you realise this, you can see the letters for what they are, full of careful observations and love of that life on the land but also frustration with the local people and the shepherds. You can be open about such things with a fellow outsider who shares the life, but you cannot verbalise them to a native.

There was a kind of hierarchy in that shepherding world, with anyone who bred great sheep, or cattle or sheepdogs, near the top; those who could gather a difficult fell with their dogs were also held in high regard. Lower down the scale were folk who worked hard and were useful in other practical ways, such as in the lambing fields, like Moscrop, and to an extent 'Mrs Heelis', and down at the bottom were those who did things no one local understood or valued much, like being the author of children's books. Potter might have scorned such a value system, but I think over time she came to share it. She went native. The historians and biographers say she bred fine Herdwick sheep and was a noted judge. I am not sure that is quite the whole truth either; instead she wisely forged a formidable, if slightly strained, partnership with her shepherd Tom Storey. She respected his shepherding skills, and with her land, flock and money he made a mark on the breed. They had set off on the wrong foot, when she assumed as the flock's owner she would choose which sheep they would take to the show. Storey set her straight by telling her that he was the shepherd and they would not show until he thought the flock was good enough, and if she did not like it she could get another shepherd – that is how the Lake District worked. But to her very great credit, she found a way to combine their talents and bred some excellent Herdwick ewes.

My favourite picture of Potter is when they won the female championship at the Eskdale Show, the pinnacle of the breed's achievements for a Herdwick ewe (no.141). In the photograph Storey holds the ewe, called 'Water Lily', and Potter peers over its woolly back, with the prize ticket in her hand. Her face is a mixture of immense pride and a touch of wickedness in her smile: she knew they had got one over on the old shepherds who usually dominated the prizes. These Herdwick shepherds are terrible men to deal with, she had written in a letter to Moscrop, and that day she landed a blow against them and no doubt earned a little respect.

There is something about a farming life that consumes you. You are not doing it properly unless you are thinking about it in your every waking moment. This is basically what happened to Potter. The Lake District farming life swallowed her up until the writer of children's books almost ceased to exist. Her publishers wrote to her constantly, encouraging her to work on new children's books, but she had become something else. 'Beatrix Potter' was replaced by 'Mrs Heelis', another woman entirely, with her letters full of sheep fluke, cows calving, buying farms and, towards the end, stopping the National Trust managers – to whom she entrusted her farms, but who did not know a fraction of what she did – from making a poor job of it. Her letters reveal something else a little sad. She wanted to write about this farming world that now filled her thoughts but was nervous to do so because she thought she might be laughed at; in her age, and still in ours, to take rural life too seriously was to risk ridicule. She therefore found a kind of halfway-house solution in writing *The Fairy Caravan* (1929), a Lakeland children's fantasy in which the proud Herdwick sheep talk (no.138). Although it is much loved by some, I think that it is not as successful as the earlier books, despite its charms. Curiously, her private letters reveal there was a book she could have written but which never happened: a memoir or book for grown-ups that told the story of the work of the farms and the farming people. I think she could have done it but she did not quite dare, or did not believe the world of books and readers wanted it. I would have loved that book.

James Rebanks

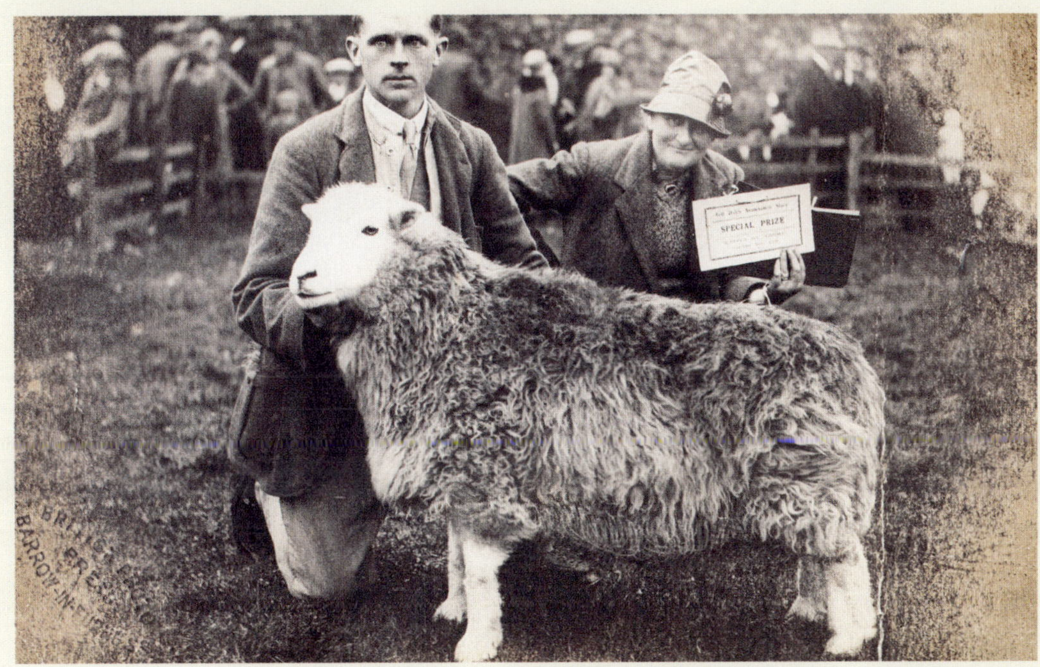

141.
Tom Storey and Beatrix Heelis with prize-winning ewe named 'Water Lily', at the Eskdale Show, 26 September 1930
Photographic print, published by the British Photo Press
National Trust, 242421

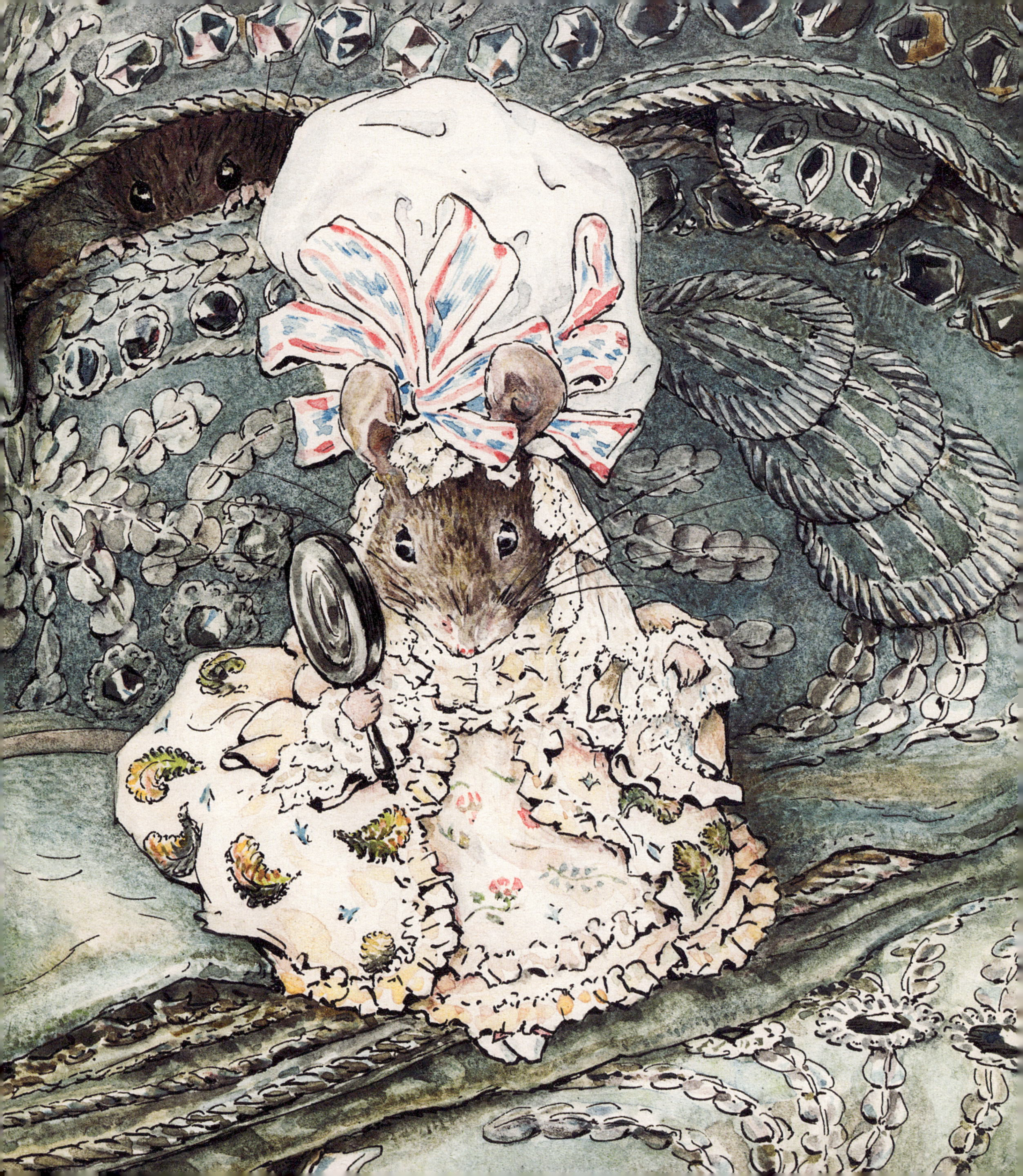

Drawn from Nature

Selected Potter Protagonists

Peter Rabbit

Peter and his sisters Flopsy, Mopsy and Cotton-tail go on a foraging outing, in typical rabbit fashion. Peter's good little sisters follow Mrs. Rabbit's instructions to stay in the lane and, most importantly, to avoid the garden of Mr. McGregor. Peter ignores the advice and gets in over his head, literally, as he becomes trapped in the bird netting in the garden. Peter is an unwilling action hero, impulsive and nervous. It is only with encouragement from the sparrows that he exerts himself to escape danger. This lightly moral tale comes right in the end and Peter just about manages to emerge unscathed, except for losing his clothes.

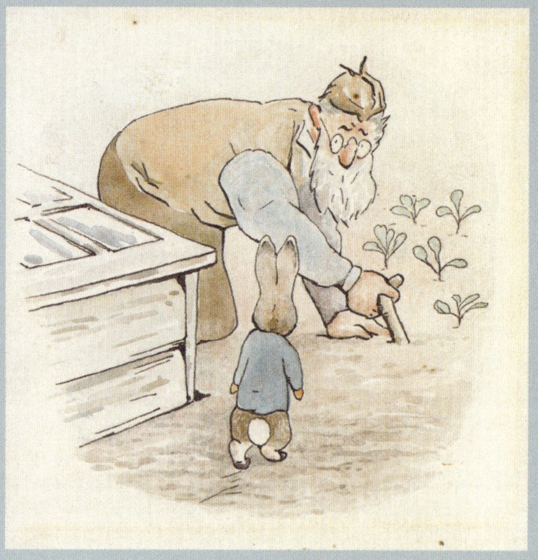

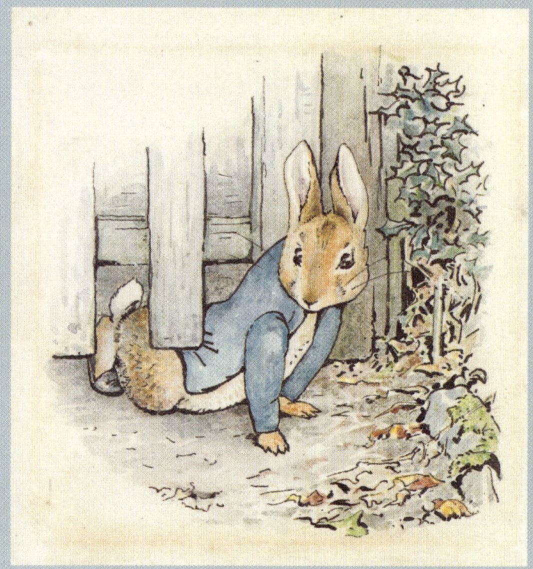

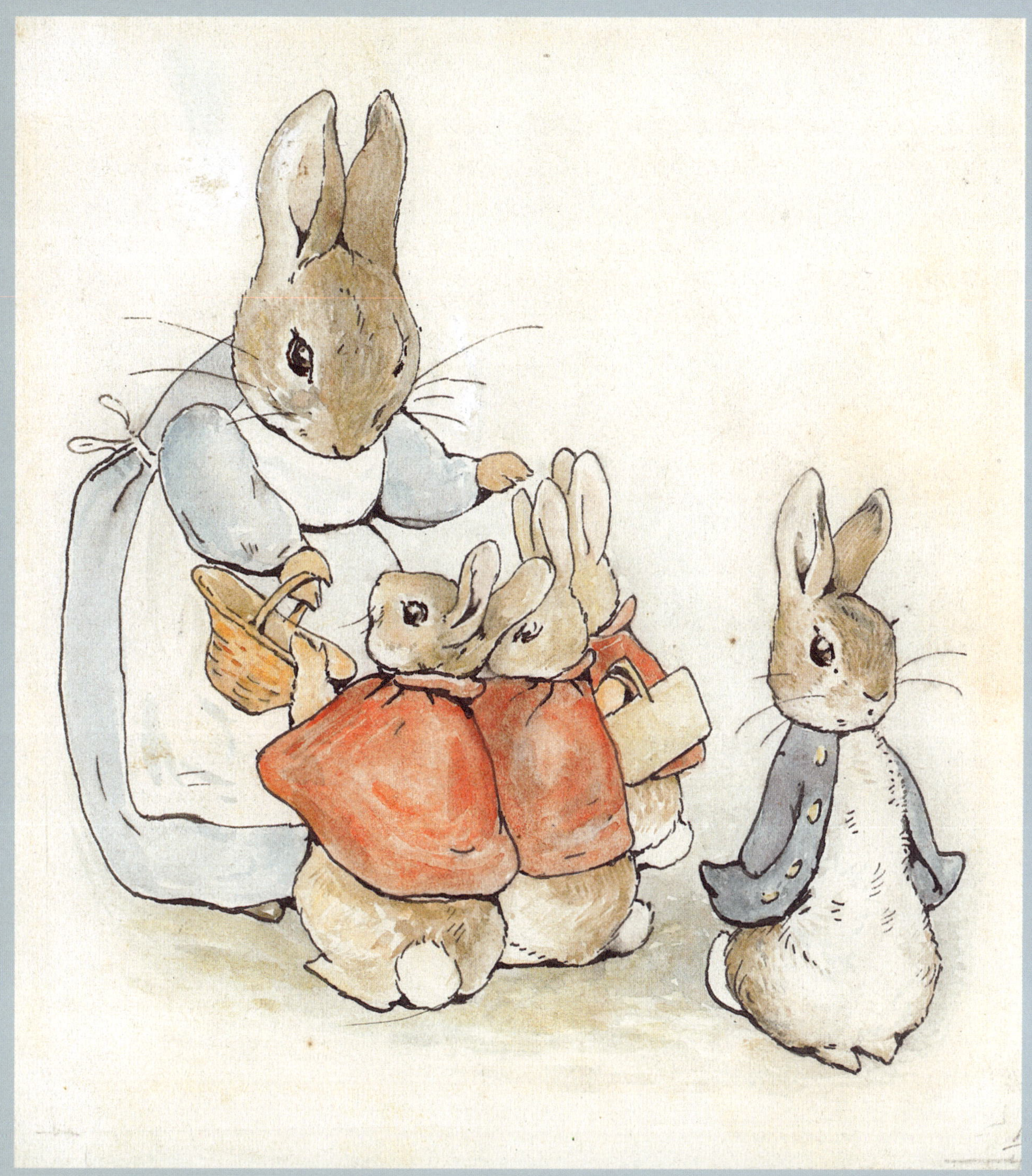

142, 143, 144.
The Tale of Peter Rabbit artwork, 1902
Watercolour and ink on paper
Warne Archive

Lady Mouse

The Tailor of Gloucester *takes place on Christmas Eve, the only time it is said that 'beasts can talk'. As the exhausted tailor sleeps, industrious mice sing nursery rhymes together as they finish embroidering a coat, while the cat Simpkin is a loner who is preoccupied with hunting them. This story, based on a Gloucester ghost story and Potter's favourite, references literature from William Shakespeare to the tale of Dick Whittington and the costume of one of the mice resembles that of the little girl in the famous painting* Cherry Ripe *by John Everett Millais.*[1]

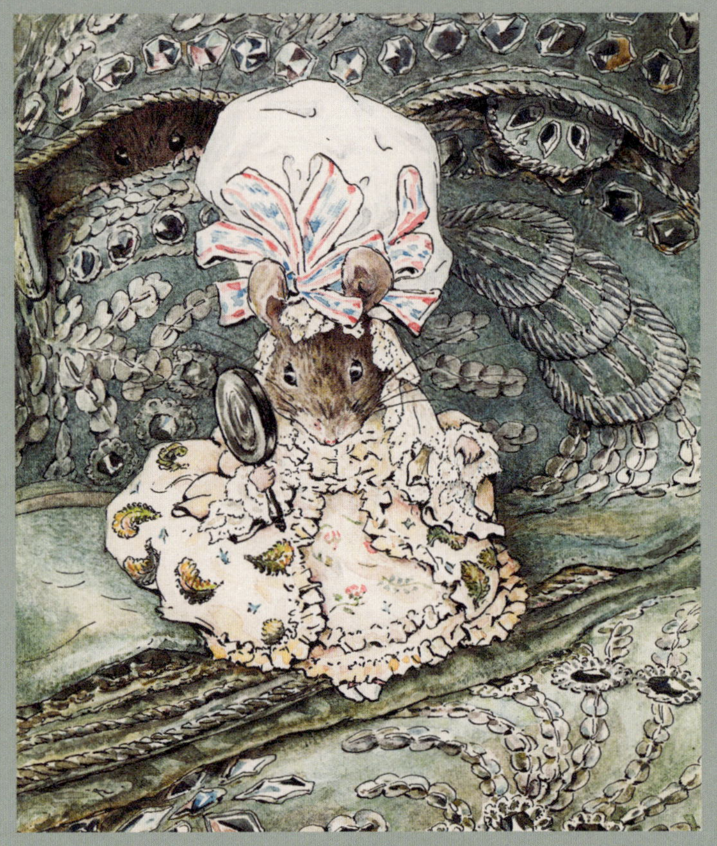

145.
The Tailor of Gloucester artwork, c.1902
Watercolour and ink on paper
Tate, A01091

Tomasina Tittlemouse

Mrs. Tomasina Tittlemouse is a woodmouse whose 'terribly tidy' character contrasts with her visitors, the 'creepy-crawly people' and Mr. Jackson, the toad. Mrs. Tittlemouse discovers a way to keep her home in order, by serving Mr. Jackson acorn-cups of honeydew through the window. She suffers many intrusions when preparing her home for hibernation but is too amiable a host to turn her visitors away. Mrs. Tittlemouse's meticulous nest-making reflects the behaviour of woodmice in nature, who live in complex multiple-chambered burrows and regulate the insect population from within.

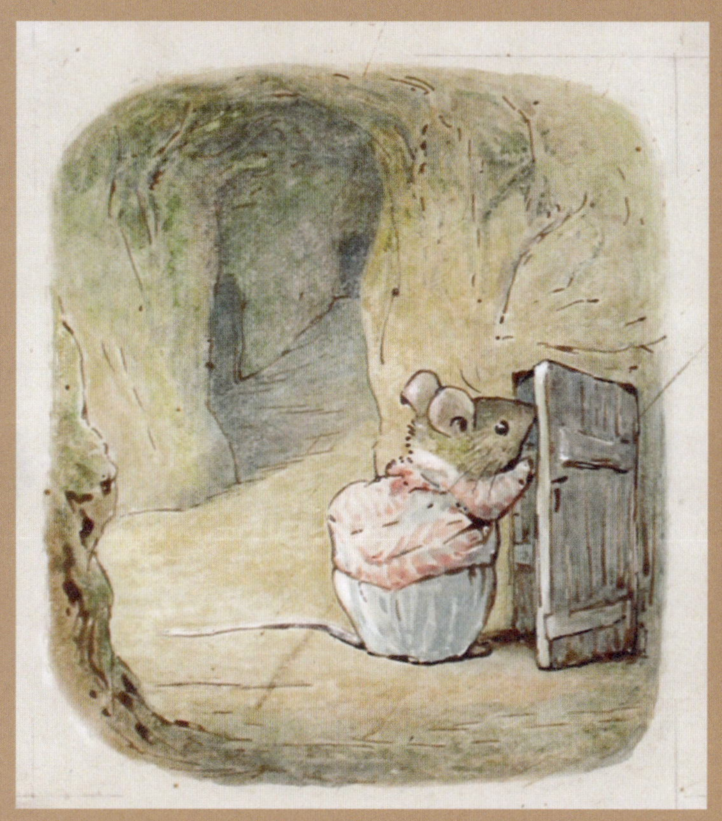

146.
The Tale of Mrs. Tittlemouse artwork,
January–June 1910
Watercolour and ink on paper
National Trust, 243047

Squirrel Nutkin

Squirrel Nutkin refuses to conform to nature, having as yet no fear of predators. The 'excessively impertinent' squirrel brazenly insults Old Mr. Brown the Owl, until the latter attacks and snatches off half his tail. A real squirrel informed the distinctive character of Nutkin (see no.42) and the story was inspired by the red squirrels who were said to mysteriously appear on St Herbert's Island at nut-gathering time and then disappear. Potter also knew of an American story about squirrels using rafts and their tails for sails.[2]

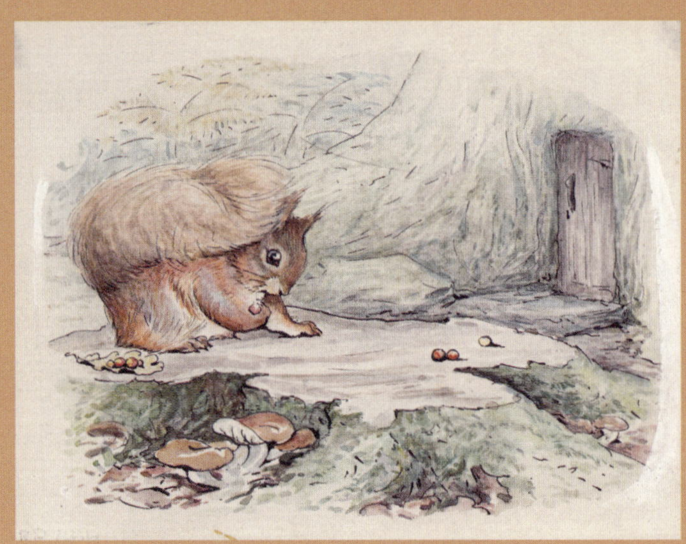

147, 148.
The Tale of Squirrel Nutkin artwork, 1903
Watercolour and ink over pencil on paper
National Trust, 243224, 243220

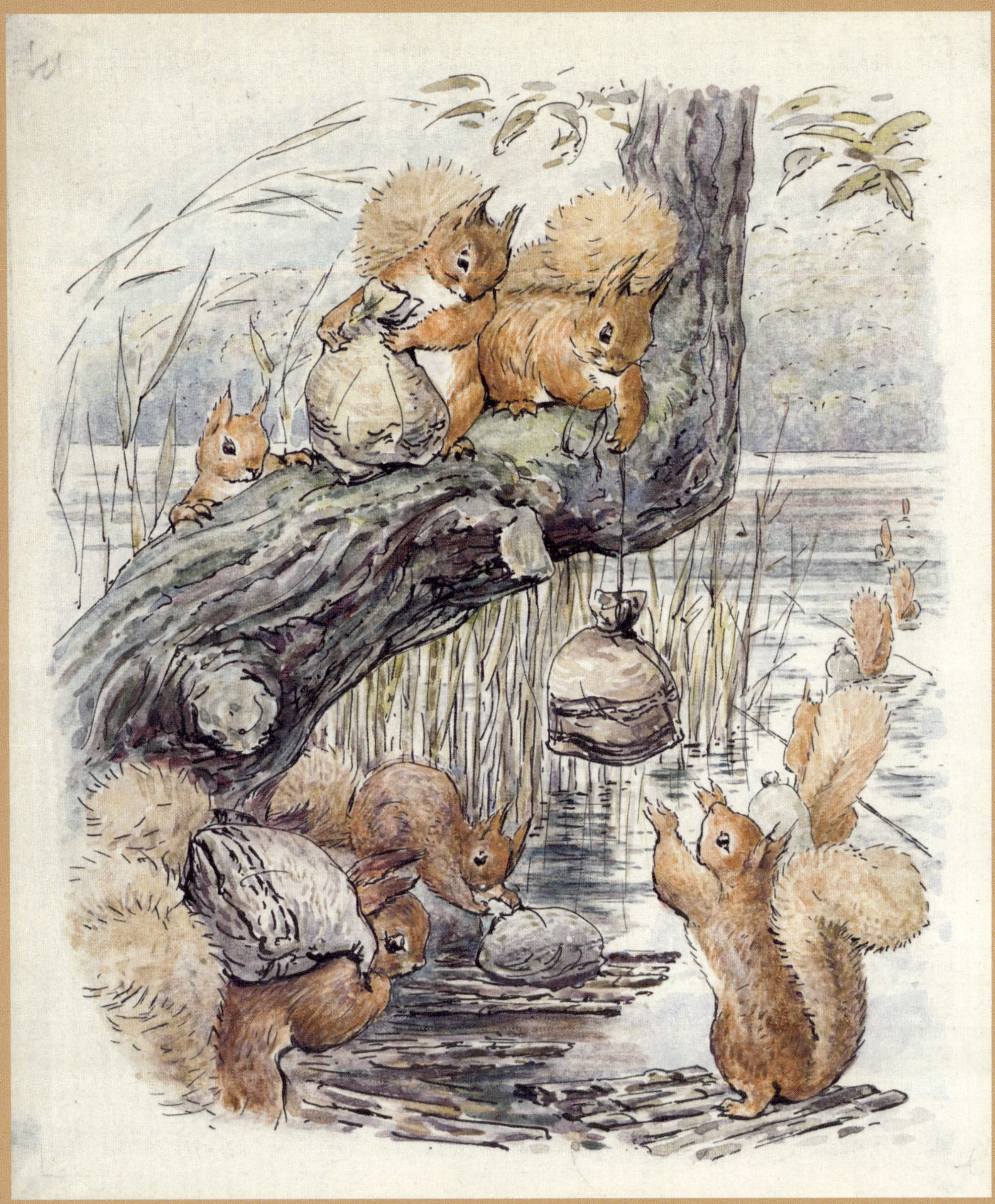

Benjamin Bunny

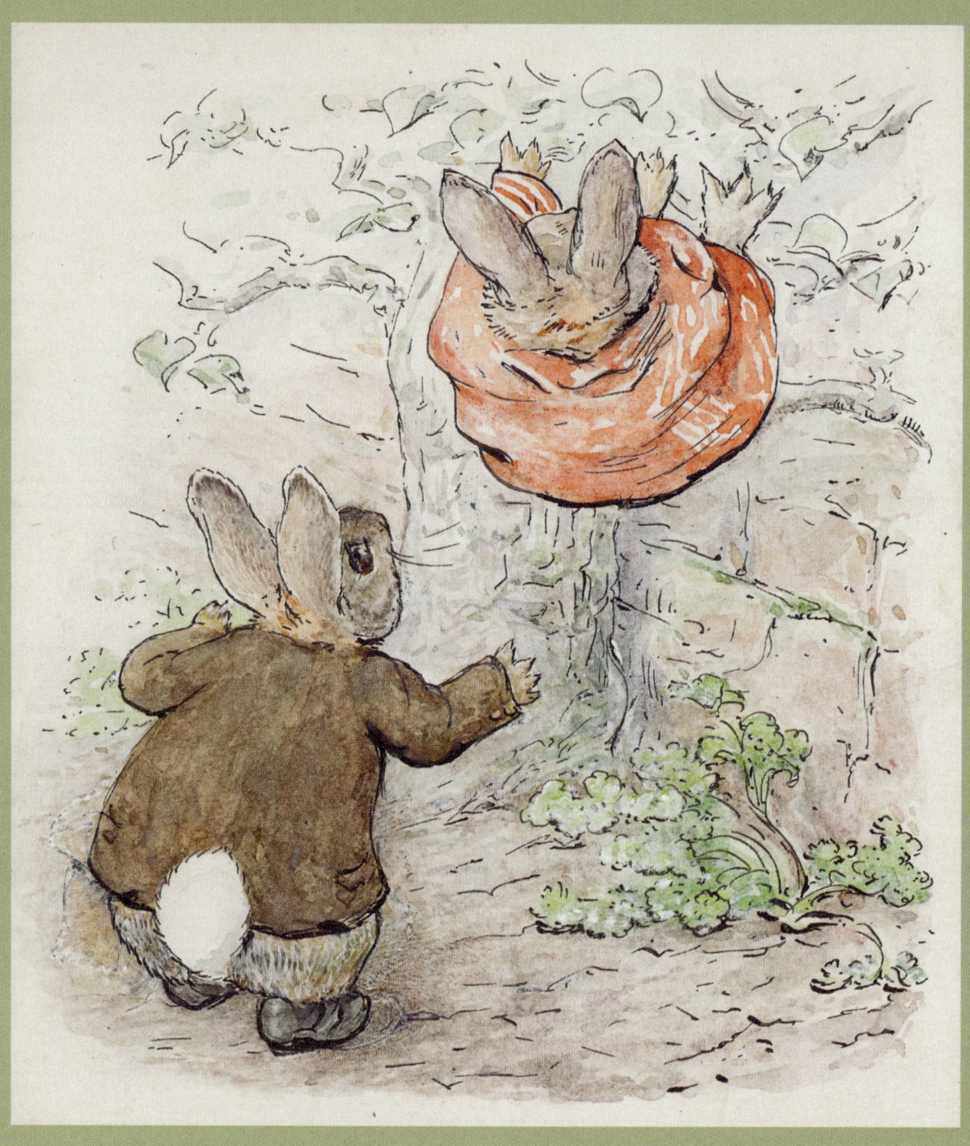

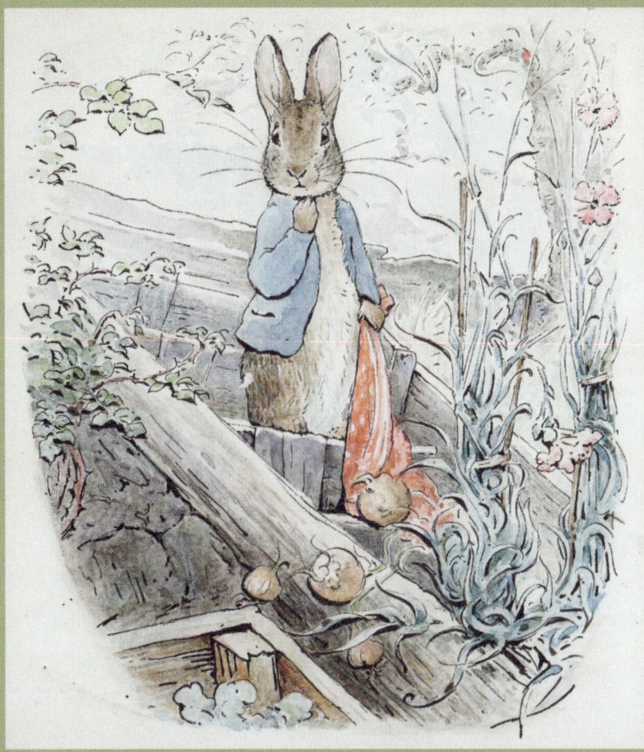

Still nervous from his earlier adventure, Peter is the reluctant accomplice in his second visit to McGregor's garden. This time his cousin, fearless mischief-maker Benjamin Bunny, persuades him to return to salvage Peter's clothes from the scarecrow. The pair can't resist lingering to sample the vegetables and end up having to be rescued by Old Mr. Bunny, Benjamin's father. The difference in character between Peter and Benjamin matches that of Potter's two favourite pet rabbits – Peter was placid compared to 'charming rascal' Benjamin.[3] In these drawings, Potter made use of real features from Fawe Park garden in the Lake District to add a sense of adventure and exploration.

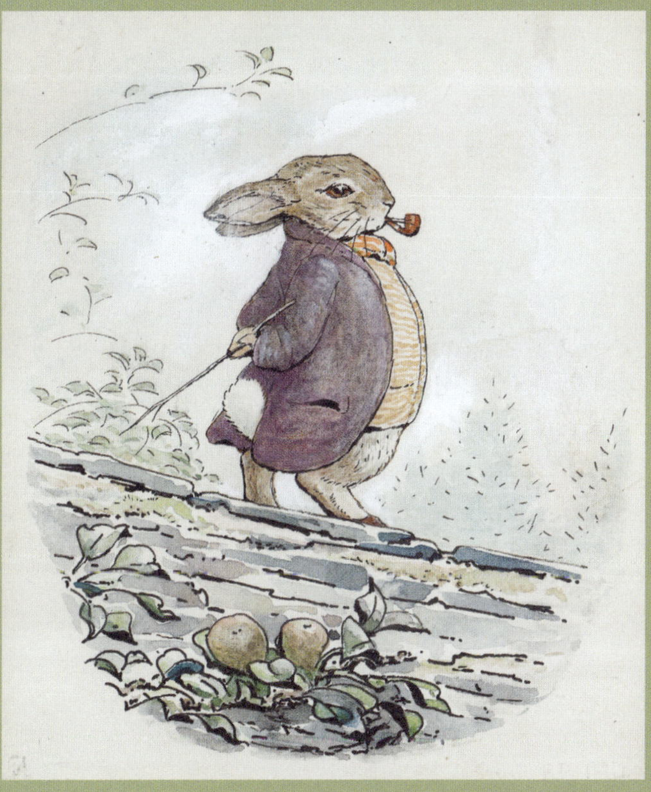

149, 150, 151.
The Tale of Benjamin Bunny artwork,
November 1903–March 1904
Watercolour and ink on paper
National Trust, 242940, 242949, 242956

Mrs. Tiggy-Winkle

Proud of her skill at starching, Mrs. Tiggy-Winkle does the laundry for many clients, including some characters from Potter's other stories. The many hours Potter dedicated to capturing the expressions of her own pet hedgehog, Mrs. Tiggy, translate into some of the most animated of any of her characters. The character of Mrs. Tiggy-Winkle was inspired by a real laundress, the heavily petticoated 'delightfully merry…as brown as a berry' Kitty MacDonald.[4]

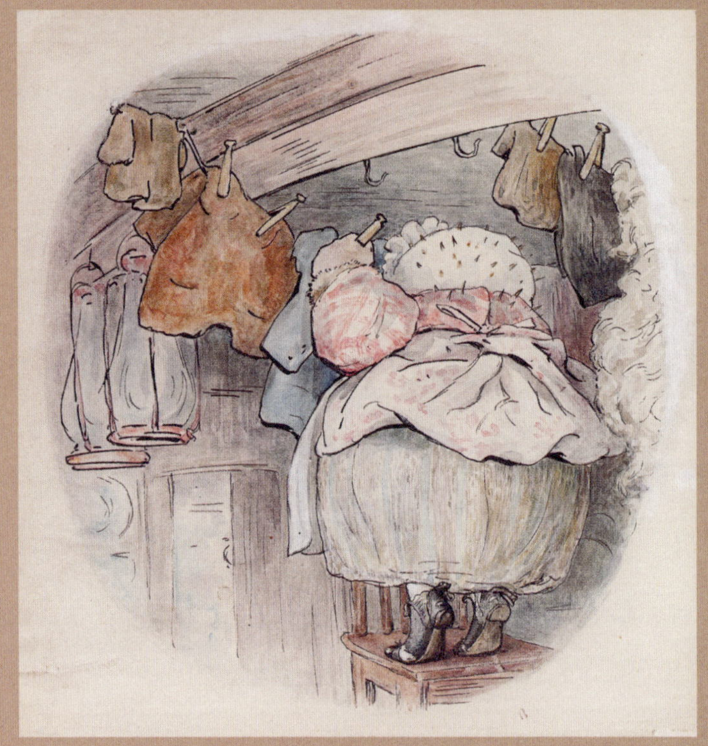

152, 153.
The Tale of Mrs. Tiggy-Winkle artwork, November 1904–July 1905
Watercolour and ink over pencil on paper
National Trust, 243307, 243312

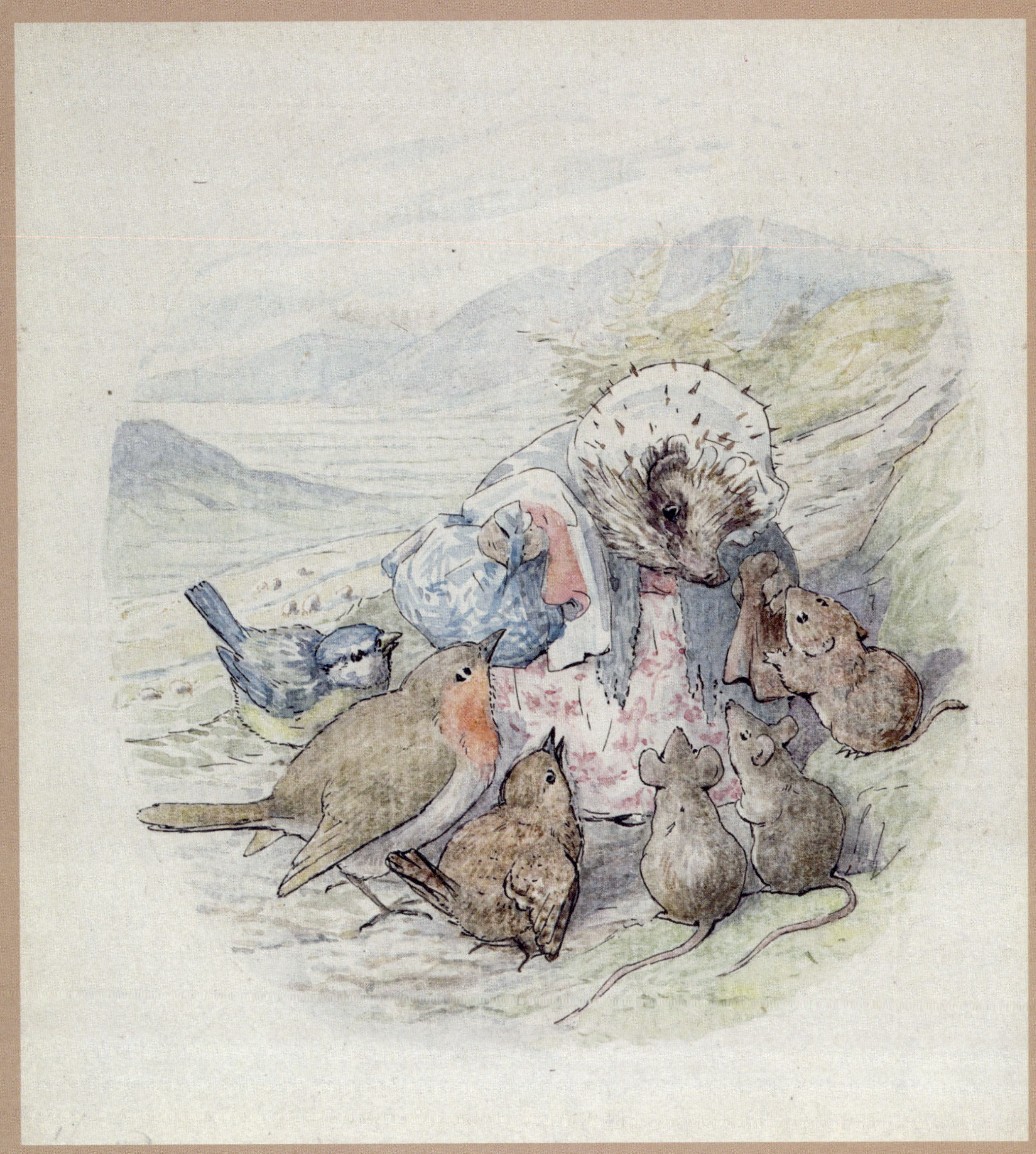

Ribby and Duchess

The cottages and colourful gardens of Sawrey and Hawkshead provide the setting for this humorous tale of etiquette and village gossip. Not wishing to eat mouse pie or to offend Ribby, her feline hostess, the dog Duchess sneaks into the house with something more palatable – ham and veal – but fails to switch pies. Thinking at first that she has swallowed the tin patty-pan from her own pie, she discovers that she has, after all, eaten mouse. Her strange behaviour ends up offending her hostess anyway. While the model for Ribby was likely one of many farm cats of Sawrey, Potter based proud Duchess on a pedigree Pomeranian dog owned by her housekeeper.

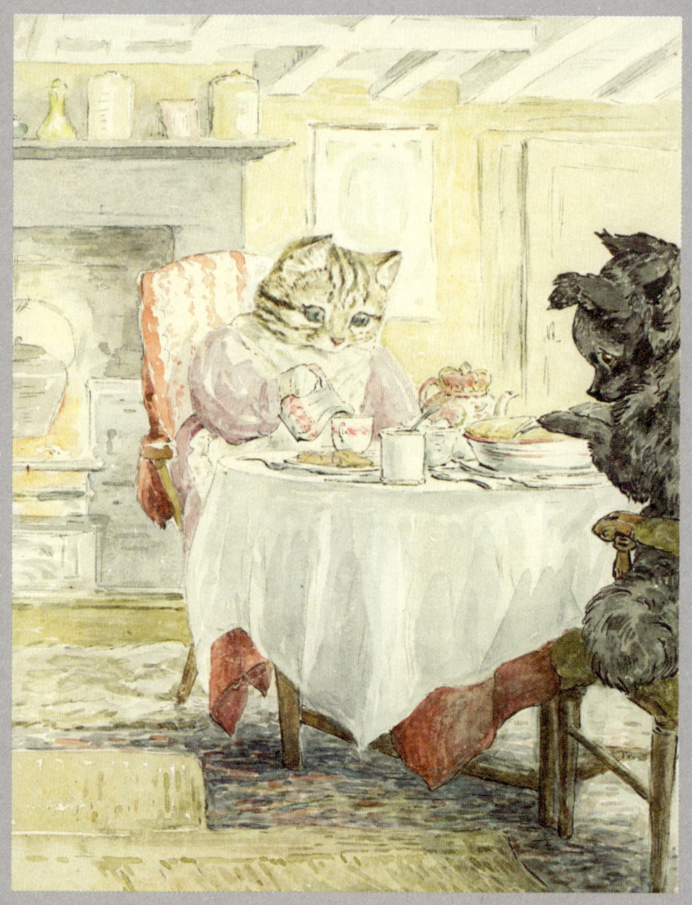

154.
The Pie and the Patty-Pan artwork, March–June 1905
Watercolour and ink over pencil on paper
National Trust, 243465

Tom Thumb and Hunca Munca

Potter exploited the acquisitive nature of mice to create the delightfully mischievous characters Tom Thumb and Hunca Munca who sneak off with some of the contents of a doll's house after causing havoc in the kitchen when they discover the food is not edible. The doll's house that features in the story was the one built for Winifred Warne by her uncle, Norman (Potter's publisher and fiancé) and was the kind where 'one cannot sit down without upsetting something'.[5] Norman sent Potter some dolls' house pieces and made a glass-fronted box for her pet mice to play in. She told him: 'Hunca Munca is very ready to play the game; I stopped her in the act of carrying a doll as large as herself up to the nest'.[6]

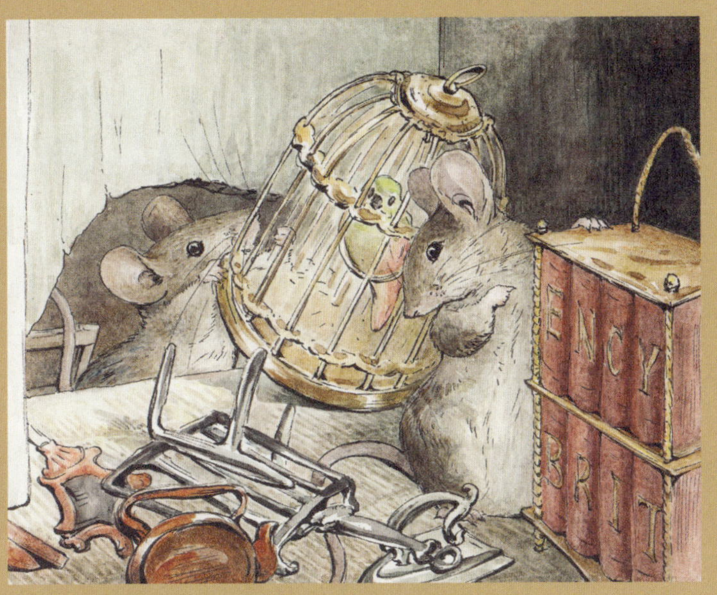

155.
The Tale of Two Bad Mice artwork,
February–June 1904
Watercolour and ink on paper
National Trust, 243032

Mr. Jeremy Fisher

In this tale of pride before a fall, Mr. Jeremy Fisher starts out quite the dapper gentleman in his stockings and dainty black shoes, but he loses his clothes when he is humiliated and forced to swim to shore. With delicate waterlilies, a glistening trout and the striped shell of a snail in Jeremy's larder, Potter captured the exquisite details of the natural world, set against the romantic backdrop of the hills and valleys surrounding Sawrey, her future home. An air of gentility (Jeremy appears in a 'sprigged waistcoat' and 'maroon tail-coat') reinforces the humour of the narrative.

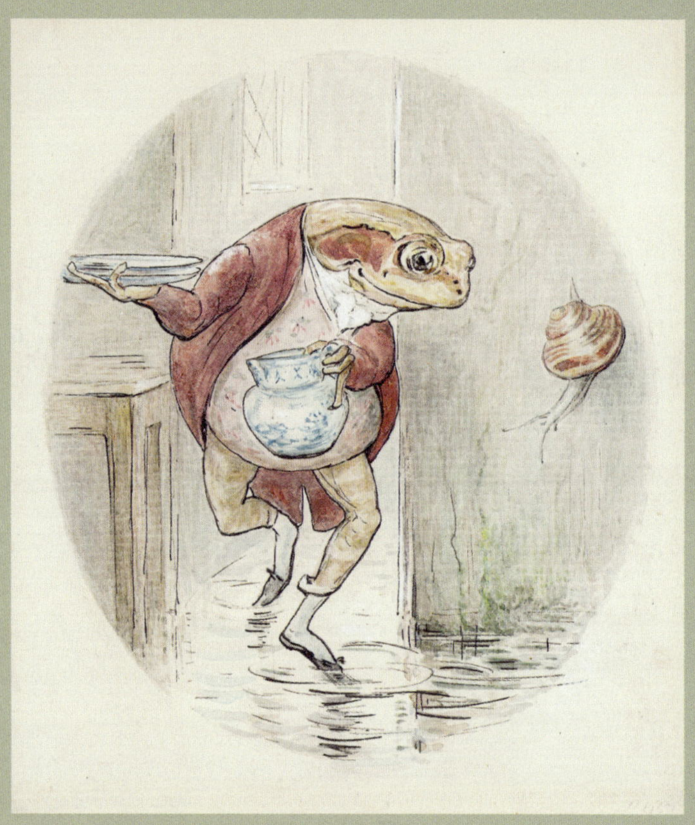

156, 157.
The Tale of Mr. Jeremy Fisher artwork, c.1906
Watercolour and ink over pencil on paper
National Trust, 243189, 243190

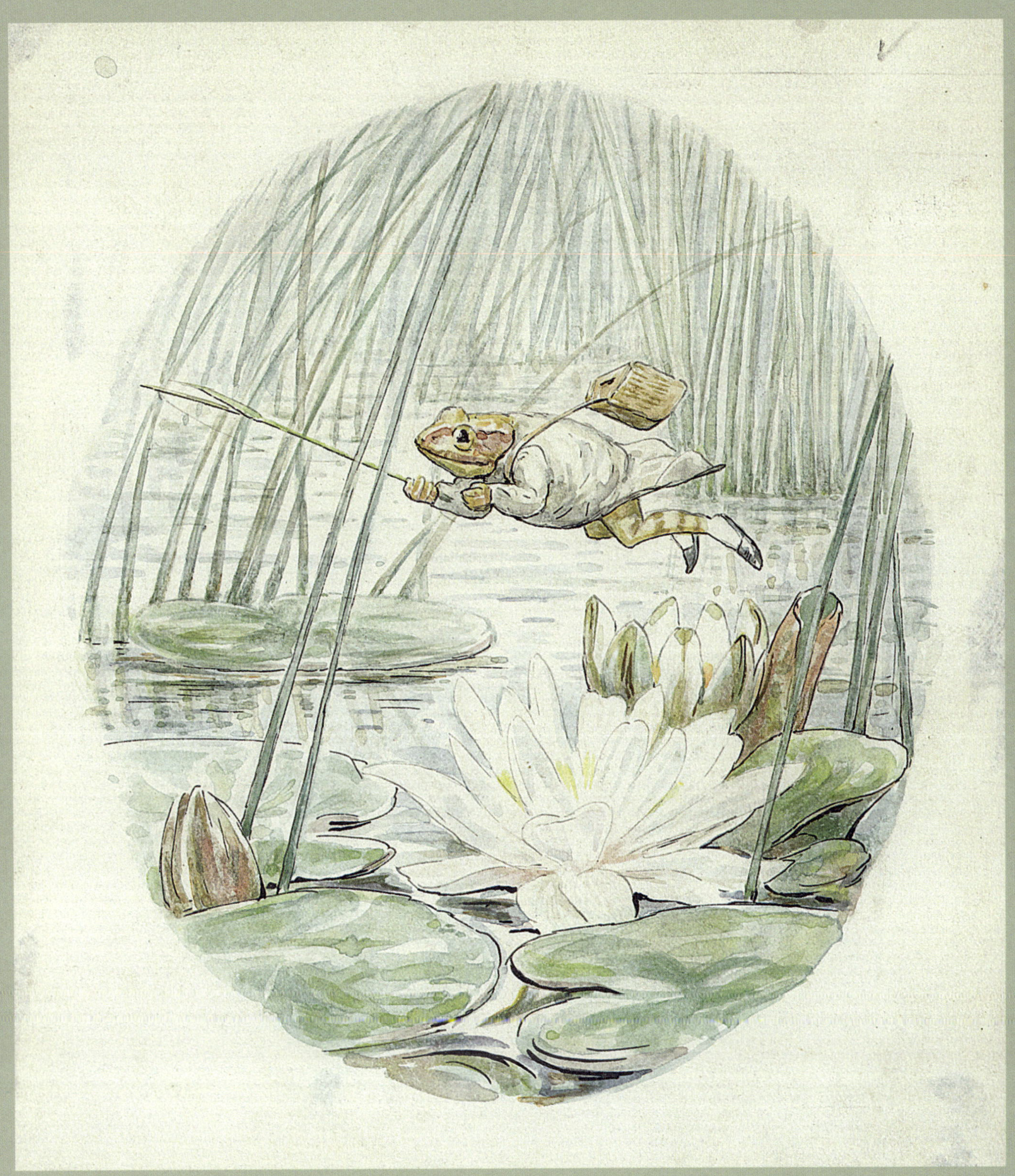

Fierce Bad Rabbit

Planned as a panoramic strip and partly told using pictures, this is a story about predators and prey. The fierce rabbit preys on another rabbit and steals his carrot, oblivious to the human predator behind him with a gun. The moment he is shot is expertly visualized by Potter as a confusion of lines, eyes, carrot and bob-tail. Potter's first story aimed at very young children was written in response to Louie, publisher Harold Warne's little girl, who thought that Peter Rabbit was much too well-behaved. Potter's panoramas were turned into book format from 1916 because booksellers struggled with the concertina format.

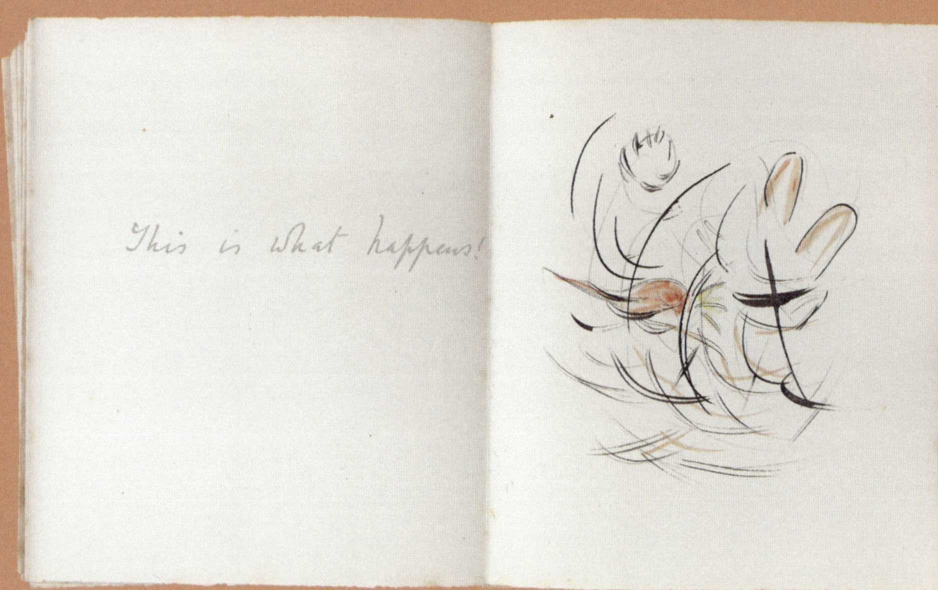

158.
The Story of a Fierce Bad Rabbit, section from a manuscript panorama, dated 23 February 1906
Watercolour and ink over pencil on paper
National Trust, 242210

Miss Moppet

The Story of Miss Moppet *is another predator and prey story, which was also originally designed as a panorama. Potter's illustrations shift between the characters' different perspectives. The kitten Moppet's razor-sharp eyes contrast with the pretty pink ribbon around her neck. She devises an ingenious trap to catch a mouse by wrapping a duster around her head to rouse his curiosity, but then the inexperienced kitten causes him to escape by playing with him like she would a ball.*

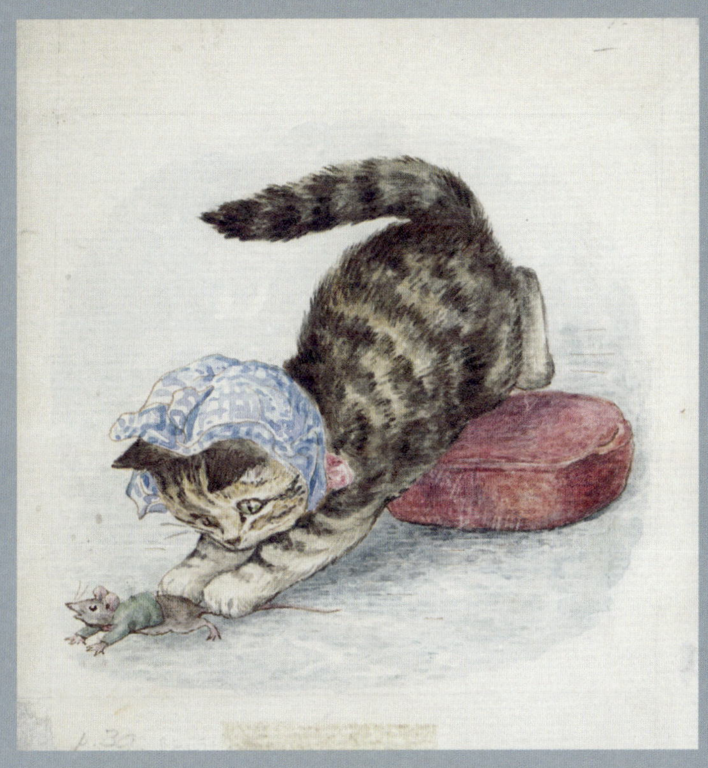

159.
The Story of Miss Moppet artwork, 1906
Watercolour and ink over pencil on paper
National Trust, 243249

Jemima Puddle-Duck

Jemima Puddle-Duck lives at Hill Top. Desperate to hatch her eggs safely, Jemima takes flight from the fields above. Her shawl and poke bonnet are reminiscent of a bygone era and it is tempting to view the character of the gullible duck as an homage to Jane Austen's Lydia Bennet.[7] *Jemima's adventure, after falling for the charms of the dashing 'sandy whiskered gentleman', ends in her rescue by the brusque but handsome sheepdog, Kep. The story was based on Potter's experience at Hill Top, her first farm, where the manager's wife, Mrs Canon, used hens to hatch duck eggs.*

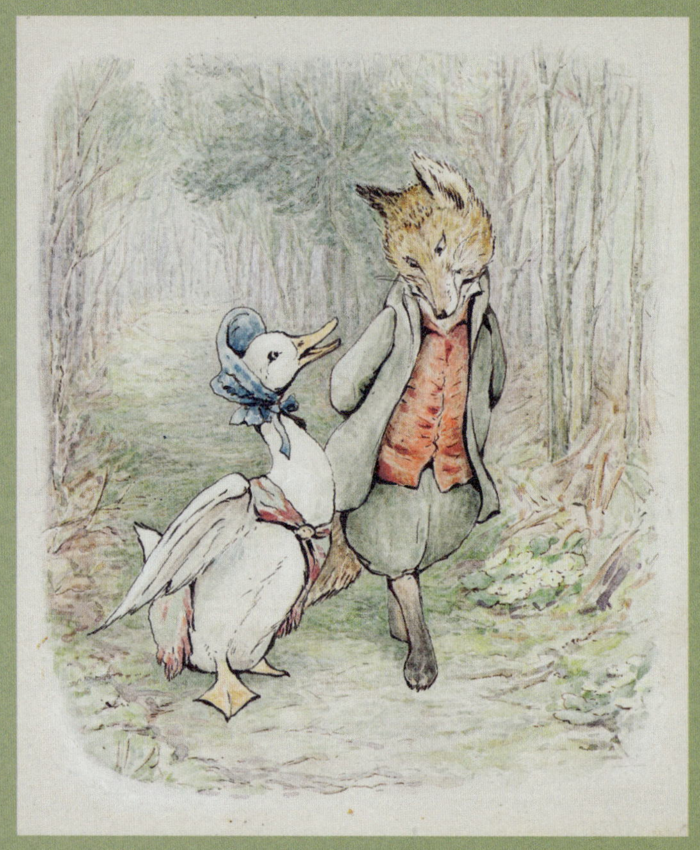

160, 161.
The Tale of Jemima Puddle-Duck artwork, 1908
Watercolour and ink on paper
National Trust, 243073, 243080

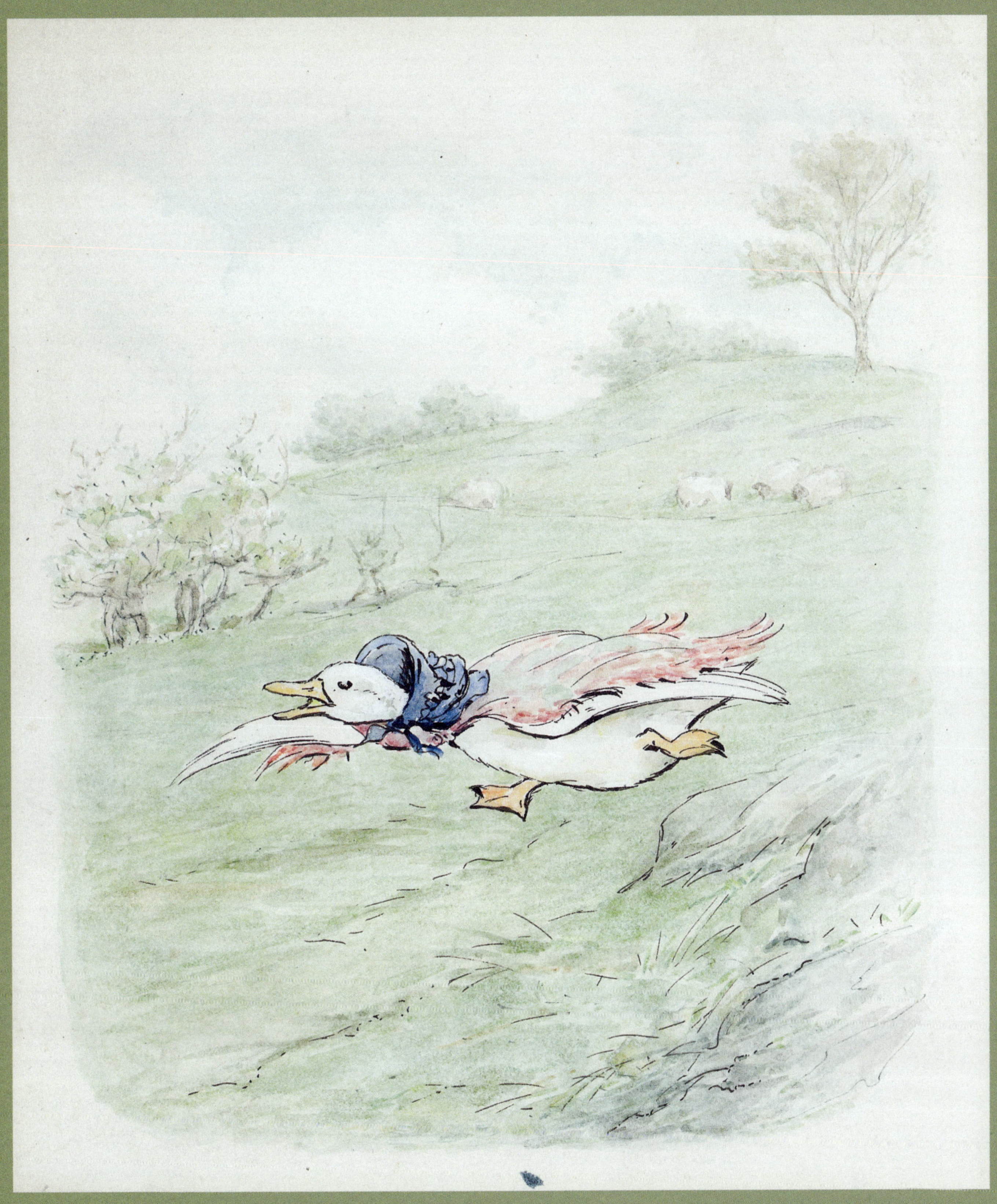

Tom Kitten

The Tale of Tom Kitten *is about good manners, or rather, a lack of them. Tom and his sisters Mittens and Moppet get up to all sorts of trouble, upsetting their mother Tabitha Twitchit by discarding their 'elegant' but 'uncomfortable' clothes. Potter modelled Tom's movements on a tabby kitten she borrowed, which she described as a 'fearful pickle'.*[8] *Irises, azaleas and St John's Wort crowd into the garden illustrations. At the time Potter was enjoying planning the garden at Hill Top, 'a case of the survival of the fitest [sic]'*[9] *in its haphazard mix of traditional flowers, herbs, fruit and vegetables.*

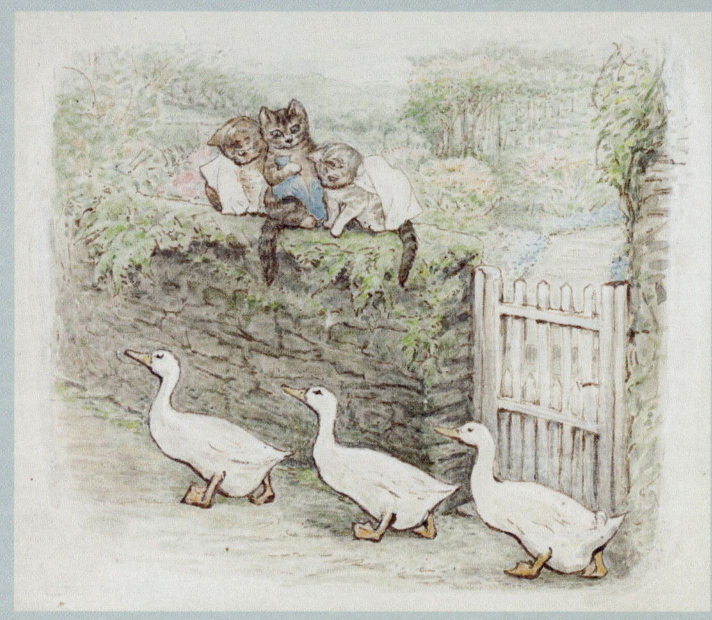

162, 163.
The Tale of Tom Kitten artwork, July 1906–June 1907
Watercolour and ink over pencil on paper
National Trust, 243332, 243328

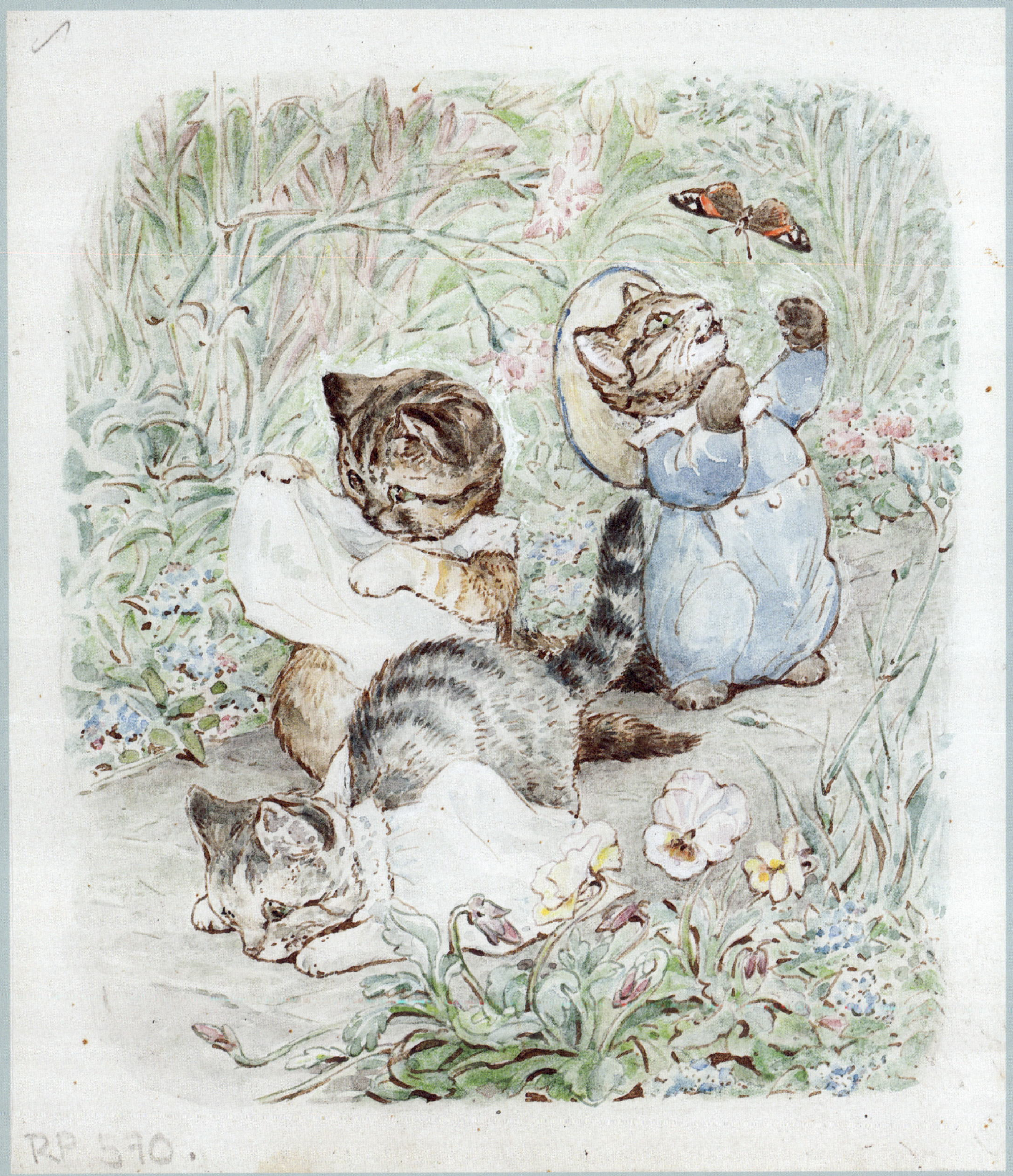
R.P. 590.

Samuel Whiskers and Anna Maria

In this second adventure featuring Tom Kitten, Tabitha Twitchit's wayward son explores the fireplace and becomes lost amongst the confusing network of chimneys. He almost ends up as dinner for the gentleman rat Samuel Whiskers and his resourceful wife Anna Maria, who run around the farm-house gathering ingredients for the prospective feast. Tom is rescued from beneath the floorboards by the carpenter while Whiskers and his wife escape, using a wheelbarrow resembling Potter's own. For this tale, Potter drew upon real-life experience of some unwelcome – and ingenious – rat visitors to her farmhouse at Hill Top.

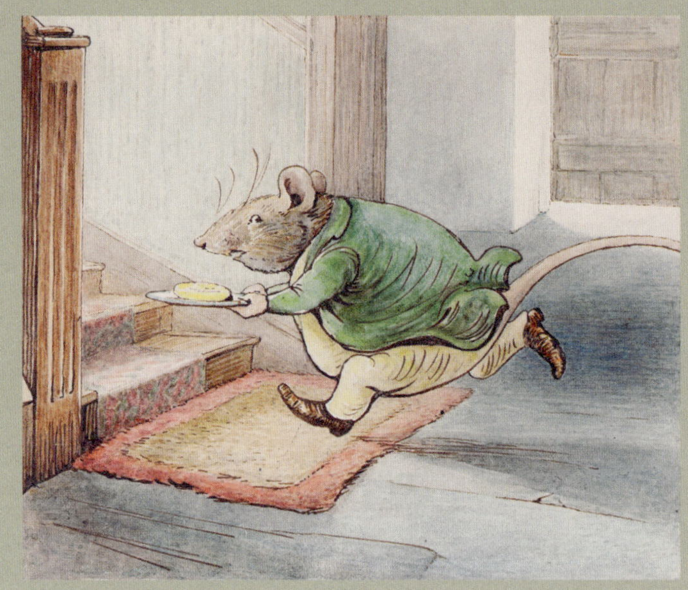

164, 165.
The Roly-Poly Pudding; later renamed *The Tale of Samuel Whiskers* artwork, 1907–July 1908
Watercolour and ink over pencil on paper
National Trust, 243403, 243415

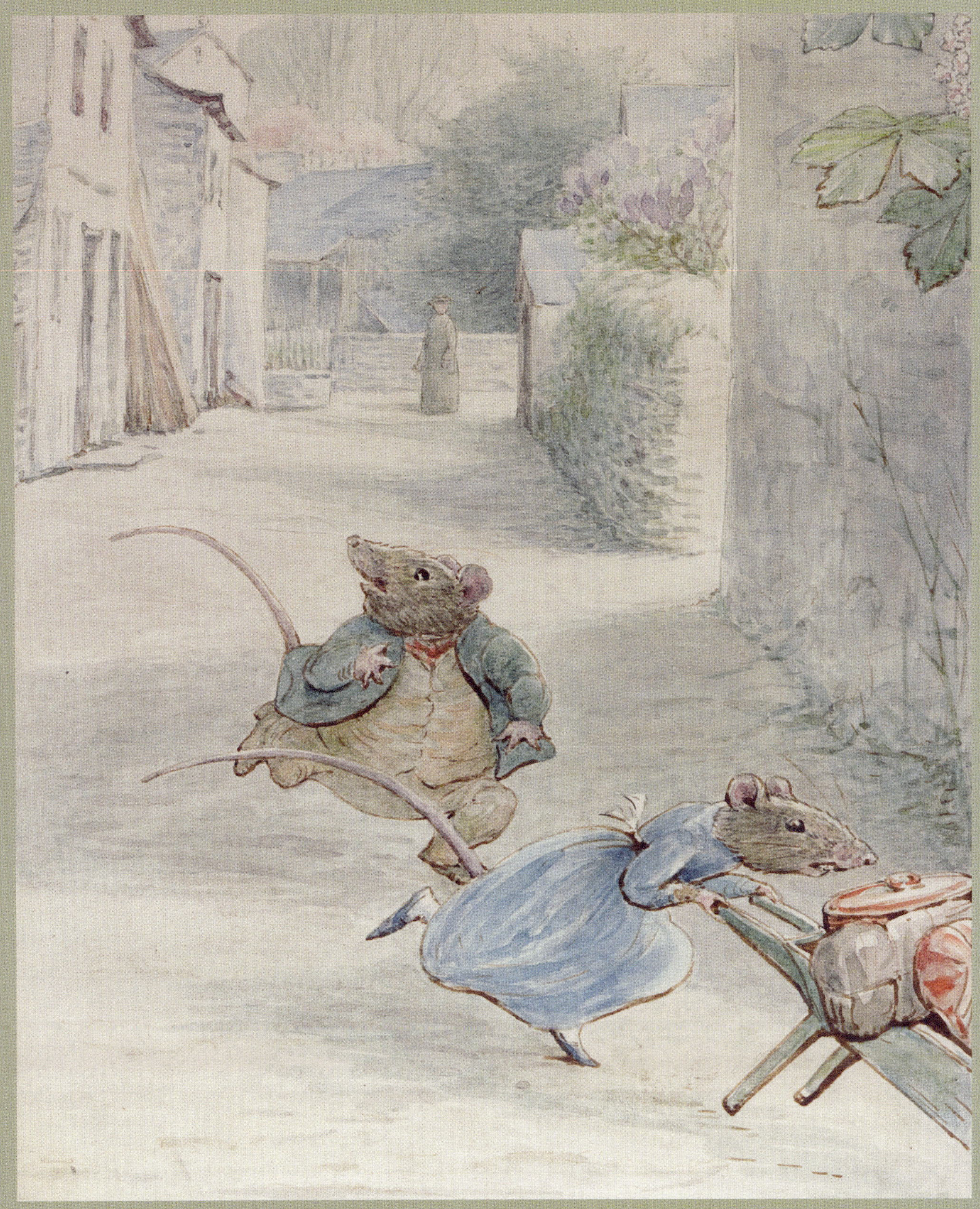

Mr. Tod and Tommy Brock

The Tale of Mr. Tod *combines a kidnap adventure with humorous slapstick and is unusual for giving the villains centre-stage. Mr. Tod the fox wants badger Tommy Brock to get out of his house. Pretending to be asleep, Tommy watches Mr. Tod set up an elaborate trick involving a bucket of water. He escapes unscathed and leaves Mr. Tod waiting in vain for the trick to work. While he is distracted by this, Peter and Benjamin rescue the Flopsy Bunnies. Potter was fascinated by dialect and takes the names of Tod and Brock from local words meaning fox and badger. Her story was partly inspired by an 'Uncle Remus' fable.*

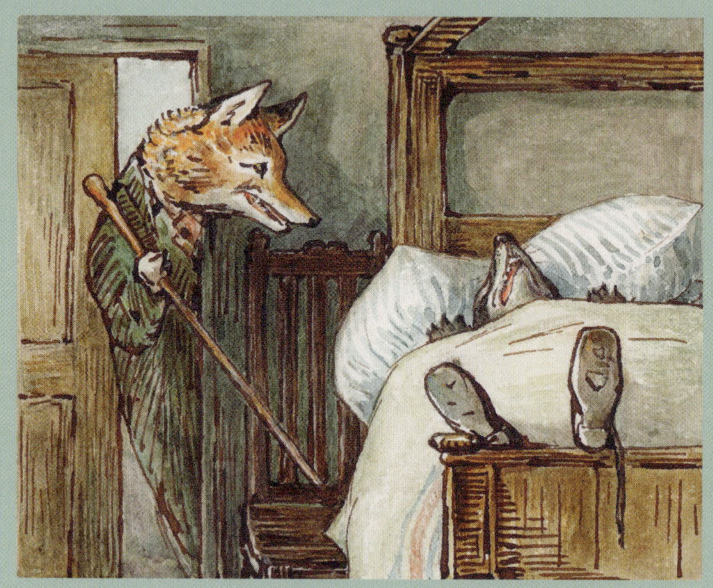

166.
The Tale of Mr. Tod artwork, 1912
Watercolour and ink over pencil on paper
National Trust, 242846

Pigling Bland

In The Tale of Pigling Bland, *Potter balanced an idealized view of rural life with the realities of farming. She depicted herself as the farmer, impressing upon Pigling and Alexander the importance of their paperwork (at that time, pigs required a licence to be transported over a county boundary). Alexander loses his papers and is turned back leaving Pigling to carry on alone. During his adventure, Pigling finds a soul mate and they run away together. Potter was adamant that the book was not autobiographical, but it is tempting to compare Pigling and Pigwig's happy ending with her own: she married William Heelis within weeks of its publication.*

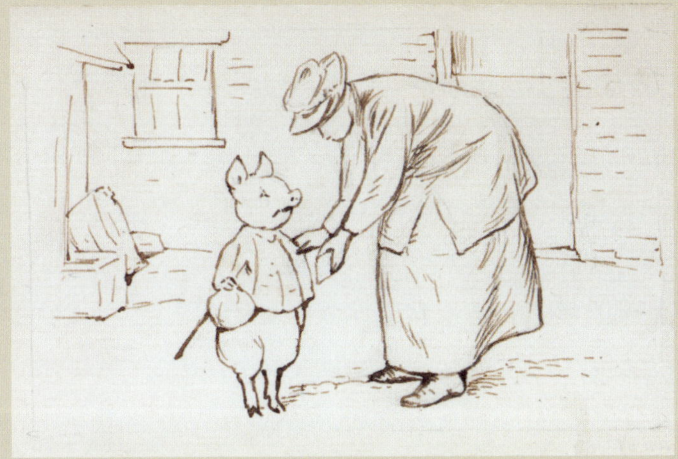

167.
The Tale of Pigling Bland artwork, May–September 1913
Ink over pencil on paper
National Trust, 242807

Appley Dapply

An early manuscript from 1905, Appley Dapply's Nursery Rhymes *contains 30 rhymes reflecting Potter's passion for animals and nature. Characters range from Appley, a little brown mouse who raids cupboards for treats, and Mr. Pricklepin, a hedgehog with 'never a cushion to stick his pins in', to an 'amiable guinea pig' with impressively coiffed hair. A rhyme about a fairy ring of toadstools reflects her great interest in fungi. Potter was influenced by the style and metre of traditional nursery rhymes, which she had studied from the 1890s. The book was finally published in 1917 with a smaller selection of verses.*

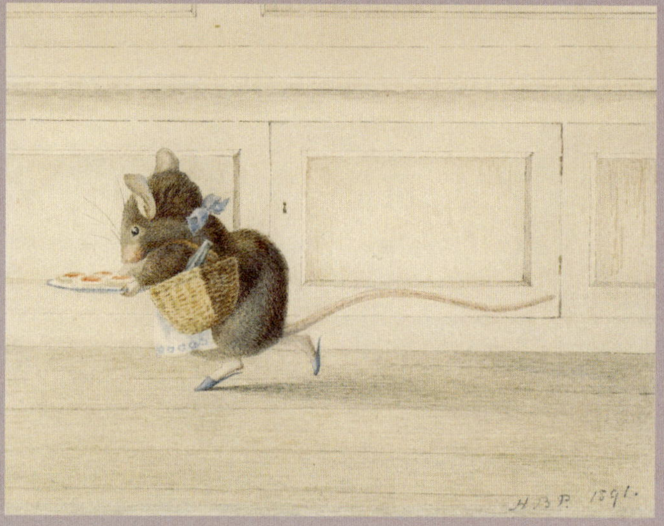

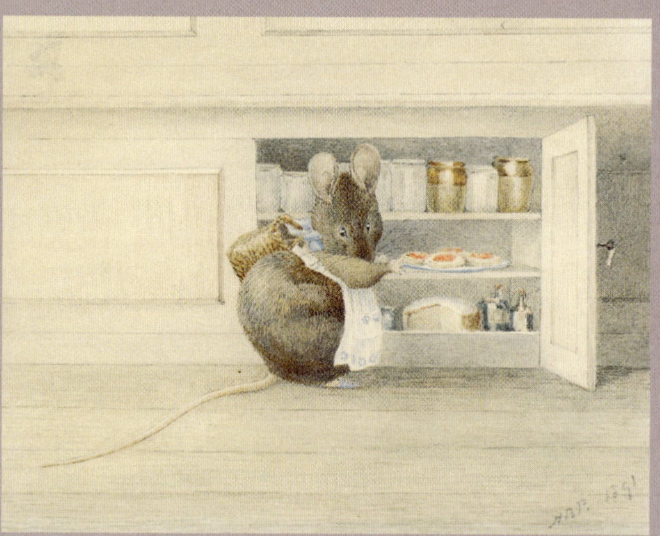

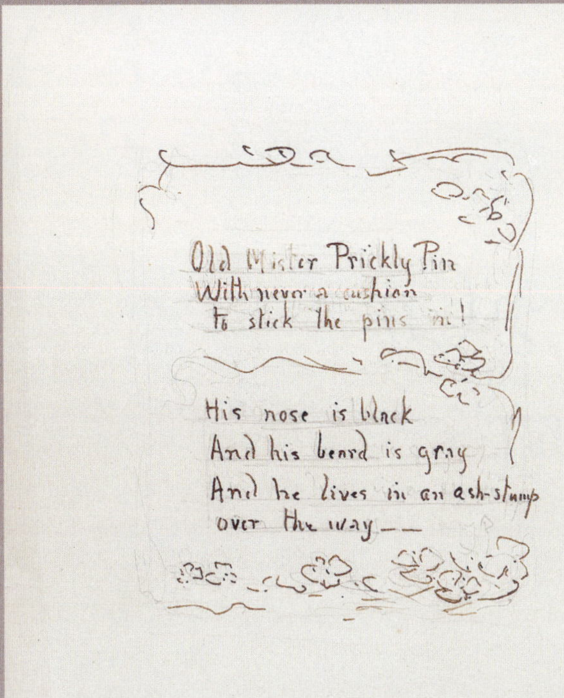

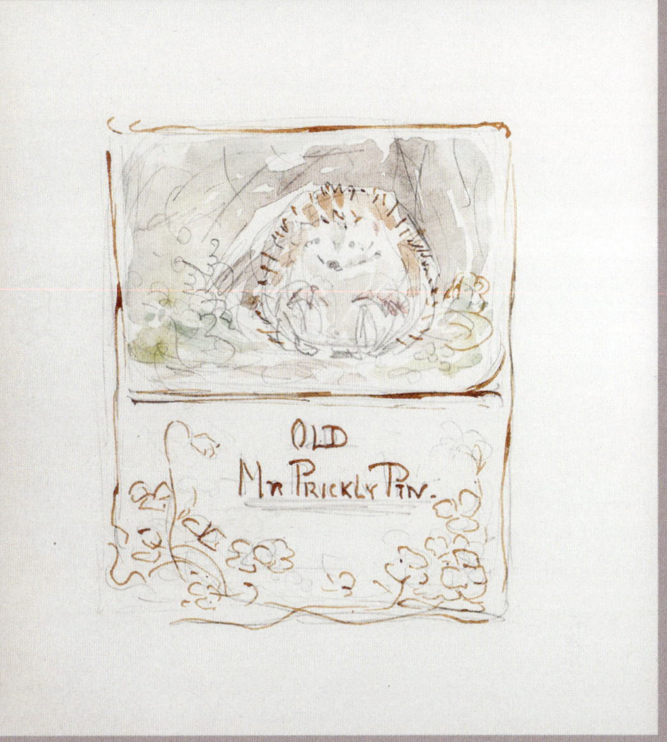

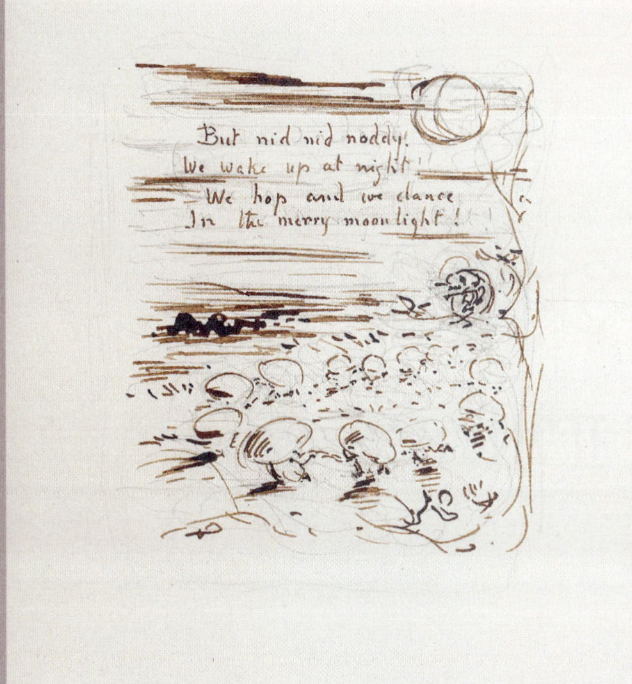

168 Opposite
Appley Dapply, 1891
Watercolour on paper
V&A: LC 29/A/1-2, given by the Linder Collection

169. This page
Appley Dapply's Nursery Rhymes, pages from a manuscript, 1905
Ink and pencil on paper
National Trust, 242235

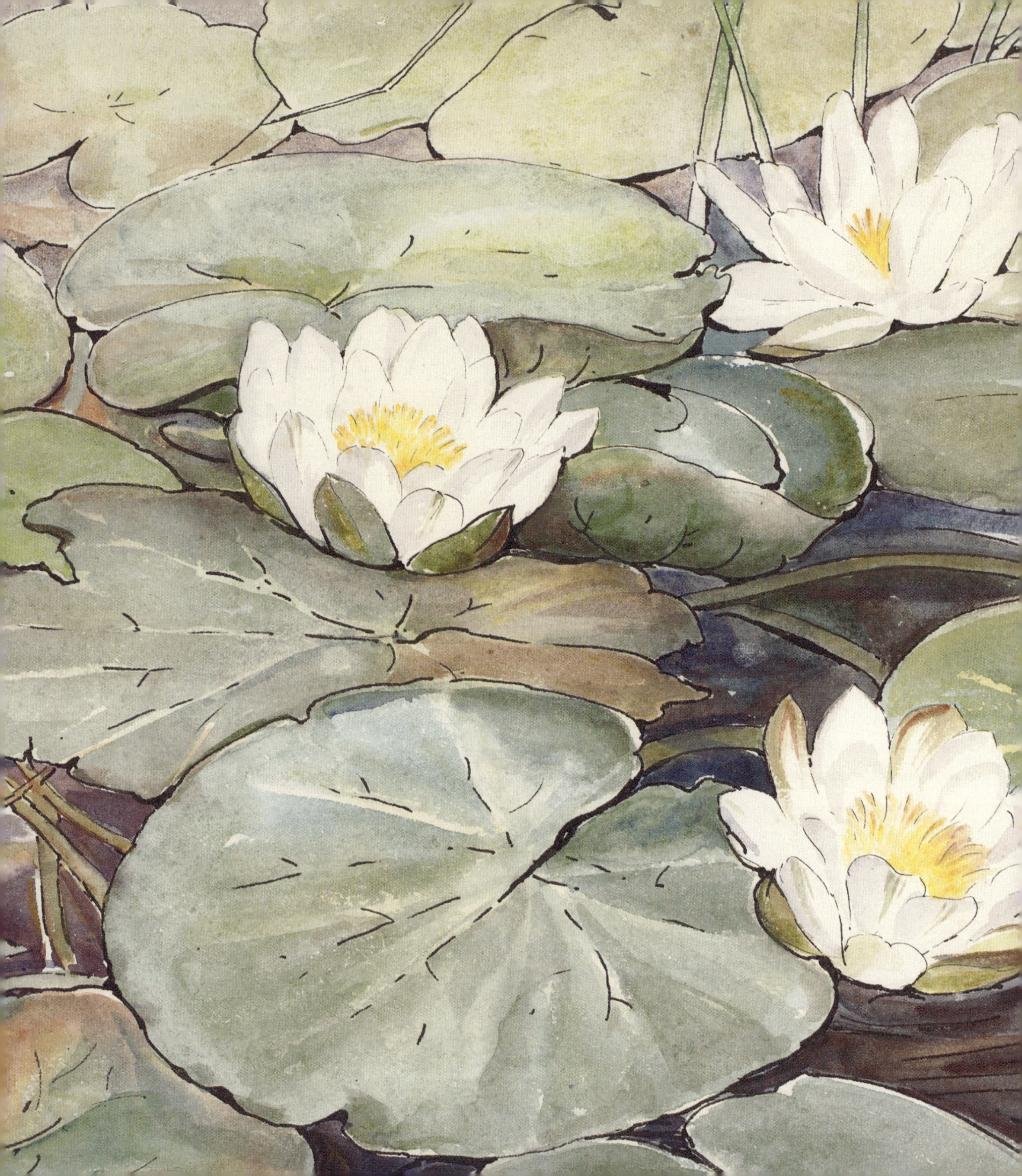

Notes and References

Notes

Full references are given in the Bibliography, p.204. Page numbers are not given for Journal, or for letters in Morse 1982 and Taylor 1989, which are organised chronologically.

Introduction

1 Morse 1982, p.213, Beatrix Potter's reply to a request for biographical information for Mahony Miller et al. 1947.
2 *Journal*, 25 July 1884.
3 Potter, May 1929, quoted in Morse 1982, p.207.
4 Ibid.
5 'A Christmas Fairy Tale', *Tailor and Cutter* (24 December 1903), vol.39, p.779, quoted in Lear 2007, p.165; Lear 2007, p.182.
6 UNESCO World Heritage Site designation, whc.unesco.org/en/list/422/ (accessed 2 February 2021).
7 https://www.lakedistrict.gov.uk/caringfor/policies/whs/what-is-a-world-heritage-site (accessed 2 February 2021).

Town and Country

1 Referring to her feelings when visiting the countryside around Camfield, her grandparents' home.
2 Sheppard 1983, vol.41, p.210. The house was built by John Spicer in 1863–4.
3 Ibid. Rupert paid £3,700 for the lease, equivalent to approximately £350,000 today.
4 Hobhouse 1986, vol.42, pp.196–214, 395–413: four Metropolitan District Railway stations were built between 1865 and 1869; Sheppard 1973, vol.37, p.3: between 1861 and 1881 the population rose from 70,108 to 163,151.
5 *Journal*, 8 June 1883.
6 Potter referred to her 'unloved' home in response to a request from Bertha Mahony Miller, editor of *The Horn Book* magazine, for biographical information c.1943 (see Morse 1982, p.213); for the Saunders' fires, see *Journal*, 20 March and 9 October 1885.
7 Morse 1982, letter to Marian Frazer Harris Perry, 13 July 1936.
8 Caused, for example, by radical protests by supporters of working-class suffrage or Irish Home Rule (see *Journal*, 16 March 1883, 27 May 1885, 18 December 1885 and 9 February 1886).
9 *Journal*, 18 March 1885, on a trip to the theatre to see *The Private Secretary*; while on a trip to Holborn she 'found the drive most interesting', *Journal*, May 1890.
10 *Journal*, 5 July 1883, 21 June 1883 (13 and 18 June), swimming; 30 March, 19 May 1883, Round Pond; 1 July 1882, Zoological Gardens with 'Miss Worseley'.
11 The South Kensington Museum moved there in 1852, and the art schools in 1857. She attended the art schools, visited the art library and was aware of the Print Room. The Natural History Museum, as it is now known, was a branch of the British Museum and was completed in 1881. The Royal Albert Hall opened in 1871 (see Bryant 2011).
12 Beatrix helped as she grew older, especially when her mother was ill (see, for example, *Journal*, 11 October 1895 and 26 August 1892). She did, however, receive a substantial gift of some shares from her father around 6 May 1895, worth £5,000, which is equivalent to approximately £540,000 today.
13 She had her first driving lesson on holiday at Bush Hall, Hertfordshire, *Journal*, 1 August 1884. 'I never touched anything...', describing an accident at Troutbeck, *Journal*, 26 August 1896, when she 'was banged into another female driving a gig'. She was usually chaperoned by her maid Elizabeth Harper, by a housemaid, by her governess and companion Annie Carter or by her former governess, Florence Hammond.
14 Several relatives became Liberal members of Parliament. Beatrix's journal frequently follows political events and reveals excitement during general elections from as early as 1886 (when she was 20), despite not being eligible to vote herself. *Journal*, 18 March 1885, *The Private Secretary* at the Globe Theatre near Aldwych; 3 June 1885, Eduard Strauss at the Imperial Inventions Exhibition of 1885, on the site of the present-day Imperial College. Potter was much taken with Strauss at the time, although she later claimed no love of music.
15 Madeline Davidson was governess 1875–8, and Florence Hammond 1878–83; Bertram also had a Latin tutor, Mr Stocker.
16 Potter, May 1929, quoted in Morse 1982, p.208, 'thank goodness, my education was neglected'.
17 *Journal*, 17 July 1883, 'Have finished Dr. Arnold, am doing Virgil, like it so much'; 17 May 1884, 'Have begun Cicero, easier than Virgil'.
18 *Journal*, c.1891, 'Memories of Camfield Place', music lessons are mentioned in a semi-fictional account of her grandparents' home written to an imaginary correspondent, Esther; *Journal*, 26 December 1896, Julius Oscar Brefeld.
19 *Journal*, 4 November 1884.
20 Taylor 1987, p.39.
21 *Journal*, 25 April 1883.
22 Potter, May 1929, quoted in Morse 1982, p.208.
23 Annie had lived in Germany. She married Edwin Moore in 1885, and was the mother of some of the child recipients of Beatrix Potter's picture letters.
24 See her painting of Wray Castle library, where she stayed in 1882 (V&A: BP.231, Linder Bequest LB 78).
25 Potter, May 1929, quoted in Morse 1982, p.208.
26 Morse 1982, letters to Mrs Ramsey Duff, June 1943, and to Anne Carroll Moore, 17 January 1940. Books by Juliana Horatia Ewing and Maria Edgeworth survive in Potter's library, Duke Collection, V&A: AAD/2006/4/19-31.
27 Morse 1982, letter to Helen Dean Fish, 8 December 1934.
28 Potter, May 1929, quoted in Morse 1982, p.208.
29 The sixth, 1862 edition of *A Book of Nonsense* survives in Potter's library, Duke Collection, V&A: AAD/2006/4/49.
30 Morse 1982, letter to Marian Frazer Harris Perry, 30 March 1939. Elizabeth Wetherell was the pseudonym of Susan Warner.
31 Taylor 1989, letter to Helen Dean Fish, 8 December 1934.
32 Potter, May 1929, quoted in Morse 1982, p.208.
33 Morse 1982, letter to Marian Frazer Harris Perry, 4 October 1934.
34 *Journal*, 8 December 1883, commenting on the artist's death.
35 Morse 1982, letters to Helen Dean Fish, 8 December 1934, and to Jacqueline Overton, 7 April 1942.
36 John Cook Wilson?; Morse 1982, letter to Helen Dean Fish, 8 December 1934, in which she estimates her age as six or seven; her copies of *Through the Looking-Glass* (dated 1876) and *Alice's Adventures in Wonderland* (dated 1879) survive.
37 She was ten in 1876; *Journal*, 5 June 1891; Beilby and Bewick 1797 and Bewick and Cotes 1804.
38 See Taylor 1989.
39 Taylor 1989, letters to Jacqueline Overton, 7 April 1942, and to Janet Adam Smith (Mrs Roberts), 2 February 1943, referring to an article by the latter which mentioned Randolph Caldecott, William Blake, Robert Palmer, John Constable and Thomas Bewick as the 'Immortals'.
40 *Journal*, 8 February 1884; the watercolours for *The Three Jovial Huntsmen* were purchased for £80.
41 *Journal*, 28 May 1883. Lessons with Miss Cameron lasted from November 1878 to 10 May 1883.
42 For example, V&A: BP.895, Linder Bequest LB 61, a spray of rose leaves, June 1880; the handwritten notes were tucked inside Potter's paintbox, part of the Herbert loan held in the V&A.

[43] Second Grade; the documents survive at the Cotsen Library, Princeton: a receipt dated 12 April, the admission card for an examination on 22 April, two evening sessions, and a list of results dated 21 May 1880. Such plaster casts were made from buildings and sculptures specifically for use in the schools of art and many still survive in the V&A's cast courts and collection.
[44] *Sty Head Tarn*, V&A: BP.308, Linder Bequest LB 1132, made in 1900 from the original by John Constable, 12 October 1806, V&A: 177–1888; *Margaret and Mary Gainsborough*, V&A: AR.4:385-6-2006, Joan Duke Collection, made in 1895 from the original by Thomas Gainsborough, 1758, V&A: F.9.
[45] Copies by Potter of John Flaxman's illustrations survive at the Cotsen Library, Princeton; *Journal*, 19 February 1885.
[46] Another example of a clay model is V&A: BP.865, Linder Bequest LB 1872; Bush Hall, *Journal*, 4 October 1884.
[47] *Newton from near Tower, Gorse Hall*, c.1850–60, V&A: AR.4:415-2006 (AAD/2006/4/415), Duke Collection. Bertram also kept sketchbooks: for example, 'The stag and the dog or other tales', V&A: BP.785, Linder Bequest LB 1107.
[48] Potter's reaction to the Royal Academy Winter Exhibition.
[49] Some of the Potters' collection is at Manchester Art Gallery. Helen received *Bird's Nest and Blossom* (c.1850; Manchester Art Gallery: 1933.31) by William Henry Hunt as a gift before her marriage.
[50] *Journal*, 19 March 1884, Christie, Manson and Woods, 22 March 1884. *Stella* (1868) by John Everett Millais is now in Manchester Art Gallery: 1908.12.
[51] *Journal*, 28 March 1884.
[52] Reeve 2000, p.10.
[53] Japanned furniture still survives at Hill Top, National Trust.
[54] *Journal*, 5 June 1891; *Journal*, 4 February 1890, on the Winter Exhibition, addressed to Esther.
[55] *Journal*, addendum to entry of 13 January 1883, c.1886.
[56] *Journal*, 13 August 1896.
[57] *Journal*, 13 January 1883; Maria Anna Angelika Kauffmann (Angelica Kauffman).
[58] *Journal*, 15 December 1883, Doré Gallery, '[Gustave Doré] one of the greatest of artists in black-and-white', although the display was of watercolours and she thought the general presentation gaudy; 'Phiz', Hablot Knight Browne; Gustave Doré.
[59] *Journal*, 16 July 1884. She is quoting a line from Gilbert and Sullivan's play *Patience* (1881).
[60] See *Journal*, 7 January 1896, for her visit to the art library.
[61] Letter to Norman Warne, 27 March 1903, Warne Archive: 'I have been looking at them for a long time in an inconvenient dark corner of the goldsmith's [*sic*] court, but had no idea they could be taken out of the case.' The candidate for the Tailor's coat has recently been identified, based on the frilled cuffs, as a brown striped silk coat thought to have had the cuffs added for use as a theatrical costume, V&A: 169–1898.
[62] *Journal*, 1 February 1886: she visited Lady Eastlake with her mother, and looked at the artworks on the wall; Mrs A has not been identified; Potter's first lesson on 22 November ('tomorrow') is mentioned in *Journal*, 21 November 1883.
[63] *Journal*, 29 November 1883, 'Do not like my drawing lessons'.
[64] Verso of the drawing no.27. The garden at Tenby partly inspired the backgrounds to *The Tale of Peter Rabbit*, 1902.
[65] *Journal*, 8 May 1884, 'the future is dark and uncertain', and 31 December 1885, 'I wonder why one is so unwilling to let go of this year? not because it has been joyful, but because I fear its successors – I am terribly afraid of the future.'
[66] *Journal*, 4 October 1884.
[67] Morse 1982, letter to Mrs Ramsay Duff, [June] 1943; *Little Sunshine's Holiday* (1871) by Dinah Craik.
[68] *Journal*, 14 March 1893, staying at the Osborne Hotel, Torquay.
[69] *Journal*, c.12 June 1894, 'We...poked about delightfully'; *Journal*, 15 August 1895, 'After a time I began to slither and slide down the grass slope to Limefit Farm'.
[70] *Journal*, 26 September 1894.
[71] *Journal*, 14 March 1893. Kent's Hole is a cavern in Torquay, Devon.
[72] Journal, c.12 June 1894. It was during the same holiday that she visited Gloucester and obtained the visual and literary source material for her *Tailor of Gloucester* story.
[73] *Journal*, 28 May 1895.
[74] Edmund Potter (1802–1883) became Liberal MP for Carlisle, 1861–74, and moved to Queen's Gate in London after handing over his calico printing business at Dinting Vale to his eldest son, Edmund Crompton Potter (1830–1883), in 1861; 'hideous', *Journal*, p.445, written c.1891; about her grandmother, *Journal*, 2 July 1884.
[75] *Journal*, p.444, written c.1891. It is thought that Potter imagined herself as Fanny Burney, an author she admired, writing to her sister, Esther (see Lear 2007, p.72). She saw herself dressed in muslin and reflected in mirrors.
[76] According to a semi-fictional account of the house, *Journal*, pp.444-50, written c.1891.
[77] *Journal*, 28 March 1884.
[78] *Journal*, 28 May 1895.
[79] Ibid.
[80] They took their carriages and ponies with them too. Between 1861 and 1900 they had at various times butlers (Henry Louch, then George Cox), housemaids (Sarah Wallant, Jane Peens, Elizabeth Harper, Catherine Fraser and Isabella Dewar, and later Annie Woodford, then Elizabeth Wooff, and kitchen maid Ada Head, then Maria Shelbourne), cooks (Sarah Lowe, then Sara Harper) and a coachman and groom, Albert Reynolds and David Becket, who lived in the mews behind.
[81] See, for example, lengthy descriptions in letters and diary of holidays in Falmouth, Cornwall, and Lennel near Coldstream on the Scottish Borders, in 1893 and 1894 respectively (see nos 38, 39); and the family of the artist John Everett Millais stayed in a house nearby, see Godfrey 2015.
[82] Potter's first holiday home before 1871 was Tulliemet, Perthshire. The gentlemen fishermen on the River Tay inspired Potter's Jeremy Fisher character.
[83] *Journal*, 8 May 1884.
[84] *Journal*, 11 May 1882 and 10 July 1882. On 21 July 1882 Potter gives a detailed description of the history of the house.
[85] *Journal*, 19 August 1882.
[86] Hardwicke Drummond Rawnsley, according to Nettleton 2005, p.84. The phrase apparently comes from a local resident's response when asked for directions to Rawnsley's vicarage: 'yon's the most active volcano in Europe'.
[87] *Journal*, 20 April 1886.
[88] *Journal*, 4 September 1896, 29 September 1892 and 17 November 1896.
[89] *Journal*, 16 August 1885, referring to Windermere.
[90] *Journal*, 10 August 1895.
[91] In response to a request from Bertha Mahony Miller, editor of *The Horn Book* magazine, for biographical information c.1943 (see Morse 1982, p.213).
[92] Ibid.

Holiday Haunts

[1] Godfrey 2015, p.4.
[2] Murray 2011, p.19.
[3] Ibid., p.36.
[4] William Wordsworth's *Guide to the Lakes* was first published in 1810; Gambles 2011, p.7.
[5] Walton and Wood 2013 p.137.
[6] Walvin 1978, p.11.
[7] Ibid., p.47.
[8] Godfrey 2015, p.10.
[9] Walton and Wood 2013, p.14.
[10] *Journal*, 21 July 1882.
[11] *Journal*, 19 August 1882. Today, the real cost equivalent would be approximately £6,376,000.
[12] *Journal*, 26 August 1896.
[13] *Journal*, 1892, p.220, written around April.
[14] Ibid.; Taylor 1989, p.13.
[15] *Journal*, 1 October 1894.
[16] Ibid.
[17] *Journal*, 18 August 1894; *Journal*, 10 October 1894.
[18] Ousby 1990, p.97.
[19] Ibid.
[20] *Journal*, 19 April 1895.
[21] Ousby 1990, p.98.

Under the Microscope

[1] Location based on an inventory of 1914, a photograph of the house (no.7) and a surviving view of the schoolroom interior (no.40), which shows a grand interior and a fireplace location suggesting that the schoolroom was at the back of the house.
[2] See Taylor 2007, pp.75, 92, not including the family of snails.
[3] Ibid., p.76, around 10 rabbits. William Gaskell wrote of Tommy in a letter to Potter in 1877, V&A: BP.878(iii), Linder Bequest LB 1317.
[4] Quoted in Dennison 2016, p.66.
[5] *Journal*, 30 May 1885, 'Mr Benjamin H. Bounce', also known as Bouncer.
[6] *Journal*, 12 September 1892.
[7] *Journal*, 18 November 1895. The picture letter featuring the story of Peter Rabbit was composed on 4 September in 1893 (V&A: LOAN:PEARSON PLC.1-1991 [nos 76–9]). Peter Piper died on 26 January 1901, aged nine; Beatrix Potter, letter in *The Field: The Country Gentleman's Newspaper*, 11 January 1902, letter to Frederick Warne, 8 May 1902, Warne Archive.
[8] *Journal*, 27 April 1882; 16 April 1892.
[9] *Journal*, 4 October 1884, Snowdrop; 9 October 1885, Bobby; 4 October 1884, Phyllis.
[10] *Journal*, 19 July 1883. Bought for 1/6 (1 shilling and 6 pence).
[11] *Journal*, 16 September 1884.
[12] Letters to Walter Gaddum, 6 March 1897 and 14 January 1899, V&A: BP.878(i and ii), Linder Bequest LB 1461 and 1462.
[13] *Journal*, 18 March 1884, mentions that Punch died on 11 March.
[14] *Journal*.
[15] *Journal*.
[16] *Journal*, 18 December 1886.
[17] Taylor 1989, letter to Miss Wyatt, 27 November 1920. Tom Thumb also featured in an earlier illustration to the fairy tale as the boy Tom Thumb's mount, 1896, V&A: Linder Collection LC 21/A/4.

18 *Journal*, 21 March 1883. Sara (or Sarah as in the census) Harper was the cook.
19 *Journal*, 8 December 1883, including footnote 31.
20 These two dates are combined in Potter's journal.
21 *Journal*, 1 October 1892.
22 *Journal*, 2 August 1883.
23 *Journal*, 19 July 1883.
24 *Journal*, 1888, draft to *The Times*.
25 'Representative...' comes from the dedication in *The Roly-Poly Pudding*; later renamed *The Tale of Samuel Whiskers*, 1908; Taylor 1989, letter to Elizabeth Booth, 12 June 1943 and to 'Dulcie', 16 November 1923, and Taylor 1992, p.182, letter to 'Dulcie', 16 November 1923.
26 Amato 2015, p.202.
27 Bertram Potter, letter to Beatrix from The Grange, 12 October [1884?], V&A: BP.795, Linder Bequest 1359. Bertram went to school at The Grange, Eastbourne, on 16 September 1884, leaving Beatrix in charge of his pet bat.
28 *Journal*, 11 November 1895. The reference to glass eyes suggests the practice of taxidermy.
29 *Journal*, March 1889.
30 Referring to Blackburn 1862.
31 *Journal*, 5 June 1891, at Putney Park, London.
32 For Potter's copies, see Andrews 1842 and White 1862, both in the collection of the National Trust, Hawkshead; 1882 edition of Sowerby and Johnson 1855, annotated inside with the date 12 October 1884, at Daito Bunka University, Tokyo, see Lear 2007, p.77; Sowerby 1855–6.
33 William Charles Lucy, corn merchant, geologist and honorary curator of the Museum of Gloucester, who Potter's aunt Sophia Hutton suggested she visit at his London home, Campden Hill Square, located west of Hyde Park, quite close to the Potters' home; 'ousel', quoted from Shakespeare, Henry IV, Part II, Act 3, Scene 2.
34 Lear 2007, p.77; and according to Lear 2011, p.46, they owned Philip Henry Gosse's *Evenings at the Microscope* (1859).
35 *Journal*, 14 March 1893. Ada Smallfield had a bowl of sea anemones that she 'got' at Torquay.
36 *Journal*, 13 June 1896, referring to what is now known as the Natural History Museum.
37 Journal, 28 October 1892 and 23 November 1895, Natural History Museum. She used a 1/6 lens. In 1896, when she temporarily lost it when it rolled off the table into the hearth, she bought a new 1/8 lens from R. and J. Becks in Cornhill, London, although: 'Cinderella found the [old] lens in the *last* spoonful but one of the middle-sized ashes', *Journal*, 20 and 30 November and 6 December 1896.
38 *Journal*, 23 November 1896, 'I have been drawing twelve Plates for Miss Martineau'; see also 21–3 March 1896. The Potters knew the family of James Martineau (1805–1900) at Gordon Square, London, probably through their Unitarian connections; Caroline ('Crinoline') Martineau was his niece, see *Journal*, 19 November 1884. Morley Memorial College for Working Men and Women emerged in 1889 from a weekly 'Penny lecture' series held at the Royal Victoria Hall.
39 Her father was Henry Bolingbroke Woodward. Gertrude studied at the schools of art at the South Kensington Museum, as did Potter. Her sister Alice B. Woodward became a childen's book illustrator like Potter.
40 *Journal*, 28 May 1895, 'Gwaynynog'; c.12 June 1894, 'Harescombe'; 7, 10, 15 August and 14 September 1895, 'Troutbeck'; 17 November 1896, 'Huddinknoll quarries', Gloucestershire; 6 October 1894, 'cold chisel'.
41 Ordovician geological period. Information provided by Prof. Richard Fortey.
42 Some survive at the Cotsen Children's Library, Princeton University, including one based on an engraving by M.C. Cooke from a scientific journal.
43 *Journal*, 27 and 30 April 1896; *Journal*, 27 and 30 April 1896; a few remains made their way into museum collections. The artefacts drawn by Potter may have belonged to John Whichcord (see Jay and Hall 1990, p.16). He lived near Bucklersbury during the excavations and L.A.M.A.S. 1868, pp.551–2, mentions a temporary display at one of their meetings near by there of finds from the 'immediate neighbourhood' lent by members, including Whichcord and the archaeologist John Edward Price (d. 1892). Pickle Herring Street information provided by Potter when gifting the drawings to the Armitt Museum.
44 Charles McIntosh (sometimes spelled Macintosh).
45 *Journal*, 26 and 27 April 1895, and also 27 and 30 April 1896, 'I was specially interested in an object similar to the Bucklersbury drawn by me, which I took to be a weight of a steelyard.' William St John Hope (1854–1919), George E. Fox (1833–1908).
46 The field of entomology at the time incorporated arachnids, on which Pocock was an expert, *Journal*, 13 June 1896; *Journal*, 9 and 13 July 1895, 'Mr Lucy'; Potter mentions taking photographs of fossils on 8 June 1895.
47 *Journal*, 21–3 March 1896, 'who lectures there on physiology'. Mrs Rose lectured at Morley College from 1892 to 1901 on natural history and botany.
48 *Journal*, 7 January 1896.
49 *Journal*, 30 December 1896. For George Murray, (1858–1911), Keeper of Botany from 1895, and Annie Lorraine Smith (1854–1937), see Lear 2007, p.107. Potter was referring to botanist Simon Schwendener's theory of lichens being compound plants of fungi and microscopic algae; Potter and her uncle Henry Roscoe 'do not believe in' the theory according to a letter to Charles McIntosh, 22 January 1897, National Library of Edinburgh.
50 *Journal*, 29 October 1892.
51 Coates 1923. Coates used the spelling 'Macintosh'.
52 *Journal*, 29 October 1892.
53 Ibid., 'spluttered candle' (see Mary Noble in Jay, Noble and Hobbs 1992, p.60); letter to Charles McIntosh, 10 December 1892, National Library of Edinburgh; Charles McIntosh, letter to Beatrix Potter, 10 January 1894, Armitt Museum and Library.
54 *Journal*, 19 May 1896; 13 June 1896; 17November–11 December 1896.
55 Earliest c.1885, V&A: Linder Collection LC 16/B/2; later dated drawings evidenced by microscopic drawings at the Armitt Museum and Library beyond the date of Potter's Linnean Society paper mentioned in a letter of 21 September 1897, AMATL. AMLC.1958.4718, for example, dated 17 January 1898, and AMATL.AMLC.1958.971, dated October 1907.
56 Taylor 1992, p.225, letter to Nancy Dean, 30 July 1940; *Journal*, 17 November 1896.

Miss Potter, the Mycologist

1 See Ainsworth 2006.
2 Taylor 1989, letter to Charles McIntosh, 12 January 1897.
3 *Journal*, 7 December 1896.

A Natural Storyteller

1 All quotes to this point from *Journal*, May 1890.
2 Letter to Beatrix Potter from Frederick Warne, 12 November 1891, Warne Archive.
3 *Journal*, May 1890.
4 Ibid.
5 Ibid.
6 *A Happy Pair* 1890, unpag.
7 Taylor 1992, p.23, letter to Noel Moore, 4 September 1893.
8 Letter to Caroline Clark, quoted in Lane 1978, p.32.
9 *Journal*, 19 August 1882, 'slate chimney-pieces'; *The Tale of Benjamin Bunny* 1904, 'a pear tree', p.33.
10 *Journal*, 4 October 1884.
11 Letter to *The Field: The Country Gentleman's Newspaper*, 11 January 1902.
12 From an inscription written in one of her privately printed editions of *The Tale of Peter Rabbit*, 'exorbitant sum' (see Linder 1987, p.110); Taylor 1989, letters to Frederick Warne, 8 May, 1902, and to *The Field*, 11 January, 1902.
13 Cotsen 2004, pp.110–11, letters to Eric Moore, 21 August 1892, and to Noel Moore, 21 August 1892.
14 *Journal*, 18 November 1895.
15 *Journal*, 5 September 1895, 'condescended to jump'; *Journal*, 18 November 1895, 'shrieks of amusement'.
16 Taylor 1992, p.28, letter to Noel Moore, 4 February 1895.
17 Ibid., p.62, letter to Marjorie Moore, 26 January 1900, 'nonsense'; Morse 1982, p.208, 'scribbles'.
18 Taylor 1992, p.43, letter to Eric Moore, 8 August 1896.
19 Linder 1987, p.xxv.
20 V&A: BP.785, Linder Bequest LB 1107.
21 Taylor 1989, letter to Mrs Fruing Warne, 26 September 1905.
22 Letter to Bertha Mahony Miller, quoted in Linder 1987, p.xxv.
23 *Journal*, 8 May 1884.
24 *Journal*, 17 November 1896.
25 *Journal*, c.1891, 'Memories of Camfield Place'.
26 Taylor 1989, letter to Norman Warne, 8 June 1905.
27 *Journal*, c.1891, 'Memories of Camfield Place'.
28 Taylor 1989, letter to Norman Warne, 12 February 1904.
29 Morse 1982, p.208.
30 Taylor 1992, p.66, letter to Marjorie Moore, 13 March 1900.
31 Taylor 1989, letter to Norman Warne, 9 November 1903.
32 *Journal*, 5 June 1891.
33 Taylor 1989, letters to Norman Warne, 5 February 1903, 'strong and distinct', and to Norman Warne, 21 March 1903, 'something to rest the eye'.
34 Ibid., letters to Arthur Stephens, 23 February 1941, 'idiotic prancing rabbit', and to Norman Warne, 21 March 1903, 'rather heavy'.
35 Ibid., letter to Norman Warne, 15 December 1903.
36 Taylor 1992, p.72, letter to Norah Moore, 25 September 1901. Several years earlier, Potter had sent a letter to Noel Moore on 26 August 1897 from the Lake District about 'an American story' in which 'squirrels go down the rivers on little rafts, using their tails for sails'. See Taylor 1992, p.50.
37 Printed dedication in *The Tailor of Gloucester*.
38 Taylor 1989, letter to Harold Botcherby, 17 February 1913.
39 Transcripts from Taylor 1992, p.91.
40 Taylor 1989,
41 Taylor 1992, p.64, letter to Winifred Moore, 26 January 1900.
42 Taylor 1989, letter to Norman Warne, 10 April 1904.
43 *Journal*, 17 November 1896.
44 Taylor 1989, letter to Bertha Mahony Miller, 25 November 1940, 'amongst the wild flowers'; *Journal*, 17 November 1896, 'tiny fungus people'.

45 Taylor 1989, letter to Millie Warne, 17 November 1909.
46 Ibid., letter to Norman Warne, September 1903.
47 *Journal*, 25 February 1886, 'weasel'; Taylor 1989, letter to Betty Harris, 4 September 1930, 'an elderly sheep'; *Journal*, 19 November 1884, 'a wood-louse diving'.
48 *Journal*, 1 August 1892.
49 Taylor 1989, letter to Harold Warne, 14 July 1912.
50 *The Tale of Mrs. Tittlemouse* 1910, p.58.
51 *Journal*, 25 July 1896.
52 *Journal*, 7 August 1883.
53 Taylor 1989, letter to Norman Warne, 6 April 1904.
54 Ibid., letter to Bertha Mahony Miller, 25 November 1940.
55 *The Tale of Little Pig Robinson* 1930, 'prosperous uneventful lives', p.18; *The Roly-Poly Pudding* 1908, 'hold his head still', p.51; *The Tale of Tom Kitten* 1907, 'eat our customers', p.12.
56 Taylor 1989, letter to Marian Frazer Harris Perry, 4 October 1934.
57 Morse 1982, letter to Bertha Mahony Miller, 18 February 1942.
58 Letter to Noel Moore, 4 September 1893.
59 *The Tale of Peter Rabbit* 1902, 'Kertyschoo', p.58; *The Tale of Mr. Jeremy Fisher* 1906, 'Ker-pflop-p-p-p', p.58; *The Tale of Squirrel Nutkin* 1903, 'Squeak!', p.79; *The Tale of Two Bad Mice* 1904, 'bang, bang', p.39; *The Tale of Peter Rabbit* 1902,'scr-r-ritch scratch', p.76.
60 *The Tale of Squirrel Nutkin* 1903, p.75.
61 Taylor 1989, letter to Harold Warne [September 1908], 'common Lancashire'; *The Tale of the Flopsy Bunnies* 1909, 'done it a purpose', p.75.
62 Taylor 1989, letter to Norman Warne, 3 February 1905, 'children like conversations'; *The Pie and the Patty-Pan* 1905, 'My Great-aunt Squintina', p.40.
63 *The Tale of Tom Kitten* 1907, 'hot buttered toast', p.28; *The Tailor of Gloucester* 1903, 'little live lady mouse', p.33; ibid., 'little twittering tunes', p.57; *The Tale of Squirrel Nutkin* 1903, 'spread out his tail', p.16; *The Tale of Mrs. Tittlemouse* 1910, 'particular little mouse', p.16; *The Tale of Peter Rabbit* 1902, 'came up with a sieve', p.52.
64 Morse 1982, p.208.
65 *The Tale of Squirrel Nutkin* 1903, p.75.
66 Taylor 1989,letter to Harold Warne, 12 March 1908.
67 *The Tale of Peter Rabbit* 1902, p.15.
68 Morse 1982, p.209.
69 *The Tailor of Gloucester* 1902, 'a snippeting of scissors', p.63; *The Tale of Squirrel Nutkin* 1903, 'a flutterment', p.70; Taylor 1989, letter to Harold Warne, 20 August 1909, 'piled up adjectives'; *The Tailor of Gloucester* 1903, 'most beautifullest coat', unpag., private edition; *The Tale of Mr. Jeremy Fisher* 1906, 'great big enormous trout', p.58; *The Tale of Little Pig Robinson* 1929, 'fatterer', p.96.
70 Taylor 1989, letter to Norman Warne, 16 June 1904.
71 *The Tale of the Flopsy Bunnies* 1909, p.9.
72 *The Tailor of Gloucester* 1903, pp.9–10.
73 *The Tale of Mr. Jeremy Fisher* 1906, p.28.
74 *The Tale of Peter Rabbit* 1902, p.45.
75 *The Tale of Mr. Jeremy Fisher* 1906, pp.57–8.
76 *The Tale of Jemima Puddle-Duck* 1908, 'The gentleman opened the door', p.40.
77 *The Tale of the Flopsy Bunnies* 1909, 'they were very improvident and cheerful', p.10.
78 *The Tale of the Pie and the Patty-Pan* 1905, 'bowed to one another', p.20.
79 Morse 1989, letter to Helen Dean Fish, 19 September 1930.
80 *The Tailor of Gloucester* 1903, p.9.
81 Lewis Carroll described his Alice story as a 'fairy-tale'.
82 *The Tale of Mrs. Tiggy-Winkle* 1905, p.84.
83 *The Tailor of Gloucester* 1903, p.80.
84 *The Tale of Little Pig Robinson* 1930, pp.68–9.
85 Taylor 1989, letter to Norman Warne, 20 October 1904.
86 *Appley Dapply's Nursery Rhymes* 1917, p.44.
87 Taylor 1989, letters to Lady Mary Isabel Warren, 23 December 1919, 'pot-boilers', and to Fruing Warne, 4 March 1921, '*atrocious*'.
88 Ibid., letter to Harold Warne, 18 November 1911.
89 *Journal*, 30 October 1892, 'wonderful portrait'; 'Brer Rabbit in a garden': Brer Rabbit illustrations include V&A: Linder Collection LC 8/A/1-4 and LC 8/B/1-3, see no.017.
90 Manuscript is in the Warne Archive.
91 *The Tailor of Gloucester* 1903, '*Tip tap*', p.34; *The Tale of Tom Kitten* 1907, 'pit pat paddle', p.45; *The Tale of Benjamin Bunny* 1904, 'trit-trot', p.9; ibid., 'pitter-patter', p.69; *The Tale of Mrs. Tittlemouse* 1910, 'Tiddly, widdly', p.51; *The Tale of Squirrel Nutkin* 1903, 'They had stolen it', p.52.
92 'Brer Rabbit's astonishing prank', in Joel Chandler Harris, *Nights with Uncle Remus* (Boston: James R. Osgood and Company, 1883), p.21.
93 Taylor 1989, letter to Anne Carroll Moore, 30 March 1939.
94 Morse 1982, letter to Marian Frazer Harris Perry, 10 February 1928.

Beatrix Potter, Entrepreneur

1 *Journal*, May 1890.
2 Letter to Mr Warne, 1 September 1917, Warne Archive.
3 Letter to Mr Warne, 7 April 1923, Warne Archive.
4 Letter to Mr Warne, 19 December 1917, Warne Archive.

Living Nature

1 Morse 1982, letter to Bertha Mahony Miller, 25 November 1940.
2 Letter to William Heelis from Donald MacLeod Matheson (Secretary of National Trust), 23 December 1943, National Trust Archive.
3 Brunskill 2002, ch.1: 'The Region and its Study'.
4 Wordsworth 1995, 'Book XIV: Conclusion', p.537.
5 Williams-Ellis 1938, esp. E.M. Forester, 'Havok' (pp.44–7) and Kenneth Spence, 'The Lakes' (pp.240–55).
6 Letter to John Bailey (Chairman of National Trust), 15 February 1930, National Trust Archive.
7 Hyde Parker 1981, p.25.
8 Morse 1982, letter to Bertha Mahony Miller, 20 November 1942.
9 Taylor 1989, letter to Millie Warne, 14 October 1905.
10 Taylor 1989, letter to Millie Warne, 23 August 1910.
11 Draft letter to Bertha Mahony Miller, 11 October 1940, Collection of National Trust (NT242302).
12 Ibid.
13 Hyde Parker 1981, p.25.
14 Ibid, p.40.
15 Manuscript (1930) of the description of Hill Top for a sequel to *The Fairy Caravan*, 1929, Collection of National Trust (NT242234.2).
16 Taylor 1989, letter to John Stone, 5 June 1940.
17 V&A: AAD/1981/6/226, Linder Archive, 'The Hill Top notebook of ideas' begun by Ethel Hartley in 16 August 1944.
18 Wordsworth 1835.
19 Murphy 1987 (2002), letter from John Ruskin to Canon Hardwicke Rawnsley (date not given).
20 Letter to Bertha Mahony Miller for publication in *The Horn Book*, May 1942.
21 *Journal*, 10 August 1895.
22 Heafing is the term used for the instinct whereby ewes will return to the part of the fell on which they were raised to raise their own lambs. Usually a 'landlord's flock' is handed on with the tenancy of the farm, to ensure that the 'heaf' is not lost. At Troutbeck Park Farm, Potter decided on a landlord's flock of 750 mature ewes, 250 two-year-old ewe lambs (gimmer twinters) and 175 one-year-old ewe lambs (gimmer hoggs).
23 Recollections of Tom Storey, transcription from an interview for the National Trust (interviewer unknown but possibly Elizabeth Battrick), summer 1984.
24 Lletter to Professor J.B. Buxton, Royal Veterinary College, London, 9 February 1938, Archives of The Royal Veterinary College, University of London.
25 Recollections of Tom Storey, transcription from an interview with Gordon Hall at the National Trust, 2 November 1983.
26 Taylor 1989, letter to Bertha Mahony Miller, 25 November 1940.
27 Letter to John Bailey, 15 February 1930, National Trust Archive.
28 Letter to Samuel H. Hamer (Secretary of National Trust), 28 October 1929, National Trust Archive.
29 Letter to Samuel H. Hamer, 25 October 1929, National Trust Archive.
30 Letter to John Bailey, 15 February 1930, National Trust Archive.
31 Letter to Samuel H. Hamer, 20 October 1929, National Trust Archive.
32 Letter to Caroline Clark, 8 April 1934, Collection of National Trust (NT242270).
33 Morse 1982, letter to Bertha Mahony Miller, 13 December 1934.
34 Letter to Donald Matheson, 17 October 1939, National Trust Archive.
35 Taylor 1989, letter to John Stone, 5 June 1940
36 Scoular 2012, letter to Rt Hon. Samuel Cunningham, 7 November 1942.
37 Letter to Caroline Clark, 15 February 1937, her cousin, née Caroline Hutton, Collection of National Trust (NT242272), see 'Town and Country'.
38 Wordsworth and Wilkinson 1810.
39 Letter to John Bailey, 15 February 1930, National Trust Archive.

Mrs Heelis, Farmer

1 Wordsworth 1974, p.206.

Drawn from Nature: Selected Potter Protagonists

1 At the start of *The Tailor of Gloucester*, Potter uses the opening quotation to William Shakespeare's play, *Richard III*: 'I'll be at charges for a looking glass, and entertain a score or two of tailors' and also refers to 'old songs that ever I heard of, and some that I don't know, like Whittington's bells', with its oblique reference to Dick Whittington.
2 Letter to Noel Moore, 26 August 1897.
3 *Journal*, May 1890.
4 *Journal*, 1 August 1892.
5 Letter to Norman Warne, 20 April 1904, Warne Archive.
6 Letter to Norman Warne, 12 February 1904, Warne Archive.
7 Jane Austen, *Pride and Prejudice* (London: Military Library, 1813).
8 Letter to Millie Warne, 18 July 1906, Warne Archive.
9 Taylor 1989, letter to Caroline Clark, 13 December 1930 (her cousin Caroline, née Hutton).

Bibliography

Books written and illustrated by Beatrix Potter (first publication in English and privately printed editions are included)

The Tale of Peter Rabbit 1901
Beatrix Potter, *The Tale of Peter Rabbit* (London: privately printed, 1901)

The Tale of Peter Rabbit 1902
Beatrix Potter, *The Tale of Peter Rabbit* (London: Frederick Warne & Co., 1902)

The Tailor of Gloucester 1902
Beatrix Potter, *The Tailor of Gloucester* (London: privately printed, 1902)

The Tale of Squirrel Nutkin 1903
Beatrix Potter, *The Tale of Squirrel Nutkin* (London: Frederick Warne & Co., 1903)

The Tailor of Gloucester 1903
Beatrix Potter, *The Tailor of Gloucester* (London: Frederick Warne & Co., 1903)

The Tale of Benjamin Bunny 1904
Beatrix Potter, *The Tale of Benjamin Bunny* (London: Frederick Warne & Co., 1904)

The Tale of Two Bad Mice 1904
Beatrix Potter, *The Tale of Two Bad Mice* (London: Frederick Warne & Co., 1904)

The Pie and the Patty-Pan 1905; later renamed *The Tale of the Pie and the Patty-Pan*
Beatrix Potter, *The Pie and the Patty-Pan*; later renamed *The Tale of the Pie and the Patty-Pan* (London: Frederick Warne & Co., 1905)

The Tale of Mr. Tiggy-Winkle 1905
Beatrix Potter, *The Tale of Mr. Tiggy-Winkle* (London: Frederick Warne & Co., 1905)

The Tale of Mr. Jeremy Fisher 1906
Beatrix Potter, *The Tale of Mr. Jeremy Fisher* (London: Frederick Warne & Co., 1906)

The Story of Miss Moppet 1906
Beatrix Potter, *The Story of Miss Moppet* (London: Frederick Warne & Co., 1906)

The Story of A Fierce Bad Rabbit 1906
Beatrix Potter, *The Story of A Fierce Bad Rabbit* (London: Frederick Warne & Co., 1906)

The Tale of Tom Kitten 1907
Beatrix Potter, *The Tale of Tom Kitten* (London: Frederick Warne & Co., 1907)

The Tale of Jemima Puddle-Duck 1908
Beatrix Potter, *The Tale of Jemima Puddle-Duck* (London: Frederick Warne & Co., 1908)

The Roly-Poly Pudding 1908; later renamed *The Tale of Samuel Whiskers*
Beatrix Potter, *The Roly-Poly Pudding*; later renamed *The Tale of Samuel Whiskers* (London: Frederick Warne & Co., 1908)

The Tale of the Flopsy Bunnies 1909
Beatrix Potter, *The Tale of the Flopsy Bunnies* (London: Frederick Warne & Co., 1909)

The Tale of Ginger and Pickles 1909
Beatrix Potter, *The Tale of Ginger and Pickles* (London: Frederick Warne & Co., 1909)

The Tale of Mr. Tittlemouse 1910
Beatrix Potter, *The Tale of Mr. Tittlemouse* (London: Frederick Warne & Co., 1910)

Peter Rabbit's Painting Book 1911
Beatrix Potter, *Peter Rabbit's Painting Book* (London: Frederick Warne & Co., 1911)

The Tale of Timmy Tiptoes 1911
Beatrix Potter, *The Tale of Timmy Tiptoes* (London: Frederick Warne & Co., 1911)

The Tale of Mr. Tod 1912
Beatrix Potter, *The Tale of Mr. Tod* (London: Frederick Warne & Co., 1912)

The Tale of Pigling Bland 1913
Beatrix Potter, *The Tale of Pigling Bland* (London: Frederick Warne & Co., 1913)

Tom Kitten's Painting Book 1917
Beatrix Potter, *Tom Kitten's Painting Book* (London: Frederick Warne & Co., 1917)

Appley Dapply's Nursery Rhymes 1917
Beatrix Potter, *Appley Dapply's Nursery Rhymes* (London: Frederick Warne & Co., 1917)

The Tale of Johnny Town-Mouse 1918
Beatrix Potter, *The Tale of Johnny Town-Mouse* (London: Frederick Warne & Co., 1918)

Cecily Parsley's Nursery Rhymes 1922
Beatrix Potter, *Cecily Parsley's Nursery Rhymes* (London: Frederick Warne & Co., 1922)

Jemima Puddle-Duck's Painting Book 1925
Beatrix Potter, *Jemima Puddle-Duck's Painting Book* (London: Frederick Warne & Co., 1925)

Peter Rabbit's Almanac for 1929 1928
Beatrix Potter, *Peter Rabbit's Almanac for 1929* (London: Frederick Warne & Co., 1928)

The Fairy Caravan 1929a
Beatrix Potter, *The Fairy Caravan* (Ambleside: for the author, 1929)

The Fairy Caravan 1929b
Beatrix Potter, *The Fairy Caravan* (Philadelphia: David McKay, 1929)

The Tale of Little Pig Robinson 1930
Beatrix Potter, *The Tale of Little Pig Robinson* (Philadelphia: David McKay, and London: Frederick Warne & Co., 1929)

Sister Anne 1932
Beatrix Potter, *Sister Anne* (Philadelphia: David McKay, 1932)

Wag-by-Wall 1944
Beatrix Potter, *Wag-by-Wall* (Boston: The Horn Book Inc., 1944)

The Tale of the Faithful Dove 1955
Beatrix Potter, *The Tale of the Faithful Dove* (London: Frederick Warne & Co., 1955)

The Sly Old Cat 1971
Beatrix Potter, *The Sly Old Cat* (London: Frederick Warne & Co., 1971)

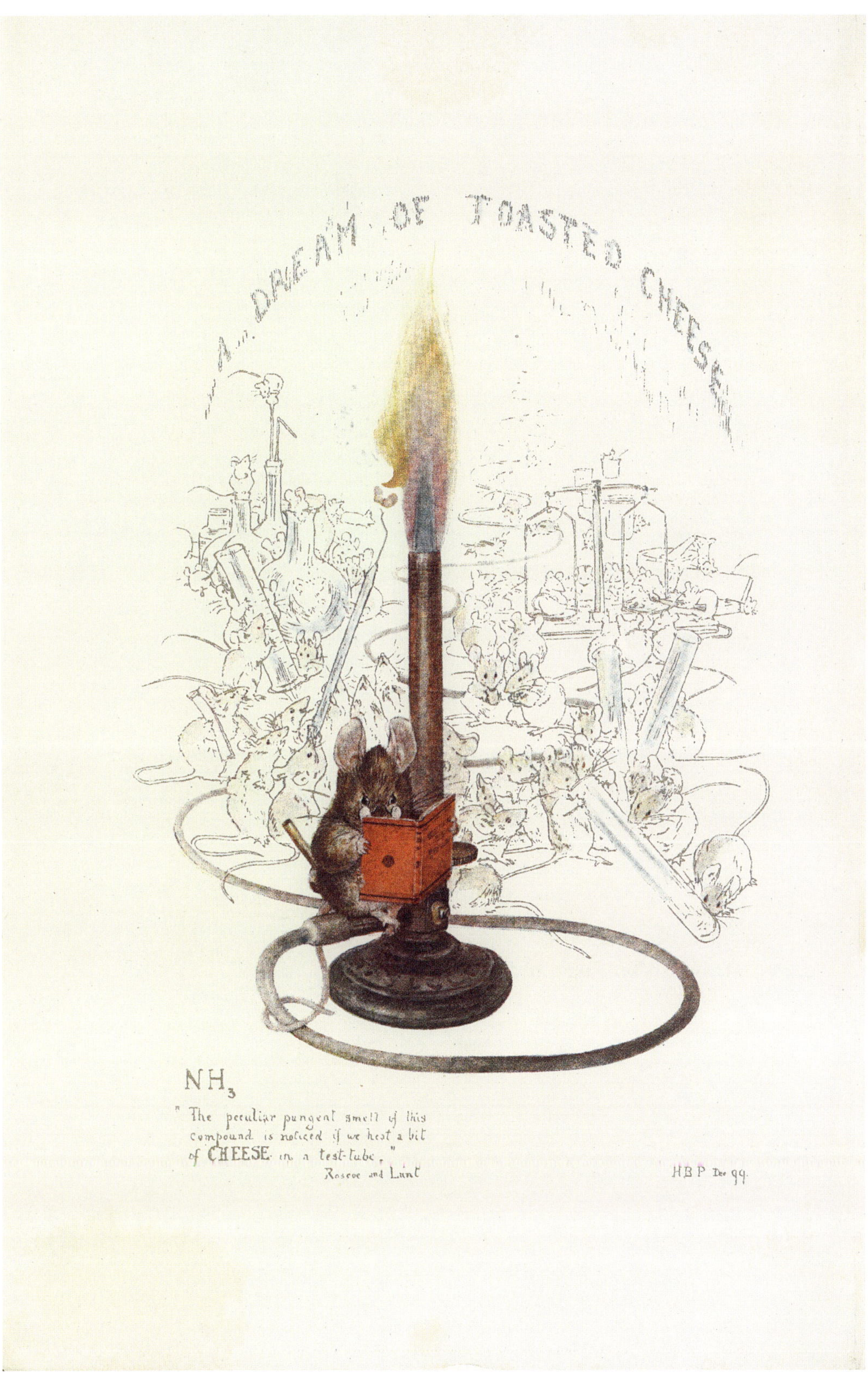

170.
Dream of Toasted Cheese, 1899
Watercolour and ink on paper
Private collection, given to Sir Henry Roscoe to celebrate publication of his textbook *Inorganic Chemistry for Advanced Students*

The Tale of Tuppenny 1973
Beatrix Potter, *The Tale of Tuppenny*, illustrated by Marie Angel (London and New York: Frederick Warne & Co., 1973)

Sources

Ainsworth 2006
Geoffrey C. Ainsworth, *Introduction to the History of Mycology* (Cambridge: Cambridge University Press, 2006)

Alderson 2007
Brian Alderson, 'Sources on the Nursery Bookshelf', in *Beatrix Potter: Sources of her Inspiration, Beatrix Potter Studies XII*, papers presented at The Beatrix Potter Society Conference, Ambleside 2006 (Exeter: The Beatrix Potter Society and Studio Publishing Services Ltd., 2007), pp.35–48

Alderson 2009
Brian Alderson, 'Tekkin' a Trip', in *Beatrix Potter: Fables to Faeries, Beatrix Potter Studies XIII*, papers presented at The Beatrix Potter Society Conference, Ambleside, July 2008 (Exeter: The Beatrix Potter Society and The Studio Publishing Services Ltd., 2009), pp.11–19

Amato 2015
Sarah Amato, *Beastly Possessions: Animals in Victorian Consumer Culture* (Toronto: University of Toronto Press, 2015)

Andrews 1842
James Andrews, *Andrews' Art of Flower Painting* (London: Tilt and Bogue, 1842)

Arkle and Dashwood 1984
Phyllis Arkle and Joan Dashwood, *The Real Sawrey* (place unknown: privately published, 1984)

Avery 1994
Gillian Avery, 'Beatrix Potter and Social Comedy', *Bulletin of John Rylands University Library of Manchester* (1994), vol.76, no.3, pp.185–200

Bartlett and Whalley 1995
Wynne Bartlett and Joyce Irene Whalley, *Beatrix Potter's Derwentwater* (Hawes: Leading Edge, 1995)

Battrick 1995
Elizabeth Battrick, *'The Most Active Volcano in Europe': Canon Hardwicke Drummond Rawnsley* (Keswick: National Trust, 1995)

Battrick 1997
Elizabeth Battrick, 'Canon Rawnsley and the National Trust', in *Beatrix Potter and the Lake District, Beatrix Potter Studies VII*, papers presented at The Beatrix Potter Society Conference, Ambleside, July 1996, pp.27–38 (Trowbridge: The Beatrix Potter Society and Redwood Books, 1997)

Beilby and Bewick 1797
Ralph Beilby and Thomas Bewick, *A History of British Birds* (Newcastle: printed by Sol[omon] Hodgson for Beilby and T. Bewick, 1797)

Bewick and Cotes 1804
Thomas Bewick and Henry Cotes, *A History of British Birds* (Newcastle: printed by Edward Walker for T. Bewick, 1804)

Blackburn 1862
Jemima Blackburn, *Birds Drawn from Nature* (Edinburgh: Edmonston and Douglas, 1862)

Brunskill 2002
R.W. Brunskill, *Traditional Buildings of Cumbria: The County of the Lakes* (London: Cassell, 2002)

Bryant 2011
Julius Bryant, *Art and Design for All* (London: V&A Publishing, 2011)

Cameron Cooper 2007
Gilly Cameron Cooper, *Beatrix Potter's Lake District* (London: Frederick Warne & Co., 2007)

Carpenter 1990
Humphrey Carpenter, 'Excessively Impertinent Bunnies: The Subversive Element in Beatrix Potter', in Gillian Avery and Julia Briggs (eds), *Children and Their Books: A Celebration of the Work of Iona and Peter Opie*, with a foreword by Iona Opie (Oxford: Clarendon Press, 1990), pp.271–98

Christie 2011
Ann Christie, '"Nothing of Intrinsic Value": The Scientific Collections at the Bethnal Green Museum', *V&A Online Journal* (Spring 2011), no.3, http://www.vam.ac.uk/content/journals/research-journal/issue-03/nothing-of-intrinsic-value-the-scientific-collections-at-the-bethnal-green-museum/ (accessed 14 February 2020)

Christie, Manson and Woods 1884
Christie, Manson and Woods, *Catalogue of the Valuable Collection of Ancient Chinese Enamels and Porcelain, and Other Objects of Art, of Edmund Crompton Potter, Esq., Deceased, Late of Rusholme House, near Manchester* (London: Christie, Manson and Woods, 1884)

Coates 1923
Henry Coates, *A Perthshire Naturalist: Charles McIntosh of Inver* (London: T. Fisher Unwin, 1923)

Craik 1871
Dinah Craik, *Little Sunshine's Holiday* (London: Sampson Low, 1871)

Crouch 1963
Marcus Crouch, *Britain in Trust* (London: Constable Young Books Ltd, 1963)

Denis 1997
Raphael Cardoso Denis, 'Teaching by Example: Education and the Formation of South Kensington's Museums', in Malcolm Baker and Brenda Richardson (eds), *A Grand Design: The Art of the Victoria and Albert Museum* (London: V&A Publications, 1997)

Dennison 2016
Matthew Dennison, *Over the Hills and Far Away: The Life of Beatrix Potter* (London: Head of Zeus, 2016)

Denyer 1991
Susan Denyer, *Traditional Buildings and Life in the Lake District* (London: Victor Gollancz, 1991)

Denyer 1997
Susan Denyer, 'Beatrix Potter and the Decorative Arts', in *Beatrix Potter and the Lake District, Beatrix Potter Studies VII*, papers presented at The Beatrix Potter Society Conference, Ambleside, July 1996, pp.39–51 (Trowbridge: The Beatrix Potter Society and Redwood Books, 1997)

Denyer 2011
Susan Denyer, 'The Lake District – From Wordsworth to World Heritage', in *Beatrix Potter and the Natural World, Beatrix Potter Studies XIV*, papers presented at The Beatrix Potter Society Conference, Ambleside, July 2010, pp.93–108 (Exeter: The Beatrix Potter Society and Studio Publishing Ltd., 2011)

Fedden 1968
Robin Fedden, *The Continuing Purpose: A History of the National Trust, its Aims and Work* (London: Longmans, 1968)

Fedden 1974
Robin Fedden, *The National Trust: Past and Present* (London: Jonathan Cape, 1974)

Findlay 1967
Walter Philip Kennedy Findlay, *Wayside and Woodland Fungi*, with colour illustrations by Beatrix Potter, R.B. Davis and E.C. Large (London, Frederick Warne & Co., 1967)

Foster n.d.
Vere Foster, *Vere Foster's Complete Course of Painting in Watercolours, with Instructions, by E. Duncan, John Callow, Harrison Weir, Rowbotham F.E. Hulme, Needham, W.G. Smith, Fitch, French, Coleman, and Other Eminent Artists, Part I – Flowers* (London, Belfast: Marcus Ward & Co.)

Gambles 2011
Robert Gambles, *Escape to the Lakes: The First Tourists* (Carlisle: Bookcase, 2011)

Godfrey 2015
Rowena Godfrey, 'Visitors to Perthshire', in *Beatrix Potter and Scotland, Beatrix Potter Studies XVI*, papers presented at The Beatrix Potter Society Conference, Birnam, June 2014 (Exeter: The Beatrix Potter Society and Studio Publishing Services Ltd., 2015), pp.1–16

Going 1985
William T. Going, 'Beatrix Potter, Peter Rabbit, and Pre-Raphaelitism', *Journal of Pre-Raphaelite Studies* (1985), vol.6, no.1, pp.68–75

Golden 1990
Catherine Golden, 'Beatrix Potter: Naturalist Artist', *Women's Art Journal* (Spring/Summer 1990), vol.11, no.1, pp.16–20

Goldthwaite 1987
John Goldthwaite, 'Sis Beatrix' (Part One), *Signal* (May 1987), no.53, pp.117–37; 'Sis Beatrix' (Part Two), *Signal* (September 1987), no.54, pp.161–77

Gosse 1859
Philip Henry Gosse, *Evenings at the Microscope; or, Researches among the Minuter Organs and Forms of Animal Life* (London: Society for Promoting Christian Knowledge, 1859)

Gray 1803
Thomas Gray, Mr Gray's Journal, including *Sketch of a Tour from Lancaster, Round the Principal Lakes in Lancashire, Cumberland, and Westmorland* (Carlisle: F. Jollie, 1803)

Greene 1964
Graham Greene, *The Lost Childhood and Other Essays* (London: Penguin, 1964)
Gristwood 2016
Sarah Gristwood, *The Story of Beatrix Potter* (London: National Trust, 2016)

Hankinson 1993
Alan Hankinson, 'Canon Hardwicke Drummond Rawnsley', *Cumbrian Life* (September/October 1993), vol.30, pp.25–7

Hardwicke 1866
Robert Hardwicke, *Hardwicke's Science-Gossip* (London: Robert Hardwicke, 1866–1893)

Hobbs 1989a
Anne Stevenson Hobbs, *Beatrix Potter's Art, Paintings and Drawings Selected by Anne Stevenson Hobbs* (London: Frederick Warne & Co., 1989)

Hobbs 1989b
Anne Stevenson Hobbs, 'Beatrix Potter's Writings: Some Literary and Linguistic Influences – with a Scottish Slant', in *Beatrix Potter before Peter Rabbit, Beatrix Potter Studies III*, papers presented at The Beatrix Potter Society Conference, Perth, July 1988 (Norwich: The Beatrix Potter Society and Gallpen Press Ltd., 1989), pp.28–40

Hobbs 2005
Anne Stevenson Hobbs, *Beatrix Potter: Artist & Illustrator*, exh. cat., Dulwich Picture Gallery (London: Frederick Warne & Co., 2005)

Hobhouse 1986
Hermione Hobhouse, 'Southern Kensington in Retrospect', in *Survey of London: Volume 42, Kensington Square To Earl's Court* (London 1986), pp.395–413, at British History Online, http://www.british-history.ac.uk/survey-london/vol42/pp395-413 (accessed 14 February 2020)

Hoskins 1955
W.G. Hoskins, *The Making of the English Landscape* (London: Hodder & Stoughton, 1955)

Houlton 2019
Sophie Houlton, 'The Gifts of Beatrix Potter in the Conservation History of the National Trust', in *Beatrix Potter: A Lasting Legacy, Beatrix Potter Studies XVII*, papers presented at The Beatrix Potter Society Conference, Bowness-on-Windermere, July 2016 (Dawlish: The Beatrix Potter Society and Black Swan Printers Ltd., 2019), pp.55–67

Hyde Parker 1981
Ulla Hyde Parker, *Cousin Beatie: A Memory of Beatrix Potter* (London: Frederick Warne & Co., 1981)

Jay and Hall 1990
Eileen Jay and Jenny Hall, *The Tale of London Past: Beatrix Potter's Archaeological Paintings from the Armitt Collection* (London: Frederick Warne & Co. for the Armitt Trust, 1990)

Jay, Noble and Hobbs 1992
Eileen Jay, Mary Noble and Anne Stevenson Hobbs, *A Victorian Naturalist: Beatrix Potter's Drawings from the Armitt Collection* (London: Frederick Warne & Co., 1992)

L.A.M.A.S. 1868
Transactions of the London and Middlesex Archaeological Society, Volume III, Annual General Meeting of 17 April 1868 (London: 1870)

Lane 1946
Margaret Lane, *The Tale of Beatrix Potter* (London: Frederick Warne & Co., 1946, revised editions 1968, 1985)

Lane 1978
Margaret Lane, *The Magic Years of Beatrix Potter* (London: Book Club Associates, 1978, revised edition 1979)

Laws 2009
Emma Laws, 'The Art of the Potter Family: the Duke Collection at the Victoria and Albert Museum', in *Beatrix Potter: Fables to Faeries, Beatrix Potter Studies XIII*, papers presented at The Beatrix Potter Society Conference, Ambleside, July 2008 (Exeter: The Beatrix Potter Society and Studio Publishing Services Ltd., 2009), pp.70–91

Lear 2007
Linda Lear, *Beatrix Potter: A Life in Nature* (London: Allen Lane, 2007)

Lear 2011
Linda Lear, 'A Crowded Universe of Small Things', in *Beatrix Potter and the Natural World, Beatrix Potter Studies XIV*, papers presented at The Beatrix Potter Society Conference, Ambleside, July 2010 (Exeter: The Beatrix Potter Society and Studio Publishing Ltd., 2011), pp.43–58

Lightner 1997
Karen J. Lightner, 'The Fairy Caravan "Explained"', in *Beatrix Potter and the Lake District, Beatrix Potter Studies VII*, papers presented at The Beatrix Potter Society Conference, Ambleside, July 1996, pp.60–74 (Trowbridge: The Beatrix Potter Society and Redwood Books, 1997)

Linder 1987
Leslie Linder, *A History of the Writings of Beatrix Potter* (London: Frederick Warne & Co., 1987)

Lucie-Smith 1979
Edward Lucie-Smith, *Furniture: A Concise History* (London: Thames and Hudson Ltd, 1979)

MacDonald 1986
Ruth K. MacDonald, *Beatrix Potter* (Boston: Twayne Publishers, 1986)

Mahony Miller et al. 1947
Bertha Mahony Miller et al., *Illustrators of Children's Books*, 1744–1945 (Boston: The Horn Book Inc., 1947)

McGeachie 2010
Lynne McGeachie, with a foreword by Judy Taylor, *Beatrix Potter's Scotland: Her Perthshire Inspiration* (Edinburgh: Luath Press, 2010)

McLean 1989
Ruari McLean, 'Children's Books during the Childhood of Beatrix Potter', in *Beatrix Potter before Peter Rabbit, Beatrix Potter Studies III*, papers presented at The Beatrix Potter Society Conference, Perth, July 1988 (Norwich: The Beatrix Potter Society and Gallpen Press Ltd., 1989), pp.8–14

Mitchell 1998
W.R Mitchell, *Beatrix Potter: Her Life in the Lake District* (Giggleswick: Castleberg, 1998)

Morse 1982
Jane Crowell Morse (ed.), *Beatrix Potter's Americans: Selected Letters* (Boston: The Horn Book Inc., 1982)

Murdoch and Woof 1984
John Murdoch, Robert Woof, *The Discovery of the Lake District: A Northern Arcadia and its Uses* (London: Victoria and Albert Museum, 1984)

Murphy 1987
Graham Murphy, *Founders of the National Trust* (London: Christopher Helm Ltd, 1987, revised edition 2002)

Murray 2011
John R. Murray, *A Tour of the English Lakes: With Thomas Gray and Joseph Farington RA* (London: Frances Lincoln, 2011)

'Museum Displays at South Kensington Museum', in *Rethinking Pitt-Rivers: Analysing the Activities of a Nineteenth-century Collector*, 2011, https://web.prm.ox.ac.uk/rpr/index.php/article-index/12-articles/282-museum-displays-at-south-kensington-museum.html (accessed 14 February 2020)

The National Trust n.d.
'The Most Active Volcano in Europe': A Short Life of Canon Hardwicke Drummond Rawnsley, Vicar of Crosthwaite, Keswick 1883–1917 (Keswick: The National Trust, n.d.)

Nettleton 2005
John Nettleton, 'Canon Rawnsley – Europe's "most active volcano"!', in *Beatrix Potter's Family and Friends, Beatrix Potter Studies XI*, papers presented at The Beatrix Potter Society Conference, Birnam, August 2004 (Exeter: The Beatrix Potter Society and Studio Publishing Services Ltd., 2005), pp.49–59

Noble 1986
Mary Noble, 'Beatrix Potter and her Funguses', in *Beatrix Potter Studies I*, papers presented at The Beatrix Potter Lake District Study Conference, July 1984 (Norwich: The Beatrix Potter Society, 1986), pp.41–6

Ousby 1990
Ian Ousby, *The Englishman's England: Taste, Travel and the Rise of Tourism* (Cambridge: Cambridge University Press, 1990)

Potter 1929
Beatrix Potter, printed from a letter as '"Roots" of the Peter Rabbit Tales' in *The Horn Book Magazine* (May 1929), vol.5

Potter 1930
Beatrix Potter, with illustrations by Katharine Sturges, *Sister Anne* (Philadelphia: David McKay, 1930)

Potter 1966 (referred to as Journal throughout)
Beatrix Potter, *The Journal of Beatrix Potter from 1881 to 1897, Transcribed from her Code Writing by Leslie Linder* (London: Frederick Warne & Co., 1966, revised edition 1989)

Potter 1970
Beatrix Potter, with illustrations by Marie Angel, *The Tale of the Faithful Dove* (London: Frederick Warne & Co., 1970)

Potter 1973
Beatrix Potter, with illustrations by Marie Angel, *The Tale of Tuppenny* (London: Frederick Warne & Co., 1973)

Potter 1977
Beatrix Potter, *Dear Ivy, Dear June: Letters from Beatrix Potter* (Toronto: Published for the Friends of the Osborne and Lillian H. Smith Collections, Toronto Public Library, by Other Press, 1977)

Potter 1987a
Beatrix Potter, with illustrations by Pauline Baynes, *Wag-by-Wall* (London: Frederick Warne & Co., 1987)

Potter 1987b
Beatrix Potter, with illustrations by Pauline Baynes, *Country Tales: Little Mouse, Daisy and Double and Habbitrot* (London: Frederick Warne & Co., 1987)

Price 1888
John Edward Price, *The Archaeological Review* (June and July 1888), vol.1, nos 4 and 5

Puleston 1873
John Henry Puleston, assisted by John Edward Price, *Roman Antiques, Recently Discovered on the Site of The National Safe Deposit Company's Premises, Mansion House, London* (London: Nichols and Sons, 1873)

Rawnsley 1923
Eleanor F. Rawnsley, *Canon Rawnsley: An Account of his Life* (Glasgow: Maclehose, Jackson, 1923)

Rawnsley 1987
Rosalind Rawnsley, 'HDR – A Lover of His Fellow Men', *Cumbria* (October 1987), vol.37, pp.409–11

Rebanks 2015
James Rebanks, *The Shepherd's Life: A Tale of the Lake District* (London: Allen Lane, 2015)

Rebanks 2020
James Rebanks, *English Pastoral: An Inheritance* (London: Allen Lane, 2020)

Reeve 2000
Glynis Reeve, 'A North Country Lass: Beatrix Potter's Roots in the Millscapes of the North West', based on a lecture presented to The Beatrix Potter Society Conference, 21 October 2000 (Glossop: privately published, 2001)

Rollinson 1981
William Rollinson, *Life and Tradition in the Lake District* (Lancaster: Dalesman Books 1981)

Schafer 1999
Dale Schafer, 'How Beatrix Potter's Childhood Reading Influenced her Writing Style', in *Beatrix Potter as Writer and Illustrator, Beatrix Potter Studies VIII*, papers presented at The Beatrix Potter Society Conference, Ambleside, July 1998 (Exeter: The Beatrix Potter Society, 1999), pp.39–49

Scoular 2012
Clive Scoular, *Dear Mr Cunningham: Letters from Beatrix Potter to the Right Hon. Samuel Cunningham* (County Down: Clive Scoular, 2012)

Sheppard 1973
F.H.W. Sheppard (ed.), *Survey of London: Volume 37, Northern Kensington* (London, 1973), at British History Online, http://www.british-history.ac.uk/survey-london/vol37 (accessed 14 February 2020)

Sheppard 1983
F.H.W. Sheppard (ed.), *Survey of London: Volume 41, Brompton* (London, 1983), at British History Online, http://www.british-history.ac.uk/survey-london/vol41 (accessed 14 February 2020)

Sowerby and Johnson 1855
John Edward Sowerby (illustrations) and Charles Johnson (text), *The Ferns of Great Britain* (London: J.E. Sowerby, 1855). Supplementary section, *The Fern Allies* published 1856

Sowerby and Pierpoint Johnson 1858–60
John Edward Sowerby (illustrations) and Charles Pierpoint Johnson (text), *British Wild Flowers, Illustrated by J.E. Sowerby, Described, with an Introduction and a Key to the Natural Orders* (London: J.E. Sowerby, 1858–60)

Sparke 1986
Penny Sparke, *Furniture: Twentieth Century Design* (New York: E.P. Dutton, 1986)

Taylor 1987
Judy Taylor, *Beatrix Potter: Artist, Storyteller, Countrywoman* (London: Frederick Warne & Co., 1987)

Taylor et al. 1987
Judy Taylor et al., *Beatrix Potter, 1866–1943: The Artist and Her World* (London: Frederick Warne with the National Trust, 1987)

Taylor 1989
Judy Taylor (ed.), *Beatrix Potter's Letters* (London: Frederick Warne & Co.,1989, reprinted 2001)

Taylor 1992
Judy Taylor (ed.), *Letters to Children from Beatrix Potter* (London: Frederick Warne & Co., 1992, reprinted 2002)

Taylor 1993
Judy Taylor, *'So I Shall Tell You a Story...': Encounters with Beatrix Potter* (London: Frederick Warne & Co., 1993)

Taylor 2007
Judy Taylor, '"An Affectionate Companion and a Quiet Friend": Beatrix's Pets as Sources of her Inspiration', in *Beatrix Potter: Sources of her Inspiration, Beatrix Potter Studies XII*, papers presented at The Beatrix Potter Society Conference, Ambleside, July 2006 (Exeter: The Beatrix Potter Society and Studio Publishing Services Ltd, 2007), pp.74–85

Victoria and Albert Museum 1984
The Discovery of the Lake District: A Northern Arcadia and Its Uses, exh. cat. (London: Victoria and Albert Museum, 1984)

Walton and Wood 2013
John K. Walton and Jason Wood (eds), *The Making of a Cultural Landscape: The English Lake District as Tourist Destination, 1750–2010* (Farnham: Ashgate, 2013)

Walvin 1978
James Walvin, *Beside the Seaside: A Social History of the Popular Seaside Holiday* (London: Allen Lane, 1978)

Waterson 1994
Merlin Waterson, *The National Trust: The First Hundred Years* (London: BBC Books and National Trust Enterprises, 1994)

Weideger 1994
Paula Weideger, *Gilding the Acorn: Behind the Façade of the National Trust* (London: Simon & Schuster, 1994)

White 1862
Adam White, *The Instructive Picture Book, or a Few Attractive Lessons from the Natural History of Animals* (Edinburgh: Edmonston and Douglas, 1862, 5th edition)

Williams-Ellis 1938
Clough Williams-Ellis, *Britain and the Beast* (London: J.M. Dent & Sons Ltd, 1938)

Wordsworth 1835
William Wordsworth, *Guide to the Lakes, Fifth Edition* (Kendal: Hudson and Nicholson, 1835, reprinted London: Francis Lincoln Ltd, 2004)

Wordsworth 1974
The Prose Works of William Wordsworth, Vol. 2, edited by W.J.B. Owen and Jane Worthington Smyser (Oxford: Oxford University Press, 1974)

Wordsworth 1995
William Wordsworth, *The Prelude: The Four Texts (1798, 1799, 1805, 1850)* (London: Penguin Books, 1995)

Wordsworth and Wilkinson 1810
William Wordsworth (text) and Joseph Wilkinson (illustrations), *Select Views in Cumberland, Westmoreland, and Lancashire* (London: R. Ackerman, 1810)

Zach 2016
Emily Zach, with a foreword by Steven Heller, introduction by Linda Lear and afterword by Eleanor Taylor, *The Art of Beatrix Potter: Sketches, Paintings, and Illustrations* (San Francisco: Chronicle Books, 2016)

Catalogues of Collections

National Book League 1971
The Linder Collection of the Works and Drawings of Beatrix Potter (London: National Book League and Trustees of the Linder Collection, 1971)

Whalley and Hobbs 1985
Anne Stevenson Hobbs and Joyce Irene Whalley, with the assistance of Emma Stone and Celia O'Malley, *Beatrix Potter, The V&A Collection: The Leslie Linder Bequest of Beatrix Potter Material: Watercolours, Drawings, Manuscripts, Books, Photographs and Memorabilia – Catalogue* (London: Victoria and Albert Museum, 1985)

Hobbs 1996
Anne Stevenson Hobbs, *The Linder Collection of the Works and Drawings of Beatrix Potter: Catalogue of Works on Paper* (London: Trustees of the Linder Collection, 1996)

Cotsen 2004
Margit Sperling Cotsen, *The Beatrix Potter Collection of Lloyd Cotsen: Published on the Occasion of his 75th Birthday (Introduction and Notes to the Story Letters by Judy Taylor)* (Los Angeles: Cotsen Occasional Press, 2004)

Archives, Library and Museum Collections

Armitt Museum and Library, Ambleside

Beatrix Potter Gallery, National Trust, Hawkshead

British Museum, London

Derbyshire Record Office, Matlock

Frederick Warne Archive (held at the Victoria and Albert Museum, London)

Free Library of Philadelphia

Hill Top, National Trust, Sawrey

Lillian H. Smith Collection, Toronto Public Library

Lloyd E. Cotsen Collection, Cotsen Children's Library, Princeton University Library, Princeton

London Metropolitan Archives, London

Manchester Art Gallery, Manchester

The Morgan Library and Museum, New York

Museum of Fine Arts, Boston

National Library of Scotland, Edinburgh

Perth Museum and Art Gallery

Tate Britain, London

University of Leeds

Victoria and Albert Museum, London

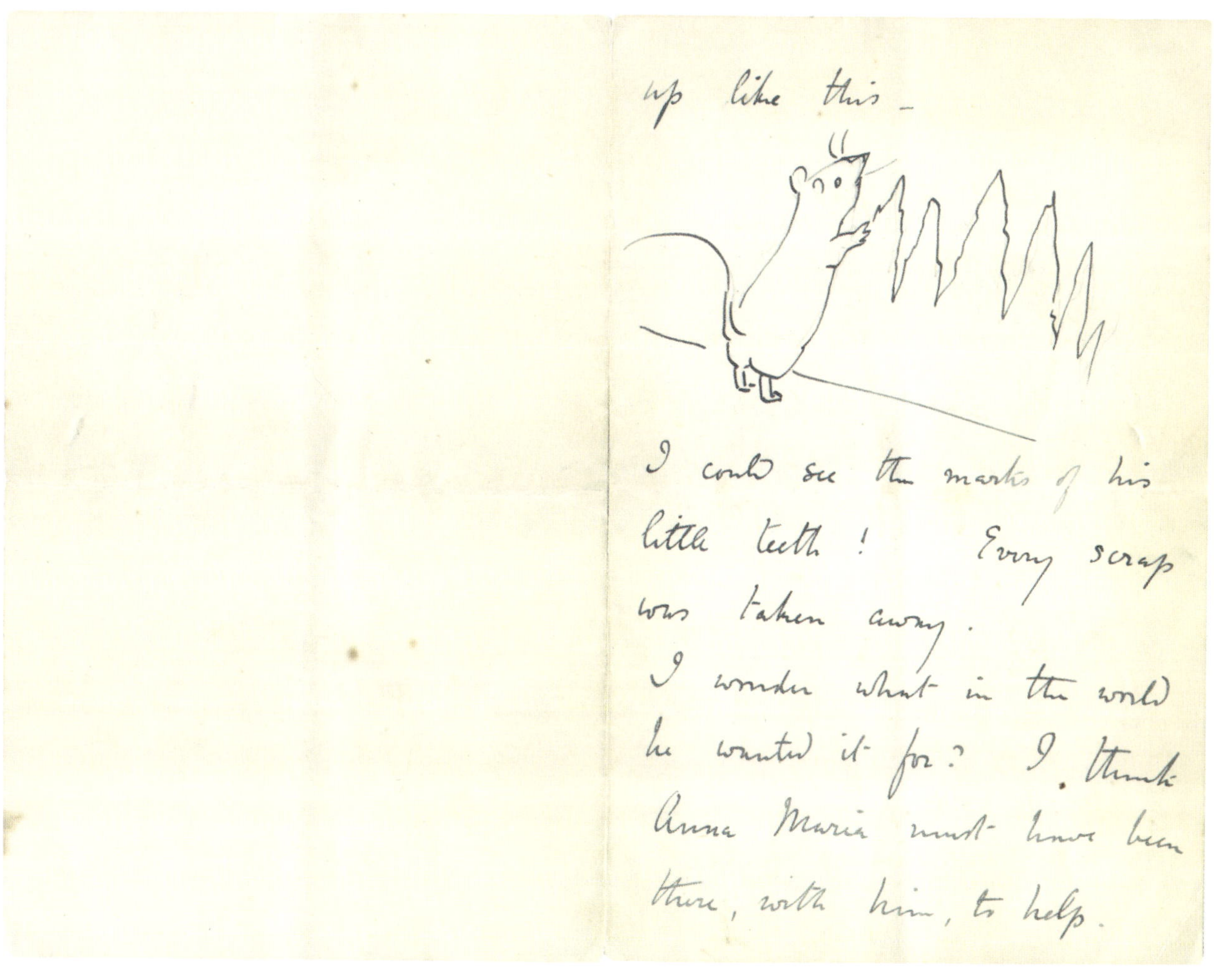

up like this _

I could see the marks of his little teeth! Every scrap was taken away.
I wonder what in the world he wanted it for? I think Anna Maria must have been there, with him, to help.

171. Below
Picture letter by Beatrix Potter sent to Winifred Warne, from Meadhurst, Sidmouth, 29 December 1908
Ink on paper
Private collection

Acknowledgements

A large exhibition requires the collaboration, enthusiasm and support of numerous people. We would like to extend our thanks to Frederick Warne & Co., including Susan Bolsover, Thomas Merrington and Sara Glenn for their interest in the exhibition, and to the Linder Collection and Jack and Audrey Ladevèze for their continued support of the V&A and the Beatrix Potter collections. The exhibition which this book accompanies was curated in partnership with the National Trust, for which opportunity we thank Hilary Grady, Director, and Tarnya Cooper, Curatorial Director.

We would like to give special mention to the National Trust project curator Liz Hunter MacFarlane for the considerable work she did to help develop the narrative and object list with the V&A's exhibition curator; also Helen Antrobus for taking over from Liz from February 2021 with enthusiasm and sensitivity to the work already achieved. Lucy Shaw, Assistant Curator, deserves thanks for her invaluable contribution in providing Annemarie Bilclough with research assistance and support in developing the object list.

Several individuals have assisted us with our research or by providing expert opinion: we thank Hilary Ainsworth, The Beatrix Potter Society, Helen Duder, Richard Fortey, Selwyn Goodacre, Christiaan Jonkers, Libby Joy, Tanya Loi, David Pepper, Derek Ross and Anne Stevenson Hobbs for being so generous with sharing their knowledge and their time to answer questions. Libby Joy receives special thanks for acting as reader for several of the essays' authors.

For advice and help with access to other Potter collections, Annemarie Bilclough would like to thank the following: Sue Osman and Deborah Walsh at the Armitt Museum and Library; Susan Benson and Anthony Hughes of Cumbria Archive Centre; Caitlin Goodman and the Rare Books Department at the Free Library, Philadelphia; Meghan Melvin at the Museum of Fine Arts, Boston; Amy Fairley and Mark Simmons at Perth Museum and Art Gallery, Katherine Harrington of Royal Botanic Gardens, Kew; Andrea Immel from Cotsen Children's Library and staff of the reading room at the University of Princeton Library, as well as Brianna Cregle and AnnaLee Pauls for image research; Philip Palmer and reading room staff at the Morgan Library and Museum; Lluis Tembleque Teres at the Museum of London; Douglas Rainwater and Hannah Williamson at Manchester Art Gallery; Jason Burch, Charlotte Hopkins and Michael Melia of the London Metropolitan Archives; Rosie Dyson of the University of Leeds Library; Christopher Coutlee at Toronto Public Library; and David Thompson and study room staff at Tate Britain, London.

The exhibition benefited from a number of key loans and we acknowledge the generosity of the following: Armitt Museum and Library; The Beatrix Potter Society; Frederick Warne & Co.; Free Library, Philadelphia; Phillip Herbert; Lloyd E. Cotsen Collection, Princeton University Library; Manchester Art Gallery; National Library of Scotland; Perth Museum and Art Gallery, Murray Roberts; Pearson PLC; the Royal Academy of Arts, Tate Britain and Andrew Lloyd Webber.

The exhibition design team has shown enormous enthusiasm both for the project's aims and the original material. Our thanks go to Keith Flemming and Sor Lan Tan of Flemming Associates for project management, V&A Design Studio for 3D design, Nina Jua Klein Studio for exhibition graphics, and Michael Grubb Studio for lighting. This book would not exist without the contributions of the authors and the diligence of our Publications team: Editor Rebecca Fortey, Head of Content Tom Windross, Managing Editor Coralie Hepburn and Production Manager Emma Woodiwiss. We are grateful to Charlie Smith and Emma Young for their handsome book design.

For help with our research and other assistance and advice our sincere thanks also go to colleagues and former colleagues within the V&A and the National Trust including Julius Bryant, Keeper of the V&A's Word and Image Department, for his steer on the exhibition narrative content; additionally, Rachel Conroy, Judith Crouch, Catriona Gourlay, Elizabeth James, Sophie Johnson, Jenny Lister, John Moffat, Susan North, Suzanne Smith, Ioan Waight, Laura White and Harvey Wilkinson and the staff at Hill Top for their help and support in various areas of expertise.

An exhibition of this size relies on a large team from departments across the Museum, some of whom come on board in the later and crucial installation stages and cannot be named individually. We thank the V&A project team: Olivia Oldroyd and Roo Gunzi from Exhibitions; Conservation liaison Clair Battison, and Conservators Zoe Allen, Sophie Croft, Louise Egan, Lara Flecker, Chris Gingell, Caroline (Nina) Jimenez Gray, Elizabeth-Anne Haldane, Ana Logreira, Dana Melchar, Katrina Redman, Jane Rutherston and Bhav Shah; the V&A's Framing team; Lenny Cherry, Corinne Jones and Bryony Shepherd from Interpretation; the Technical Services installation team; Marion Crick, Richard Davis, Sarah Duncan, Charlotte Hazeldene and Ellie Atkins from the Photographic Studio; Sara Mittica from Registrars and Anna Fletcher from Touring; from Development, Lorna Killin and Julia Brown, and from Press and Marketing, Mel Caplan, Jordan Lewis, Anne McAteer, Laura Mitchell, Shannon Nash, Piera Orizzonte and Catherine Poust; Fred Caws, Anthony Misquitta and Andrew Tullis for their considerable help in navigating intellectual property; Harriet Curnow and the Learning team, and the Events, Digital, Visitor Experience and Security teams, and Margaux Soland and Elizabeth Lovatt from V&A Enterprises. From the National Trust we thank Conservators Nigel Blades, Caroline Cotgrove and Emma Schmuecker; Rights Manager Chris Rowlin; Heather Caven and Fernanda Torrente from Collections Management; Tom Freshwater from Partnerships, and for their support at the initial concept stage: John Chu, Matthew Cowpe, Tim Pye, Nami Ralph, Annie Reilly and Nicola Walker.

For their oversight and wholehearted support of the project from its inception we thank Dr Tristram Hunt, Director of the V&A; Linda Lloyd-Jones and Daniel Slater, former and current V&A Heads of Exhibitions; Rebecca Lim, Head of FuturePlan Programme; Alex Stitt, former Director of Audiences, Commercial and Digital; Antonia Boström, Director of Collections, and Helen Charman, Director of Learning.

Finally, the following people provided the V&A and National Trust curators with moral support in various ways over several years of exhibition planning: Steven Bilclough, Darren Booker and Glynys Hunter.

Credits

Author Biographies

Annemarie Bilclough is the Frederick Warne Curator of Illustration at the V&A. She was co-author with Emma Laws of *Winnie-the-Pooh: Exploring a Classic* (2017) and contributed to *Alice: Curiouser and Curiouser* (2021).

Richard Fortey is a prize-winning scientist, author and television presenter. His books include *The Hidden Landscape: A Journey into the Geological Past* (1993), *Life: An Unauthorized Biography* (1997), *The Wood for the Trees: One Man's Long View of Nature* (2016) and *A Curious Boy: The Making of a Scientist* (2021).

Sara Glenn has been the Commercial Curator for the Warne Archive for 21 years. Managing the collection on behalf of Penguin Random House UK, Sara has curated many successful touring exhibitions around the world featuring original Peter Rabbit manuscripts, illustrations and ephemera, bequeathed to her publisher by Beatrix Potter.

Liz Hunter MacFarlane was Collections and House Manager for the National Trust for 20 years. She was Project Curator for the National Trust for *Beatrix Potter: Drawn to Nature*.

Emma Laws is Director of Collections and Research at the Devon and Exeter Institution. She previously worked as Curator at the V&A for over 20 years and was co-author with Annemarie Bilclough of *Winnie-the-Pooh: Exploring a Classic* (2017).

James Rebanks is a farmer and shepherd in Matterdale, and author of the best-selling *The Shepherd's Life: A Tale of the Lake District* (2015) and *English Pastoral: An Inheritance* (2020).

Lucy Shaw is Assistant Curator at the V&A, where she works with the Beatrix Potter and Children's Books Collections. Previously she worked as a cataloguer of Prints, Drawings, Paintings and Photographs.

Image Credits

Frederick Warne & Co is the owner of all rights, copyrights and trademarks in the Beatrix Potter character names and illustrations.

Photographs of all V&A collection objects are © Victoria and Albert Museum, London. Any additional crediting is included below.

Numbers refer to illustration numbers.

Courtesy of The Armitt Museum and Library Centre 56, 61, 64, 67–69, 71, 72 68
© The Trustees of the British Museum 96
Courtesy of the Free Library of Philadelphia, Rare Books Department 9
Courtesy of Jonkers Rare Books, Henley-on-Thames 41, 17
Courtesy of Leeds University Library 42
Courtesy of The London Metropolitan Archives (City of London) 7
Manchester Art Gallery, UK/© Manchester Art Gallery/Bridgeman Images 11
Courtesy of The Morgan Library & Museum. MA 2009.1. Gift of Colonel David McC. McKell, 1959 37
Courtesy of The Morgan Library & Museum. MA 2009.12. Gift of Colonel David McC. McKell, 1959 81
Image used courtesy of the National Library of Scotland 70
© National Trust/Liz Hunter MacFarlane 129, 139
© National Trust/Robert Thrift 18, 130, 140
© National Trust Images/Val Corbett 135
© National Trust/J. Hardman 12
Courtesy of National Trust and Frederick Warne & Co. Photo © National Trust/Colin Liddie 60, 98, 119, 120, 138, 146–51, 154, 155, 158, 166, 167
Courtesy of National Trust and Frederick Warne & Co. Photo © National Trust/Robert Thrift 29, 30, 32, 45, 57, 65, 87, 89, 91, 115, 118, 126, 134, 141, 152, 156, 160–64, 169 and front cover
Courtesy of National Trust and Frederick Warne & Co. Photo © National Trust Images 22, 153, 159, 165
Courtesy Pearson PLC. Photo © The Victoria and Albert Museum 76–79
Courtesy of Perth Museum & Art Gallery, Perth & Kinross Council 62, 63
Courtesy of Princeton University Library 2, 8, 12, 39, 46, 74, 121, 137, back cover
Photo © Tate 4, 26, 145
Private Collection 171
Courtesy of Toronto Public Library 123
Courtesy of The Victoria and Albert Museum and Frederick Warne & Co. 1, 3, 5, 6, 10, 13–17, 19, 21, 24, 27, 28, 31, 33, 35, 36, 38, 40, 44, 47–49, 51–53, 55, 58, 59, 66, 73, 75, 80, 82–86, 90, 92–94, 95, 97, 99, 100, 102, 103–5, 111, 112–14, 116, 117, 122, 124, 125, 128, 132, 133, 136, 160, 168, 170
Courtesy of Frederick Warne & Co. Photo © Frederick Warne & Co. Ltd. 101, 106–10, 142–44

Index

Illustrations and captions are in italics.

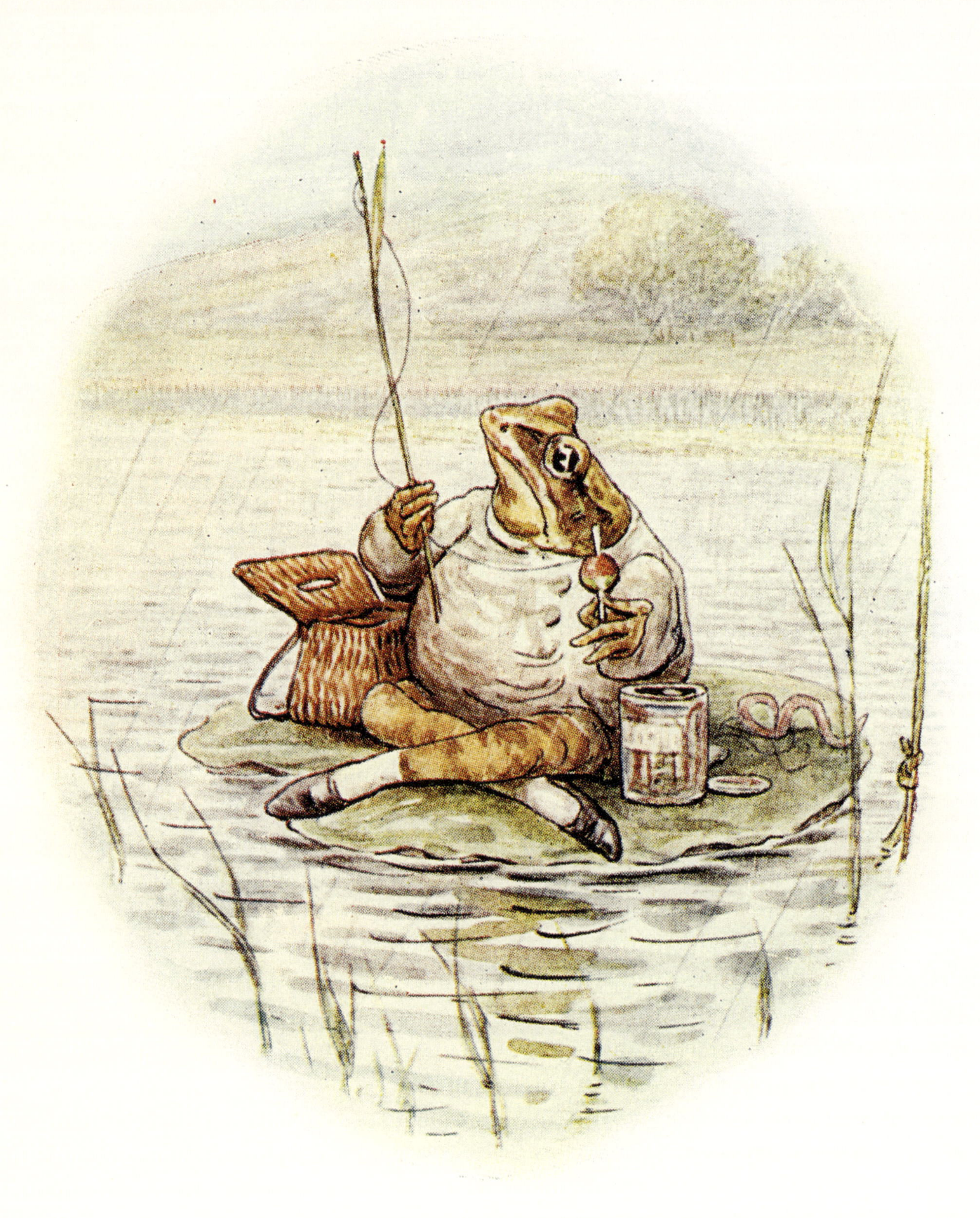